DEDICATED

TO

GEORGE MACDONALD, LL.D.

WORKMAN, PREACHER, AND POET

SOMNIA MEDICI

SOMNIA MEDICI

BY

JOHN A. GOODCHILD

LONDON
KEGAN PAUL, TRENCH, & CO., 1 PATERNOSTER SQUARE
1884

(The rights of translation and of reproduction are reserved)

PREFACE.

THE composition of the verses and tales contained in this volume has been one of the relaxations of a medical man, to whom circumstances have given long periods of leisure in the practice of his profession. I date it from my southern home, in the hope that one or two of the pieces may interest my friends upon the Riviera. For the rest, I am content to pour my driblet of weak wine into the flood of contemporary English verse as an addition to the bulk, rather than to the bouquet of the whole; so subscribe myself, dear reader, yours sincerely,

J. A. GOODCHILD.

CASA GRAZIA, BORDIGHERA, ITALY.

CONTENTS.

	PAGE
Schöne Rothraut	1
A Common Story	3
Under the Laurels	6
A Withered Rose	8
On a French Picture	11
A Resemblance	14
Cold as Ice	15
Winnie	18
Lines for Music	22
Song	24
In a Studio	26
Honour	33
The Tale of Rabbi Joseph	84
The Idiot	117
Love and Vanity (a psychological enigma)	128
Marriage Wishes	132

CONTENTS.

	PAGE
FRIEND OR FOE (A PSYCHOLOGICAL ENIGMA)	133
A DRESDEN BEAUTY	137
PEARLS	139
THE LANDS BEYOND THE SEA	141
THE 'CLAIM OF BLOOD'	144
THE RESTORATION	151
'ANTIVIVISECTION' (SONNET)	160
'ANTICS'	161
THE PRAISE OF FOLLY	162
MOLOCH	164
HIS SIDE AND HERS	166
THE STAR IN THE EAST	167
SONNET	168
THE BREATH OF LIFE	169
SONNET (IN MEMORIAM)	170
SONNET	171
SWALLOWS OF THE RIVIERA	172
A PRAYER	17
SONNET (THE OLIVE)	176
THE FIRST LESSON (ODE)	177
DAMOCLES	185

SCHÖNE ROTHRAUT.

TAKE as gold this old tradition
 Of the royal-rendered wage,
Guerdon of love's mad ambition
 In the true heart of a page.

He, his passion vainly hiding,
 Worn and pale with hopeless pain,
Through the summer woods was riding
 Close beside his mistress' rein.

'Why so sad, my page?' and turning,
 Gazed she straight into his eyes.
''Tis thy thought my bosom burning
 With a flame that never dies.'

Flushed she then, but answered, 'Carest
 Thou to feed the flame I bring?
Look me full, and if thou darest,
 Kiss the daughter of the king.'

Stark he stood, all wonders mingling,
    Then from heart to finger-tips
Rushed the heated life-blood tingling
    As he seized upon her lips.

Crushing newborn awe with laughter,
    Said she, 'Thus must end thy pain;
See thou never more hereafter
    Lookest for like grace again.'

Spake he glad: 'Each leaf that glitters
    In the sun thy gift hath seen;
Every bird that sings and twitters
    Knoweth where my lips have been.

'And the winds from dawn to vesper,
    Blow they north or blow they south,
Softly in my ear shall whisper,
    "Thou hast kissed Schöne Rothraut's mouth."

'Every floweret of the meadow,
    Every bird upon the tree,
In life's sunshine or its shadow,
    Shall bring back my joy to me.'

A COMMON STORY.

LEFT long since a little maiden,
   To a woman's hope and fears,
Weary now and heavy laden
   With the burden of the years,
Patiently she bendeth under,
Waiting one to part asunder
   Every bar and dry her tears.

He went westward gaily, deeming
   In new lands to gather gold.
What is left her but her dreaming,
   Sitting lonesome in the cold,
Whispering the old tale over,
Weaving fancies round her lover,
   Longing for his arm's enfold?

In the years since these were parted
   Hath his love or hers outran?
If he left her open-hearted,
   Yet the boy is not the man.

Is he, with set eyes upon her,
Striving up the steeps of honour,
   Working what the boy began?

He will, if he come hereafter,
   Find her reft of youth's first glow,
All the dimples, all the laughter,
   Faded. Has he strength to know
Something higher, something truer,
Than the fair sweet child her wooer
   Kissed at parting long ago?

Heart of woman inly bleeding
   Through slow hours of dull unrest,
Is thy tender bosom feeding
   Changeling love that drains the breast,
Till the charms of old that bound it,
Cast no more their spells around it,
   And deserted is thy nest?

Mammon all his slaves oppresses,
   And his wares are dearly bought,
Weighed against love's young caresses
   In the years that went for naught.

Though she dream the old romances,
Though he guard his early fancies,
   Which knows now the other's thought?

Oh, 'tis weary weary waiting
   At hope's close-barred outer gate,
Till his greeting through the grating
   Bid thee rise and hear thy fate.
May thy heart which never faltered,
Gathered to a breast unaltered,
   Find glad entrance with its mate.

UNDER THE LAURELS.

A NIGHTMARE.

Under the laurels low dropped she down,
Under the laurels heartbroken, lone,
Love on the sorrels made its last moan.

'What is that, darling?'   'Nothing, heart's nearest;
Blackbird or starling that which thou hearest.'
'Nothing else, darling?'   'Nothing, heart's dearest.'
Low 'mid the laurels ceaseth the moan,
Now, from the laurels sound comes there none,
Under the laurels life is nigh flown.

'Why shake with chill, love?'   'Over my grave,
Spirit of ill love, my soul doth crave.'
'What ill can kill love?   Love should make brave.'
Cold on the laurels shines down the moon,
Under the laurels heartbeats are none,
Love 'neath the laurels stiffens to stone.

UNDER THE LAURELS.

'Good-night.' 'Good-night love.   So soon to part,
Why at my sight love, love didst thou start?
What ill can fright love clasped heart to heart?'
Cold o'er the laurels night-winds have blown,
Damp on the sorrels dewdrops have shone,
Here midst the laurels night is nigh gone.

'Once more good night love :   Heart to heart fold.'
'What is unright love? Love thou art cold.'
'Warmed by thy bright love, lo, I am bold.'
Back through the laurels, true love alone,
Over the sorrels false love is gone,
Here midst the laurels shall he atone.

'What this my trouble? why should I fear?
If love be double, both loves are dear,
Love's but a bubble not worth a care.'
Over the laurels black clouds do frown,
Under the laurels love waiteth on,
White on the sorrels, ghostly and wan.

In the grey morning, chilly and drear,
Death-cold and scorning, what finds *He* here,
Stretched in dread warning, snow-white and clear?
Deep through the laurels cometh his groan ;
Stark on the sorrels falleth he prone ;
Love 'neath the laurels no more alone !

A WITHERED ROSE.

HEAVEN, in pain for our spirit's dearth,
Sent this rose midst its gifts of worth
To sing glad songs of the skies on earth;

Young and fresh in its early bloom,
With tender colour to brighten gloom,
And to sweeten the world with its heart's perfume.

Heaven took thought for its rose as well,
When later, down from its garden fell
A lily of Eden on earth to dwell.

A fragrant lily, with heart as white
As untrodden snow on the mountain's height,
Or the silver moon of a southern night.

Earth's storms beat fierce on the tender guest,
But Heaven gave haven of earthly rest,
And the lily lay warm on the rose's breast.

Then the world grows glad with the joy of the rose,
When the red red heart of its rapture glows,
And its incense breathes in each breeze that blows.

But Heaven had heed of its lily too,
Lest, though safe from storm 'neath the rose it grew,
Its petals be dimmed by grief's earthly dew,

Its fragrance wax faint with the earthly toil,
Its whiteness get taint of earth's darker soil,
Or the vagrant bees its honey despoil.

From Heaven came a breeze that returning bore
Its lily back to its own bright shore,
And its rose was alone upon earth once more.

Alone? Nay up, where the lily lay
Ere the wind of Heaven caught it away,
Sprang a speedwell into the light of day.

A tiny flower, but the tender hue
Of eyes which mirrored the vault of blue
Showed the speedwell had come from Heaven too;

And the rose, through mists that the dews had made,
Gazed down on the floweret beneath its shade,
Then lifted its head to the skies, and prayed.

A WITHERED ROSE.

The speedwell lives but a day to show
The hues of Heaven to the rose below,
Then back to its garden above must go.

The rose bowed its head in its grief alone,
When the last glad gift of the skies was gone,
And yearned for a sun that unclouded shone.

'Oh take me home to the garden rare,
Where my leaves may their stains of the earth repair,
And my stem may a richer burden bear.'

A little while, and the rose once more
Shall back return to the heavenly shore,
Its mission to earth fulfilled and o'er.

But though old and withered, its fragrance sweet,
Still gladdens souls parched in the noonday heat;
Till the rose and the lily and speedwell meet

LINES ON A FRENCH PICTURE.

DOUBT and terror and sore distress
   In those sweet blue eyes, and why?
She is lovely and pure; health, youth, the power
To enjoy are hers. Let her take the hour,
      And the sunshine sky
         With its happiness,
           For her dower.

See! she beholds on her right
   A chamber, squalid and bare,
Where her sisters stifle and starve and freeze
As they bend dim-eyed o'er their wasted knees,
      And they toil in care
         Through their dim wan light
         To their darker night.
           Must she sit with these?

No! she may turn if she will
   To mount on the riotous car
Which pleasure drives down the steep incline,
Where lie sparkling trinkets and pools of wine ;
     There, thick perfumes are
        Her fears to kill,
          Down that fearful hill
             Where the corpse lights shine.

Shall she remain where beauty fades,
   And youth no harvest reaps ?
To toil for the scanty dole of bread
And that sordid shelter overhead,
     Till she sleeps
        In the shades
           With the dead ?

A narrow choice : the sole escape
   Lies down that broad hillside,
Down where the myriad gaslights glow
Till Paris flames like a hell below,
     Where the lost abide.
        Of such a shape
           Are her musings now.

LINES ON A FRENCH PICTURE.

She fronts us with eyes that plead.
   Well may her tears downflow.
Look at her ; give good heed ;
For her riddle is hard to read.
      Far and wide
      Are such tangles tied
         To be loosed in woe
         BELOW !

A RESEMBLANCE.

I saw her first where warm the sunbeams fall
   In the November air,
'A daughter of the Gods, divinely tall,
   Divinely fair.'

In Paris next I met her. As I gazed
   Each feature seemed the same;
Slow drew I near and read with eyes amazed
   The world-known name—

'Venus of Milo.' Pride may quench the pain
   Of idle hopes or fears.
My homage lies but where the world's has lain
   Two thousand years.

COLD AS ICE.

A WINTER pool of virgin ice,
   Cold, hard, and deep ; in vain I tried
To thaw thy surface and entice
   An answering ripple from thy tide.
Hard as the diamond, never love of mine
Might crimson all thy depths with ruddy wine.

And he who bought thee seemed fit mate,
   Snows in his heart, snows on his brow,
He wore thee with a fitting state,
   The costliest gem in all his show ;
And for a brilliant hard and bright and cold,
He made a heavy setting with his gold.

But some faint trace of spring that dwelt
   Beneath the snowdrifts, made him press
Thy surface cold, inclined to melt
   Its brilliance with his limp caress
Of chilly softness, bringing not a thaw,
But rending all the ice with treacherous flaw.

It crackled here, it trembled there,
  And half its lustre fled away.
Its hardness scarce had strength to bear
  The dull foul weight that on it lay,
Moist with dank leaves of autumn, and the mould
Which gathers on dead hearts when youth is cold.

To thy cold mirror, flecked and starred
  And treacherous with hidden shame,
Yielding below, though surface-hard,
  There came a youth with torch aflame,
Who lit above the unknown depths a fire,
Piled with dead weeds and thorny stems of briar.

Till thy cold hidden springs gushed forth,
  No longer crystal as of yore,
But turbid in their bubbling wrath,
  And dark with earth-stains red as gore;
For he that drew them loved not them nor thee,
But broke the ice up in pure fantasy;

And when the turbid runnel flowed
  Too swiftly, rising up in haste,
Cut muddy channels to a road
  Where all was spent and run to waste

In muddy pools amidst the muddy sand
That trodden underfoot was cursed and banned.

Then the ice crashed to pits below
   All noisome with the hurtful breath
Of rotting garbage.   Ice and snow
   And ashes pile those caves beneath;
Whilst he who drew the waters fled; and I,
Who loved, look down and marvel where they lie.

WINNIE.

You are waiting for me to-day, Winnie; you picture me at your feet
To flatter your pride with homage. I come not. I should but greet
With a curse, and I dare not curse for the thunder in the sky;
But I tremble, tremble for you, Winnie. It is Heaven that strikes, not I.
Pause, guard yourself for a moment, ere the bolt strike on your head.
I have heard from my cousin Frank, and my cousin Frank—is dead.

It has fallen, Winnie, Winnie, it has struck you in your sin;
Red as blood athwart your darkness, it has pierced to the lie within.

Are you blinded and dumb and pulseless? are you
    dead beneath the blow?
Or shrivelled in flame as I was but a few short hours
    ago?
Oh, Winnie! I dreamed not, guessed not, as the stars
    above me shine,
I knew not that Frank had loved you, and the curse
    is yours, not mine.
Have you a heart that you ventured to traffic with
    idle mirth
In the seemings of other love, when the truest heart
    upon earth,
The bravest, the best, was your own? You are vile,
    and this I say,
'It is well for my cousin Frank that he died ere he
    saw this day.'
'Tell Winnie,' he wrote to me, 'as I lay in fever and
    pain,
My one sweet hope upon earth was to look on her
    face again.
This dream is over; but say to my darling that God
    above
Will reward her tenfold for all she has given of truth
    and love.'

And you—but I will not curse you. Would heaven that I could screen
From the curse. Oh, Winnie, Winnie, the gladness that might have been!
Gladness, never, never, no gladness for him or for me.
We were both deceived, both blind; it is well that he cannot see.
Had he lived but a short space longer the truth had destroyed the lie;
For the truth prevaileth alway, and the falsehoods are born to die.
But the falsehood had slain him then, he had never endured this pain,
This knowledge that love was false, and that loving trust was in vain.
Did you deem him a doll in a scarlet coat to be played with and thrown aside?
Did you dream that he could forget, that my cousin Frank would have lied?
He has sent this trinket for you to wear at your heart for his sake;
It will burn like a coal red hot, but shrink not from scorch or from ache.

Press it close down on your breast, guard, cling to it.
  Heed it well;
If you wear it not in due penance now, it will blister
  your soul in hell.

Heed not my ravings, Winnie; I am giddy and mad
  with pain,
And my heart is bleeding for yours, though we never
  may meet again
Till we three be met together. Will you stand up
  then by his side
And tell us the damning spot has by pain been
  purified?
Or will your foul—Nay, my Winnie, I swore that I
  would not curse,
But would shun your face in my darkness till this
  vapour of lies disperse;
For I know not falsehood from truth and love, and
  my spirit has gone astray.
Oh, Winnie, Winnie, Winnie, how I loved you but
  yesterday!

LINES FOR MUSIC.

WILD the lintwhite's warbling trill—
        Ruby Mayo, Ruby Mayo,
On the bramble-tangled hill—
        Ruby Mayo, Ruby Mayo.
True love could not tame the tongue
Of a wilder maid who sung
In the days when we were young,
        In our springtime—Ruby Mayo.

Love went forth at pairing time—
        Ruby Mayo, Ruby Mayo;
Found the maiden in her prime—
        Ruby Mayo, Ruby Mayo.
Fairer than the briar rose,
Careless as a stream that goes
Laughing, leaping from the snows
        Down the mountain—Ruby Mayo.

LINES FOR MUSIC.

Love that dreamed had viewed his mate—
   Ruby Mayo, Ruby Mayo;
Love that wooed had long to wait—
   Ruby Mayo, Ruby Mayo.
Love that thought to win his quest
Fell to earth with wounded breast,
Pierced by thorns around the nest
   Love lay bleeding—Ruby Mayo.

Had the nest been warmer found—
   Ruby Mayo, Ruby Mayo,
He had healed him of his wound—
   Ruby Mayo, Ruby Mayo.
Love that lingered long in pain,
Perished, killed by cold disdain.
Love can ne'er grow warm again
   On a cold heart—Ruby Mayo.

Narrow woman turning grey—
   Ruby Mayo, Ruby Mayo,
All our flowers are dropped away—
   Ruby Mayo, Ruby Mayo.
We had lost our brighter day
When the cold hail beat in May,
Though the lintwhite whistled gay,
   In her thorn brake, Ruby Mayo.

SONG.

A SONG, a song of a bird,
   Of a little brown bird ;
I and my little brown bird,
   And love was the third.
She had but a single note
       In her throat ;
But the single note was sweet
         Tweet tweet, sweet tweet tweet.

A plaint of my bird alone,
   Love and I had flown.
I had left her my love, my own,
   Just for a moment lone ;
And the song froze in her throat,
     The one note
Of her little love-song sweet,
     Tweet tweet.

Oh, my bird, my bird, my bird,
   Oh, my little shy bird ;
I and my little dead bird,
   And grief is the third ;

And grief has her song by rote,
        The love-note,
But he cannot sing it sweet
            Tweet tweet, sweet tweet tweet.

IN A STUDIO.

No, not mine, Signor. Thank God that I
Paint no such phantoms to give the lie
To the truth. Sapristi, it is not well
To summon lost angels out of Hell.

From Heaven you say. Yes, so to you
It may be. Listen : your angel slew
My comrade Martin, and such a deed
May rather from Hell than Heaven proceed ;
But sit, Signor, on the sofa there,
And judge her yourself if you have the care.

My comrade Martin, and near in blood,
The blithest soul in our brotherhood,
Young, brilliant, handsome, and free of stain
As our fair young Raphael come again,
Might have clambered up to the highest place
In our art had he 'scaped from that demon's face ;

But he met with a woman proud and light
And handsome; you know her perchance by sight,
The Countess of Voltri. You know her? Yes.
Then, Signor, you give perchance a guess
That she sought his homage. She did in fine,
As to-morrow she'd seek for yours or mine.
No, not her portrait. You think that you
See a trace of her features showing through.
No! the Countess is fair, but this I say,
No demon beauty with strength to slay
Such a soul as Martin's; yet ever he
Sketched out her face in his reverie,
And painted her often, gave new grace
To each subtle change of the woman's face;
And all good portraits; but still he toiled
Upon fresh studies. He was not foiled
By her form or features. Martin knew
That he gave the lady all her due,
But cursed them, and swore he had painted ill,
And craved fresh sittings, and others still.
So, toiling ever the long day through
At these self-same features, Martin grew
Haggard and thin, till I fain had torn
Him from her. I said she had overworn

Her reputation, and others were
Of greater honour and not less fair :
And he answered, 'Aye, but I seek to find
A subtle something that lies behind,
A wonder of beauty ; it will not stay
On my canvas now, but it will some day.'

The Countess was pleased that the common voice
Named her the handsome painter's choice.
She had thrown a charm, or so they said,
And he painted nothing but just her head,
A head worth painting though all the same.
They knew not he ever missed his aim,
And painted not for the Countess' whim,
But to grasp a shadow that fled from him :
But she perhaps learnt that he loved her not,
Or had portraits enough, so she forgot
His hungry gloom, it disturbed her rest,
And she liked a more cheerful lover best :
So she sat no more, and my friend was left
With his visions, raging like one bereft
Of his senses. We saw him never more,
For he thrust us forth, and he shut the door

Of his room. Pepìna his servant-maid
Tells me he ever after staid
Within, and that always overhead
Hither and thither she heard him tread
For a week, and the door was not unshut,
Save at midnight to take the victuals put
For his use on the sill, and he never took
But bread and water. She tried to look
Through the keyhole, but found it stopped. At last,
When for days he had hardly broke his fast,
She heard his easel drawn forth and guessed
From the hammer strokes that disturbed her rest
That he stretched a canvas. Then days passed by
Whilst his food untouched on the sill did lie,
And he gave small signs, but at length one night
She started and woke from sleep in fright
To hear him singing. She said the voice
Was of heaven, but though it bid rejoice
And triumph, it curdled her blood with fear,
And she fled without that she might not hear ;
Then she came to me with the morning sun,
And I knew that Martin's task was done ;
So I burst the door, and stiff and cold
He sat, the friend I had loved of old,

His glazed eyes fixed in a ghastly stare
Full on the face of that demon there,
With the angel depth in her tender eyes
And her lips like a rose bloom of Paradise.

So, I knew how his soul had seen
The face of the angel that might have been
For the woman that was. Perchance in youth
It had dwelt within her, for this is truth,
That of spirits of evil since man's fall,
Those likest angels are worst of all ;
And this vampire phantom which Martin wooed,
Had sapped his spirit, and drank his blood.

Has the Countess seen it ? Oh, yes ; she came,
Came on the arm of her newest flame ;
Said she was sorry my friend was gone,
She really fancied that he alone
Could hit her features ; then, an aside
To her friend, '*He* went mad before he died.'
Then to myself, 'I have heard the man
Has painted me lately,' and with her fan
She tapped his cheek as she whispered low,
'I mean *you* to buy it before I go.'

IN A STUDIO.

So I answered her back : 'If my cousin died,
It is no fresh food for your famished pride,
And this last picture that Martin drew
Is the face of a fairer fiend than you ;'
And I drew the curtain. She turned to gaze
With an angry mocking smile on her face,
But she could not front it. Her proud eyes dropped,
I fancy her heart for one moment stopped ;
She grew so deathly her friend sped round
To save her from falling to the ground ;
And twice she raised up her head to look
Once more at the picture, but could not brook
Its gaze ; then she seized me by the arm
As with sudden action to break the charm,
She hissed, 'Tear, burn it, and I will pay
Its price thrice over.' I answered : 'Nay,
You at least shall know that this spirit vext
May cross you in this world as in the next.'

Signor, I turn it. Here on its right
Is a sketch of Capri, the evening light
Fairly caught. Next a vintage subject. Then,
This large group of our Naples fishermen.

The Coliseum.   You say that none
Of the pictures please you, save this alone.
Name my own price, you will buy but this,
Demon or angel whiche'er it is.
Nay, Signor, I sell not the living lie.
When the Countess lies dying yon fiend shall die.

HONOUR.

An Egotism.

I.

A CHILLY morn and a leaden sky;
A parting scene of days long gone by;
The grey-haired father, and Kate, and I.
  'Honour, my boy, Honour and Truth.'
It is my father's last farewell,
Too light in the ears of heedless youth;
But it rings in the heart now he that spoke
Raises his prayer no more to bless;
And the echo that after woke
Rang deeper in bitterness,
Till my heart was well-nigh broke.

And little Katie. Ah, pretty Kate,
You too are sad for your old playmate.
How she can sob and kiss and cling,
The little winsome petulant thing,

With her hot face pressed upon my shoulder
Right in the gaze of each beholder.
  I am flushing a rosy red,
    I, who am eight years older,
  Stiffer at every tear that is shed,
    Hot with shame, but colder.
Yet there she lies, with the tiny head
Pressed warm upon my shoulder.

'Kate, my child, we must let him go.
  Frank, my boy, GOD bless thee!
Katie dear, it is sad I know,
  And harder still to press thee;
But a little maiden like thee must grow,
So Katie, dear one, let him go.
  Frank, my boy, GOD bless thee!'

II.

Four years? Aye, it is strange to think,
  In this silence of tropic night,
  Of Katie in bridal white.
Four years. Aye, as the moonbeams sink
  Katie sinks out of sight.

At home a bridal morn,
Here it is heavy night.
She walks in diamonds bright.
Here Dian veils her horn.
Brighter are diamonds.   Stars that blink
As a moon goes down.   Yes, the moonbeams
    sink,
And Katie sinks from sight.

III.

Alone in the world.   Aye, no man
   Is kin to me if I come ;
Neither man, nor child, nor woman,
   In a home that is not home.
I may press the Father's hand
     Nevermore,
Nor will little Katie stand
     At the door.

IV.

All as of old.   The yews upon the lawn
Are watching over tombs.   The windows close
Shut in the ghostly spirit of the house.
Each door is fast ; it is but early dawn

And all is sleeping. If the veils be drawn
Will it awake? I know not. All is dead
As the dull mist of morning overhead.
I will not enter to disturb its peace:
So 'requiescat' for the hour. I tramp
Slowly the devious shrubbery paths. I cease
At the old arbour, mossy, green, and damp.
Yonder's my window in the basement, shaped
An arch, within, by heavy darkness draped.

How oft have I ere daybreak stolen out
With rod or gun, to bring an early prey
From pool or pasture; gaily painted trout,
Or partridges, or conies brown or grey,
That sought a luckless meal with early day.

Lo! sudden is the heavy curtain raised
So swift, methought it vanishèd away
Into a heavenly vision as I gazed.
A woman standeth there in white array
Too lovely to be earthly, slender, tall,
Crowned with the shimmering gleams that
    golden fall

In lustrous wavelets earthwards from her brow,
Raised for one moment to the skies, and now
Eclipsed in shadow.   All abashed I hold
My breath—a statue—till the heavy fold
Droops down once more ; then creep forth mean and base
Barefooted.   Holy was my resting-place.
And I, the man of many doubts and cares,
Held in my house an angel unawares,
Who in some mortal habit or disguise
Walks in my burial place of memories,
To fold their napkins, roll the stone ? who knows ?
But, looking eastwards, lo ! a sudden rose
That tinges all my tomb from base to leads,
Methinks the creeping roses raise their heads
To greet the sunrise.   Well, 'tis idle all,.
And dreams fade out if sunlight on them fall.

v.

Someone is leaving the garden door,
   And I am waiting beneath the trees.
This is the vision that came before,
   Now I may catch it before it flees.

Ah, dainty maiden, the look you bore
Is the same, if your angel garb no more
   Blows free in the morning breeze.

Aye, but I know you, for your blue eyes
   Have a colour of nothing below the sky,
And that black robe is a tissue of lies,
   The wings are under and you may fly;
Fly away as the dewdrops rise,
Soar like the lark that rising dies,
   Dies into deep blue sky.

Stay, but only one moment, stay!
I am passing across the grass.
Hush! she starts and she looks my way,
Now, now will the vision pass?
Nay, nay, it is open day,
And this is a mortal lass:
She is no fairy freak to fade,
But the sweetest, kindest, purest maid,
See, she has grasped my hand.
Maiden white in my yew tree's shade,
No mist-born fancy are you to fade,
But the fairest woman in any land.

VI.

I am the master of Windon Hall
  And of many an acre broad.
Acres broad, I would give you all
  Aye ! my heritage and hoard,
Could my gift a smile in answer call
  From the guest beside my board.

There is my aunt sits at the foot,
  A comely woman and kind,
The widow of a peer to boot,
  And somewhat to state inclined ;
There she sits in her sable suit
  With her solemn man behind.

But Margaret lightens the gap between,
  My aunt's niece Margaret.
My aunt has pearls that might deck a queen,
  But none so golden set
As the lustrous oval that shines between
  The locks of Margaret.

Aunt, I may kiss your comely brow,
  I have tasted your kindly lips,
You have pressed me whilst fondest tears downflow.

I touch but her finger-tips
When Margaret bends with a lily's bow.
Aunt, I could give you all, you know,
   For the thrill from those finger-tips.

VII.

How goes the world with our little Kate,
My father's ward, and my playmate,
   So wilful and unsteady?
Yet such a bonnie bright little maid.
I must not call her Kate, I'm afraid,
   For Kate is now 'My Lady.'
Just fourteen when I left, you know,
And I was not here to watch her grow;
So I see the child that loved us so,
   Not Kate—four years my 'My Lady.'

The aunt sits silent and rather stiff;
Perhaps Katie and she have had a tiff.
   Ah well! I should not wonder.
But Margaret? nay, it is not a frown
But sorrow, that bends her eyebrows down,
   For I caught a glisten from under.
It's an awkward question, that's evident.

I must find out, though, all that is meant.
Our sweet little Kate! It is small content
   To see I have made a blunder.

VIII.

Oh this is horrible! The pretty child—
My father's darling, and his holy trust
From one he loved—trod down by one defiled,
A slave of brutal rage and savage lust—
And none to help her. All alone are we,
But she is bound in chains, and I walk free.

My father! oh thank God he did not know,
Or I had loved his memory the less.
Ah Katie, this had bowed his spirit low
Had he but known: or was it this did press
Upon him ere he died? I, far removed,
Felt sorrow shake the hand of him we loved.

Here is a letter; one that I must read
In silence. 'Tis the voice of olden days
Speaking from shadow. Grant me help to heed
A spirit that my call shall never raise
Hereafter. What will be its last commands,
Tear-blotted, scrawled in haste by dying hands?

It is my Father who speaks, and he cries from his grave :
'On to the rescue, on ! Save her, our darling save !'
He who had striven in vain, wounded and fainting in fight,
Sends forth his only son to battle, to strike for the right.
Yes, he had sworn to his dying friend in the days long past
That the child, unfriended else, should be kept by him to the last ;
And by all of his should be held in a loving and sacred charge
As the holiest thing that they had—to be guarded with life and fame,
And Honour. Aye, and he held his Honour forth as a targe
Where the storm might beat as it list, it were idle to speak of shame.

'Honour and Truth.' He grasped the sword in his hand that slew
The falsehood. But where is he may part the false from the true ?

And blinded by smoke of battle one falls in a righteous cause.
If she have wrongs to avenge, yet she is his by the laws,
And his by her oath. She is bound in hand and soul alike.
She is his armour of proof. Where is it a foe may strike
But he wound her first? Ah, Father, thy sword is in feebler hands,
But I kiss the cross on the hilt—will strive what the blade commands.
Father, be thou my guide. If a demon hold her in thrall,
Nay, a million fiends, I stand ready to answer our Katie's call.
Long, long ago, I had dreams that were dreamed in idleness,
But the dreams were all of home, and Kate in her loveliness:
Is she as fair as the child was? Fairer, my aunt says. Yet
Was ever a shadow so fair as the light of Margaret?

Pouted passionate lips and eyes of the deepest brown,
Was it your smile that bewitched us most, or the childish frown?
The wild and innocent mirth, or the sudden shadow of wrath
That cleared in a shower of tears and kisses when love came forth,
And lighted a lovely rainbow of smiles on the tear stained face
Raised into loving eyes as you clung in our arms' embrace?
Aye, little Katie, I come, I come at thy call to my fate.
Katie dear, it is thine not mine if I come too late.

IX.

Here for ten days beneath his roof;
Signs there are, but they lack of proof.
This is a hound but fully trained,
A varnished scoundrel evil-grained.
Look at his shaven rounded chin,
His close-cropped head, his well-groomed skin,
The eyes a little blood-shot. Aye,
That's where these brutes refuse to lie

But show their nature. What a chest
The dog has! What a powerful arm!
'Tis a fine animal, but best
Chained up where it can do no harm.

And here's My Lady, little Kate
That was, tied up with such a mate.
But Kate is no more Kate to me:
The thing is done—so let it be.

Yes, for we meet all three at table;
We stroll all three down to the stable;
We take long gallops through the heather
And, but last night, we danced together.
For Kate, My Lady, is not too proud
To grant me every grace allowed
My Lord's most intimate retainer;
But I craved more, or I was vainer.
It's wiser, better, to be gone.
This is no farce to carry on.
All here's too painful. If I hate
The civil brute who killed our Kate,
Here is My Lady still alive,
Nay, seems, for all I see, to thrive;

A cold and scentless flower, 'tis true,
But fairer blossom never grew.
So marble white! Such stately pose!
'Tis a camellia! 'Twas a rose!
Lot's wife! Her pillar! But the salt
Seems lacking; there I am at fault.
She lacks all savour. 'Tis a queen
Of puppets worked by a machine:
But very lovely! Could her cold
Form shape into a marble mould,
It were perfection. Artists dote
On every contour of its throat.
There is a poet here will rave
Night after night upon its wave
Of ebon tresses, when the hour
Of man and pipe comes.—Grapes are sour.
I thirsted for the fray. My foe
Feasts me instead. 'Tis well to go,
Nor cause a scene. He's over-civil,
And I could wish him at the devil.
That's all. I will not hear the talk
Of servants; it's no road to walk
That leads through kitchen gossip; yet
One does hear hard things to forget.

But there she stands and makes no sign,
She's frozen this old flame of mine;
She has forgot her early days,
And all her childhood's loving ways,
And childish tempers.   That is well:
Temper would make her lot a hell.
  But Kate is eight years older,
  Eighty long years colder.
  My Lady would not bend her head,
  Warm upon my shoulder.

x.

'Frank, you will kill me if you stay!'
'Kate, Kate!'   She has fled away;
And I like a fool struck dumb, when I might have known
  Katie a child again,
  Katie in grief and pain,
Katie to solace and help; but my chance has flown.

'Frank, you will kill me if you stay.'
Then were it manly to flee away,
And to leave our Katie frozen to ice or stone?
  Hope on, for help is near,
  Child of our home nest dear;
Kate has a fellow-nestling, he is not flown.

'Frank, you will kill me if you stay.'
She looked like some helpless thing at bay
As I came on her here in the thicket all alone.
This was no statue cold,
Kate in her living mould!
Katie to cherish and kiss though the years have flown.

'Frank, you will kill me if you stay.'
It will ring in my ears to my dying day.
But was it a shriek, or a prayer, or a dying moan?
Ah, Kate! I cannot say.
Kate, I can only pray
For guidance to strike in the dark ere the day be flown.

XI.

Oh a fool! I am but a fool. But was ever a villain so vile,

From the sole of his varnished boot to the close-cropped convict head,

As this sporting swindling viscount, with his low card-sharping smile,

Till I dashed his leering waxen mask into blotches of purple red?

For the sneering sniggering brute that grinned full-gorged in its sty
Stirred a fiercer devil in me to spring, like a beast, at his throat,
Craving nought but his blood. Oh, why did I strike him? Why?
If I scarred a scoundrel's skin it was only through Kate that I smote.
There he stands by the fire at his ease and inspects his nails!
There the hound's bloodshot eyes look up from its paws and leer!
Could you filter a meaner wretch from the foulest dregs of the gaols?
Has it a heart? or a brain? But at least it has ears and shall hear;
Yes, he can listen and grin? Would that a thunderbolt strike
Full on those odious fangs! But the justice of Heaven is blind,
And lightning that falls from the sky strikes the good and the evil alike.
The gust of a passion in me fans him like a flattering wind.

Yes, he is cold whilst I burn in the hottest furnace of rage,
Just a touch of warmer malice, but no honest heat of shame.
These are days of sewage.   This the whitened garbage of the age,
That, deodorised, will smoulder, will not kindle into flame.

How can I talk of Katie to him? and what to him is the tale
Of my father's trust from the grave, or our Kate in her childish prime?
I must speak with a courteous caution, only to know I must fail.
'Lady Northolt' drags sadly on lips that kissed Kate in the olden time.
Then with a mocking candour, too shallow to merit belief,
As a lie even half believed, he confessed himself 'ill at his ease
With himself.' (Yes, ill-content were the fiends, and the dying thief
Who turned from the Lord. For Satan's a difficult master to please).

'He was sorry he married so early. Believed himself
  wholly bewitched.
I had known her a child, but begad could not picture
  the power that she had
To charm when the pair of them married.'—He saw
  not my hands how they twitched,
Or had checked himself then in his virtuous mood as
  he strutted and swelled.
'They were better apart, no doubt. They were never
  too well agreed.
The fact was both had a temper.'—Why, where will
  the rascal end?
'He had had a hint when he married. Was sorry he
  did not heed.
But he knew very well at the time that I was the old-
  est friend.
He had heard too much of it since, from her, and a
  quiet life
Was all he desired.' (Good God! 'twas 'a quiet
  life' that he said.
Yes, a carnival orgie of peace!) 'But he could not
  get on with a wife,
A wife with a will of her own, and damned fanciful
  whims in her head;

And I had the earliest claim.   'Twas the easiest thing to arrange.
There must be some gossip of course, but the tale would blow over in time,
But he would be free once more, and My Lady be glad of the change!'
But I struck the last lie down his throat, so I lost the details of his crime.
Yes, his blood-dabbled cheek has been reddened for once with a frenzy of hate.
He may groom himself now as he please; he will carry my mark till he die.
But the deeper scar is on her.   He was armoured all round by our Kate,
And where is our Honour? if truth should dwell in a villain's lie.

XII.

Margaret! Margaret!
You are hard! you are cold!
And your brow, when we met,
'Twixt its gold,
Shone as fair but faster set
Than of old.

HONOUR.

Oh Margaret! Margaret, I may not complain.
One that had sight of Eden may well grieve
Before the angel; but the conscious stain
Will bow his forehead humbly to receive
Thy judgment. Would that thou and I might trace
This thing free-souled together. Thy fine wit
Would probe it deeper. If one heart could face
Another wholly, wholly guess of it,
Thou would'st have pity; mightest yet repair
The subtle flaw; thou hast the keener eyes.
Were this again to act, I know not where
The hidden mischief to our honour lies.
'Twere all as one. I would not have the thing
Done or undone, but carried far away.
'Tis a vague nightmare with a dusky wing
That blinds me in the common light of day.
All visions of a brighter hope have ceased,
But there lies Katie strangling in the gloom,
With none to help her, whilst a loathsome beast
Coils in gross circles on my father's tomb.

XIII.

    Speak but thy soul's desire.
    Child, for thy comfort come
    Home to thy own dear home,
    Home of the honoured sire.
        Nay, Kate, keep back !
    Words that are wiser said :
    Here shall her footstep fall
    Never, till 'neath his pall
    One human dog lie dead.
        Dreams all !   Dreams all !

Dreams ! yes, dreams that had riddles of fate,
For here, in our house, is Kate, our Kate,
    And here are strong arms to hold her.
Our child is alive again, was dead.
Here she lies, with the tiny head
    Pressed warm upon my shoulder.

Oh ! 'tis the ghost of Kate, our Kate !
Look in her eyes, they are mad with hate
    In their lurid, deathly smoulder.
And her brow is fresh gashed with livid red.
Kate, stand back !   'Tis a Gorgon's head
    That was pressed upon my shoulder.

XIV.

Kate, I have sworn that while we live
You shall have all that is mine to give.
This house is yours, as his and mine.
Our oath was alike. It is always thine.
My arm, my Honour, are yours for aid.
They are poor enough. They have been betrayed,
Tried and found wanting. Poor attire
Is the whitest robe in such outer mire
As we've crossed in fight ; and here our ground
Is boggy and treacherous all around.
And you must rest here ; and I must go
To cry for a succour. No, Kate, no.
   We are older, weaker, wiser, colder.
I am your brother and love you so,
That never again shall your head lie low,
   Pressed upon my shoulder.

XV.

How these excellent women love one another !
This might draw tears out of eyes of stone ;
And my warm-hearted aunt lets hers run over,
But the torrent is squandered on me alone.

'No, my dear boy, I will not receive her.
Let her go back.   She has done you a wrong.
It's a horrible tale !   It is best you should leave her.'
'Aunt, shall I grind at the press with the strong
Whilst the blood of our Kate gushes red from under?
Or stand at my ease in the jeering throng
To idly gossip, and stare, and wonder,
Watching her lashed by his merciless thong?
Yes, look at Margaret standing steady !
Margaret ! Margaret ! you can hear.
You have a heart for the poor and needy,
And our aunt has ever a ready tear ;
But I swear that both of you, one and other,
Would stand with the Pharisees and stone.
You have pity for me as a foolish brother,
But a sister is nothing when trodden down.
Why do *you* stand with your dove's eyes flashing,
As I were some reptile and did you shame ?
My words are but drops on a statue plashing.
The pure cold marble is void of blame.

You were right, my aunt.   It is best to leave her.
But my father's house is her home by right ;
And its door is wide open to receive her
Winter and summer ; so, aunt, good-night.'

XVI.

It's the devil's counting-house.   Here we go
To see what the devil has got to show
   To a man that want's amusing.
He's a merry devil and laughs 'Ho-Ho!'
Like a pantomime fiend.   At Monaco
The devil's the proper person to know,
   He's so civil and disabusing.

Where are his horns? and where are his hoofs?
Hidden no doubt, but we see no proofs
   That his dart is upraised for slaying.
Here, he welcomes you polished and bland
As that old bald maestro, baton in hand,
Who leads the really magnificent band.
   It is 'Orpheus in Hell' they are playing.

In the palmy garden are cosy seats
For coffee and cognac, nice retreats
   For a closer observation.
In his modern Eden down here at least
Is every stupid and noisome beast;
And nymphs and satyrs renew their feast
   In this high French cultivation.

Look at the palace; stucco and gilt,
With statues of Fortune; here the jilt
Stands brazen without a rag on.
'Tis for her that the place was built,
To dance her cancan or Gallic lilt
With sordid Saint Georges who come to tilt
   For her sake with a gilded dragon.

Here is her janitor prim and neat
As a pompous prig at a Sunday-school treat.
   He tells me I'm not respectable
Without a card; and the ushers frown,
But call to my aid a person named Brown
Who will lend me his: and *his* name goes down.
   Why this is really delectable!

Dame Fortune's boudoir! No doubt her imps
Are those garlic-eating, white-chokered pimps
   Who have set her ball a spinning.
See, it is settling, 'rouge pair et manque.'
I suppose the chance was against the bank,
For a ripple of teeth from the foremost rank
   Proclaims that the owners are grinning.

Dull as a chapel, I must confess !
I must risk a louis ; I can't do less,
　　But I did not come to squander.
Watch that vagabond's face of distress,
White with a horror he can't repress :
Is he gazing at death and its bitterness ?
　　Why, where will my fancy wander ?

That's the Duke of Aldborough shuffling along.
I saw our archdeacon just now in the throng.
　　Here's Sir John Jobson the minister.
'Who would think of finding you here, Sir John ?
That's a dangerous measure your folk are upon.
And how's your new Brummagem hand get on ?'
　　And off goes Sir John looking sinister.

That woman yonder's at war with fate ;
I have seen that look in the eyes of Kate,
　　And gold will never content her.
Moore's ' Peri that wept at heaven's gate '
Need not have been so disconsolate ;
She was all right, though she had to wait.
　　But how shall these Furies enter ?

There's an old death's head that lacks a shroud !
It's a strange menagerie, that's allowed,
   If one goes on picking and choosing.
But the Gallic houris are not endowed
With too many charms, and not too proud
For thieving. This very various crowd
   Fails to be strictly amusing.

I remember that blackleg. 'Frank, my boy,
I've read all about it, and give you joy.'
   Can it be to me that he's speaking?
Yes, by Jove ! and to save a row,
I suppose I must toss back his blackguard bow.
I hardly thought I was quite so low.—
   Just hear that Dutchwoman shrieking.

'Read all about it.' Yes, I'll be bound
That some Society Journal's hound
   Is gnawing a succulent bone of it.
Where are this week's papers? Here—one, two,
   three.
That's all; but enough. How glad we should be
To have mirrors like these of Society,
   Reflecting the highest tone of it !

'Scandal in high life.' Then what is low?
My name, you villain! Well, well, I know
   You must eat; and it's no use swearing.
But you need not lie to such an extent.
Write a better tale if you must invent.
'*We* write from rumour.' I'll not resent
   The new pinchbeck pin *We* are wearing.

'The lady's at Monaco, We hear.'
Would it be worse, Kate, if you were?
   For our Honour's an inky bubble
That bursts to bespatter a page of 'Truth.'
Truth and Honour are nowadays printer's proof,
And his proof is sufficient to damn them both,
   As vexation of spirit and trouble.

And Kate might be here; for that girl, like Kate,
Has the selfsame restless demon of hate,
   And must deaden its nightmare fancies
With poison. Her sickness is long past cure.
Can I picture Margaret walking pure
In this Comus revel? But why endure
   The torture of such romances?

I am off from this paradise of the lost
To some quieter Eden along the coast,
    Where these hounds will lose scent in their
        tally-hos.
For I shrink when a vile mosquito sings,
Though by deeper wounds his are surface stings.
The Italians, who care for none of these things,
    Will act the parts of my Gallios.

XVII.

I lit a beacon on my soul's dark sea,
That so each vagrant thought that questioned me
Sailing thereon, no more be pressed on me,
But reach one haven, there at rest to be.

A calm, deep-bosomed, peaceful as a mere,
Where no wild storms confuse the listening ear,
And hopes which mock in outer mist appear
Bubbles no more, but one bright crystal clear.

There all vague barques that sought forth far and
    wide
Unresting, into quiet waters glide,
And 'twixt twin hillocks of its shore abide
Safe from all strife, at peace and fortified.

So, on my sea, the light which streamed o'erhead
Drew every hulk to where it shone.   It led
Through weeds, that though they tossed thereon were
    dead,
And pathless wastes wherein they wanderèd

My little fleet ; which spread all sails to gain
That refuge where the passions stir in vain,
No more to scatter, or incur again
The restless fury of the hurricane.

Then warm south wind arising filled their sails,
Coasting by lands where pearly light prevails,
Beholding sun-warm slopes, and sighting dales
Flower-fragrant, musical with nightingales.

Here lay their harbour : but a bar unseen
Severed the wave from that still bay within,
Nor was there any open way to win
An entrance to the peace that lay therein.

Then darkness grew, till in the sky above
The star-guides failed ; and that warm light which love
Had lighted, fell.   The storm had might to move
The firm foundations and the site thereof.

Oh ! wherefore was there any beacon lit ?
If only that the mists should smother it ?
If only that the tide pass over it,
And the deep womb of darkness cover it ?

Whilst the dark waves arising more and more
Wreck all, and rise in waterspouts and roar,
Passion to drive them ; and their doubts before,
Upon the hidden rocks about the shore.

XVIII.

'Oh, rare pale Margaret.' The line runs in my head.
I'm ill and drowsy, reading books in bed.
The laureate's Margaret was rare, and mine
Finds some description in his opening line.
Suppose, as I have nothing else to do,
I scribble out my lines to Margaret too.
    'Oh, rare pale Margaret, on thy lofty throne
    An angel in derision looking down.'
Nay, I am foolish and I do thee wrong,
I may not worship ; let me give thee song.

HONOUR.

    Margaret cold !
        Nay, do not frown.
    See, I am humble,
        Fallen prone.
If I never arise
Need your calm blue eyes
        Look down?

    Snow on the hilltop,
        Fever below.
    Heaven's cool breezes
        Freshly blow
On yon snowy peaks ;
They fan not my cheeks'
        Fierce glow.

    Up through the clouds
        The mountain horns
    Know these hot noontides'
        Brighter morns.
Here slow heat dozes
On sickly roses
        And thorns.

Could I but reach
That lofty land,
There might my vision
Wide expand.
It is far to wend
With no guide to lend
Her hand.

Up steep hill paths
My soul will set,
It lacks wing to fly,
Margaret.
If it fail and die,
May the calm blue sky
Forget.

Heat ! heat ! what a filthy steam !
There is a stream ! I saw it gleam.
No ! no ! only the glow,
Sun on a rock, a block, a mock !
I turn, I burn, there is flame below.
A furnace ! a furnace ! He's there to blow ;
He sneers, he jeers ; why, her tears are molten solder!
Kate is down there ! I can see her glow.

HONOUR.

No, Kate, no!
Kate! Hate! You are burning, go
Heart apart to smoulder.
Kate—Fate! and my heart is tow.
It stares! it glares! it has caught me—
Oh! it flames upon my shoulder.

Smoulder! moulder! choking smoke.
Kate! Kate child, hands off! I shall choke.
Nay, I'm not angry, Kate, you know.
Kiss me, kiss me—don't stoop low.
I'm going on, Kate, up the stair,
We shall find it cool up there.
Where has the child run off to? Where?
Sorry to miss her evening kiss.
Kiss! hiss! kiss! Hist, it's a serpent's hiss!
There's the brute on a tombstone,
I think it has swallowed Katie down.
Look at its eyes—they are red with sin.
What a tomb to bury our Katie in!
That's her shroud! Nay her ghost's too proud
To walk in filthy vesture.
That brazen jade in this crawling crowd
Shall use it to hide her gesture,

Prancing, dancing.   Here's Sir John !
'How does your Brummagen hand get on?
Vanished !—very uncivil.
Naked nymphs—what a noisy band
Follow a hollow bâton, a wand ;
No, it's the civil devil.
Down, down, down, they are gone.
I'm going on, on, on—on over the rubble,
On, on, on, on a bubble.
On ! on ! *Honour !*
Weak, weak, seek the peak
Up in the snow !   Golden hair !
Gold, cold, frozen there ; asleep, asleep.
Sleeping, sleeping.   I am creeping, weeping, creeping
    up the stair,
Ends there, blue air, blue air.
There's a flower that cures grows there.
    Blue air !
I creep, I creep.   Steep asleep ; sleep deep ; deep
    keep ; keep blue eye,
Keep weep ; weep, die.

    In this hot gloom as I ponder,
      Waking in pain on my bed,

HONOUR.

Eyes that for ever grow fonder
   Look down in love on my head;
Eyes in a picture up yonder.
'Tis but a painted Madonna
   Hangs on the dun plastered wall;
But the eyes of her would not dishonour
   The master, the greatest of all,
Who painted the Virgin Madonna.
Gentian-blue eyes of a spirit,
   Heavens of pity unfeigned
Love-drawn on earth, ye inherit
   Tints of the flower that I gained,
Brought home from far hills of the spirit.
HE that was born of this woman
   Knew how a heaven of love
Might enter a heart that was human;
   HE, who had sorrow to prove
All spirits that dwell in a woman.
I, who am fevered and dreaming,
   Watch my flower grow in her eyes.
Margaret's? Nay, I was scheming
   Only in idle surmise
Gotten of fever and dreaming.

HONOUR.

Orange ! whose virginal blossom
   Lights thy dark shadows with bloom,
Send one white star from thy bosom,
   Let me drink in its perfume.
For the air of my chamber is tainted,
   They have shut out the air and the day ;
I pine for those presences sainted
   In these close hot horizons of grey.
Oh for sweet scents of the meadow !
   Oh for a couch in the breeze,
Amid flowers in the flickering shadow
   Arched by the grey olive-trees !
But this blossom brought in from the garden
   Breeds fragrance. Some freshness is there
In this snowflaky thing. Will it harden
   A crystal, or melt in this air?
Could but its fine subtle essence
   Reach, not the brain but the soul,
Grief might shrink out of its presence,
   Leperous thought be made whole.
Such a spirit might flow from a maiden
   More fair than this flower from the tree,
And these shadows, gold-freighted be laden
   With fruit. But this thought may not be.

Here comes the sunbeams striving
    Into my chamber at last.
It looks like the land of the living,
    And my valley of shadow is past.
But, oh ! how the clouds go sweeping
    On in the howling blast !
Weak, I am weeping, weeping
    For a sun that is overcast.

XIX.

A lawyer's budget. Confound the thing !
Why are they sending their trash to me ?
I was getting better. Suppose I fling
Their gift on the fire. But I'll look and see.
Oh that's his move ! Well, at least he knows,
This Minotaur, that the legal maze
Is safer shelter than coming to blows,
As they used to do in the good old days.
' Particeps criminis at the suit
Of John Dalrymple, commonly called
Lord Northolt.' So is the savage brute
His bull : which nobly littered and stalled,

Thoroughly soaped, and gorged with food,
Held a high place at the cattle show,
'Highly commended' for noble blood,
With a ticket marked 'Dangerous' down below.
'Deferred to next session.' 'Three months reprieve.
Worry and bother for three months hence !
'Long and Lawson will gladly receive
Any instructions for my defence.'
Defence ? Why, what have I left to defend ?
Kate ? Well, yes, I suppose I must.
I will stand by Kate to the weary end
If only to answer my father's trust.

XX.

'Frank, I must see you before I die.'
Nonsense, she's always dying ! And yet,
As the telegram falls to the floor, I lie
'Neath the eyes of the spirit of Margaret.

Now if this woman would really die !
'Truth and Honour.' Ay, don't forget.
'Truth and Honour.' I well may sigh
For aid to my vision of Margaret.

If we must meet before we die,
My eyes will be weary if yours are wet ;
For mine have been straining to the sky
To catch the last glimmer of Margaret.

Yes, we must meet before we die.
Both are caught in the self-same net ;
But I sicken, for blacker clouds go by,
That have hid me from sight of Margaret.

XXI.

Rain, rain, and a broken pane,
Beating, sleeting into the train.
Rain, rain, and a pain in twain,
Beating, eating an addled brain.
Pain, pain, and dirty rain,
Filtered through filth it leaves its stain.
Rain, rain, and on again.
Rumble, tumble, a jolting train !
Mumble, jumble, and daylight's wane !
Fumble, stumble, but hope is vain !
Rain, rain, hiding the plain

A rumble, a tumble, a mumble, a jumble,
    A feeble brain.
  I stumble, I grumble. A mist and a stain,
    And rain, rain !

XXII.

I am coiling up again
For another night in the railway train.
How strange it is that every place is
Filled with the dear old English faces !
I'm foolish ; for it is not strange,
But anyway it's pleasant change.
And pleasant are familiar tongues ;
And pleasant, air that fills your lungs.
' Pleasant ' 's a word I have not said
For some time since, I am afraid :
But still it's nice to look about
And see how warm the lights peep out
'Neath eaves of English cottages.
The Frenchmen boil their pottages
By no such fire as that which gleams
From each warm hearth in ruddy streams :
For English hearths, like English hearts,
Seem warmer than in other parts.

HONOUR.

    That woman yonder in the corner
Has a warm heart. I need not scorn her
That she is stout. She thinks I'm ill,
And offers wraps to keep out chill.
'No, madam, thanks; I am not cold.
Give me your baby here to hold
One moment for you, whilst you are getting
Your bags put safely in the netting.
Believe me, I can hold it steady.
See how it takes to me already!'

The little dumpling—how it crinkles
Its face into a hundred wrinkles
To smile. Its soft fat tendrils linger
Quite lovingly clasped round my finger.
My pretty one! may no mishap
Befall thee lying in my lap!
Yes, little babe, it's long ago
Since I have held a baby so:
Not since I was a boy of eight,
And proud to nurse a baby—Kate!
Yes, I remember.—Would that she
Were once more but this babe to me!

Then if she wept a passing while
'Twas easy to call back her smile;
Now tears unsolaced bubble up,
And she must drink the bitter cup.
O baby! you have done no harm
But nursed on my unloving arm,
Lie all forsaken in the cold.
My heart is worn, it's growing old,
If I who nursed the babe disdain
To seek it solace in its pain,
But left it wounded, wet with mire,
By my cold hearth without a fire;
Cold hearth of home! my English heart
Was hard and frozen, far apart.

'O baby! I'm not fit, you see,
To hold a child upon my knee.
Go back.   You well may start from sleep,
To stare afraid at me, and weep.'
She fears—the Psyche in this child—
A changing love, a thing defiled.
She slept with love, and wakes to find
Love fled, and sorrow left behind.

HONOUR.

Well may you turn from me, and clutch
The breast of her who loves you much.
You know that there is safer rest
Than that you found on this cold breast.'
A hollow cage of hardened bone,
The bird inside was froze to stone.
Nay, I know not ; it may revive
In its own nest again and live.
The hearth is cold, the fire burnt low,
But yet may kindle up and glow
Till some warm light and comfort come
And glad once more the dear old home.
I must kneel low, and strive to raise
The sluggish embers to a blaze ;
And take once more upon my knees
The child I left alone to freeze :
Chafe the cold limbs—our child was ill,
And so a little frost might kill.
Oh ! 'twas a cruel thing to do,
To leave this girl that loved us so
To hear the storms outside, with fright,
Cold and alone, at dead of night,
Whilst shrilling sharp a wailing wind
Blew through the chambers of her mind.

HONOUR.

Well might our Kate ere this be dead
To see such ghosts around her bed
As that man-brute who gashed her brow
Bending to give a fiercer blow,
Whilst she lay open to a thrust
That bows her honour to the dust.
Please GOD I am in time to save
Our little Katie from her grave.
Katie! I have been foolish, loath,
And idle.   Now I keep my oath.
The outside world may scoff in vain:
We two will bear it, and remain
Brother and sister to each other;
A sister child; an elder brother.
Sure we may find some comfort still
In mutual faith through good and ill.
If all alone and shunned by friends,
We two are twins to our lives' ends.
We two must strive that home suffice
In warmth; for all the world is ice.
Safe within doors such winter cold
May be defied, though o'er the wold
The winds drift snow through all our life.
Thou hast no husband; I no wife.

The parent birds are long at rest
And we lone nestlings in our nest.
Outside the fowler spreads his gin ;
But 'Truth and Honour' bide within.

XXIII.

'My Lady has wished, sir, for you to arrive.'
GOD be thanked ! then our Kate is alive.
Up the stairs to the silent room :
All is shrouded ; it's like a tomb.
Tread soft—she may sleep. A short step back
At that white keen outline edged with black
Of our Kate ; drained out, if purified
By tears.—I kneel, I am at her side.
'Katie !' Oh what a glad sweet look
In the open eyes ! I cannot brook
Their light of welcome. My tears fall fast.
'Katie dear, I am come at last.'

'Frank, I knew that you would come
If your little Katie called you home.
Why did you leave me, Frank ? you knew
In all the cold world I had only you.'

'I was a heartless guardian.
 Katie, forgive! My tears must sue.
  Katie, sister, pardon.
 My moods are gone. Frank's here instead
 To raise your pillows, smooth your bed.
  Frank has been growing older
 In faith and trust. Nay, lay your head
  Once more upon his shoulder.'
'Frank, I have known how all behind
 Was falsehood. Your sister read your mind,
  My kindest foolish brother.
 You were kind all through; but could not find
  That my love was never other.
 And Frank, I feared that if I should die
 You might be unhappy. Men are shy
  And slow to read love's token.
 I have a sister. Love her. Try:
  Or else her heart is broken.
 See my nurse. She's a *sister's* cap,
 But it can't hold *all* her gold in its flap,
  Though it becomes her rarely.
 Turn and look. You are in my trap.
 Oh! Frank, I feared! It is lucky hap
  To catch both birds so early.'

XXIV.

Child, is it pain to be dying?
Hearing glad songs of the spring,
Birds to their lovers replying
Whilst scythes of the grass-cutters ring
That grass on green fields may lie dying.
While our gladness that dwelt in the shadow
Sings round thee in brightness of day;
The breezes come in from the meadow
Sweet with faint breath of the hay.
Child! the grass fades not in shadow!
Yea, she is glad in our gladness.
Home, and warm sun are her lot;
Gone are the frosts and the madness,
Floods of old sorrows forgot
In a short summer sunshine of gladness.
Margaret is her Madonna,
Took up her sorrowful heart,
Loved it, and set it in honour.
I had my visions apart
Far from our maiden Madonna:
Mine was the blurred blotted vision
Gotten of fever and dreams,

Clouded by wrath and derision;
Katie lay warm 'neath its beams
Safe with the sun of her vision.
Watch how they love one another,
Sisters in loving and truth;
Differing else. But Kate's brother
Bows down in sorrow and ruth
Alike to the one and the other.

XXV.

We are three that look forth at harvest
    On earth in her bridal veil;
But one of us gazes farthest
    And saith to the bridegroom, 'Hail.'
Sees the golden mesh of the netting
    Sun-woven, touch gold more bright,
The robe of the bridegroom setting
    On his sky-broad couch of light.
Sees fields that looked love to heaven
    Reach all at the even time,
For the sun bends low at the even
    And they have but a step to climb.

So her eyes that grow fonder, fonder,
   Are brimmed with the mellow beams :
Clear pools where the sunset yonder
   Is mirrored in golden gleams.
For the love from a soul upspringing
   Looks close on its golden crown,
Whilst ours to grey levels clinging
   And sorrow-dimmed look down.
'Katie !' 'Her soul advances,
   We are barred by our prison grate.'
'She will answer us one day, Francis,
   If we stand where we are, and wait.'

Yes, a smile of welcome is in her eye,
   If the sweet still lips be colder.

Her memory may not unhonoured lie,
   Whilst we live on earth to uphold her.

Before all the world her head is high ;
   At rest upon love's shoulder.

THE TALE OF RABBI JOSEPH.

ADAPTED FROM DE QUINCEY.

JOSEPH BEN JOSAPHAT, a rabbi gray,
Knelt from high noon till eventide to pray;
Then, risen, gazed afar o'er Mamre's plain
To watch the twilight's lingering citron wane;
And saw a sudden mote that moved. A deer
Perchance? Nay, 'twas a man in haste. Drawn near,
He paused respectful, knelt him down, and bowed,
Hands laid on breast, before he gasped aloud:
'Swift, holy rabbi! Swift a sheep to tend;
A daughter of our race draws nigh her end.
One grievously tormented. Fiends of hell
Gather against the child of Israel.'
   The rabbi girt his robe: a friend to all
His race, he answered gladly at their call;
And with his guide passed from the cavern's mouth
Unto the grove of Hebron by the south.

There, found a palace built of wood and stone
And ivory, rich as that which Solomon
Gave the Egyptian woman. Heavy palls
Of Sidon's broidering waved on painted walls
'Twixt fluted stems with brazen capitals.
All priceless things lay scattered without heed;
The Persian crystal, and the Indian bead;
The perfect forms of Greece, and bowls by hands
Of Sinim wrought, the farthest of far lands.
All these the rabbi heeded not, but passed
Into the richest chamber, and the last,
All gold and amber. In its close recess
Lay one of unimagined loveliness
Wrapped in soft silks of Shiraz, but a glow
Of flame unsteady flickered on her brow,
Or left it ash-white, and her eyes' black wells
Shrank not in light. Reflective shadow dwells
In such defies the sun, they watch near wings
Of Azrael, sunless are his shadowings.

The sufferer shivered as the rabbi laid
His palm upon her burning brow to aid
A heat, no freshness of the night-breeze fanned,
With the cool contact of his pitying hand.

She turned like one tormented. As a leaf
Shivers and shrinks in the sirocco's breath,
So every muscle shrank. Each tendon thrilled
Like bowstring springing ; and the rabbi skilled
To mark, knew now that one of the unblest
Had seized that lovely dwelling for his rest.
Then drew he forth an unguent from his gown,
Which wise men of old time had handed down.
'Such Daniel made and touched therewith and healed
The herb-fed king, and led him from his field
To sit upon the throne.' Therewith her lips
He touched, then nostrils, eyes, and finger-tips.
Next he made fire of shittim wood, thereon
Laid aloes, frankincense, and cinnamon,
And as the fume rose, bore her from her bed
And mid the vapours bended down her head.
Then died all fire from out her face again,
It froze to one blue mask of icy pain.
She shrieked as one in torture, but the lips
Moved not ; her glassy eyes had no eclipse ;
No breath stirred, but 'twas horrible to hear
The blasphemy, the hate, the filth, the fear,
The shriek for mercy, and the viler note
Of mocking laughter from that moveless throat.

'Spare me this incense torment. Spare
To smite mine ears with sound of prayer.
Is vengeance wanting? Lo! the sky
Is thick with wings of those that fly
Hither, at bidding of the Lord,
To cleave me with the venomed sword.
Look forth! each holds a flaming scourge
Thrice knotted. What hast thou to urge?'

When midst a storm the sudden lightning's shock
Hurls down some mighty pinnacle of rock
Upon a tiger leaping in the grasp
Of death, so sudden sprang she in his clasp
Maddened with dread. Her eyeballs from their caves
Leapt out like souls accursèd from their graves,
Despairing, hating, seeing nought but dire
Tormenting fiends behind, in front but fire.
Then issuing forth, the parting demon tore
With one last agony the shape he wore,
To one last scream of helpless hate gave vent,
And fled despairing to his punishment.
Slowly the breath returned to that weak frame,
And, gazing up, she spoke the Rabbi's name,
Who slowly rising, in his aged arms

Took the frail burden of her mortal charms,
And gently laid it where to east a ray
Shone through the porch and heralded the day.
A fresh sweet breeze, by thyme and violets
Balsamed with perfume, cooled the steaming sweats
Of Israel's daughter; but her face still bore
The marks of many sorrows gone before;
And though the spirit speaking was her own,
She told its tale in many a varied tone
Of joy or anguish : and the Rabbi heard
That tale rejoicing, but he spake no word.

'Listen and fear ! I for a while
Was dweller in the land of Nile ;
Rich, powerful, courted, hated, vile,
A murderer, adulterer,
A sensual king's worst minister.
I fell ; and stript and bare,
I sought the wild beast's lair ;
In raging heat, accurst,
Tortured by pains and thirst,
I found a refuge from the glare,
An empty tomb, and entered there.

Amidst foul bones that stank
Corrupt, I failed and sank,
An outcast parched and lone,
Who late stood by the throne.
Each dried limb shrank
To skin and bone,
But thirst was nought
Beside the thought
Of hate, my own.
Joy ! could I drink a flood
Of the accuser's blood !
Joy ! could I tear
The heart laid bare !
Watch with a gloating eye
The fierce despair,
The agony !

'I tore myself.   I thrust
My nails into the dust.
I cursed with failing breath.
My tongue clave to my teeth.
E'en hatred failed, and soon
I sank into a swoon.

'I woke, a pitcher to my mouth.
Who is it that would aid my drouth?
An aged man and sinister,
He seemed the devil's minister.
I cursed, and he the while
Sat with a listening smile,
Approving what I said
By motion of his head.
Stronger, I cursed again, and he
Proffered his drink once more to me.
"What fiend art thou?" I said; "wouldst give
Life to a hate that loathes to live?
It starves and perishes with heat.
I spue thy water, spurn thy meat.
I burn for blood. Revenges sweet,
I crave nought else. I will not eat."

'The old man turned. His glance
Pierced through me like a lance.
His mouth curved to a smile
So bestial, so vile,
I, even I, felt fright
To read that look aright.

He spoke. "A lucky fate
Is thine, to satiate
A thirst that is so sore
In floods of human gore.
I had ere this perceived
The fire in which you grieved.
Hate filled thy heart with flame.
My hatred is the same,
And I myself will give
Thine fuel by which to live:
The hearts of those who sent
Thee into banishment,
Their fortunes, and their lives,
Their children, and their wives,
Are thine. Lo! I thy friend
Have saved thee to this end,
Will raise thee from the dust,
Will satisfy each lust,
Will give thee wealth and power
And Egypt for thy dower.
Oh, son of Abraham
(Friend of the great I AM)—
Now for a hundred years
Cast off all doubts and fears.

Rule all men at thy will,
Torture, and burn, and kill.
Spend wealth, nor fear decrease,
Drink wine and live at ease.
The fairest of the land
Are all at thy command.
All's thine, all at thy feet,
Till once again we meet,
Then shalt thou dwell with me
And must my servant be;
But that's a distant day
A century away.
A hundred years to cloy
Thy vengeance, and enjoy
All things thy burning heart
Can dream of wealth and art,
And beauty and success.
Behold, I give no less."

'I grasped the old man's scorching hand.
I stood upright at his command.
I watched him fill a golden cup;
I seized it, paused not, drank it up.

I sucked it to its utmost drain,
I felt it burn into my brain.
I looked around, and he was gone,
  And in the tomb I stood alone.

'None could have known me as I stood;
Fresh tides of youth coursed in my blood.
No more myself, the form I bore
Was stronger, comelier than of yore;
No longer naked as before,
The richest broidered robes I wore,
And arms with jewelled hilts, each thing
Worthy the ransom of a king;
Whilst yellow-glistening in the gloom,
Were piles of gold that filled the tomb.
I took small heed of what was shown,
My vengeance filled my heart alone,
And I rejoiced. 'Twas bliss to know
I held the scales of joy and woe;
And such revenge might be my own
As never yet the years had known.
I would wrench forth such bitter cries
From foes in mortal agonies

As Hell had hardly heard arise;
A vengeance should my soul devise,
To shake men's hearts, appal the skies.

'I drank my fill. I lashed the state
Of Egypt with the rod of hate.
I was the tempting fiend who school'd
The vilest kings that ever ruled,
A nation's shame, mankind's disgrace,
A dastard and a mongrel race.
I had revenge, invented woes
Too fierce, too nameless to disclose,
For all who in my former life
Had dared contend with me in strife.
I had my spies. The lightest breath
Was laden with the dread of death,
Till men dare hardly speak my name
So swift so sure my vengeance came;
And foes, in torment, hid apart
The hatred that devoured their heart.
I feasted to excess. I drank,
I wallowed in all vileness rank.
No surfeit on my strength prevailed,
No purposes of evil failed.

At length, when I had drainèd dry
All pleasures to satiety,
Could no fresh sensual crimes invent,
Devise no fiercer punishment,
It grew my chief delight to win
My fellows to my life of sin,
Construct the snare or spread the gin,
That innocence was taken in.
An easy task. That bestial court
Was but the foulest, last resort
Of crimes that in another place,
If found, had need to hide their face.
Here, they walked open, looked not down,
Danced naked, blushed not, wore the crown.
I bought old age, corrupted youth,
Set falsehood high, trod down the truth,
Prompted oppression, closed the door
Of justice to the wronged and poor.

'And sitting thus in my estate
I feared no foe, controlled no hate.
Ofttimes assassins lay in wait
To slay me, ambushed at my gate.

I feared them not. My spies revealed
The shadows where they lay concealed,
And hunters, stealing forth to slay
The tiger, met it in their way,
To fall themselves its latest prey.
So all the land lay still. Men fled
My presence, smitten sore with dread ;
No promise there that time would stay
My hand. I lived without decay,
Unchanged, more awful day by day.
I hardly watched the years roll by ;
I hardly deemed that I could die ;
I knew not that my time drew nigh ;
The changeless dial of the sky
Watched all men change save only I.

'We held an orgie that the morn
Beheld reluctant. Pale and worn
The king sat. I alone arose
As fresh as at the twilight's close.
The old man, changeless in his might
To sin. The youth, at morning light
Nerveless and feeble. Lo ! a train
Of camels wending o'er the plain,

From the far desert come, to bring
The Arab tribute to the king.
I looked. Though these and he were met,
Both should be fishes in my net.
I would be king myself, and rule,
No longer guide this fainéant fool:
Lust roused him to no fresh excess;
False, but too feeble to oppress,
He was too weak for wickedness.

'I watched the string of camels wend
Across the plain, and towards me bend,
Halt at the city gate. I might
Have seen the sheik himself alight,
Save that I turned and saw the king,
Drunken, cast off his covering,
And reeling feebly to my side,
Gaze down upon the prospect wide.
'Twas but a push. He reeled and fell
Mid slaves who raised a hideous yell,
Desisting sudden from their sport,
To raise their master from the court
Dead, without doubt; and I the while
Turned back with a contemptuous smile,

To shrink in terror from the eye
Of him I met in days gone by,
The desert sheik. I knew the hour
Was his, and fled my dream of power;
I sickened 'neath his loathsome stare,
And snatched a dagger in despair,
Striving to plunge it in my side.
His mastering hand my thought denied,
He dropped my arm again and smiled
On one as helpless as a child,
And smiling said, "The years are flown,
And I am come to claim my own.
  I who am Sammael,
  Prince in the lowest hell,
  Lord both of man and beast
  In all this sensual East,
  Come hither now to claim
  Thee, child of Abraham,
  (Loved of the great I AM).
  Though of that race divine,
  Now art thou surely mine.
  Pass then to Hell's despair,
  Wait till I claim thee there."

'His visage flashed with flame.
His voice as thunder came.
I fell before his feet.
He raised his spear to beat
A chasm to the glow
Of endless fires below.
Sudden, I heard a groan
Of anguish break his tone.
A gleam of lightning shone
And wrapped him, like a gown,
Writhing from head to feet,
In white and awful heat;
The radiance from the eyes
Of one from Paradise
Who fights with powers of Hell
For sons of Israel.
The foul fiend sent a ruddy dart,
Thrice venomed, downwards at my heart.
The angel caught it on his shield
And smote with lightnings blue and steeled
Such blows he could not choose but yield,
And giving back he groaned aloud,
Then vanished in a thunder cloud;

Whilst the avenger looking down
Rebuked me, anger in his frown:

'"Son of man, thou that hast sinned,
Traitor and worst of thy kind,
Know that the Infinite Mind
Sends me to scourge and to bind.
Thou of thy race wert the bane,
Stained with all sensual stain,
Cursed with the curses of Cain.
Mercy—is judgment and pain.
Thou as a beast shalt be fed,
Gall of affliction thy bread,
Scorch of the sun on thine head.
No man my vengeance hath fled.
       Kneel! I have said."

'I saw him bend to touch my brow.
I shrank as from a mortal blow;
I felt a sudden stab of pain
Shoot through my forehead, numb my brain.

I bounded out of the palace gate,
I leapt down the terraces, elate;

I swam through the Nile, and I scoured the sand
With a force that I cared not to understand.
I sped o'er the plains like a rushing wind
Till I lost the last trace of the towers behind,
And saw but the desert levels dry
With their flickering rim 'neath the scorching sky.
I marked out a tent where the Arabs slept,
And a strange thirst filled me as on I swept.
They arose from their rest as I drew more near
With a savage clamour, and shrieks of fear.
There was one who rushed forth and hurled a lance.
I felt the dull point from my shoulder glance,
And maddened I sprang with a savage roar;
He was down 'neath my feet in a pool of gore,
My teeth in his throat, whence the stream ran red.
I sated my drouth whilst his comrades fled.
I left his carcase, I neared the brink
Of a pool, and I bent me down to drink.

 'It was a blood-stained lion's face
 That from the pool returned my gaze.

  'I leapt. I clove the air
  With howls of fierce despair.

I shuddered at the sound,
And started bound on bound.
My mane adown the wind
Streamed stiffly out behind.
My blazing eyeballs, hot
As fiery coals, saw not.
I shunned not thorn nor shock
Of precipice or rock.
My sole desire to fly
This loathsome shape and die.

' And e'en its savage strength
Grew faint with toil at length.
Its shuddering limbs grew wet,
Its glaring eyeballs set,
Its feet were flayed.   I fell
To heritage of Hell.
I loathed this bestial form
Now weaker than the worm ;
I shuddered that the day
Could mark me as I lay.
I longed for shades of night
To bury me from sight ;

But there with calm bright eyes,
The stars gaze and despise;
The unruffled moon looks down,
And the still mountains frown.
I would have hid my ills
In caverns of the hills:
But there the awful face
Of Sammael filled each place.
Small rest, small refuge there
From terror or despair.
I could not die. The beast
Rose up, and won its feast
Upon the wolf that came
To profit by its shame.
The angel's word was sure,
Perforce I must endure.

'I had endured. The sun had risen
Uncounted ages on my prison.
The thoughts that filled my tortured mind
Traced all the paths that lay behind,
Saw all my sins in letters clear
Of blood, the tale from year to year

Horrible, ghastly.   Lo, the scroll
Spared not one jot, contained the whole.
But all the present was the brute's,
And had its bestial attributes.
It had the instincts of its form,
And shivered in the winter storm,
Or blistered neath the cloudless sun,
Until at length, at length, begun
Decay ; and all its mighty thews
Grew stiff and feeble with disuse.
Its eyes grew dim, its jaws grew weak,
It scarce had strength its prey to seek ;
It dragged its feeble carcase old
To profit by a shepherd's fold,
And as the trembling beasts, dismayed,
Fled bleating, lo ! there came in aid
Their shepherd, and my slow dim eyes
Watched him approaching with surprise.
In sight of this old man and poor,
I dreamed of hope unfelt before.
Nay surely, surely 'twas the same.
I drooped my head in sudden shame,
And sought to breathe the angel's name.
Then, kneeling humbly in the dust,
My heart received his sudden thrust.

I sprang in pain. A scorching light
Flashed, and burnt blue, and died in night.

'I was wrapped in a garment of heavy dew
As I slid from the womb of the night anew.
I swam in a vapour that all around
  Quivered and writhed with the thunder's sound.
I reeled as a lightning blazed, and then
Thick darkness enveloped me round again.

              d through the swirl
              st, and I clove the whirl
              t, as I strove to soar
              around me, behind, before.
              sped. I was failing fast.
              ghtness above at last?
              l o'er my head
              ke, and the sun shone red.
              y from the dome downbent
              he clear bright firmament,
              my sin and its punishment.
              on he gazed upon,
              ing heart drew a scream alone,
              in its walls of bone?

It hovered with mighty wings outspread
In circles, or through the ether fled
Like an arrow by some strong bowman sped.
I gazed on the shadowed form that fell
On a wreath of vapour. I read the spell;
An eagle now, it was mine to soar
Through realms of wonder undreamed before.
Lo! far beneath me in blazing light
Lay the changing seas of the cloud-realm white,
Lapping shining forms clad in bright attire,
The mountain islets, each snowy spire
Standing a finger to point a road
From the cloudland up to the light of God.

But still the beast! oh, still the beast,
I must dip my beak in the bloody feast,
And stoop from the paths of that higher way
To sate my appetite day by day.
Summers and winters, sun and storm,
Passed me, and still I bore this form.
The sordid meal of the eagle o'er,
The soul used the eagle's wings to soar
Far from the land of slow beasts and trees,

To float alone on the wild fresh breeze,
And behold all wonders of lands and seas;
To gaze on the little things that man
Has toiled like the careful ant to plan,
Or contemplate desert mountains trod
Of no man, raised by a thought of God.
I saw on their summits the smoke that curled
From the awful fires of the under-world.
I sailed o'er the forge of the thunder brand,
And marked where it smote in the Master's hand;
I harked to the never-ending roar
Of the tides that pulse on the ocean's shore.
I followed the clouds that unceasing roll
At the Master's bidding from pole to pole,
Drawers of water, slaves that toil
With burdens of corn and wine and oil,
And all good gifts; and high above
I saw that the sun looked down in love,
A servant; and now I dared to gaze
Upon him undazzled, nor shunned that face
Which alone in the firmament apart
Had searched every wound of the lion's heart,
And had broken his spirit by slow degrees
To seek for his pardon upon his knees.

So all these things working slow but sure,
Gave me the hope of a final cure
For my sin, and poised aloft my moan,
"Would I had known, oh, would I had known!"

'It may be a century had flown,
Ere all I have spoken became my own.
In moments only by slow degrees
Was faith worked out and my soul at ease.
Ever the eagle's instinct broke
The threads of my hope as they awoke,
And severed the webs from my toiling mind,
To leave them streaming adown the wind;
But at length one morn as a radiance soft
Of gold from the world's edge rose aloft,
And climbing to heaven yet wrapped the earth
In embraces golden, I mourned the dearth
Of those below me who could not see
The glory, the rapture, revealed to me,
And I spake to the sun as he rose to view,
"Would God that they knew—would God they knew!'

'A storm uprose. An awful sound
Of gathered whirlwinds hurtled round.

The hurricane came swooping past;
I reeled, a feather in its blast,
And caught with failing sight the eyes
Of him, the Son of Paradise,
My soul's tormentor. Yet methought
It was a kindlier glance I caught.
Then in that rushing mighty wind
A lightning flashed, and I was blind;
And down the whirlwind's eddying rings,
Drifted to earth with broken wings.

'It was high noon when I awoke
In a mud dwelling filled with smoke.
Strange forms around gave wondering cries
Of gladness when they saw me rise.
What was I now? A peasant's child,
Born midst the mountains steep and wild;
Who, last night fallen into swoon,
Had waked past hope that summer noon.
In all the neighbouring mountain glades
She was the loveliest of the maids.
Therefore her kindred's hearts were glad
To find the choicest thing they had

No more in fear of death.   They sold
Their pearl next day for heavy gold
To a slave merchant who approved
My form.   'Twas such as monarchs loved.
He bore me neither sad nor gay,
But musing, patient, far away.
I was the sultan's toy, his sport,
When first I entered at his court ;
Sat with the sensual at their feast,
Where every jest betrayed the beast ;
Gazed helpless at each cruel show—
The murderous lash, the headsman's blow ;
Obeyed the tyrant on the throne ;
But kept my secret prayer my own,
"Oh, would to God that these had known !"

'Another took my place.   The brow
That once approved was frigid now.
"Modesty !   'Twas a harem slave.
Himself had smiled and she looked grave.
Enough !"   My tender back was flayed
By scourges, and my debt was paid.

'Then was I passed from hand to hand,
Obedient to each new command.

Each one more brutal, more unkind,
And each more bestial in his mind.
I would have shown them, if I could,
Things higher than they understood;
All sinking, as I saw full well,
In oozy slime cast up by Hell.
I strove with some. There was no gain,
Save of an increase to my pain.
None would turn back, and none believed
The bitterness in which I grieved;
But heaped worse insult. If they gave
Smiles of approval to their slave,
It was worse torture, for their smile
Was Sammael's own, corrupt and vile;
And my cold forehead brake in dew—
" Would God they knew—would God they knew!

'Though soiled by these, I still was fair,
And each new day brought new despair;
Till at the last my tempter came,
No more the old man, but the same.
A strong fierce youth, he gazed on me,
And droopèd his eyes as modesty

Prevailed; then at my feet he knelt
To speak the love his bosom felt;
And well his voice was tuned to move
My heart that only longed for love.
So my soul yearned to one who came
To seek me in my servile shame,
Spake me as equal, nay, obeyed
The lightest sign my finger made.
Though soft and tender unto me,
A wild son of the plains was he;
And he would bear me from the sink
Of cities, fresh, sweet air to drink.
So I believed him. Sore oppressed
And wretched, love might yet be blessed.
I gave assent. He strained my form
In wildest rapture. 'Twas a storm
Of passion girt me, and his kiss
Burnt through my lips, a fire, a bliss,
Too fierce, too piercing to endure.
'Twas the heart's blister, not its cure;
For gazing into eyes that sent
Flame to mine own, I read the intent—
The purpose of the fiend of Hell,
And shrieking Sammael's name, I fell.

THE TALE OF RABBI JOSEPH.

Ah, God, 'twas dreary.   Soon he came
Once more.   I called on Abram's name;
But nought prevailed to make him flee.
He offered now fresh baits to me—
Freedom, repose, long nights of ease,
Long days of joy, ay, all the peace
My bosom craved ; but I reviled
His offers, spake myself the child,
Self-willed no more, of Abraham,
Obedient to the great I AM.
I might have spoken unto stone :
He offered now a queenly throne,
Where I might sit and win all hearts,
Might serve my race, encourage arts,
And be a nation's joy and pride,
No more to servile masters tied,
But free to grace with my right hand
The noblest chief in all my land.
'Twas vain.   My soul had learnt a way
To scorn its prison house of clay.
Though this be soiled and must endure,
The soul within might yet be pure.

'Then foiled, he bore me hither.   This
His palace, and all here is his.
For here he deemed that from the brink
Of pleasure stumbling, I might sink,
This body lapped in all that could
Break down its strength and hardihood.
Here oftentimes, as now this night,
He drove my spirit forth in flight
Into the darkness, and this breast
Received the demon as its guest,
That I might find it feeble when
My wandering soul came home again.
In all its pains I had my share,
Ay, often was I nigh despair;
But now methinks 'twas given me
This night my angel's face to see,
And lo from a great sun he smiled,
And spake in comfort, "Abram's child,
The sun that shineth in his might
Shall be thy resting-place this night."
Soon may I take his hand to go.
Oh, rabbi, think'st thou this is so?'

The rabbi bowed his head in holy fear,
Perchance he deemed that awful Presence near;

Then prayed aloud the prayers for those who dwell
Beneath the shadowy wings of Azrael,
Daughters of Jacob. Soon the damsel spake:
'Lo, thou art weary, father, for my sake;
And now for me, my father, pray no more,
But pray that God send peace to Zion's shore.'
The rabbi prayed, and as he wept, her voice
Blent with his own, whilst tongues that did rejoice
Filled all the air with songs of wondrous love
That from the earth ascending died above;
And Rabbi Joseph raising not his head,
Yet knew within his heart her spirit fled
With others upwards, and the golden cord
Loosed, was drawn heavenwards by her loving Lord.

Then turned he from the gate, and, looking back,
Saw but the hillside, chilly, waste, and black,
And the wide plain before was void and bare.
His visions faded and that palace air;
Or—was he dreaming now? The rabbi took
The scroll he carried of the Pentateuch;
There was his tear upon the lines he read,
Whilst perfume lingered by sweet incense shed,

And, gazing upwards at the risen sun,
He deemed he saw a mote die thereupon.

Lo! are not these things written in the book
Of Rabbi Joseph? He who will may look
Upon the writing. All is entered there
In his own script with conscientious care.
But credible? Nay, friends, for faith is rare,
And all *things* bubbles, dreams that burst in air

THE IDIOT.

LOITERING through drowsy pathways of my life,
I came upon an orchard land, apart
From all the stirs that fill the outer world.
Here, sitting down, I dozed amongst the rest,
Or, half awake, I watched them, marking all
The rustics and their queen, who, snowy-haired
And velvet-tippeted, around her court
Wandered each day with praises or rebukes
For those who questioned not her kindly sway.
She seemed the only gentlewoman there,
Dwelt at the Hall, an apple-faced old maid
With soft grey eyes ; and all who saw her doffed
Their caps respectful, save an aged man,
Fourscore perchance, whose vacant eye bespoke
The loss of reason. Scanning him again,
I saw he was not of the rustic mould,
But something worse or better. Day by day
He sat dejected on the self-same seat,

Regarding neither wind nor rain, his eyes
Set on one window of the ivied Hall.
Nor spake he to the passers-by ; but oft
I saw the old maid trotting on her rounds
Regard him with a tender glance, and touch
His shoulder with a thin and mittened hand,
And, standing thus, would follow up his gaze
To the same window. Sometimes in his ear
She spoke soft words ; but he, as deaf and blind,
Gave back no answer. Once I saw a tear
Brushed from her eye, departing ; and I asked
Of one who knew the village chronicle,
The old man's name, the old love's history.
She, starting back at my request, amazed,
Agape in wonder at my ignorance,
Called all the powers to witness it ; and then,
Glad with a chance that never rose before,
Told all the story as I tell it here,
Save that I after found one little thread
To weave into its pattern. Now the tale :

Nigh fifty years before : The mighty days
Of the great conflict fresh in all men's minds,
Ay, even down in sleepy Wittenden
A thing to brag of over drowsy ale,

THE IDIOT.

How old George Barford's son had won his stripes
At Waterloo; and Widow Beddoes' boy
Had fallen. Local heroes of renown.
The last a poacher—'None the worse for that'
The farmers said, but said it *afterwards*.
Suddenly flashed into the village life
A gay lieutenant in the Navy, son
To the last vicar, bearing on his coat
The medals which he won at Trafalgar;
Son of the village which for twelve long years
Had missed the cheery echoes of his voice,
That rung in stronger accents than of old,
But glad as ever; gladdest when his shout
Had cheered his sailors clambering up the sides
Of some great Spanish vessel from the deck
Of his small sloop. So all the village made
Him hero of the hour. Chief at the Hall
The stately welcome of his father's friend
Its widowed mistress, holding by her side
Her little daughter, sunny-haired and fresh,
A country daisy, with an open eye
Regardant of the sun. And all the warmth
Which tropic suns had gendered in his blood
Flushed to his face beholding. He recalled

A shy sweet infant whom he used to bear
Down sunny lanes to roll amidst the hay;
Or raised upon broad shoulders to draw down
The topmost filberts in the coppices.
And now the child was gone, or lingered yet
But in unsullied childish faith in one,
Her earliest hero, and perchance her last.
But he that met her, little hero-like,
Cast down his eyes and stammered : till the dame,
Who wished him well for his good father's sake
Pronounced him awkward. But she brought him in
And made good cheer, and drew forth all the tale
Of Nelson, told afresh with moist blue eyes
And lips that quivered. Soon she made a feast
To half the county gentry; they should know
How Wittenden had borne its little part
In making up the annals of the time.
So half the county met to hear and praise;
And the young squires who owned contiguous lands,
And thought, perchance, to better their estate,
Looked black as thunder when they saw him lead
The heiress down the avenue of elms
To the great booth erected for the feast.
She, timidly observant, as she sat,

THE IDIOT.

Thought only 'Is there any like him?' 'None'
Her bosom answered.   He on his side saw
No other eyes, save those two speedwells turned
In trust to watch his lips, which, all unused
To tell the story of his own success,
Moved clumsily enough until he reached
The praise of England's hero and his own.
Then, with a sudden glory in his eyes,
The voice that rang amidst the battle smoke
Burst forth as when he shouted from the mast,
A tattered flag of Gallia in his hand ;
And ringing, dropped to utter tenderness
And manly pathos o'er the hero's fall.
So all who heard him marvelled, but a few
Smiled, or grew frigid, marking the clasped hands
And streaming eyes of her who sat beside
Unconscious save of him and of his thought.
He also, turning, caught her thus entranced,
And knew his hope, and felt it like a flood
'Whelm all his being.   But the dame, removed
By the long table, nothing marked or guessed.
Thereafter, the feast finished, and the folk
Returning homeward through the mazy lanes,
There came one hour of peace at early eve

When these two pacing down the avenue
Turned to the Grecian temple on the right
And shared their gladness, told the same old tale
Eve heard of Adam in their paradise.
And he, in Eden sitting with his Eve,
Was like a child that sees the present joy,
Nor dreams of any sorrow till it comes.
Till that returning homeward to the Hall,
Her arm in his and humid were her eyes,
His also filled with joy that verged on tears,
They found the old dame frigid and sedate,
With formal courtesy, and boding brows
That questioned of their converse. Nothing loth,
He rushed in sailor fashion on his fate,
And blurted all his tale into her ears,
That listened unresponsive. 'Nay,' she said,
' Her daughter, poor Sir William's only child,
Was but an infant, knowing now in nought
Would learn her station later. Much she grieved
That one who, older, should have thought it shame
To trifle with her inexperience,
Had wronged their hospitality, and brought
A sorrow to a house that had deserved
A kindlier treatment.' Then she bade 'adieu,'

Scorning to ban him for his father's sake,
And also that perchance she felt some touch
Of pity for the misery and shame
That crimsoned all his cheek, and seamed his brow
With veins that filled to bursting. Tottering forth
With strong limbs feeble to support the weight
Of sorrow in his bosom, he laid hands
Upon his nag that stood before the door,
And clambering slowly to the saddle, drove
The spurs into his unexpectant side,
Who, starting wildly, galloped down the lanes,
And o'er the open fields that lay beyond,
And out into the bosom of the night,
As wolves were at his heels. And the fierce wolves
That tore his master's bosom, goaded him
Beyond his strength to flee them, till he fell
Heart-broken; and his master, helpless flung
Forth on the thirsty earth that drank his blood,
Lay senseless, with the crisp curls steeped in gore.
'Twas thus a shepherd found him at the day.

Carried from thence into a hospital,
The life that girt its limbs to flee, returned
To find its mansion stripped of every sense

Save some vague memory of departed love.
Thus was his body decently interred,
Not in a grave, but in asylum walls,
And ate, and drank, and slept, as though the soul
Were still its tenant, as perchance it was,
Though wrapped in such a sleep as that which wraps
The good King Arthur in Avilion.
So there his remnant lingered, till at length
The village mistress, passing from her throne
Made room for her successor, the pale maid
Who long obedient to her mother's will
Had lingered with clipped wings within the cage;
And finding now her liberty at last
Took small advantage save for fuller works
Amongst her poor, and that she journeyed forth
To greet the shadow of old love, and strove
To give such tenderness as might repair
The outward blemish of his darkened house.
Not that he knew her. Hardly knew the place
Save for one spot, the old moss-covered seat,
Whence in the summer evenings long ago
He watched her curtain waving in the wind
To catch her shadowed outline. Here he sat
The long day through. She took him in at eve

And played to him to soothe him, but he strode
Forward and back the long night through in grief,
And only on that seat found any rest.

   Such was the tale; and here's the thread I found
To bind it: for I won the old maid's grace
By some slight works of service to her poor;
And so she took me in, and cockered me
With country dainties, luscious clotted creams,
And melons from her hothouses, and pines,
And various cakes washed down with home-made
    draughts,
Some cloying and some nasty. To refuse
Were treason, so I drank against my will.
And soon it happened that for some slight call—
A trifling cough, I think, that craved my skill—
I was admitted, marshalled by her maid,
Into her maiden chamber, bright with chintz
And flowers, and great old china gods that leered
Upon their mistress, but their swollen bulks
Full, not with knavish mirth, but lavender.
Here, when her handmaid had laid bare her throat,
I saw a large flat locket from a chain
  Hang, worn and polished, on her wrinkled breast.

She saw my eye fall on it, and she drew
It from her heart and set it in my hand
Without a word, as one who felt that I
Knew all it spoke of. I, who touched the clasp
With reverence, saw a faded miniature
In vapid nerveless stipple. Just a face,
Handsome enough if well and truly drawn;
But simpering lips and eyes of stony glare
Robbed it of beauty, save that in my thought
I set it by the poor old shade below
And saw the contrast. As I gave it back,
Kissing her withered hand in gratitude
As for a secret shown in sacred trust,
She simply said, 'I wished that *you* should see
The real John Somers.'

'The real John Somers,' kind old loving heart,
I cannot see him here. If eyes of love
May gaze through fifty years and see his spring
Of life run fresh with waters, it is well.
He, too, may deem he sees his real maid
In some disordered flashes of his trance.
But neither sees the other till the veil
Upon the souls of both be lifted up.

Then shall he know what love and patient trust
Are his for ever ; and the maid he loved,
Turning like Mary from the sepulchre,
Behold the real John Somers. Not the shade
She loved in youth, but, being purified
In a new birth, in glory strange and bright
And lovelier than this shadow of her dreams.

LOVE AND VANITY.

He was my pupil. I loved him well,
   For he flattered my pride in a hundred ways.
He was young and trusting. He could not tell
How love founded on love of self, will sell
   Itself for the love of praise.

I loved him still, but I loved him less,
   For an idle jealousy dimly burned
When, his young face glowing with happiness,
He sought me out that he might confess
   His secret of love returned.

Then I must see her that I might know,
   And his transports of loving rapture share;
So I gazed on a face where the gentle glow
Of beauty shone, like a moon on snow,
   To illumine a soul as fair.

I loved him no more, for my love was hate,
   Hate I dared not show for the love of pride.
My dream had been ever of such a mate;
I had risen higher, methought, had fate
   Bestowed on me such a bride.

LOVE AND VANITY.

Now, this beardless youth, with his shallow brain,
   And frank bright manner and honest brow,
I deemed had robbed me; but loathed in vain,
I dared not alter, nor dared complain,
   How his friendship galled me now.

But sorrow was his, for her life was bound
   By feeble ties to its dwelling-place.
Cold winds from the north were sharp to wound
The tender English bud that they found
   Exposed to their chill embrace.

Then we carried her southwards, he and I
   And her brother. He and I, were apart,
But he knew not, and lauded each pondered lie
Which met his frank love with hypocrisy;
   For I was merry at heart.

, At least not his.' That was all my thought.
   'Not his, not another's,' I whispered low,
As I watched the battle of those that fought
With fortune, and aided them well, for nought
   Of my aid could stay the foe:

So the day came on when defeat was nigh,
  Her spirit unfolded its wings for flight,
And we stood together to see her die;
I Judas-blasted, whilst he rose high
  In her love's reflected light.

He turned and said, 'Let the tender care
  Of loving hands do her service still.
None else shall our office of tendance share,
Till you and I and her brothers bear
  The form we have loved so well

'To its resting place;' and I bowed my head,
  Nor dared refuse—for he knew not me;
But I shivered before a new-risen dread,
And knew as I gazed that the maiden dead
  Had awful eyes to see.

For the veil of deceit had been torn aside,
  The veils I had woven with heedful care
To serve as a shelter for hate and pride
And the love of self; they were all descried
  And their nakedness made bare.

How they shrivelled and shrank from the dead girl'
    sight,
  By her pity blasted and not by wrath,
As I helped them robe her in garments white,
And strewed on her bosom the blossoms bright
  Which the southern suns bring forth.

Her eyes still fail not, nor yet will cease
  From probing the foul unseemly wound,
Though I seek with my tears to win release
From their searching terror, and sue for peace
  Bowed low on her grassy mound.

I am rightly judged, for my sin was great,
  But 'Spare me, spare me,' I whisper low.
If I cannot love him, I *will* not hate,
But will give him—what? That my toil, my fate,
  And my coming years must show.

MARRIAGE WISHES.

A UNION pure, a union true,
   Of mutual faith begot,
Where earthly trials are but few,
And each new year binds trust anew—
   Be this, my friend, your lot.

Success be yours. United bear
   All trouble that may come,
Do you her woman's weakness share;
May her love lighten all the care
   Which meets you in your home;

And hand in hand together climb
   The path that leads on high;
That thus this morning's merry chime
Ring in a marriage, not for time,
   But for eternity.

FRIEND OR FOE?

SHE was alone, and I was alone.
Her strength for the battle of life seemed gone.
Rest she wanted, and friends, and ease:
          I could give her all these.

With a careless bounty I oped my store.
She touched it not, though her need was sore;
I saw her shrink, and read in her eyes
          Distrust and surprise.

My pride was touched. To myself I said,
'I will bow before me that graceful head,
And order myself so that in the end
          She shall call me friend.'

But she was restive. 'Twas hard to tame
The maiden tremors that went and came;
Doubts of herself, and doubts for me,
          That made her to flee.

My touch was gentle, her spirit meek ;
My wish stood firm, and her soul was weak ;
So she stretched forth her hand to my hand that gave,
   And rose from her grave.

Then I was glad that her virgin pride
Was humbled and trustful by my side,
Proud that my wiles such trust could bring
   To so wild a thing—

Proud as one who has lured to his will
Some forest creature with subtle skill.
So her beauty, her gladness, and all she had
   She owed to my aid.

I had given her all that I had to give,
Hope and ease and the strength to live ;
I made her take them, then why be sore
   When she asked for more?

Asked with chaste eyes what I might divine
From the hand that fluttered to rest in mine,
Or from cheeks where the blushes a moment stayed.
   Then I waxed afraid.

FRIEND OR FOE?

I had given much, then why ask me now
For a gift given elsewhere long ago,
Or cast away?   Could she not perceive
        'Twas not mine to give?

Then I grew wroth.   I was smitten sore
By those trustful eyes that expected more.
I had given freely.   She still should be
        A debtor to me.

But I fled from her presence ill at ease
With myself and her, as a wizard flees
From a ghost he has raised, and my pride was low
        As I turned to go.

Between us stretches the ocean wide,
But her candid eyes from the further side
Can still reproach, and they ask me still,
        'Did I well or ill?'

Pride bade me tame her, and so my pride
By her grateful trust should be satisfied.
I bent her to love me, but in the end
        Have I been her friend?

In the aftertime, in some unknown place,
When we two are standing up face to face,
Though she bless me or curse, yet all the same
   I must blush for shame.

A DRESDEN BEAUTY.

CHARMING? Oh yes. You are rosy and white;
Blue eyes; porcelain teeth set a-row
In the daintiest mouth; sunny smile; you are right,
And the word just describes you, I vow.

I should like you to keep, underneath a glass shade,
Ever smiling and rosy and fair,
To gaze on each day. I should not be afraid,
For your babble could not tire me there.

Would you like it? I think so, don't doubt it, in truth,
For each lounger would pause to admire.
Admiration and bloom of perennial youth,
What more could your fancy desire?

Admiration you have. If you ask me for mine,
I grant it at once as your due.
It is lucky for both that you cannot divine
Why I never could give you love too.

Fate has treated you well. You have more than you
    need
Of beauty to kindle desire.
It is all that you want, and your mind would not heed
Such a love as it could not inspire.

You are doomed, my fair friend, to be wedded one day
To love, not of gold, but of dross.
If *he's* decently civil, I think I may say
You will never discover your loss.

PEARLS.

'See yonder purple mountain—there,
    Where all the heavens are gold, love;
Let's build the rosy towers in air
    Which shall our lives enfold, love.'
'It's rather bare, it's rather drear,
    It must be rather cold, love;
A villa here were nicer, dear,
    The tower up there's too old, love.'

'Well, gaze where yonder peak of snow
    Against the sky shows faint, love;
'Tis a white marble temple now,
    And you its patron saint, love.'
'Why, Charlie, dear, too far you go;
    What pictures queer you paint, love;
For should I so an image grow,
    'Twere too absurd and quaint, love.'

'Just see that little tiny boat,
   A speck twixt sea and sky, love;
Oh, could we there for ever float
   Together, you and I, love!'
'No, Charlie, you forget your throat;
   You're hoarse, and, by the bye, love,
You've no great-coat. I cannot vote
   That we your scheme should try, love.'

'The sun has gone and left behind
   The lonely evening star, love;
Were you that star, how sweet to find
   And worship from afar, love.'
'Now, Charlie, you are quite unkind,
   Our evening you would mar, love;
You ought to find, I speak my mind,
   It's nicer as we are, love.'

'Well, well, let's go. Perhaps you're right;
   But still, upon the whole, love,
I fear you miss the full delight
   Romance yields to the soul, love.'
'Romance! well, yes; for though it's bright,
   'Tis damp here on this knoll, love.
I'm glad though, quite, we came to-night,
   You've been so very droll, love.'

THE LANDS BEYOND THE SEA.

'WHAT is there lying beyond the sea?'
'Come, little Blanche, and sit on my knee.
There is lying a lovely land of spring,
Where the rose has no thorn, and the bee no sting,
Where the bright sky is flecked but with April showers,
And the air is sweet with the smell of flowers,
Meadows of violets and daffodils
Fresh with the spray of a thousand rills,
Whilst glad bright songs of the parent birds
Fill the soft wind-whispers with loving words;
And this land lying beyond the sea
Is your own land, Blanche—it is lost to me.

'Further, we reach the enchanted land
Where beautiful castles of cloudland stand,
A warmer land where the ladies bright
Bind each their favour on gallant knight;
And the knights are handsome and strong and true,
And one perchance is awaiting you.

'Tis a beautiful land, and its fruits are fair,
But harbours dragons of doubt and care,
And here and there in some lonely spot
A lady lies weeping her prisoned lot.
We hope that the best of its gifts may be
For you, my pet; they are not for me.

'Next we enter an upland plain,
Wealthy with pastures and golden grain,
A land of summer, a fruitful soil,
But also a land of care and toil;
With happy homesteads, and orchard meads,
But a soil productive of many weeds;
Children's voices, and harvest songs,
By fierce deep torrents of human wrongs;
Still, happy, for those who do not shirk
Their allotted share of its harvest work;
So this land lying beyond the sea
May be glad for you, and perchance for me.

'Then we slowly climb up the lofty hill,
Where the snows are lying white and chill,
And high on the distant crest may find
A shelter to gaze on the view behind,

A little haven of rest ere we
Launch forth on the waves of a further sea;
And as we turn to look back again
On the track we have travelled across the plain,
May we see it, with grain and orchards fair,
The fruit of the seeds we have planted there;
So the hill that hangs o'er the clouded sea
Shall be happy resting for you and me.'

'What is there beyond the further sea?'
'Nay, that, little Blanche, is not known by me.
Do you see the red sun nearly set?
He shines upon lands that are fairer yet,
Sands all bathed in one golden light,
Where the sun no more goes down at night,
Filled with flowers that can never pale,
Watered by streams that shall never fail,
As they stream from the heights of that golden shore,
Summits where thought has no wings to soar.
Blanche, my darling, I trust that we
May find such a shore to the further sea.'

THE CLAIM OF BLOOD.

A Ballad of Revenge.

PART I.

A STORY of bitter vengeance,
   A tale of a bitter wrong,
How the Lady Hilda laid 'Claim of Blood'
   On her father Earl Rolf the Strong.

Fair was the old Earl's daughter,
   He had never a child beside,
But if he toyed with her silken locks,
   It was less in love than pride.

To the one fair child of his house
   He was not all unkind,
But her eyes sought love in his inmost heart,
   Sought, but they could not find.

Yet love had his birth within her,
   And grew as the maiden grew,
The love of her cousin Siward,
   Bravehearted and strong and true.

So two young hearts in their springtime
  Throbbed harmonies true and sweet
As nightingale's nesting song, and sure
  As the tides unchanging beat.

The old Earl knew their wooing,
  And looked for the thing that came.
The lad was no changeling son of his race,
  And hereafter should bear his name.

'These, last of their stock, should wed,'
  With a mighty oath he swore,
'That the old tree yet might bring forth seed
Unmingled, a stalwart stubborn breed
  As their ancestors of yore.'

But his vow as a thread was broken,
  The hope of their lives undone.
With royal greetings to Rolf the Earl,
Came command to yield his child, his pearl
  To the King of Lochlann's son.

That he through his only daughter
  Might father a line of kings,
Twin hearts must break of a broken troth
He heeded not for his mighty oath,
  Nor the two betrothal rings.

L

But they 'scaped from his grasp of iron,
    In secret the pair were wed.
Of his own unbending stock they came,
And in two young hearts there was kindled flame
    That has molten his bars like lead.

Then they fled no man knew whither,
    And no word the old Earl spoke,
For his pride would not pursue them,
Though his inmost spirit slew them
    For the purpose that they broke.

'Twas midst the falling leaves they fled,
    And solitary wore
The hours of old Earl Rolf until
    The autumn came once more,
Forth went he then with hounds and men
    To chase the savage boar :
And riding farther than his wont,
    Left all alone, he found,
'Mid the thick forest's deepest shade,
    A plot of open ground,
And herbs grew there that spoke of care ;
    And at the edge there stood

A little cot with thatch of fern
  And builded all of wood.
There, sitting happy by the door,
  His only child he sees,
Whilst bending down in loving care
Her husband trifles with a fair
  Sweet babe upon her knees.
Forth blazes the long-smouldering hate,
  Poising his hunting dart,
He hurls the cruel weapon straight
  Into his nephew's heart.

PART II.

The king sat in his banquet hall,
  His chieftains there were met,
In a high place amidst them all
  The brave Earl Rolf was set.
Save that his pride had had such fall
  He had sat higher yet.
There came a woman to the throne
  As white as is a shroud,
Withered with famine and despair,

And none there was that knew her there
  As crying forth aloud,
They heard her by God's judgment swear,
  And make 'the Claim of Blood.'
Then at that woman's cry, the king
  Rose up from off his seat,
For, claiming blood, all they that claim
For murder foul, or woman's shame,
  Take hold on the king's feet.
Gazing in wonder, said the king,
  'Oh, woman, what art thou?
And who is he that did thee wrong?'
'It was the tiger, Rolf the Strong,
  Who sits beside thee now,
Who, coming stealthily and hid
  Like a wild beast from view,
Skulked like a coward in his seat
To slay the man he dared not meet
  My husband brave and true.'
'Oh, woman, lived there any man
  From whom Earl Rolf would hide?'
'Siward; the hero of a line
Whose blood is blent, oh king, with thine,
  A warrior skilled and tried.'

THE CLAIM OF BLOOD.

'If this be true,' then said the king,
   'And thou deniest not,
Sir Earl; though these have been thy shame,
   Yet will I here allot
Large fine for crying wrong, and blame
   Of treacherous hurt God wot,
But "Claim of Blood," I disallow.'
   Then on his speech broke short
And shrill her cry. 'I urge my cause
   'Gainst one who broke thy forest laws,
Thy bloody laws of sport.'
Forth from her withered breast she drew,
   And hurled before the throne
An infant's body cold and blue,
   And starved to skin and bone.
'Shall not the wretch this babe who slew,
   For his vile deed atone?
Thy law of blood is strong and sure,
   That forest beasts with young
In pairing time shall dwell secure
   Thy woods and wilds among.
This law unkept wilt thou endure
   At hands of Rolf the Strong?'
'Thou shouldst have askèd at his hand

>   The wherewithal to eat.'
> 'Blind of the blind;' she answered then,
> 'What hind eats in the tiger's den?
>   The stag is there for meat.'
>
> Then spake Earl Rolf. 'I plead not here.
>   This woman hath just cause;'
> And the king bowed his troubled head,
> 'Thyself hath spoke thy doom,' he said,
>   'That knew the forest laws.'

THE RESTORATION.

PART I.

How the Sisters and Maids builded God's House at Wittenden.

De Witten, it is not a name
Graved deeply on the shield of Fame ;
Only the genealogist,
Poring some old black letter list,
May find the name and titles written
Of Hugo Pyevor, Lord of Witten.
A fighting baron, so 'tis said,
Who for the White Rose lost his head,
And dying left his 'minished lands
Of Witten to the maiden hands
Of daughters twain, their names unknown,
Of whom we learn this fact alone,
That chancing upon times of peace,
They gave their substance and increase,
And all the best they had, to found
A house of God upon their ground,

Which in its beauty might maintain
Its own with many a prouder fane.
Though small, as suited well their hoard,
Yet, being builded to the Lord,
It lacked not any beauty man
In a sincerer age might plan.
The piers and buttresses upbore
A fairy roof, all fretted o'er
With carven work and tracery
Of fairest stone wrought painfully;
Whilst cunning men of Flanders came
To kindle all the lights with flame,
And on its golden-panelled choir
Glowed colour of a softer fire;
For some Italian wanderer painted
Lank sweet-faced lines of figures sainted,
The earliest preachers of the Word,
And midmost, breaking bread, their Lord.
So when the lovely church was done,
It stood, an anthem carved in stone,
A silent work of praise the poor
Might see and feel beside their door;
And those two sisters, passed away,
Beneath its marble pavement lay,

Marked by memorial brass on which was written,
Systers & maydes doughters of ye Lord Wityen
To ye glorie of God.

PART II.

How Time and Man dealt with God's House at Wittenden.

Just for a moment let our thought
See what four centuries have brought,
What loss through time or man's despoil,
And what the gain of pious toil.
Three hundred years passed swift away
With little symptom of decay,
Only that some of Cromwell's men,
Coming by chance to Wittenden,
Tore out most of the painted glass,
And broke the old memorial brass.
Then, hating images, effaced
The figures in the chancel traced,
Scratched with their swords all paint and gilding,
But did small damage to the building.

But in revenge, the softening touch
Of Father Time had added much
Of value, gifts of golden moss
And lichen grey repaired all loss
And damage, with a varied pall
Of colour on the outer wall;
So this stood fairer than before,
Though in the church the loss was sore.
Then all the churchyard elms, grown high,
Found voices in a rookery,
That cawed and chattered o'er each stone,
With tear-dewed mosses overgrown,
Bearing 'Resurgam' written o'er
Such names as all the hamlet bore,
  Stubbs, Beddoes, Barford, here, and then
Stubbs, Beddoes, Barford, there again;
Or, cherub-capped, where alien names
Of reverend Samuel John or James,
All 'Vicars of this Parish,' slept
As shepherds with the sheep they kept.

But just a hundred years ago,
When all the Church's wheels ran slow,
And idle shepherds of the sheep
Were wont a drunken watch to keep,

THE RESTORATION.

And churchwardens were men of power,
And 'churchwarden' was written 'boor';
George Blenheim Stubbs and William Saltash
Daubed the church with a coat of whitewash,
And, lest old Time too soon should cancel
Their outrage, wrote it in the chancel;
As also, how 'Dame Hannah Beddoes
Left certain lands in Deadmen's Meadows,
Likewise that tenement and ground
Called "Lesser Farisy," to found
An almshouse.'—Since, the church remained
Unaltered, and grew weather-stained.
Without, once more the whitewash peeled
Slow from the walls, and thus was healed
The worst disaster; but within
'Twas still an eyesore, though its skin
Grew grey with age and chipped a little,
Enough to show its hold was brittle,
And such a broom as swept the floors
Might soon have sent it out of doors.

Such fortunes did the church betide,
Till the last slumbrous vicar died;
And such our present vicar found it
When first he cast his eyes around it;

And, as a man of taste and lettered,
Saw how its state might well be bettered.
'Need not come down.' 'There seemed no harm in it;
In fact there was a certain charm in it;
If many things the eye offended,
He thought at least they might be mended.
The neighbouring landowners, no doubt,
Would do their best to help him out,
If the expenditure exceeded
The prime cost absolutely needed;'
So shortly afterwards from town
An architect was summoned down
To draw his scheme of renovation;
And this began 'The Restoration.'

PART III.

Shows how God's House at Wittenden was Restored A.D. 1884.

The church was builded with such care
It wanted nothing of repair.
Outside, a little weather-beaten,
Within, a few stones flawed or eaten;

THE RESTORATION.

Outside, two inches of hard scraping
Soon polished every cranny's gaping;
Within, each little chink's disaster
Was smothered up with yellow plaster;
And all the spots of gold and paint,
Dim outlines of each vanished saint,
Last vestige of the Church of Rome,
Were painted out with monochrome;
Which, later on, was neatly spotted
With fleur-de-lys. The windows, dotted
With many odds and ends of stained
Glass, that since Cromwell's time remained
Unshattered, now were taken out;
A needful thing without a doubt.
How can a church look trim and neat
Unless its windows are complete?
So now, best green cathedral glass
Fills every pane. The ancient brass,
Broken and worn, yet had its history
So finds a refuge in the vestry;
For all the floor, of marble chequers,
With three old slabs of ancient vicars,
Is now removed, and tiles from Minton
Are laid, bright-glazed, with such a glint on.

THE RESTORATION.

The vicar's zeal, now fairly sated,
Yet seized the pulpit antiquated.
He did not care for preaching boxes,
So had an eagle down from Coxe's.
The old carved boards, though rather shabby, yet
Made up into a handsome cabinet.
'Tis in his study, for a taste
Refined abhors old things to waste.
And now once more the church all through
Is very near as good as new.
The yellow plaster, at some distance,
Looks much like stone.   Aloft, a mischance
Is that the scraping and the peeling
Blurred the fan-tracery on the ceiling,
Marred much of the carved work in sooth.
However—left it clean—and smooth.
Smoother it is at least, and cleaner,
Though some folks fancy it looks meaner
The vicar's taste, who in reality
Has shown much zeal and liberality,
Has patched it with such pious care
As will leave marks for many a year.
The vicar is so proud and satisfied,
The old maids' ghosts may well feel gratified,

To find their work, so smartened, may
Befit our more enlightened day,
Nay, trust their humble efforts will
Please ages more enlightened still,
That looking on their brass will groan
In the old church for old days gone.

'ANTIVIVISECTION.'

WAILINGS of silly women, led astray
   By full-fed ignorance, or sentiment
   Fostered of falsehood. Not that these invent
Their tales of horror. Meaner spawn than they,
Hired agitators, scent their meal, and bray
   Persistent. O'er their work of love downbent,
   The foemen of disease are discontent
With the disturbing clamours, and their way
Beset with gadflies; but they will endure
   Whilst truths increase, and blatant falsehoods die,
Whilst nature yields her hidden gifts of cure,
   Whilst human sorrows for compassion cry.
Time will disperse, with certain hand and sure,
This swarm of buzzing idlers, whose obscure
   Humanitarians foul Humanity.

'*ANTICS.*'

THERE is a people in these latter days,
    Agnostics, Knownothings, or Nihilists,
    Anti-logicians, Anti-scientists,
Anti-religionists, or any craze
That brings their names before the public gaze,
    Vague angry voices wandering in mists,
    Unteachable, dense matter that resists
Knowledge and truth, corpse-candles whence no blaze
For guidance shines, mind-jungles where no ray
    Of light can pierce through the bewildering maze,
Their function blind negation of the day.
    Knowledge, advancing, heeds not, nor delays
For antic 'Anti' dust that clouds her way,
    Drifting in angry gusts that fools upraise.

THE PRAISE OF FOLLY

Ye scholars, ye who nothing take,
    And think therefrom to form a God;
Yet know that man may nothing make,
    Nor vap'rous gas, nor earthen clod.
Oh, all ye scholars, and your schools,
Ye are but fools, ye are but fools.

Ye twist the thin thread of your thought,
    And tell us the poor tangled skein
May be into a garment wrought,
    Of shelter from the storm and rain;
But all the spoil on all your spools
Weaves webs for fools, weaves webs for fools.

And ye who deem that man alone
    Unhelped may reach a perfect state,
Unpurified sit on God's throne,
    And toil alone is truly great;

Oh, ye vain toilers, all your tools
Are blunted fools, are blunt-edged fools.

And ye who cry that wider laws
   Will leave man happy and at rest.
Know ye not that the final cause
   Of peace lies hid in every breast?
Oh, blinded rulers, he that rules
Is fool of fools, is fooled by fools.

Ye too, who seek inglorious peace,
   Believing all creation still,
Can ye not mark each year's increase
   In knowledge of a higher will?
Yet ye recoil, your courage cools,
Faint-hearted fools, faint-hearted fools.

And ye who childlike seek a light
   By which a wider space to scan,
And striving slow from height to height,
   Would teach of love to every man,
From icy poles to Afric pools,
Are this world's fools, God's finer tools.

MOLOCH.

'Doctor, is it a lie?
I'm an ignorant woman, but you,
You ought to know if it's true.
If they burn my baby
They'll burn me, and may be
You too.
Why didn't you, didn't you say,
When you saw it would die yesterday,
That they'd burn it?   That is, if you knew.

'Am I mad?   Yes, I am,
Out o' my sense and blind,
For I know you were nought but kind
To my poor little lamb.
So I thought when it pined at the breast
That it wanted for nought but rest.
However was I to know
They could treat a poor innocent so?
I thought it was all for the best.

But parson a while ago,
He came in and said
That I ought to have sent for him
Before it was dead;
And he told me how
They were burning it now,
And would burn it for ever in Hell because I had been
    so slow.
And I could not answer a word. The beast! he
    ought to know.

'But when he said, "Let us pray,"
I spat and I screamed,
And the whole world seemed
Turned up the wrong way.
I stormed and I cursed
Till my heart nigh burst,
To think of the brutes they must be, if it be as he say.
I don't care what they'd do to me, so they spare my
    lamb,
And I'd strangle to go and help it. Mad? Yes, I am.'

If one out of darkness curse and rail at a spirit of evil,
Her curse is not to the Lord, but her priest's man-
    fashioned devil.

HIS SIDE AND HERS.

His was the idle word, the foolish lapse
   From truth in time of trial.
Thine was the right of censure, and perhaps
   Of parting and denial.

His was the humble seeking after peace,
   The true, the long repentance.
Thine the remorseless scorn that would not cease ;
   Thy lips pronounced his sentence.

His was the frantic deed of mad despair,
   The plunge beneath the river.
'Tis thine to sit and gaze dull-eyed on care
   Alone, alone for ever.

THE STAR IN THE EAST.

When the rainbow hopes of our youth are faded
    Where sunlight and storm-cloud blended,
When the rosy glow of our sky is shaded,
    When the love-song of birds is ended,
    And mists lie thick on the meadow,
    Slowly out of their shadow
        Riseth the Star.
'We beheld its light in the East, and are come to praise from afar.'

SONNET.

NONE mourn this hideous sodden heap of clay.
    Loveless it lived, defiled by every lust,
    Deformed by every passion. Dust to dust !
Ashes to ashes ! Idle 'twere to pray
O'er such a carcase. Only hide away
    Its noisome horror from the daylight. Thrust
    It forth uncared for and unwept to rust
In secret. Let its memory pass away.

Man, who art thou that judgest ? See the mute
    And pitying dog that licks the dead man's hand.
    We ask not what it was that formed the band
Betwixt them, but we may not well dispute
    Some *cause* for love there. One will understand
And love this *something* better than HIS brute.

THE BREATH OF LIFE.

In glad spring morning uprose the breeze,
Whispering dreams to be understood;
Whispered low in the dreamy wood,
Whispered under the shady trees,
Whispered ever that God was good.

Dying sounds in the noonday glare,
Freshness of morn is soon forgot,
Heavy scents in the torpid air
Now uprose as the sun grew hot
Round sluggish waters where God was not.

Clouds from the east hung overhead,
Rose the tempest in sudden might,
Flowerets sodden and crushed and dead
Float in the flooded torrent's bed,
'Neath a tempest black as night.

Eve, and the storm is lulled to peace.
Eve, and the clouds are backwards rolled.
Eve, and the golden lights increase.
'Fresh and sweet, though its breath be cold
The breeze sinks down into gates of gold.

IN MEMORIAM.

E. NEVILLE ROLFE, M.A., *Canon of Gibraltar.*

PAIN, blindness, weariness are cast aside;
Weak limbs, dark eyes, your way is smooth and plain
In pleasant places where the harvest grain
Warm in love's sun grew ripe till eventide.
There, where thy treasure is, shalt thou abide.
No murmur dulled, no sloth curtailed that gain
Of fruitful labour, rich and free from stain,
Given in full trust to One that likewise died,
Who, risen, speaks: 'I say to thee, arise,
Enter thy Master's joy.' From the dark eyes
Drop scales, and 'mid that light where Jesus is,
Behold! Thy throne and crown not otherwise
Set than for higher service. 'Tis in this
The loving humble servant finds his bliss.

SONNET.

Her days were spent in prison, for disease
    Got hold upon her youth, and vexed her sore
    With pain's disablement, and shut the door
Of her outgoings; but within dwelt peace.
Patient, she watched the sluggish years increase
    The weary chains of feebleness she wore,
    And unreluctant bowed her head before
The appointed angel of her soul's release.

She brings her gift of patience; all *she* had,
Who lacked her childhood's sports and youth's delight,
Who drank her cup in silence; but when bade,
Entered into the Temple and was glad.
And He who takes her offering will not slight
Her toll, but store it with the widow's mite.

SWALLOWS OF THE RIVIERA.

WE English, lovers of our homes, are yet
Spiers of empty places, and our hands
Plant English homes in many distant lands;
Yet are we English always, nor forget.
But if strong founders of new realms regret
Their English homesteads, may not rather we,
The sick, the weary, pale and ghostly bands
Who gather sunshine by the southern sea;
Basking like flies when Autumn strips the tree,
To thaw the freezing streams of life, in mind
Reach back for the familiar days, and yearn
For love and home and summer to return?
Then northwards go rejoicing those that find
Fresh springs of life; but some are left that pined
Through all the balmy sunshine to discern
The friendly faces, feel the friendly kiss,
And rest in green sward of our English shore,
Heart-hallowed by the kin that went before,

Or by some love of childhood; even this,
Though peace be now, it has been pain to miss.
But these and those sent home with longings sore,
Some token of their being. Day by day
Sped little gifts that spoke of love away;
And many paint a scene where swallows flit
On toys of wood or clay with legend writ
Of 'Nous reviendrons,' or 'Je reviendrai.'
The shops are full of them. The theme is fit
To take the fancy. 'Tis of hope they speak,
And joy's return, and comfort for the weak;
Yet could I never like them. Though the thought
Be hopeful, sadder food I could not seek
For contemplation. Sad are those that bought,
Lives unfulfilled, imperfect lives that sought
Renewal or completion. Thus each one
Telling of hope to come, speaks sorrows past,
Dark places where the shades of death were cast
On life and love, when homesteads glad with sun
Grew dark with rainclouds. If the storm be done
And life reopens, yet the passing blast
Has nipped the fruitful labours of the year,
Perchance has checked the growth of after years.
So these fond gifts are sprinkled all with tears:

The hope is witness both to bygone fear
And sorrow of to-day, though hope be there.
If hope be absent, sadder still appears
The gift, a witness to dreams unfulfilled,
Where hope was but a longing, disbelieved,
Sent home in wish to solace those that grieved
With false foundations where a hope might build;
Sent forth with mute repressions, throbbings stilled
In aching hearts that faltered not, but knew
The heart-beats numbered. 'Figures white and frail,
Ye near your night-time. All may read the tale
And see the " Finis " written, save the few
Your love would blind, and blot the end from view
With the last drops pressed forth from hearts that fail.'
So mothers in far England fondly keep
The symbol of the swallows, and they pray
For the returning nestling, till the day
That peace has brought to their belovèd sleep;
But watchings manifold to those who weep
To read the legend 'Je reviendrai.'
Yet were the swallows symbols. One who cared
For each and all has watched the unsteady flight,
Guiding it through the darkness of the night,
And warming 'mid the frost till forth it fared
Home with young wings into the summer light.

A PRAYER.

Lord, Thou hast known my trials, being tempted.
    Lord, Thou hast known my sorrows, being tried ;
Weak as myself, from sin alone exempted,
    Bearing sin for me, being crucified.

Thou, Lord, alone art now my consolation,
    Whom, like to Peter, I have oft denied.
Work out in me Thy work for my salvation,
    Bought by Thee dearly, being crucified.

Thou knowest all my thoughts of evil, hidden
    E'en from myself, but none from Thee may hide.
Show them to me, and after Thou hast chidden,
    Take them far from me, being crucified.

THE OLIVE TREE.

Fair, sweet, and quiet rest; and fruitfulness;
   And colour blending all strong lights of day
   And high contrasting hues with softest grey;
With much of grace, the olive doth possess:
With these contented, dons no gaudier dress
   For the bright annual festa of the May;
   Repining not though sun or rain delay,
Nor emulous to tower above the press.

So many a Dorcas, widow, wife, or maid,
   Life-rooted in her quiet sunny place,
Sifts evenly her sunshine and her shade
   Through life whose quiet labours leave small trace;
And the last lightning gleaming on her face
   Shall find her bearing fruit, and not afraid.

THE FIRST LESSON.

GOD touched the sleeping essences of man
   And said, 'Be born
A child ; and as a child go forth to scan
Thy garden playground, stocked with flower and thorn,
   Walled in by tracts unknown.
   These keep I for mine own,
But lend thee here an open book to teach
   The things within thy reach
    Of thought or touch.
   Behold ! all such
Are thine to know. Moreover, there is One
Will be thy help beyond. Mine only Son
   Shall teach thee to discern
    Things that thou couldst not learn ;
    My own humility,
    My love for thee,
My toil and tenderness for smallest things,
Mine all, and safe beneath the sheltering wings

Of their All-father.   For no jot is lost,
No atom wasted, of the endless host.
No breath but stirs obedient to the call
Sent through the Infinite to guide them all,
'Mid times and spaces where no eye may see
Save Mine, but each least fragment marked by Me,
The Eternal Soul that wraps infinity.'

  The newborn babe that's blessed,
  In love's warm arms caressed,
  Nought knows, or cares to know
  Save love ; and even so,
  Reposing on a fonder breast,
God's child lay naked on love's side and knew
Only his Father smiling in the blue
Of parent love that girt him ; without shame,
  As in love's bosom still,
  Trusting in that from whence he came,
   He feared no ill,
   His life, his will,
All love's ; and every need from love's own side
Drank in content, and slumbered pacified.
  There nursed, he learnt his alphabet of love,
   The birds, the flowers,

The changing wonders of the sky above.
  The rivulets, the showers,
All spake their Father's tongue, and claimed his
  brotherhood,
Children alike of Him who 'saw that they were good.'

But he that thinks the Father keeps His best
From His own child, hath never any rest,
Grasping for things forbidden, that his eyes
May look into some fancied paradise
  Other than God's. He deems
  That, could he shape his dreams,
  He might build up a place
  Where he and all his race
   As Gods might sit
   To fashion it
According to their will, hid from the Father's face.
  Froward he thinks to fill
  God's seat, for children still
   Deny their littleness,
   Not caring to confess
Entire dependence on another's will,
  Entire indebtedness.
  Sitting in halls of space and time,

They hear through walls a chant sublime,
    That mighty chime
That pulses through infinity,
Its echoes of divinity,
And catching one stray chord of the vast harmony
    They mirror faults in it. They idly fling
    A plummet on a string
    Of finite thought and sense
    Down through the deep immense,
And boast it as the full recording measure
Of the unknown, reserved in the eternal treasure.

    Knowledge, His gift, is good.
    The tree hath wholesome food.
    The wise man and the poet,
    Who take good seed and sow it,
Eat and are filled. They watch each growing frond,
    And know it
    A finger pointing to wide realms beyond
    Thither it sends forth shoots
    Rich with fresh fruits,
All sweet at heart with sun ; but they that find,
    And hasty gnaw the rind,

THE FIRST LESSON.

Fill all their bosom with an empty wind,
  A flatulence of mind.
  Whilst others, seeking evil,
  Stoop to the earthy level
And gather husks; nay, bending prone,
  Deem such alone
  (Refuse the devil
Shook from dead branches down)
Sole fruit upon the highest summit grown.

  We are but children all,
  Who creep, or run, or fall,
The universe our school, this earthly ball
Our playground. Listen, for the Father's voice
  Bids us rejoice.
  He sends us toys
  To learn from, sport with, not to make.
We cannot fashion them, nor break
  Beyond His power to mend;
  For He will keep each wait
  Stored by Him to the end,
That after children may behold it safe.
If we, like our own little ones, be loath
  To play, and curious seek the springs

That move our toys, mayhap the growth
Is stunted stooping, and the soul hath feebler wings
　　To carry it beyond its rest on *things*
　　Into the heavens.　We search out the machine,
And gazing thereupon think to discern
What all its endless wheels and forces mean ;
　　And if we humbly learn
　　To worship the all-powerful skill
　　Of Him who wrought it of His will
There is a gain, but heavy is our cost,
The charm, the poetry of our toy is lost.
　　　For he who scans his frame,
　　　To study how it came
Forth into life, will take his tools and try
Each secret till he leaves it bare and dry.
One takes a spark out of his battery
　　　To stir a hideous laughter
On a dead face, and when he gazes after
　　On the glad laughing features of his boy
　　　Will mark like muscles twist.
　　　What is romance to the anatomist,
　　Or beauty such as hers who ruined Troy,
　　But of his old intricate female toy
Constructed like another ?　Take the flower that blows

THE FIRST LESSON.

'Neath the March hedges, when the melting snows
Leave sodden grass-banks bare : a heaven-born thing
Of joy to childhood, but to him who knows
And searches, common toy of cellulose
Less worthy thought than many. Could he bring
His childhood's eye to study the primrose,
His winter were the nearer to the spring ;
  And great his gain, for faith
  Is blessed. Who could breathe
At ease, if pent in prison walls where death
Stood as blank loss of all ; save hope came there
Of love beyond the grave, and present care.

Fellow children, ye who love your dolls or break them,
 Melt the wax and sift the sawdust, ye are free.
There are lessons in them all if ye will take them,
 And the lessons writ in all of them agree.
  Things the youngest child may read in,
  And the poorest help his need in
   With the key.
Initial, heading all the endless scroll,
The key which hath unlocked the sapphire gate
Through which the vapours of creation roll

Distilled to starry spray. The aureole
Which crowns the patience of the saints who wait.
The Bethel ladder angel hosts descend.
The index cipher on the dial plate,
Pointing through all its numbers to a goal.
The bourn wherein all crossing orbits blend.
The unhorizoned girdle of control,
Whereon the seeming headstrong bolts of fate
Find out a master curve to which they bend.
The thread on which from heaven depends the soul
About the fringes of a robe of state
That warms and shelters and enwraps the Whole
In one great seamless garment none may rend,
Love's measureless Omicron circle without end.

DAMOCLES.

A Story of Paralysis.

I.

Ah! I awake. I look up. I behold
A terror that lightens in air,
The torture they dreamed of, of old,
The sword that hangs down by a hair.
Firepointed, double-edged steel
Presses my bosom laid bare.
I look. Death is poising it there.
I breathe. My breast swells, and I feel.
I would stir. The close point of it keen
Pricks deep, and I dare not appeal.
Friends cannot help me or heal.
Change may not come to my scene.
Toil is a thing that has been.
Life hath no joy to reveal.

Knowledge quivers and will,
Flies in the web of my brain;
But the body is still.
The sword shall kill
Ere I turn to my life again.
Ere I raise my head
From its rest, I am dead,
Dead with a deathly pain;
For the sword hangs low on its slender thread,
And thereby shall I be slain.

II.

I cannot struggle or flee
This sword that hangs over me.
Would that the cord were free,
And death was the striker's fee.
The flesh would still enlace
The spirit in strait embrace,
But the parting pang must be
For flesh that shudders to see
The bare blade hung in its place
On the thread of my destiny;

Stirring in faintest wind,
Keener than mortal brand,
I know of a phantom that lurks behind,
And a sickle is in his hand.
Yea, he hath taken stand
To sever the fragile band.
He keepeth his sword-point free from rust
Till he speeds it down in his final thrust,
When the moment toll
Of my parting soul.
Next moment? next year? or when it must.
Till then life's current shall slowly roll
Through thirsty sand and dust.
Then, the dust shall drink the whole.

III.

All the earth is empty show.
Here I have no part or lot,
Drifting with stagnation slow
Buoyed by a dead river's flow
On a life that alters not.
From my bark that sways no jot
I can never rise to row ;

Can but dread the coming gale,
Feel the softened timbers rot.
If I hear the tempest blow
I can never shorten sail.
Waterlogged upon the tide,
Can I to yon lily reach?
Nay, 'twould drown this fragile boat,
Sinking slow by sunny beach
Where a myriad lilies float.
I drag past green meadows wide
Filled with flowers, and *all* denied.
Onward helpless to yon breach
Rocky-gated, where I note
Crested waves that leap outside.
   There the sea-gulls screech.
   Vulture-like they gloat,
Knowing where my bones shall bleach
'Neath the death-wave tossed in pride
   Whence their screams deride.

IV.

All my laughter, all my tears,
All my kisses, all my strife,

DAMOCLES.

All my warmer throbs of life,
Are as pictures of past years.
All my present is to sit,
Like one opium-drugged and dumb,
Watching players go and come
From my sofa in the pit.
All my future is the scene
On a stage, an outside tale,
Gay, romantic, trite, or stale,
Played before its shifting screen.

I can never play my part,
Strut with others on my stage,
Join their laughter, brave their rage,
Clasp the heroine to my heart.
I shall never sing aloud
Joys of love, or pangs intense
Of my injured innocence,
Or portray the oppressor proud,
Or the fool, with wit and sense,
Superhuman gifts, endowed,
Charming laughter from the crowd
Of his saner audience.

I gaze idle. None will stop
On that stage where I have been,
Till the night fall on the scene
And for me the curtain drop.

v.

Dying sparkles leap and fall
Till the last light leaves my wall,
Till the last faint crackles fail ;
And a voice behind them all
Sobs alone its ceaseless wail,
Sighs beneath the mourning veil.
Wakeful, midnight-wrapt, and still,
Still with cords that cease to thrill
Jarred by hammers of the day,
I can hear it, hushed or shrill,
Till the tense cords loosened sway,
Streamers, wind-born every way.
On sad seas of wandering wind,
Sobbing for the day behind,
Sighing for the day before,
Never rest or peace to find
On a waste, where pulse no more,
Breakers on a bounding shore.

DAMOCLES.

Sobbing 'neath dark voids of sky,
Sighing as the clouds go by,
Wailing loud, it shudders past;
Rises shrieking, but to die
Struggling on with fainter blast,
Idly, blindly, to the last.
Lo, it sinks into a moan!
Surely now its strife is done!
Hush! it sleeps, it finds its goal;
Nay, it wakens with a groan,
Mourns and wails without control,
Breaks in sobs that shake the soul.
Mourner over all lost springs,
Dirge of youthful hope it sings,
Death of all 'mid passing pain.
Low on earth's cold breast it clings
Sobbing with the soughing rain
O'er her graves where all was vain.
All was vain, and all was nought,
Plains whereon brave warriors fought,
Fields where lovers kept fond tryst,
Marts where myriads sold and bought,
Graves—where phantoms rise in mist,
Windblown vapours scantly wist,

Love and hope, with sin and hate,
Blended in one day by fate.
Power and beauty, toil and skill,
Fallen earthwards soon or late.
Fiercest gust of mighty will
Dropped to wailing, and lay still.
Good or bad, what matters which
If the same grave wait for each?
Noble strife, or wailing low?
Each hath grass, or marble niche,
Both must weep their trouble through,
Both must bend beneath the blow.
And the free wind strews their tomb
With dead scraps of last year's bloom
Now decayed like those beneath.
Earth hath others in her womb,
And the wind shall lend them breath,
And the wind shall wail their death.
Earth shall mourn, and mourn, and mourn
Children that no more return,
Wind her sweeper night and day,
Bearing corpses, to what bourn?
Hither? Thither? Who may say?
Wandering winds seek every way.

VI

I wake from sleep, and life is still a dream,
Dreamed in sad silences and listless hours.
No fresher gale uplifts the deathly steam
From dreary levels, whereon grow no flowers,
Nor any rise of prospect-vantage towers.
The sands slide slowly in my darkened glass;
I count the midges in their joyless round,
Or the rain plashing on the stagnant pond.
I watch the black shade on my dial pass,
And only wonder if it nears its bound.

I am outside of all. Alone! Alone!
Like Memnon watching o'er the flooded Nile.
With some dead peace in drear wide eyes of stone,
Regardant of decay, he bears no smile,
But marks small change within a weary while.
Time is to us as nothing save the dim
And unhorizoned level of the flood,
Where feeble eddies round our ankles brim,
And all around the transient wildfowl skim,
And nightly the broad sun sinks down in blood.
One day is as ten myriads of days,

And one night as a night of ages past.
We may not measure the mysterious ways,
Or reach to any compass of the vast,
To find if there be first thereon or last.

A helpless mummy, in stiff linen swathed,
Slave-borne upon a grimly pictured pall
Forth from sarcophagus to festival
In drear reminder to wild guests who bathe
Their sense in wine, dead-eyed I see them all.
One shrinks a little. One a maiden fair
Glances all idly, curious at most :
Her youth with death in life hath nought to share.
Her neighbour bends black brows in angry stare,
Then chides some hidden fear with outward boast;
But none applaud my pageant. All would grasp
The present with firm grip. The future lies
Beyond the warmth of any bosom's clasp,
Beyond the hopes and joys that all men prize,
A loveless lifeless corpse in youth's bright eyes :
Or chrysalis at most, whose rougher rind
Speaks nothing of a beauty hid from view,
With wings ungrown to sail the balmy wind,
And mouth unmeet to sip the honey'd dew,
  . all the old life perish to a new.

VII.

See the children pass me by,
   Chasing glad some painted fly:
Caught, they mourn its broken wings,
   Or send forth a bitter cry,
Knowing how the hornet stings.

One has found a lily white,
   Shouts aloud his shrill delight,
Waves his treasure to and fro
   Till it falls: so in my sight
All life's blossoms overblow.

One has from the blackbird's nest
   Brought the bird which sung the best,
And its eyes grow glazed and dim,
   Sorrow stills its song to rest;
It shall never sing to him.

One has found a stone of price
'Mid the shingles on the strand;
   All his days will scarce suffice
   For its polish and device,
Till it shatters in his hand.

One has died of chills at morn.
One sinks in a slimy tide.
 One has pierced his heart with thorn.
 All grow muddy, bramble-torn
On the weary steep hillside.

 Some are tender, and they fail,
Vanquished by the noon-day heat,
 And their gayest plays grow stale ;
 In bleared eyes all colours pale,
Wearily they drag their feet.

 But some few have found a road
Onwards to a cooler spot,
 Carpeted with softer sod,
Where the sunbeams smite them not,
And a stream runs from a grot.

 Oh! my soul would join with these,
Clasp them round, and add my voice,
 As they sit, and sing at ease
 Old-world songs, and rest at peace,
Drink the wellspring and rejoice.

VIII.

There is a bird that sings to my heart
   As she hides 'neath the chestnut spray;
She sings not for me, for she dwells apart,
   And her song is glad, not gay,
But she thrills out her love-note so true and clear,
That I listen, and love her, and fain would hear
   That shy little bird and gray.

She sings but the self-same song that was sung
   Over nests in the bramble thorn
To nestlings who learnt from a loving tongue
   Ere man on this earth was born,
Ere Pride had his bloodstained banner unfurled,
Or Mammon grubbed deep in a grosser world,
   Or the Serpent invented scorn.

There is a maiden who sits by my bed,
   A shy little maid and plain,
But the light which rests on her homely head
   Was won when a Self was slain,
And a band she has wove of that golden thread
Wherewith she has bound up the wounds that bled
   Of my heart torn through with pain.

The low soft voice of this little maid
    Runs deep, with the tender thrill
Of a quiet streamlet that sings in shade,
    If one stoop to its tiny rill,
Of the soft green mosses, and violet bloom
That dwell in the woodland's deepest gloom
    Where all voices save God's are still.

Day by day she is present there
    To give me my daily dole,
And no man hath ever called her fair;
    But her tender simple soul,
Uncrushed 'neath a burden of pain and care,
Has borne it to heaven on the single hair
    Of her love-gained aureole.

Modest and kind she sits by my side,
    Sits as my patron saint,
No painter's ideal! that's not denied,
    But a sainthood too high to paint.
For her heart uprooted from mortal sod
Hath put forth flowers, like the high priest's rod,
    Whose whiteness a tint would taint.

IX.

Winds that wandered, winds that wept
On earth's bosom whilst she slept,
And dark clouds spread wide their wing,
From your chilly couch ye leapt
Wide the entrance gates to fling
For the children born of Spring.
Let me listen as I lie
Over-canopied by sky,
On a flower-sprent carpet rare,
Watching sunflecked shadows fly
Wheeling, wavering, in air,
Song and sunshine everywhere.
Winds that tore the clouds away
From the threshold of the May,
Ye have known December's frost,
Longest night, and shortest day,
But as barriers to be crossed
Where your eddies beat and tossed
Till ye reached fresh springs again,
Fresher for the spraying rain,
Cleaner from your mist and scum.
Well it is ye had not lain

Waiting sunnier days to come
Idle, rusting, wasting, dumb.
Ye from shades where Winter lowers
Brought forth nouriture of showers.
Ye have scattered wide the seeds,
Seeds which Summer knew for flowers,
Flowers which Autumn mourned dead weeds
When ye strowed them on the meads.
Weeds that withered lay and sere
On the dead heart of last year
Scentless, tempest-tossed, and pale,
Slept 'neath snow-shrouds on the bier
Till the shroud grown bridal veil
Melted in your warmer gale.
Then the life that slept beneath
Time's old covenant with death
Woke with spirit of the morn ;
And each blade leapt from its sheath,
Earth's old children newly born,
Flowers and fruits and golden corn ;
Flowers and yellow corn and fruits
From dry seeds and rugged roots
Out of graves of earthly mould,
Where they hid their tender shoots

Neath the inner warm enfold
Of a mantle surface-cold.
Winds, no more ye mourn and mourn
For a hope without return,
For a toil without delight;
Through dead quicksets barbed with thorn
Wailing, shrieking your affright
In the dead of winter night.
But ye glide soft-voiced along,
Breathing perfume, bearing song
Of young gladness born of May,
Guard its growth to Summer strong,
Knowing harvest and decay,
Sleep and waking, night and day,
One same life that breathes alway.

X.

I dreamed this dream last night.
  I was dead:
And now that the sword had fallen
  From its thread
I was in, and of, a chaos, faintly bright.

Thick as snowdrift was it, silent, and not cold,
            Neither warm ;
Or the touch was gone.   If there I was, I dwelt
            Without form
Immingled in that utter white enfold.

If I moved, it was dead motion, like the flow
            Of a ball
On a star track, without orbit, or desire
            Thence to fall,
Or a bond to hold it near some central glow.

I passed, gliding, all untrammelled, not in air,
            But in space,
Disembodied, tireless, ceaseless ; but no rest,
            And no race ;
Nought to reach, and nought avoid, of joy or care ;

Merely the sense of being, some dumb life
            In the I ;
Past all pain, for every care and every fear
            Was laid by
With the weapons which I bore in mortal strife.

So that awful stillness at the first was peace.
   All was o'er.
I had faded to nirvana, not accursed,
   But no more.
I must be. I was a life. I could not cease.

This was harmony, complete, without the jarring
   Pipes or strings;
Passage on and on without the airy beating
   Of the wings;
It was shield of full defence, no sword for warring.

There my soul was first unweary, without trouble.
   I was nought;
Just a powerless wraith beyond the thought of heaven,
   Till, methought,
'Were it not better now to be a bubble,

Rising up and showing tints beneath the glory
   Of a day,
Then to lose this Self, and bursting be dissevered
   Into spray,
Dead indeed, not living life without a story?'

Thought thus gathered to itself again for trial,
   Straining sight
To discover if indeed there was no ending
   To my light,
This unshadowed brightness born of hope's denial.

Then this seeking woke once more a sense of strain
   And of fetter;
I could battle as it were against my peace,
   It was better
Hope should come, if sorrow brought her back again.

So this thought . . . myself . . . became a slow
  . . . revolving . . .
   In that snow-light;
The brightness without source and without shadow
   That was no light.
Dreams have such things. Speech lacks the forms
  for solving.

Now this self-thought turning slowly formed a centre
   First displayed,
As a shapeless nucleus dawning in the light drift
   Where it strayed,
Just as new-born clouds the central sky may enter.

Wheeling faster . . . still self-centred . . . nothing winning,
>Now and then
Leapt black flashes of an outer unknown shadow
>To my ken,
From the dumb—'beyond'—where life hath no beginning.

Fuller loss of self . . . oblivion . . . lay outside me . . .
>If I strained
It seemed tangled in my giddy endless brightness,
>But I gained
From this shade a sense of somewhat still denied me.

So striving, whirling on bright clouds to sever
>In my dream
I circled, till adown the light-veil widened
>One black seam,
And I gazed aghast far out into the . . . Never . . .

Then the rent flew wide, and closing back, resigned me
>Into shade.

Where one tiny glimmer round the thought wheel lingered,
   Soon to fade,
Save for help, in utter dark, where none might find me.

Here I wandered, all unguided, in vague terror.
   Life ideal . . .
A lost atom on a blind and pathless vacance,
   Pale, unreal,
Flickered feeble now and then in helpless error.

Rest there is not there, or any hope to guess of.
   'Tis to spin
Fading out through deathly shadow without limit,
   Nought to win,
Or to cast our anchor unto, or possess of;

Till, the self-light dead, on blackness came a shimmer,
   Scarce a hair
Of gold light drawn through the awful empty silence
   Stretching there,
Leading upwards, pointing downwards, with its glimmer.

This fine spirit slowly now approached self-guided
    My dark disc,
Turning feebly, and its scarce-seen golden cobweb
    Took the risk,
Touched my vortex, and around it swiftly glided;

And that weightless idle whirlpool, once so swift,
    Could not strive,
But rolled slowly up that slender gossamer,
    To re-live,
Bound once more with life, no more at will to drift.

Swifter still, and yet the fine thread did not fail
    As I spun
From the dark without beginning, till I reached
    Things begun,
And a star drift hurtled past us like a hail.

Then the golden beam became a broader bond
    Bound around me,
Round the central self escaped from the self-voids
    Where it found me,
As we coursed amid the wandering lights beyond.

So we passed through things where light and darkness blended
   Night and day.
Where young stars flashed out a moment's life and faded
   In decay;
Then on, towards one bright place where darkness ended.

Here, methought, returned again my power of striving;
   But I woke,
And the living cord which drew me towards the heaven
   Was not broke;
But the morn had broke on night to find me living.

XI.

I cannot tell her the love of my soul,
I have lost the power to speak;
And the nerves can no more control
A body half dead and weak.

DAMOCLES.

    I cannot stir in my bed;
        If I wish to call,
    I can turn my head,
        And that is all.

The body will hardly die again
As the life ebbs out of the brain;
And I have but little pain;
And little do I repine
For the life that once was mine.
I have done with the strife,
And the growth of life,
Like cut grass in the sweet sunshine.
If the sword had slain me when first it smote,
I had died like the beast
With the taste of blood in my throat.
Now, I dream of a sweeter feast.

Mine ears are open to hear
The note of the linnet clear,
As it sings of the springs
And the glad new year.
Mine eyes are open to know
That the sword which hangs so low
Is a brand in a Hand
That in mercy withheld the blow.

Since my body was laid low,
I from love have learnt to know
Self, once slaved, a soul freeborn;
Not a winged thing in the mesh
Of this web of mortal flesh
For a spider-devil's scorn.
Love has led me forth to mark
How fixed star-points pierce the dark
Of our night, how hope and trust
Are firm stays on which to lean,
Ere the clouds blot out this scene,
And the earth returns to dust.

Will she know me? Yes, I think,
If I wait on Heaven's brink.
Yes! 'for you are mine alone,
And a love first seen will shine
From my being unto thine,
As I bend to clasp my own.'
Or if not, at least love means
Something on those other scenes,
Spirits working twofold, twinned;
Surely, surely, love will seem
Something other than my dream
In the years that went behind.

What is, *is*, and what shall be
Is—but wider eyes must see ;
For the thing itself, divine,
Cannot die or be laid by,
Will not lie to God on high ;
And love's groundwork now is mine.

XII.

Dead—dead !
I caught the whisper, without,
In the town, in the street.
(My hearing wanders so far from me round about.)
I can hear the crashing of wheels—then the people's shout
Dead—dead.
I can hear the thing pass on with a muffled tread.
Where the highway and my way meet
I can hear each footfall beat
Like a hammer that strikes on lead.
Dead ?—dead ?
Nearer, nearer,
Clearer, clearer,
Till the beat of it fills my head,
And the throb of it thrills my bed.

Dead?—dead?
It comes close
To my house,
And I start with a moment's dread,
For death has paused at my door,
It falls to rest on the floor,
Voices brief
Of pain and grief,
And I know the thing that is said—
Dead!
I have no fear,
But death draws near
And looks down beside my bed;
And death is my dove, my dear,
Still spinning her golden thread;
For the love is still in her face
That she wore in her olden place.
Now, she rests with my soul instead.
Dead! Yes, I understand,
I am weak, but the thing looms grand.
Here but an hour ago,
Gone from my side just now
For a moment hence,
And before her mortal sense

DAMOCLES.

Had a time-point to rebel,
The pride of its temple fell,
And she sees the light descend,
And she hears the music swell,
    As the heavens rend.
    Surely—surely,
She hears the voice of a friend.
Father and Friend of all,
It will not be too drear.
I am happy and of good cheer,
Awaiting my final call.
I do not longer fear,
For one whom my heart holds dear
Stands by the dreaded sword,
And strengthens its golden cord,
Until it has strength to bear
And to draw me to my Lord.
I thought to have gone before,
But hers was the higher right,
And hers is the furthest flight,
Higher than thought can soar.

If there come any hither free of thought
That stands on self, and free of any shame

In lowliest labours, caring not to blame
Those things as common that their Master wrought ;
It needeth not a miracle be wrought,
Or on the head descends a tongue of flame,
To prove their spirit out of Heaven came ;
And if such Spirit stoops, 'tis not for nought.

This spirit had she, and it leads her now
Past the dim portal to the open day,
Wearing a crown of olive on her brow.
Her feet, worn out on paths her Master trod,
Passed swiftly, easily, the higher way,
Bearing her lightened burden up to God.

XIII.

'Love, what is death?' *'The dam that hoards my*
 stream,
 The ore's fierce anguish of refining trial,
The harsher prelude to my swelling theme,
 The flight which, giving grosser touch denial,
Leads upturned hearts to search the heavens for mine
 espial.'

Yes!
Death hides not love. The hoarded stream bursts
    forth
  Unto a boundless bosom. From the fire
The gold runs pure; the dross was nothing worth;
  So from dead clay the Spirit of Desire
Leaps up, to grub no more in toil for mortal hire.

Death is love's growth. Aside his robes are laid
  Of mortal childhood. In a statelier pall
Befitting his full age, all unafraid
  He enters gladly to the banquet hall,
Unshamed to join the Master's marriage festival.

If love be death, as love is certain life,
  He knoweth, Who hath made and proved them
    both,
Who bound in flesh fought out the fleshly strife,
  Gave death and life alike His hand in troth,
Blent them, and sealed their peace with love's
  fraternal oath.

Love lived and died, and lived again and grew
  Immortal. Who shall answer if it were

This thought which spurred the Indian king who
    blew
    In heavy purple steeps of burning air
The snowy bubble bulbs of love's great sepulchre?

Life houses here till nightfall in the known.
    Known? Nay, he guesses even of his tent,
Until, beneath its needful shelter grown,
    He knows that 'neath his canvas is not pent
The star that o'er him shines, and lights the
    firmament.

He finds a seat therein, where surely poised
    There is a vantage point from which to bend
His eyes on the arena many-voiced,
    Where life, chief actor, leading death his friend,
Plays many varied parts wherein their voices blend.

Life, death, and love are three, a three in one,
    All dimly seen and shadowed unto men,
Creating, warning, teaching; for the Son
    By death brought down the Spirit to our ken;
The Father gives the '*now*,' The Spirit tells the
    '*then*.'

The '*now*' is one small ripple on wide seas
  Breath-stirred to swell and fall. The '*then*'
    shall rise
A vapour joined with the creating breeze
  That o'er the waters moves, and soar through skies
Where nights no more eclipse the bright realities.

XIV.

Seedtime is here, if on the soil of time
Before the Spring the dews of heaven shower,
A swelling time if will be loving power,
A bursting time if husks be cast of crime,
A springing time ere Spring has reached its prime:
And if the worms have spared the budding flower,
And the warm light shine out above one hour,
A time of blossom reared of earthly slime.

This one thing stirring in my darkness throve,
It will not sicken in a broader light,
It cleaves unto its stem in Hell's despite,
And deeply rooted, nought shall hence remove.
Still climbing till it reach the loftiest height,
And breathe forth incense to the Sun of love.

DAMOCLES.

There is a moment when the spirit sighs,
And all my brow is wrinkled with a frown,
As eyes strained heavenwards droop from Heaven
    down;
Then the soft tear turns bitter-salt and dries,
And thirst and sickness choke the prayer that dies
Unbreathed between parched lips of sordid brown.
So, weary nigh to swoon, I seem to drown
Lost in the gulf of mine infirmities.

Poor stifling insect, clogged upon this pool
Of sluggard mud, forgotten sure am I,
Reft of my nurse, the gentle passer-by
Who helped my fever with soft hand and cool,
And buoyed me in this slough in which I lie.
' Shall love not come to pluck thee forth, poor fool?'

Mother? I did not know that you were near.
It seems so long. It seems, seems, seems, I
    say;
I do not know, it seems so far away,
Ages perhaps, since you and I were here,
And you were lying down, and I sat there,

And you were, do they call us dead ; but stay,
Pray for me, mother, as you used to pray ;
Hold me ! I'm falling, falling, mother dear.

Dark ! Is it night ? Why is it so o'ercast ?
Air, air ! I stifle 'neath these closing walls.
Where am I ? What is that thing gliding past ?
Look ! it is stopping, stopping here at last.
Listen ! She's turning this way, and she calls.
The sword, the sword ! My God, it falls, it falls !

www.ingramcontent.com/pod-product-compliance
Lightning Source LLC
LaVergne TN
LVHW061213060426
835507LV00016B/1912

NOTE ON EDITIONS

Given the uncertain accuracy of *The Complete Works*, edited by Edmund Gosse and Thomas James Wise, 25 vols (London: Bonchurch, 1925), and for the sake of consistency across the following chapters, I have chosen to refer to the edition of Swinburne's poems overseen and published within his lifetime: *The Poems of Algernon Charles Swinburne*, 6 vols (London: Chatto & Windus, 1905). However, readers will also want to consult Francis O'Gorman's excellent new scholarly edition, *Algernon Charles Swinburne* (Oxford: Oxford University Press, 2016).

Tous les grands poètes deviennent naturellement, fatalement, critiques. Je plains les poètes que guide le seul instinct; je les crois incomplets. Dans la vie spirituelle des premiers, une crise se fait infailliblement, où ils veulent raisonner leur art, découvrir les lois obscures en vertu desquelles ils ont produit, et tirer de cette étude une série de préceptes dont le but divin est l'infaillibilité dans la production poétique. Il serait prodigieux qu'un critique devînt poète, et il est impossible qu'un poète ne contienne pas un critique. Le lecteur ne sera donc pas étonné que je considère le poète comme le meilleur de tous les critiques. — CHARLES BAUDELAIRE

[All great poets naturally — fatally — become critics. I lament the poets guided by instinct alone: I consider them incomplete. In the spiritual life of the former, a crisis ineluctably arises, in which they want to rationalise their art, discover the obscure laws by virtue of which they have produced [it], and draw from this study a series of precepts whose divine aim is infallibility in poetic production. It would be prodigious for a critic to become a poet, and it is impossible for a poet not to contain a critic. The reader will therefore not be surprised to discover that I consider the poet the best of all critics.]

INTRODUCTION

Great works wait. — THEODOR W. ADORNO

The poet Veronica Forrest-Thomson writes: 'You must come to terms with T. S. Eliot/ If you are doing the twentieth century'.¹ She neglected to add that T. S. Eliot spent most of the twentieth century coming to terms with A. C. Swinburne. As Eliot recalls: 'the question' on every aspiring poet's lips in 1920 'was still where do we go from Swinburne, and the answer appeared to be: nowhere.'² Eliot's sense of the impasse presented by Swinburne's technique echoes down the century: 'I am Swinburne, ruler in mystery. / None know the ending, / Blazes a-blending in splendor [sic] / Of glory none know the meaning on [...]' wrote Ezra Pound in 1908.³ A. E. Housman was less generous: 'Swinburne picks up the sausage-machine into which he crammed anything and everything; round goes the handle, and out at the other end comes [...] noise.'⁴ According to these readers — representative of a general critical consensus since 1920 — 'Swinburne's art is out of fashion'.⁵ What further test could we need, other than that of time itself, to show that Swinburne's poetry remains just as much of a dead end today as it seemed to the architects of the new poetic over a century ago?

A book which persists in wishing to come to terms with Swinburne will make many readers feel embarrassed, especially if that book proposes to do so by attending to his 'style'. The word evokes grandeur. It veers close to tradition, the canon, genius. The reader will expect, at worst, a dilettante's anthology. Gobbets of Swinburne — the majesty of the anapaestic rhythms, the lip-smacking alliteration, and the glories of the biblical diction — will be tried, tasted and summed, against all the evidence, towards a plea for Swinburne's timeless appeal. A study that responds to Eliot's 'serious condemnation' that 'at one period of our lives we did enjoy him and now no longer enjoy him' with unrestrained delight is at risk of nostalgia, a hope that 'it may all flow again if we suppress the / breaks'.⁶ At best, one might hope for a re-run of the 'Swinburne controversy', perhaps following the example of Christopher Ricks, in which Swinburne, like Milton, is made to face the critics again and is shown to be better than anyone previously realised.⁷ However, this argument risks underplaying the challenge presented by Swinburne's verse, as if we could by argument bring his poetry near.

Such defences usually keep within the bounds of the criticism originally levelled at the artist. That this has been Swinburne's fate is registered in the frequent declarations that T. S. Eliot's essay 'Swinburne As Poet' has been refuted, while critics continue to labour under the terms of his essay.⁸ This in part accounts for the curious paradox that constitutes Swinburne studies today in which it is possible to claim that a poet about whom so much has been written is still considered marginal.[9] Since 1920 Swinburne's poetry has been read on another poet's terms.[10]

Clearly the reader's doubts regarding a study of Swinburne's style could only be assuaged if I begin by acknowledging that the time for writing like Swinburne is over and gone. Who could write like Swinburne today? Who would want to? Really to take Swinburne's style seriously, one has to begin by admitting that in art 'Truth exists exclusively as that which has become.'[11] Yet this need not be the end of the matter. Instead, approaching Swinburne's poetry as over and past may be the first step in coming to read it as more than just an historical curiosity. Compelling reasons for a study of Swinburne's style may be found if what strikes us as 'out of fashion' in fact tells us more about his peculiar place in the history of poetry. What Swinburne's style requires, then, is not lip-smacking nostalgia, or a defence against the critics, but attention to the way it lives and moves, since:

> Art can be understood only by its laws of movement, not according to any sort of invariants. It is defined by its relation to what it is not. The specifically artistic in art must be defined concretely from its other; that alone would fulfil the demands of a materialistic-dialectical aesthetics. Art acquires its specificity by separating itself from what it developed out of; its law of movement is its law of form. It exists only in relation to its other; it is the process that transpires with its other. (*Aesthetic Theory*, p. 3)

Perhaps the embarrassment provoked by the announcement of a study of Swinburne's style will only be dispelled if, in reading Swinburne anew, we can more fully understand his significance for the historical development of English poetry.

It is this question above all that I explore in this book. However, this enquiry into Swinburne's style began with a very different question: what influence did Swinburne's verse have on the subsequent development of English poetry? Reading and writing about free verse had drawn my attention to an ambivalence towards Swinburne's musicality in the work of T. E. Hulme, Ezra Pound, T. S. Eliot, H. D., F. S. Flint, and other poets who acknowledge the influence of Swinburne, yet who prioritise very different aspects of the verse repertoire in their own poems. By considering their reaction to a late nineteenth-century poet as one test case, particular facts about the conscious and unconscious motivations behind the emancipation of English poetry would, I hoped, become clear.

Instead, I became interested in the peculiar challenge which Swinburne's verse poses. Reading back into the nineteenth century, I was struck by the way his poetry frequently exceeds the expectations and the critical vocabulary of his reviewers. His work continues to divide readers: renewed interest in Swinburne's poetry peaked in the 1960s with Lang's edition of *The Swinburne Letters*. The three books of essays and over a dozen articles published since the 2009 centenary conference suggests his work is today undergoing further re-evaluation. However, criticism has yet to engage with the most challenging aspect of Swinburne's poetry: his style. Previously, I had thought of Swinburne as a point of comparison. Now I wanted to understand the peculiar position his poetry holds in English verse.

This inquiry immediately ran into two connected difficulties: firstly, since I came to Swinburne through Eliot, I remain acutely aware that to continue to argue for or against Swinburne's style risks replaying critical arguments formed at a different historical moment. Secondly, I am mindful that to read Swinburne after 1922 is also to encounter aspects of the poetic repertoire that are now largely discredited. The position of the reader today is not that of the reader in 1866. The demise of a transhistorical kind of listening epitomised by Walter Pater's scholar-reader and practised by critics such as George Saintsbury, Arthur Symons, and by Swinburne himself registers in the gathering dissatisfaction with aesthetic criticism around 1920.[12] At the same time, the break with tradition on which the development of free verse is understood to depend means that much of the knowledge we can suppose was present at a hearing of Swinburne's poetry in his lifetime has been supressed. How then are we supposed to begin to understand Swinburne's style?

Rather than arguing for or against Swinburne's poetry in the terms of past criticism, I wish to begin again by recognising that if criticism has found Swinburne's poetry challenging, this is because Swinburne's poetry challenges criticism. His poetry invites us to test the limits of our ears. Take, as one example, his poem 'Itylus' from *Poems and Ballads* (1866) in which unspeakable trauma, broken sisterhood, and a longing after an impossible happiness cumulate in a vow never to forget.[13] I could quote that refusal briefly here, but this would not prove convincing, since the poem's music is cumulative, and its power depends for its effect on the intricate interweaving of syntax, rhythm, repetition, and end-rhyme. Here is the nightingale's address to her sister, the swallow, in full:

> Swallow, my sister, O sister swallow,
>   How can thine heart be full of the spring?
>   A thousand summers are over and dead.
> What hast thou found in the spring to follow?
>   What hast thou found in thine heart to sing?
>   What wilt thou do when the summer is shed?
>
> O swallow, sister, O fair swift swallow,
>   Why wilt thou fly after spring to the south,
>   The soft south whither thine heart is set?
> Shall not the grief of the old time follow?
>   Shall not the song thereof cleave to thy mouth?
>   Hast thou forgotten ere I forget?
>
> Sister, my sister, O fleet sweet swallow,
>   Thy way is long to the sun and the south;
>   But I, fulfilled of my heart's desire,
> Shedding my song upon height, upon hollow,
>   From tawny body and sweet small mouth
>   Feed the heart of the night with fire.
>
> I the nightingale all spring through,
>   O swallow, sister, O changing swallow,
>   All spring through till the spring be done,
> Clothed with the light of the night on the dew,
>   Sing, while the hours and the wild birds follow,
>   Take flight and follow and find the sun.

> Sister, my sister, O soft light swallow,
>   Though all things feast in the spring's guest-chamber,
>   How hast thou heart to be glad thereof yet?
> For where thou fliest I shall not follow,
>   Till life forget and death remember,
>   Till thou remember and I forget.
>
> Swallow, my sister, O singing swallow,
>   I know not how thou hast heart to sing.
>   Hast thou the heart? is it all past over?
> Thy lord the summer is good to follow,
>   And fair the feet of thy lover the spring:
>   But what wilt thou say to the spring thy lover?
>
> O swallow, sister, O fleeting swallow,
>   My heart in me is a molten ember
>   And over my head the waves have met.
> But thou wouldst tarry or I would follow,
>   Could I forget or thou remember,
>   Couldst thou remember and I forget.
>
> O sweet stray sister, O shifting swallow,
>   The heart's division divideth us.
>   Thy heart is light as a leaf of a tree;
> But mine goes forth among sea-gulfs hollow
>   To the place of the slaying of Itylus,
>   The feast of Daulis, the Thracian sea.
>
> O swallow, sister, O rapid swallow,
>   I pray thee sing not a little space.
>   Are not the roofs and the lintels wet?
> The woven web that was plain to follow,
>   The small slain body, the flowerlike face,
>   Can I remember if thou forget?
>
> O sister, sister, thy first-begotten!
>   The hands that cling and the feet that follow,
>   The voice of the child's blood crying yet
> *Who hath remembered me? who hath forgotten?*
>   Thou hast forgotten, O summer swallow,
>   But the world shall end when I forget.

This lilting, bittersweet song shows an expert handling of song metre: four beats per line make it easy to divide syntax across a line or several for rhetorical effect and the *abcabc* rhyme-scheme also offers an opportunity to use rhyme to create contrast and development within stanzas (for example, in binding 'swallow' and 'follow' into a question — will she or won't she follow? — in lines one and four). However, my intuition on rereading is that the power of this last stanza, and of the last line in particular, lies not in the handling, nor in the refrain which alters the epithets which address the swallow, but in the altogether more subtle and precise placement of that ultimate word: 'forget'.

Taking my cue from the poem, I note several aspects of Swinburne's verse practice which might take me further. To begin with, I observe that the line-ends tend to fall in with syntactic units, a fact which contributes to, or perhaps, heightens my sense that individual lines retain their own rhythmical character as rising or falling. This, I realise, is largely determined by the last two syllables of the line, which may be rising, as in 'forget', or falling as in 'remember'. The reason that this is noticeable, I further observe, has to do with the way Swinburne's poem takes advantage of a natural tendency in English to go up, that is, to rise in pitch, at the end of a sentence expressing a question or conditional clause. Since pitch is one way in which stress registers in English (along with amplitude and duration) we can see his verse working with the music of everyday speech.

However, the distribution of these rising and falling lines does not fall into a strict pattern, unlike the rhyme-scheme, and the questions do not always occur in tandem with a rising line. Swinburne is altogether less monotonous, and more subtle than that. The proportions of each type of rhythm vary from stanza to stanza: in some there is a ratio of four rising lines to two falling, in some two falling lines to four rising. The only stanza where this is not determinately the case is the antepenultimate verse beginning 'O sweet stray sister' which has three of each, but which might alter were one to argue for a performance of the proper name 'Itylus' which deviated from the value usually given to it by classical scholarship.

In the first four stanzas, rising lines get the upper hand for four consecutive stanzas. A falling line might therefore be considered more unexpected in the first half of the poem. In the second half of the poem there are more falling lines than rising lines, with the exception of the penultimate verse. Overall then, I can observe that a stanza of predominantly falling lines is only slightly more unusual than the opposite, but a rising line is even less usual in the second half of the poem.

Returning to the high predominance of rhetorical questions, I note that fourteen lines out of sixty end with a question mark, and of those nine are in rising rhythm and five are falling. And as to the force of that word 'forget', this recurs seven times: twice at the mid-point of the line, and five times at the end of the line. However, syntax and prolepsis are also working together here: when the word 'forget' occurs in the middle line, on the second beat, the reader comes to expect a repetition of the word 'forget' at the end of the following line, since this happens twice.

This is a long way round to go, yet it does give us some sense of why this final sentence has such force:

> O sister, sister, thy first-begotten!
> The hands that cling and the feet that follow,
> The voice of the child's blood crying yet
> *Who hath remembered me? who hath forgotten?*
> Thou hast forgotten, O summer swallow,
> But the world shall end when I forget.

Meeting the cognate participle for 'forget', 'forgotten', in second position in the penultimate line leads us to expect 'forget' again at the end of the line. Yet this last utterance of 'forget' is, by the poem's standards, a fairly unusual one. Firstly, it makes for a rising line in a stanza in which there are predominantly falling lines, and a rising line in the second half of the poem. Secondly, this rising 'forget' appears at the end of the line, yet unlike the six other instances of 'forget' in this poem it is not a question nor a conditional clause, but a statement.

Similar, yet different, it has earned the full force of a contrast: the question is repossessed, quoted, recalling while setting to rest all those previous invitations to 'forget?' Such coordinates provide a fitting answer to the only other rising line in the stanza, the *c* rhyme, which recognises 'The voice of the child's blood crying yet'. This line is already also unexpected, a rare case of enjambment, rising after two falling lines, in a predominantly falling stanza, in the predominantly falling half of the poem. It rises, then, with the full force of a question: the child's blood, figured here as a 'cry', hangs in the balance. And this time the nightingale answers, not with a question, but with a vow: to never forget. When these cumulative expectations and associations combine with the rhetorical footwork of the last two lines, and issue in a line of monosyllables which would have me weigh every last word, one can see how the power of Swinburne's poem has as much to with his prosody as it has to do with his content. The question of how Swinburne's poem moves is just as crucial to its meaning as the question of whether he is, say, following Catullus in confusing Itys and Itylus, and thus their wrong-doing and wronged mothers, Procne, Philomena and Aëdon.

Yet how far are we prepared to go in acknowledging the meaningfulness of those extra-semantic aspects of verse, such as rhythm and repetition, in which Swinburne was so expert? How, in an era in which such intricate forms, or techniques like repetition and refrain are never used in poetry (though it might occur in choral music, hip hop, or in radio comedy for satiric effect) can we fully appreciate the subtle variation in the pace of these stanzas? And how in this generation, in which Victorian poetry critics frequently draw upon historical and social formations as the key to understanding how poetic form works, are we to cope with a poet whose working knowledge of poetic form was implicit, whose sense of his practice must be patched together from stray comments in essays or letters to friends, and who saw no need to offer a theory or treatise? Lines such as these make us aware of the limits of our critical range. As such, they are an invitation to reconsider the scope and aims of our reading.

This book, subtitled an experiment in verse history, is a response to this. In what remains of this introduction I aim to explain what the verse-historical approach — much less a theory than a set of assumptions — involves. However, before doing so, and in order that the reader might have a better grasp of the material which motivates these commitments, I want to start with an attempt to give an overview of Swinburne's style. Here T. S. Eliot's observation that it seems impossible to criticise Swinburne because our 'words of condemnation' are the same words that express his 'qualities' rings true: some of the fullest engagements with this aspect of Swinburne's style come from his detractors ('Swinburne as Poet', p. 132). Let us start, then, by revisiting the usual claims that are made against his poetry.

Swinburne's Style

'No one else has made such music in English', Pound claims, qualifying this a moment later: 'I mean has made his kind of music' ('Swinburne versus Biographers', p. 327). This sense of Swinburne's verse as unparalleled registers in the unusual extent to which his poetry goes in its aspiration towards music. Eliot recognises an unusual configuration in Swinburne between semantic meaning and musical value: 'what we get in Swinburne is an expression by sound, which could not possibly associate itself with music. For what he gives is not images and ideas and music, it is one thing with a curious mixture of suggestions of all three' ('Swinburne as Poet', p. 324). Eliot does not imply that Swinburne has music and no meaning, as critics who argue against him sometimes imply. Rather, the separation of semantic meaning and phonic patterning which he recognises in Campion's poetry cannot be said of Swinburne's verse. Adorno, in his attempt to reclaim for music a meaning that goes beyond the Romantic characterisation of music as 'emotional', dismisses Swinburne in the same sentence in which he criticises Rilke. Swinburne is understood as using, without 'energising', the 'incipient intentions' in language and so falls without the range of 'true musicality'.[14] Presumably Adorno is responding to Swinburne's virtuosity, that capacity of his to pick up a rhythm or a rhyme scheme and push it as far as it can go. Whether we agree with Adorno's definition of 'true musicality' or not, his observation of Swinburne's enjoyment in the musical aspects of verse remains untouchable.[15]

The complaint that Swinburne's poetry is merely emotional is clearly connected to his unusual musicality. Gerard Manley Hopkins recognises Swinburne's especial poetic gifts in a letter to Robert Bridges: 'I do not think that kind goes far: it expresses passion but not feeling, much less character [...] Swinburne's genius is astonishing, but it will, I think, only do one thing'.[16] Hopkins understands Swinburne's power, but needs more gradation in feeling, a more specific situation. Pound, too, offers and retracts praise when he connects Swinburne's 'art of verbal music' with Keats's discovery that poetry did not have to be 'the pack-mule of philosophy' ('Swinburne Versus Biographers', p. 326). His poetry is glorious precisely because it resists being the vehicle for ideas. In contrast to Browning, who 'wrote to a theory of the universe, thereby cutting off a fair half of the moods for expression', Swinburne achieves 'an emotional fusion of the perceptions [...] but this is of all sorts of writing the most dangerous to an author' ('Swinburne Versus Biographers', p. 328). Despite the risk that 'verbal confusion' runs, Pound will at least allow that some of Swinburne's emotions were 'indubitably real'. However, the criticism that his poetry is cut off from the world is harder to shake.

William Morris sums this up: 'But, to confess and be hanged, you know I never could really sympathize with Swinburne's work [...] it always seemed to me to be founded on literature not on nature [...]'[17] Swinburne takes him on in the 'Dedicatory Epistle' to his *Collected Poetical Works*:

> The half-brained creature to whom books are other than living things may see with the eyes of a bat and draw with the fingers of a mole his dullard's distinction between books and life: those who live the fuller life of a higher

animal than he know that books are to poets as much part of that life as pictures are to painters or as music is to musicians, dead matter though they may be to the spiritually still-born children of dirt and dullness who find it possible and natural to live while dead in heart and brain. Marlowe and Shakespeare, Æschylus and Sappho, do not for us live only on the dusty shelves of libraries. (I, p.xxi)

Swinburne's defence hardly denies that his works are bookish. He could have argued, on the contrary, that much of his writing responds to real political events. Yet he chooses instead to defend his work by arguing that books are really real.[18] Eliot offers the most total view of Swinburne's work as hermetic when he takes issue with the words of criticism customarily aimed at Swinburne's poetry: there is no point in saying Swinburne's poetry is like anything, because it doesn't refer to anything real. The sense that Swinburne's poetry is morbid is a mistake: it could not die in the first place. Eliot goes on to dismiss Swinburne, arguing that the writing he values is that which struggles to describe new objects, such as the prose of Joyce or Conrad. However, this is not before his image of Swinburne's poetry as a kind of rootless cloud-forest aptly catches the artificiality, the detachment of Swinburne's poetry.

It is a short step from Swinburne's literariness to his derivativeness, and from what appears habitual to what is unthinking. Swinburne's poetry stands accused of automatism. Housman's analogy between his verse and a 'sausage-machine', a repetitive mechanism that treats its material indiscriminately, is suggestive. Pound, too, suggests that Swinburne is more concerned with keeping his poems going: 'He habitually makes a fine stanzaic form, writes one or two fine strophes in it, and then continues to pour into the mould strophes of diminishing quality'. This also goes for Swinburne's diction: 'He neglected the value of words as words, and was intent on their value as sound. His habit of choice grew mechanical, and he himself perceived it and parodied his own systematization' ('Swinburne as Poet', p. 326).

Swinburne's verse has been dismissed as merely musical, musical in the wrong way, merely emotional, artificial (if not dead) and ultimately mindless. What it is about Swinburne's style that makes for such unusual encounters? How is Swinburne's 'verbal confusion' achieved? How does Swinburne's poetry achieve such a level of detachment from the world? Must a strong or regular rhythm be dismissed as unthinking automatism? Or might there be something more generative, even vital, about this aspect of Swinburne's technique?[19] Pound, we have seen, set Swinburne apart. Saintsbury, in a Swinburnean proliferation of genitive syntax, crowns Swinburne as 'indisputably at the head of the choir of the poets of our days' (*History*, III, p. 334). We recognise Swinburne's style when we hear it. It echoes through the triple rhythm in the first three stanzas of Thomas Hardy's 'The Voice', and throughout the third verse of Dylan Thomas's 'A Winter's Tale'. What, then, is Swinburnean? The critics have given us some directions. We might begin with his rhythm.

'"The beauty of Swinburne's verse is the sound," people say', writes Eliot ('Swinburne as Poet', p. 324). 'No man who cares for his art can be deaf to the rhythms of Swinburne', Pound admits ('Swinburne versus Biographers', p. 328). Swinburne's rhythms, in all their variety, insistence and finesse, are likely to be the first thing we notice. He is a master of those forms in which the rhythmical element dominates over other aspects of verse-craft such as syntax or diction. He takes a hint from the existing rhythmical tradition — *dol'nik*, triple rhythm, third paeonic — and refines it to create virtuosic performances. Witness 'The Triumph of Time', the chorus of *Atalanta* and his late parody 'The Poet to the Woodlouse'.[20]

Even Swinburne's detractors allow for his rhythmical achievement. Pound remarks that 'Swinburne's surging and leaping dactylics had no comparable forerunners in English' (p. 328).[21] Housman reflects that 'Not only did he create new metres, he resuscitated old: particularly the heroic couplet'. Compared to Pope or Dryden, he writes, 'You are free to like it less: it is less brisk and forthright, but its fullness and richness and variety are qualities of which one would never have supposed the couplet to be capable' ('Swinburne', p. 391). Housman also notes that 'Among Swinburne's technical achievements is his development of anapaestic verse towards a self-possession unequalled by previous examples' (p. 388). Though Housman concludes that anapaestic verse is not the best 'vehicle' in English verse, his recognition of Swinburne's *sprezzatura* as regards triple rhythm remains.

Put Housman and Pound's adjectives together and we can understand why it would be wrong to limit Swinburne's contribution to the rhythmical repertoire to a regularisation of previous forms. While 'self-possession' recognises the tight restraints to which Swinburne works, 'surging' indicates variety. Consider following Swinburne's 'Hymn to Proserpine' with a reading of the last two stanzas of Hardy's 'The Voice'. Swinburne would have never allowed the rhythm to drop off, even if this does serve to demonstrate the end of the speaker's conjuring in Hardy's poem. Swinburne's preponderance of double offbeats — what Housman calls anapaestic metre — is more regular, his verse further from the principle of alternation that governs English speech. It is perhaps for this reason that D. S. W. Harding picks Swinburne's 'characteristic swing' as his example when considering how irregular a poem's rhythm must become before we are no longer able to perceive the metrical set..[22] Song rhythm, not speech rhythm, is the instinctive basis of his verse.[23]

His experiments with syllabic verse, which often indicate their form by their title — 'Sapphics', 'Hendecasyllabics', 'Choriambics' — are accomplished enough almost to vindicate D. S. Carne-Ross's fantasy that classical metrics might be a seamless fit for English verse.[24] That a title should refer to form, rather than introducing what the poem is about, suggests how metre was for Swinburne a generative principle. One rather regrets the loss of his experiment in galliambics, for which presumptuous act of composition he was allegedly flogged at Eton, now no longer extant.

Swinburne's verse is capable of superb variation. Consider the second verse in 'A Dark Month', in which the second half of the fourth line achieves the prosodic equivalent of a hand attempting to sweep away oppressive thoughts:

> We shall not feel if the sun rise,
> We shall not care when it sets:
> If a nightingale make night's air
> As noontide, why should we care?

Or consider how variation is used in this rare case of verbal mimesis in 'At a Month's End':[25]

> Across, aslant, a scudding seamew
> Swam, dipped, and dropped, and grazed the sea:
> And one with me I could not dream you;
> And one with you I could not be.

The second line causes problems for those adapting classical metrics because the experience of promotion on 'dipped' following the stress on 'swam', a stress encouraged by foregoing alliteration, does not fit easily into a binary system in which syllables appear stressed or unstressed. In fact, Swinburne's verse frequently pitches us into difficulties like this, in which what trips so instinctively off the tongue is hard to reduce to a diagram. Frequently the placement of three monosyllables combined with linking sound effects such as alliteration will give rise to a promotion on the middle word, sometimes registering as a change in pitch, with the odd result that one sometimes feels as if one is singing Swinburne. This is ubiquitous in 'The Triumph of Time'. Often, as Veronica Forrest-Thomson also notes, promotion falls on a part of speech that is not syntactically as important, such as an adjective rather than a noun, with the result that Swinburne's verse seems to focus on the qualities of objects, rather than the objects themselves.

This detail demonstrates a more general tendency about Swinburne's style, which means admitting that in Swinburne's poetry rhythm often appears to get the better of syntax. It is not the adjective 'sweet' so much as the preposition 'of' that is rife in 'The Triumph of Time', which arises from the ease with which the phrase 'of the' fits the rhythmic requirement for a double offbeat. It is not just 'The dead red leaves' that 'lie rotten' but 'the dead red leaves of the years' (I, p. 41). Swinburne's verse is like a cobweb in which each word depends on its connection to every other. This particular collision of syntax with rhythm perhaps accounts for the hermetic quality which Eliot detects in this poem in particular.

Yet it is not that Swinburne cannot construct a verse-paragraph with an eye to word order. Long before the more rhetorical *Songs before Sunrise* (1871), and the more successful syntactical balancing acts which he achieves in the choral odes of *Erechtheus* (1876), the Huntsman's speech at the opening of *Atalanta* (1865) and the monologues of the female protagonists demonstrate Swinburne's syntactical debt to Milton and Shakespeare's early plays. Yet we get the sense that the temptation to fit syntax to rhythm is something Swinburne takes pains to resist in these poems.

Donald Davie proposes that 'Most people, if they think about the syntax of poetry at all, regard it as something neutral [...] a mere skeleton on which are hung the truly poetic elements, such as imagery or rhythm [...] But a skeleton obviously has a great deal to do with the beauty or ugliness of the body it supports'.[26] Curiously, Swinburne uses a similar image to Davie in the course of his scathing critique of Frederick Furnivall, who for Swinburne represents the new methods of dating early modern texts practised by The New Shakspere [sic] Society. His protest, more recently interpreted as a 'reticence to engage in prosodic debates', is directed against an anatomical way of treating rhythm and metre, and comes in the form of a footnote in his *Study of Shakespeare*:

> Prosody is at best no more than the skeleton of verse, as verse is the body of poetry; while the gain of such painful labourers in a field they know not how to till is not even a skeleton of worthless or irrelevant fact, but the shadow of such a skeleton reflected in water, it would seem that critics who hear only through their fingers have not even fingers to hear with.[27]

For Swinburne to theorise prosody is another case in which 'Our meddling intellect / Mis-shapes the beauteous forms of things: / We murder to dissect.'[28] Yet his implicit acknowledgement of prosody, not syntax, as core is indicative. Could it be that rhythm was, for Swinburne, the backbone of his verse-craft? Pound's estimate that 'The rhythm-building faculty [...] was perhaps the chief part of his genius' would agree with this ('Swinburne Versus Biographers', p. 328).[29]

Swinburne's diction is difficult to consider aside from the other aspects of his style. His word choice is connected to rhythmic considerations and complicated by his repetitive tendency and facility in rhyme. Timothy Steele's argument in *Missing Measures* is suggestive on this point, posing the interconnectedness of metre and diction as an historical question which modernist writers had to decide:

> Swinburne was a dead end. And why was he, and Victorian verse in general, a dead end? It was because of the numbingly emphatic quality of the verse. [...] It was because the verse almost seemed to preclude mature and flexible expression. Metrical speech [...] by nature produces degrees of emphasis. Moreover [...] meter can support elevated diction more readily than prose can, and it may thus encourage the unwary or unskilful writer to employ falsely or indiscriminately elevated diction. It may have been only natural for Ford, Eliot, and Pound, living at the particular historical moment they did, to consider removing meter from poetry in hopes of removing everything which seemed overwrought and dull.[30]

Even allowing for the sea-mews, pards and asps, Swinburne's diction is consciously literary. Housman writes of the 'great and overpowering richness' of diction in *Poems and Ballads*, 'He seemed to have ransacked all the treasuries of the language and melted the whole plunder into a new and gorgeous amalgam' ('Swinburne', p. 394). It is not just past forms that Swinburne seeks to revivify in this volume, but the English language itself. In 1866 the 'lexical colouring' of his verse had not yet reached the point of self-consciousness that made it ripe for the parodic inversion of Christian motifs that we encounter in *Songs before Sunrise*, and which made William Michael Rossetti so nervous.[31] Swinburne can even use the archaism 'sayeth', as he spells it at one point in 'The Triumph of Time', without seeming archaic. The diction of *Poems and Ballads* exhibits that doubleness of language which Adorno identifies with those highest lyric works in which 'the subject, with no remaining mere matter, *sounds forth in language until language itself acquires a voice.*'[32] However, this is not simply a lyric diction spoken in a high register, by an 'I' who has turned away from the world, as in the poetry of Charles Baudelaire ('*Je fermerai partout portières et volets* [...]'). Reading Arthur Symons, writing after Swinburne and Baudelaire, we read the word 'rent' functioning in a way we would never see in Swinburne, for whom the word denotes not the transaction required to secure a garret room, but the way lightning tears the sky, or time devours all things.

Later, Housman writes, Swinburne became 'diffuse' and 'voluble'. His work began to make use of an 'impoverished vocabulary' with frequent recourse to 'a dwindled stock of words repeated again and again'. His epithets are used indiscriminately and without much thought. We might draw up a list of things that are referred to as 'flower-soft' and never see any connection between them. According to Housman, Swinburne's diction, like that of Pope, begins to 'run in a groove': 'They impose upon all thought and feeling a set mode of speech: they are mannerisms, and consequently they are imitable' ('Swinburne', p. 394). Eliot, likewise, accuses Swinburne of using only 'the general word [...] it is not merely the sound that he wants, but the vague associations of idea that the words give him' (*Selected Essays*, p. 326). The tendency to choose words because of their 'vague associations' is given a slightly more positive spin in Pound's account: 'Unusual and gorgeous words attracted' Swinburne: 'he uses the same adjectives to depict either a woman or a sunset. There are times when this last is not, or need not be, ipso facto a fault. There is an emotional fusion of the perceptions, and a certain kind of verbal confusion has an emotive value in writing' ('Swinburne Versus Biographers', p. 328). Though Pound can detect the motive behind Swinburne's word selection, he maintains that 'this is of all sorts of writing the most dangerous to an author, and the unconscious collapse into this sort of writing has wrecked more poets in our time than perhaps all other faults put together'.

How can Swinburne be attracted to both 'the general word' and 'unusual and gorgeous words'? These claims respond to Swinburne's diction from different angles: Swinburne has a stock of nouns (e.g. flowers, foam, stars), adjectives, epithets and compounds (e.g. wild, sweet, little, flower-soft) that he makes frequent use of. As a result, anything outside this 'harem of words', as Edward Thomas puts it, or anything out of the way, seems particularly 'gorgeous' — 'tamarisk', 'Ilion', 'laurustine'.[33] Yet Swinburne's imitators were much more liable to choose 'unusual' words than he was. The noun-turned-adjective 'mazy' in Arthur Symons, or the compound 'life-fruitage' in Ernest Dowson sound like Swinburnese, but they do not appear in Swinburne.[34]

For Swinburne the 'lexical colouring' of words — the memory of the psalter or the *Song of Songs* — was an aspect of their meaning which he drew upon. Over time this colouring becomes extended to include other words used by Swinburne. We see this if we take Housman's hint and actually follow the compound 'flower-soft'. The collocation of both words occurs often before 1878, although only once in the same line. However, it is in *Poems and Ballads: Third Series* that they are first compounded, in 'A Birth-Song' (a poem celebrating the arrival of Olivia Frances Madox Rossetti), in his 'Memorial Verses for Théophile Gautier' and in the poem 'Relics'. The compound is used, variously, to refer to baby Olivia's 'flower-soft [eye]lids', Gautier's 'flower-soft word' and the 'flower-soft thoughts', which the poet recalls on smelling laurustine on his first trip to Italy. The object shifts, but the emotional connection between gifts, looked forward to, bestowed and lost is clear. This accumulating set of connections between words may be, as Eliot writes, 'vague'. Yet for Swinburne there is evidently a powerful set of associations connected to the compound. *Tristram of Lyonesse* is a poem in which the play of memory is required across all aspects of his technique. Composed at the same time as many of the poems in the *Third Series*, it makes concerted use of the compound 'flower-soft' to create a contrast, hundreds of lines apart, between the lips of Iseult of Ireland, and the attentions of Iseult of Brittany to Tristram as he lies dying. Here is the initial description of Iseult:

> Her flower-soft lips were meek and passionate,
> For love upon them like a shadow sate
> Patient, a foreseen vision of sweet things [...] (IV, p. 14)

Later the same compound is used to forge a contrast between Tristram's maiden wife, also called Iseult (of Brittany), and Iseult (of Ireland) whom he longs for:

> [...] and the breath
> Felt on his face did not his will to death,
> Nor glance nor lute-like voice nor flower-soft touch
> Might so prevail upon it overmuch
> That constancy might less prevail than they [...] (IV, p. 74)

Tristram remains faithful to Iseult of Ireland, in the absence of whom the compound must act as proxy. Again, the emotional connections, rather than the named object, motivate the diction. The final occurrence of the compound calls on all the past associations of this compound with gifts given and lost, with a loved one, and with a love that will, with all the seasonality and vulnerability implied by the yoking 'flower-soft', also pass away:

> [...] And the king
> Built for their tomb a chapel bright like spring
> With flower-soft wealth of branching tracery made [...] (IV, p. 150)

Swinburne's diction is a trade-off. The gains of 'working' words in this way allows for an exploration of 'vague associations' which inevitably build up around certain words, especially when they arrive in predictable arrangements. Eliot's example of a word that Swinburne works, 'weary', verges on opportunistic. If the online edition 'The Swinburne Project' can be relied upon in the absence of a concordance, this adjective is not an especially prominent candidate for Swinburnean diction, occurring only 47 times in Swinburne's works, when compared to red (137), soft (153) and sweet (242). Yet his word choice also risks redundancy. Swinburne's increasingly Swinburnean diction is resourceful, but resourceful in the same way that one man's attempt to make poetry from memory after being marooned on a desert island might be.

Swinburne's poetry is repetitive. From the individual letter, to the repetition of stanza forms, to over forty verses in *Songs before Sunrise*, the capacity for remembering that his poetry presumes in his reader is provocative. At times this is far from subtle. Clive James confesses that Swinburne 'would gradually turn out to be the most accomplished poet that I couldn't stand':

> Spenser, in *The Faerie Queene*, would occasionally throw in an alliterative line for effect ('Sober he seemde, and very sagely sad') but Swinburne wanted the whole poem to be that way [...] Perhaps he noticed but thought we wouldn't,

intoxicated as we were bound to be by his sonic hurtle. But for a poet to be all sound is nearly as bad as for a painter to be all paint [...] a Swinburne poem affects me like a painting by John Bratby: there is so much impasto that the only tension lies in your wondering whether it will slide off the picture and fall on the floor.[35]

James here interprets Swinburne's repetition of consonantal sounds as a confidence trick, or gaudy over-ornamentation that makes up for his lack of 'underlying strength'. Eliot takes similar issue when he reads 'grief' as being paired with 'glass' through alliteration in a chorus of *Atalanta*, protesting that it could be otherwise (*Selected Essays*, p. 326). What such accounts miss is the way in which phonic repetition is inextricable from rhythm and development. The rather static analogy with *impasto*, though suggestive, seems misplaced once we acknowledge that Swinburne's verse is always moving, 'hurtling', to use James's word, forwards. Consider, as a point of comparison, Dante Gabriel Rossetti's *scioglilingua*:

> [...] for where
> Is he not found, O Lilith, whom shed scent
> And soft-shed kisses and soft sleep shall snare?[36]

Now *this* is alliteration as *impasto*. The result is verse in three, rather than four, dimensions. And for Rossetti's portrait-poem, written onto the frame under his portrait of 'Lady Lilith', this is entirely appropriate: the poem is all about arrest. However, at its most alliterative and sibilant, Swinburne's verse is rarely like this, even where snakes feature:

> Thy skin changes country and colour,
> And shrivels or swells to a snake's.
> Let it brighten and bloat and grow duller,
> We know it, the flames and the flakes (I, p. 163)

These lines are from 'Dolores', the rhythm of which poem Pound compares to horses' hooves being lifted out of the mud ('Swinburne Versus Biographers', p. 328). Presumably Pound was responding to the thickness of phonic overlay surrounding the nodes of rhythmic intensity. Unlike Rossetti's lines, alliteration here marks the beat at least twice in every three-beat line. The rhythm is unmistakable, and this lulling, rolling languor is as much a part of our encounter as it is absent from the encounter with Rossetti's sonnet. Alliteration also works more generally to multiply our sense of and sensitivity to the connections between words. Just as Swinburne comes to exploit the 'vague associations' that accumulate around a word or compound through repetition and alliteration, so sibilance and assonance also encourage us to seek connections between like sounds that repeat, an aesthetic which is also evident at the level of the phrase. For Swinburne is a master of the refrain, whether he is seeking a suitable response-call for a ballad, the meaning of which deepens at each recurrence: 'Red rose leaves will never make wine' (I, p. 29), or a phrase from and around which to build a poem, as he does in the roundel, a form he developed.

Rhyme for Swinburne is 'the native condition of lyric verse in English'.[37] On this point, Housman and Swinburne agree. It was for Housman 'the chief enrichment of modern verse' and he respected Swinburne's facility ('Swinburne', p. 391). English is supposedly poor in rhymes, Housman argues. As a result the poet is at constant risk of embarrassment; Milton and Wordsworth are cited as examples of this fact. Dante Gabriel Rossetti only gets around this problem through the creation of new highly specific diction or 'jargon'. By contrast, for Swinburne, sonnets were 'child's play'. Four rhymes were easy. Eight to ten rhymes in a stanza of a long poem are equally doable, and he 'wrote them so that he never seemed to be saying anything for the rhyme's sake'. He was particularly good at feminine rhymes, Housman notes, and did not even resort to present participle endings ('Swinburne', pp. 391–92). Swinburne got his training in rhyme early in 'Queen Yseult', a poem he began at Oxford after meeting the Pre-Raphaelite Brotherhood, but later abandoned. Rhyming three lines together in tercets, the form challenges the poet to find not one rhyme, but at least two for every word. Over time he built up a repertoire of possibilities, which meant that he could choose to use a predictable rhyme, a less frequent rhyme, or arrange things such that rhyme hardly registers.

Swinburne's flair for rhyme is best demonstrated in the heroic couplets of *Tristram*. Swinburne can choose to reanimate rhymes that are already ancient in English, such as 'breath' and 'death'. Or he can deploy his own rhyme repertoire, to forge moments of correspondence hundreds of lines and even books apart, for example in his use and reuse of the 'god', 'rod' rhyme in *Atalanta* and later in *Tristram*. As with his diction, Swinburne expects much from his reader here. The so-called 'antiphonal' passages at the opening of the Prelude and the last canto are built from the same couplet rhymes, with one subtle variation. Can the poet honestly expect his reader, on encountering these lines, to recall the opening of the poem, some three-thousand-and-ninety-eight lines earlier?[38] Fate triumphs over love. This thought takes rhyme as its vehicle, and we encounter it via the-same-but-different.

However, Swinburne can in the same poem vary his rhymes so that, without quite achieving what Donald Davie calls the 'urbanity' of Shelley's *Julian and Maddalo*, they nevertheless flash by, propelling his verse onwards without calling attention to themselves.[39] Take this passage describing Tristram's dawn swim:

> [...] but with a cry of love that rang
> As from a trumpet golden-mouthed he sprang,
> As toward a mother's where his head might rest
> That none may gird nor measure: and his heart
> Sent forth a shout that bade his lips not part,
> But triumphed in him silent: no man's voice,
> No song, no sound of clarions that rejoice,
> Can set that glory forth which fills with fire
> The body and soul that have their whole desire
> Silent, and freer than birds or dreams are free
> Take all their will of all the encountering sea.
> And toward the foam he bent and forward smote,
> Laughing, and launched his body like a boat
> Full to the sea-breach, and against the tide
> Struck strongly forth with amorous arms made wide

> To take the bright breast of the wave to his
> And on his lips the sharp sweet minute's kiss
> Given of the wave's lip for a breath's space curled
> And pure as at the daydawn of the world.
> And round him all the bright rough shuddering sea
> Kindled, as though the world were even as he,
> Heart-stung with exultation of desire:
> And all the life that moved him seemed to aspire,
> As all the sea's life toward the sun: and still
> Delight within him waxed with quickening will
> More smooth and strong and perfect as a flame
> That springs and spreads, till each glad limb became
> A note of rapture in the tune of life,
> Live music mild and keen as sleep and strife:
> Till the sweet change that bids the sense grow sure
> Of deeper depth and purity more pure
> Wrapped him and lapped him round with clearer cold,
> And all the rippling green grew royal gold
> Between him and the far sun's rising rim. (IV, p. 127–28)

The lines spill over and over and on, verging on completion — almost — yet running on, only terminating in the last line quoted. That we hardly register the recurrence of what should be overfamiliar rhyme-pairs ('desire' and 'fire'; 'heart' and 'part') demonstrates Swinburne's tremendous facility. He learns this trick of overrunning and pausing, as he does in the penultimate line quoted, from Shelley. However, Shelley's verse does not combine this propulsive energy with the feats of repetition, or of remembering, that Swinburne's verse requires.

This play of remembering and forgetting often registers at the generic and thematic level as longing. It is never the story, but the intensity that Swinburne wants. Housman writes that Swinburne had a lack of talent for narrative, also evident in his lyric poetry: 'there is no reason why [poems] should begin where they do or end where they do; there is no reason why the middle should be in the middle, there is hardly any reason why, having once begun, they should ever end at all [...]' ('Swinburne', pp. 399–400). You could easily rearrange Swinburne's stanzas without disrupting coherency or impairing effect. In this, Housman is justified in the case of some poems (particularly the longer political odes) but the complaint takes us further away from, rather than moving closer towards, Swinburne's peculiar position: at a period in which the ascent of the novel meant that poetry had to come to terms with prose, Swinburne's poetry continually resists narrative logic in favour of lyric. Even *Lesbia Brandon*, his unfinished novel, is mainly an excuse for a setting of poems. The desire for ardent experiences to continue at the same altitude is registered in the content and themes that prove so recognisably 'Swinburnean': heartbreak, painful-pleasurable sexual encounters, necrophilia, rape.

Pound writes that 'Swinburne's actual writing is very often rather distressing [...]' ('Swinburne Versus Biographers', p. 326). That platitude is most immediately true as regards content. With the exception of the virgin huntress Atalanta, women exist to ravish or be ravished: Faustine, Lilith, Dolores, Oreithya; even 'The Sun-dew' in the meticulously wrought pastoral of the same name is carnivorous. Swinburne was fascinated by violent acts. Rikky Rooksby notes of his teenage experiments with revenge tragedy that 'The frequency with which he deployed the stage direction *"stabs the king"* became a family joke'.[40] The same goes for recognisably Swinburnean themes. It is hard to think of another poet whose greatest feats consist mainly of leave-takings, parting songs and elegies. As he admitted to the painter Joseph Knight:

> In an age where all other lyrists, from Tennyson to Rossetti, go in [...] for constancy and eternity of attachment and reunion in future lives, etc., etc., I limit love, honestly and candidly, to 24 hours, and quite enough too in all conscience.'[41]

His sado-masochistic poetics have also been interpreted, most recently by Sara Lyons, as 'part of an endeavour to find a rhetoric adequate to affirming both the joys and pains of a wholly immanent conception of life, purged of all desire for transcendence'.[42] Thematically and, as I shall suggest, stylistically too, his poetry centres on a break in the continuity of passionate experience.

A recent critic of *Tristram* recognises that: 'No English poet had done anything quite like this before. Nor was Swinburne's manner to prove readily continuable'.[43] Following the way in which the rhyme-pair 'breath', 'death', and 'sea' with its various rhyme-associates work across the poem, he concludes:

> None of them, however, is primarily amplifying or decorating any semantic or thematic point. They form, instead, a crucial part of Swinburne's verse manner of perfectly-judged, near-overload [...] Readers' brains are to be overtaxed as much as possible while still observing certain fixed and restrained constraints of rhyme and metre. The verse's virtuosity partly consists in its calling forth an answering readerly virtuosity, as though Swinburne were challenging her to [...] keep afloat in all this. ('The Insuperable Sea', pp. 531–32)

The result is 'a mode which, instead of adumbrating and then illustrating or instrumentating a fantasy, captures a phenomenology of erotic experience, permits a fidelity to the *shape* of erotic experience' ('The Insuperable Sea', p. 534). This conclusion, which is really more of a beginning, takes us deeper into this poem, since it unearths a peculiar fact about Swinburne's style: much of what happens in his poetry takes place, not explicitly — in the form of self-reflexivity, self-reference and verbal mimesis — but implicitly, in the way his verse unfolds.

Of course this does not preclude Swinburne from being, on occasion, explicit about the way his verse works. The work of remembering and forgetting is connected to the curious algolagnia with which Swinburne talks about poetry, and particularly rhyme. Amnesia must be countered with repeated, pleasurable-painful affirmation:[44]

> Things in verse hurt one, don't they? hit and sting like a cut. They wouldn't hurt us if we had no blood and no nerves. Verse hurts horribly: people have died of verse-making, and thought their mistresses killed them — or their reviewers. You have the nerve of poetry — the soft place it hits on, and stings [...] It's odd that words should change so just by being put into rhyme. They get teeth and bite; they take fire and burn. I wonder who first thought of tying

words up and twisting them back to make verses, and hurt and delight all the verses in the world for ever. For one can't do without it now: we like it far too much, I suspect, you and I. It was an odd device: one can't see why this ringing and rhyming of words should make all the difference in them: one can't tell where the pain or the pleasure ends or begins.[45]

This is rather an unorthodox view of the distinction between poetry and prose. It is not my intention to endorse an argument here about the affectivity of language according to Swinburne (or rather, the *mater dolorosa* in *Lesbia Brandon* who speaks), much less to claim any simple analogy between style and embodied experience. Yet it goes some way towards explaining the kind of poetry we are reading. Having 'the nerve of poetry' requires one to be sensitive to verse: one needs to be susceptible to get it. The idea that rhyme ties verses up, 'twisting them back', is related to this. Rhyme keeps verse in line — a disciplinary procedure, to be sure — but also, more importantly, Swinburne affirms that all verses *are* in line. To tie words up in rhyme is to somehow place them in continuity with all other words that have been 'put into rhyme'. Though Eliot would prefer the analogy of a catalyst for an explosion, rather than bondage, Swinburne's understanding of rhyme as a ripple, or shudder that goes backwards and forwards, hurting and delighting 'all the verse in the world forever', is not so different from the argument of 'Tradition and the Individual Talent' (*Selected Essays*, p. 18). Neither argument makes sense without the assumption of an unbroken continuity in the act of writing and encountering verse.

Perhaps more than any other English-language poet since, it is 'the shape of words' to which Swinburne's poetry asks us to attend. I take this phrase from the title of J. H. Prynne's lecture, 'Stars, Tigers and the Shape of Words', in which the poet sets out to test the limits of the Saussurean model of language. Between his hypothesis and his reading of Blake, Prynne happens on the example of Thomas Malkin, the gifted child of one B. H. Malkin, now usually remembered for his inclusion of several of Blake's poems in the memoir he wrote after his son Thomas's early death. Prynne draws our attention to one particular instance in Malkin's account, in which the infant is able to associate letters and sounds, pointing at coloured blocks, far in advance of being able to talk.[46] Thomas Malkin's act of association is one suggestive account of how aspects of language usually judged to be 'secondary' are in fact constitutive. Letter-form, along with sound-patterning such as rhyme, homonyms, rhythm and prosody — the entire 'shape' of words — are crucial. As Prynne argues, 'The contaminations which seep into the categories of analysis come from historical usage and development, and are especially marked in strongly formed and complex traditions of literary expression'.[47]

Swinburne was also struck by the case of Thomas Malkin, whom he doubtless came across in his early research on Blake. As he wrote in a letter to his friend the painter Seymour Kirkup, the example of Thomas Malkin had equal resonance for him:

Did you ever meet with that rare book [...] *A Father's Memoirs of his Child*, by D. A. Malkin [*sic*]? Apart from the interest of its connection with Blake, it is in my opinion the most astonishing study of physiology I ever met with [...] the instance is unique, for it is not an example of forcing, but of native and instinctive genius.[48]

This opposition of 'native and instinctive genius' against educational 'forcing' is consistent with Swinburne's later refusal to offer an account of prosodic rule and precept in his *Study of Shakespeare*. Readers of *Modern Painters IV* will note the similarity of Swinburne's use of the word 'genius' with Ruskin's definition:

> Imagine all that any of these men had seen or heard in the whole course of their lives, laid up accurately in their memories as in vast storehouses, extending, with the poets, even to the slightest intonations of syllables heard in the beginning of their lives [...] and over all this unindexed and immeasurable mass of treasure, the imagination brooding and wandering, but dream-gifted, so as to summon at any moment exactly such groups of ideas as shall justly fit each other: this I conceive to be the real nature of the imaginative mind.

Ruskin's account of the play of memory in artistic creation tallies with his appreciation of Swinburne's style, though he regretted the 'matter'.[49] His definition allows us to reflect on that aspect of Swinburne's criticism which has been interpreted as a 'refusal to engage in poetic debates'.[50] As Ruskin continues:

> they have no idea what the state of other persons' minds is in comparison; they suppose every one remembers all that he has seen in the same way, and do not understand how it happens that they alone can produce good drawings or great thoughts.[51]

In a similar way, might Swinburne's assumed reticence on prosodic matters be in fact a refusal to state what seems to him so obvious? Nick Freeman reminds us that Swinburne may be 'talking from experience' when he writes of Furnivall's folly of confusing Fletcher's style with Shakespeare.[52] Swinburne knew from practice what he was talking about: like a seasoned card player, the rules of Écarté or Preferans can be written out, yet the rule-book cannot capture the fluency that comes with an individual player's experience, practice or history. When Swinburne asserts again and again throughout his *Study of Shakespeare* that poetry appeals to the 'ear', he is not arguing 'He that hath ears to hear, let him hear', but testifying to the existence of something like a habit of hearing: proverbial, learnt, practical wisdom, which depends upon the continuity of experience. It is this, rather than any pretension to secret rules or precepts, which allows him to assert of Blake's mystical poems that they contain 'laws, strange as it must sound'.[53] It is to these poetic laws, and their practice, that Swinburne's verse expects us to attend when reading his verse and it is in this expectation that we might finally grasp the challenge and the invitation of Swinburne's style. In making this claim I am under no illusions that, for some readers, this invitation to reconsider Swinburne's style on its own terms cannot be considered without further explanation, given that it comes with a large number of assumptions that may appear extremely dubious. These assumptions must be laid out at the outset if this study is to prove answerable to these objections.

Verse History

Why, then, should a reassessment of Swinburne's value begin with his style? Why should we care about style at all? Responding to this challenge need not begin by defending our profession as critics, or a scramble to assert poetry's right to exist. Instead, I simply wish to remind the reader that whether one chooses to approach the problem of Swinburne's poetry through the lens of phenomenological, hermeneutical, structuralist or post-structuralist theories, or more recent cognitive or formalist approaches, one must still read it. No matter how uninterested a critic is in how a poem is made, no matter how far their encounter fails to register in the writing which follows reading: in the unfolding encounter between reader and poem, in the test and counter-test of knowledge and knowing, style is as inevitable as reading.

If style is as inevitable as reading, then all reading is necessarily subjective. This truism is a hard one to hold to in the current climate, in which the requirement that scholars of poetry produce knowledge — objective, reproducible, transferable — dominates our work. Yet reading, practically considered, remains remarkably resistant to these demands. It is for this reason that Douglas Oliver's experiments with reading into 'the machinery' led to a second revised definition of poetic stress as that which 'arises from our conscious belief that we have, just recently, in a notional instant, unified some of our experience of a poem's developing sounds.'[54] Likewise, for Clive Scott, 'we may read the text in such a way as to try to preserve [...] a third-person experience, as someone else's experience.' But 'this is all but impossible.'[55] It is the same with painting. Following Marx, the art-historian Michael Baxandall describes how light reflected from the art object enters the eye, falls on the retina and is conveyed by a series of nerves to our brains.[56] After this, what the eye sees is no longer uniform. Instead: 'That which we tend toward will depend on many things [...] but not least on the interpreting skills one happens to possess [...] what we may call one's *cognitive style*'.[57] What Baxandall says of painting could also be said, by analogy, of auditory perception. For Pierre Bourdieu, the requirement to reduce such experiences to a moveable abstraction is exemplified in the diagram, which is 'never more pernicious than when exerted on practices defined by the fact that their temporal structure, direction and rhythm are constitutive of their meaning.'[58] It is because I count art-objects, and especially poems, among these practices that this book contains no scansion diagrams (excepting Swinburne's own), preferring instead to describe how a line is encountered.

However, when I must characterise a poem's rhythm, I follow Derek Attridge's method of beat-analysis.[59] Here I abandon my more usual practice of staying close to the terms in which, as Baudelaire puts it, 'les poètes [...] veulent raisonner leur art' [the poets want to rationalise their art]. While to talk of the number of beats, not feet, in a line is at odds with Swinburne's own practice (as my discussion of Swinburne's relationship to Greek metrics in Chapters 1 and 4 will make clear), this is necessary on two counts. While allowing, as Yopie Prins, Meredith Martin and others have ably shown, that the critical practices surrounding metre and scansion during this period did carry cultural meaning beyond the purely practical question of how a line moves, I am more concerned with scansion as a way of communicating my encounter.[60] Scansion is a way of distancing ourselves from our initial encounter with a poem, for the purposes of communicating that experience, or comparing it with the experience of other poems, or indeed with other readers' encounters with this or other poems. Or, as George Saintsbury put it somewhat less limply:

> There are, no doubt, several differences between poetical and other intoxication, but perhaps the chief difference is this. You can test the strength of the liquids odious to Sir Wilfred Lawson in two ways, — by dipping a Sykes's hydrometer in them, or by actually imbibing and waiting to see whether they 'get your forrarder'. In the case of poetry, only the latter test is available: you are yourself the hydrometer.[61]

Assuming that scansion is a way of making available my encounter with poetic rhythm and other interweaving aspects of style, it follows that one must have the right vocabulary for the job. Yet in the case of English poetry, foot scansion remains a second-order experience. The poet Douglas Oliver raised such doubts in his revised definition of poetic stress:

> If a metric involving poetic feet is imposed on the verse, then such feet may be considered as entities to the extent which, consciously or unconsciously, they are brought into mental play. In performing verse, our conscious perception of feet would be slight at best; it is hard to hold a complex metrical pattern in consciousness when we are concentrating on so much else. Begging the question of what happens unconsciously, the problem is how the abstract metrics are actually realised in the sound of our voice. More often, it is the stresses themselves which seem to become our *conscious* structuring principle — with the post-dating and back-dating of sounds onto instants that that implies, an apparent time-bending operation that partly destroys the delimitation into poetic feet even while perhaps affirming it. The feet reappear, however, if we apply our abstracting intellect to their rediscovery. Even so, the necessity of checking such an analysis against our mental performance of a line will revive uncertainties about the foot structure at any moment of irregularity — a necessarily circular argument.[62]

Since, except in the case of a poetry composed, as Pound puts it, in the sequence of a metronome, foot scansion depends on the working principle of variation to remain coherent, scansion often hinges less on the division of repeatable clusters of sound, but upon the distribution of stress across a line. One is frequently thrown backwards — as its origin in the past participle of the verb 'to strike' implies — on the ictus itself. It therefore makes more sense to talk about the way that syllables are sounded in performance, in relation to a perceived stress, rather than abstracting the line into repeatable tendencies. However, perhaps a more compelling reason to prefer beat-analysis to foot scansion is that, in the case of certain metres in English in which Swinburne proved himself an expert, foot scansion entirely fails to live up to the task of communicating how a line moves. We shall see this most compellingly in the case of Saintsbury's own sense of how the foot system proves inadequate to describe Swinburne's work in what, following Attridge, I call the *dol'nik* rhythm, in the chorus of *Atalanta in Calydon*.

To return to the problem of Swinburne's style: to claim that reading is subjective is not to claim that it is individualistic. It has become a commonplace of recent neo-formalist approaches to claim that all readings are as valid, thereby suspending the question as to the quality of a performance. This overlooks the fact that all acts of reading are also communal in nature. In fact, to argue thus may be a false democracy which cuts short the possibility of aesthetic response. As Immanuel Kant points out, it is a quirk of aesthetic judgements that they are at once deeply subjective, yet we want to convince other people of our own experience. Thus, as Simon Jarvis has argued: 'Every time a debate gets underway on "whether" aesthetic evaluations can be proven, or "whether" they are on the contrary merely subjective, the possibility of hearing the peculiar grammar of this kind of judgement has already been foreclosed.'[63] Rather than attempting to convince my reader of the correctness of my reading of *Atalanta*, or indulging pure subjectivity, I wish to investigate its communal aspects.

If aesthetic experiences are subjective, objective and communal, then we can no longer avoid the question of competency. This is a daunting prospect in the case of Swinburne's verse. Considered against this poet, fluent in five languages (two of them dead), whose verse was paradoxically both classic and innovatory, yet whose Alexandrian attempt to conquer all forms promotes a level of stylistic self-awareness which was to prove unsustainable for the next generation of poets, Michael Baxandall's reconstruction of how the man or woman in the street experienced paintings in fifteenth-century Italy comes to look almost easy. This question of competency is further complicated by the suspicion (which for this book must remain just a suspicion) that a reader listening to poetry before the advent of free verse, which emphasised very different parts of the repertoire, may listen differently to readers now. Yet to give up Swinburne as lost is to overlook three basic continuities between 1865 and the present moment. These include: the linguistic-prosodic capacities of the English language, our ability to encounter and reflect on how a poem works in us and, lastly, our ability to discern similarities and differences in technique between poems and poets across periods.

The contribution of T. W. Adorno's aesthetics to my reading of Swinburne's poetry, and the approach which I am calling, tentatively, verse history, is pervasive.[64] Quite apart from the fact that Adorno's enquiry into the possibility of art's redemptive power against the dominance of instrumental reason has not yet had the reception that it deserves, there are at least four reasons as to why his thinking proves especially relevant to the problem of Swinburne's style. That Adorno dismissed Swinburne, on the grounds that his work did not work to harness the 'incipient intentions' of his materials, need not deter us.[65] In fact, it is through Adorno's recognition of the way in which Swinburne's work hangs in the balance between the derivative and the innovatory, constantly threatening to slip back towards the former, that we are able to grasp what makes his work so distinctive and so valuable.

Since music cannot be thought to have content in quite the same way as a novel, or a painting with a narrative subject, music has always catalysed practitioners and philosophers of art to think about the relationship between form and content. As a philosopher whose greatest number of examples are drawn from music, Adorno has good cause to rethink the concept of form in ways that prove particularly suggestive for Swinburne's style. This is especially the case with regard to the more musical aspects of Swinburne's verse, which critics have historically interpreted as having a 'confusing' — to borrow Eliot's word — relation to content. 'Against the philistine division of art into form and content', Adorno writes,

> [...] it is necessary to insist on their unity; against the sentimental view of their indifference in the artwork it is necessary to insist that their indifference endures even in their mediation. Not only is the perfect identity of the two chimerical, it would not redound to the success of the works: By analogy to Kant's maxim [that 'Thoughts without content are empty, intuitions without concepts are blind'], they would become empty or blind, self-sufficient play or raw empiria. With regard to content [*Inhalt*], the concept of material best does justice to the mediated distinction. According to an almost universally accepted terminology in all the arts, material is what is formed. It is not the same as content [*Inhalt*], even if Hegel fatally confounded the two. This can be explicated with regard to music. Its content [*Inhalt*] is in any case what occurs — partial events, motifs, themes and their elaboration: changing situations. Content is not external to musical time but essential to it, as time is essential to content; content is everything that transpires in time. Material, by contrast, is what artists work with: It is the sum of all that is available to them, including words, colours, sounds, associations of every sort and every technique ever developed. To this extent, forms too can become material; it is everything that artists encounter about which they must make a decision.[66]

Here Adorno introduces a third term, 'material', by which we might seek to rethink the relation between form and content. Working by implication, then: the poet will arrange his or her materials in a way which mediates the world. In addition to content, these materials may include recognisable forms, such as the heroic couplet or the sonnet. In fact, 'materials' may also extend to the way a poet arranges episodes, chooses from a stock of rhyme words, settles for this word or that, alters a word to fit the rhythm all the way down to the distribution of stress across individual syllables. Distinct from this, the content is what occurs within the time of reading. This understanding of the role of material in mediating form and content necessarily asks that we consider the modes of attention the poem courts as it unfolds, rather than simply thinking about plot, character, and argument as static, or by treating aspects of style such as rhyme, rhythm, and assonance as ornaments or accessories to a theme. To use a musical example (which did not find favour with Adorno): just as one would not stop at calling the 1924 performance of Gershwin's 'Rhapsody in Blue' a 'cityscape', but would start by describing the way in which, in the central section, the violins fall silent, allowing the listener to encounter a lone pianist thrashing the logic out of a musical phrase in order to understand it, in such a way so as to unite our previous and later impressions, Adorno's proposal asks us to consider how the changing verse textures, repeating rhyme-pairs and subtle rhythmic modulations at line-level in Swinburne's poetry may constitute actual events.

Yet why do form and content remain 'indifferent?' Adorno seems to be at pains here to preserve the dialectical relation between form and content by means of an all-out ban (a frequent move in his *Aesthetics*) on interpretations which seek to reduce one to the other. The impetus behind this prohibition can be grasped once we consider his call for aesthetics to rigorously rethink the concept of form and, by extension, what is meant by mediation in art.

For Adorno, form is 'the law of the transfiguration of the existing, counter to which it represents freedom' (*Aesthetic Theory*, 189). Working by implication again then, the poem gives us the world again in art, but not through an arrested or simplified understanding of mimesis whereby what happens in the world reappears in the poem in such a way as to make form reducible to content, or content reducible to form. Instead, form and content exist in close relation to each other without being identical. Really, it is a question of getting mediation right. For Adorno even a tragedy which strives towards mimesis of the most Aristotelian archetype (that which evokes pathos and identification) is still a mediation, is still a transfiguration. To pass over the mediation of the world which artworks achieve by means of their form is to overpass the potentially radical and redemptive (or, in some negative cases, instrumental) potential of poetry. It is for this reason that Adorno guards against a 'philistine' identification of form with content, a move which, he argues, belies art's truly dialectical nature.

Introducing a third term through which we might rethink the concept of form is not just splitting hairs, for it is through the form of the artwork that art can be said to have an historical truth-content. To claim this is not to suggest that form in art is simply connected, whether reflectively or causally, to forms of social life. Instead, Adorno's understanding of poetry as a 'philosophical sundial telling the time of history' claims something quite different. As he asserts in a radio broadcast called 'Lyric Poetry and Society', in a moment in which his continuing interest in lyric poetry becomes clear, 'the distance from mere existence' assumed of and within the lyric poem 'becomes *the measure* of what is false and bad in the *latter*'.[67] Put more pithily, in his later expansion of this idea: 'Art is the social antithesis of society, not directly deducible from it' (*Aesthetic Theory*, 9). This understanding is related to Adorno's sense that art works are both like and unlike empirical reality, a double-character which they achieve by means of their form. Since form is the mediating factor by which poems attain their 'step away' from the world, 'form converges with critique' (*Aesthetic Theory*, 189).

Therefore, if we follow Adorno's dialectical approach, there is no need for readers to investigate context in advance of reading, so as to decode historical meanings from the form. Instead, what proves distinctive about Swinburne's style is the way it makes a critique of society, simply by means of its form, and because it is art. From this comes a new question: not 'what is the relation between poetic form and historical events?', but 'how is history registered within the poem by means of its form?' It is this question, more than any other, which motivates my investigation into the peculiarly symphonic rhythmic textures of *Atalanta*, the iterative daze experienced when reading *Poems and Ballads* and particularly 'The Triumph of

Time', the slowing and leaping of couplets and triplets throughout *Tristram of Lyonesse* and the invention of a unique kind of ode in *Erechtheus*.

As abstract as it may at first appear, Adorno's claim about the historical truth-content of art has several practical implications for us as readers. While more recent approaches to poetry in history might ask: 'what historical circumstances are relevant to the form of this poem?', for Adorno, as I have already noted, 'Truth exists exclusively as that which has become' (*Aesthetic Theory*, 3). This somewhat gnomic proposal connects two insights at once: there is an inevitable contingency to composition which means that the original force of circumstances in which an artwork was made is never truly recoverable. Adorno's sense that art today is, in his word, 'emancipated', suggests that reading cannot start from any other moment than the one in which we find ourselves (*Aesthetic Theory*, 2).

Scholars disagree by what Adorno means by emancipation. At times he seems to be responding to the entry of non-traditional materials into art. Atonal music, abstract expressionism and the absurdist drama — *Aesthetic Theory* was dedicated to Samuel Beckett — might all be offered as examples of emancipated art, in which non-traditional materials were allowed to enter into an artwork's form. For our purposes, the liberation of verse from the apparently now traditional aspects of the poetic repertoire, such as regular metre, rhyme or a specialist poetic diction, in or around 1908 might be considered an emancipation of sorts. For the purposes of this study, this begs the question of how easy it is to hear Swinburne after the advent of free verse — a suggestion which I explore in more depth in Chapter 2. For now, I wish only to acknowledge that Swinburne's poems were made in an earlier paradigm in which an established repertoire — what I have likened to a card game, and what Pierre Bourdieu would call a *habitus* — was still fluent and active, and when to make experiments in poetry did not involve the renunciation of traditional practices in poetic making.

Adorno warns the reader against the desire for a recovery of now unfashionable artworks: 'Hopes for renaissances of Pfitzner and Sibelius, Carossa or Hans Thoma, say more about those who cherish the hope than about the enduring value of the works of such souls' (*Aesthetic Theory*, 55). The same vigilance against nostalgia is present in his interest in the poetry of Eichendorff, which I explore in relation to Swinburne in Chapter 1, and in his sense that Bach is no closer to being Bach for being played upon period instruments. Yet Adorno remains open to the idea that an artwork that is previously rejected may find its audience at a later date: 'Great works wait'. If truth in poetry 'exists exclusively as that which it has become', then the verse-historian might build on this on this to ask, practically: what techniques were available, and what use did the poet make of them? What continuities are there — unconscious and conscious, indirect and direct — between poems of this moment, and poems composed at other periods? It is questions such as these that I have tried to keep constantly before me in this study.

One final commitment that has influenced my enquiry is Adorno's development of Kant's insight that 'artworks were purposeless because they had stepped out of the means-ends relation of empirical reality' (*Aesthetic Theory*, 184). Since, as Adorno argues, any artwork deserving of the name of 'art' gestures towards an escape from the dominance of instrumental reason, it follows that a critic of art cannot seek to dominate, but must simply encounter the artwork — though no encounter is ever truly simple, as Adorno's exploration of the time, space, and the internal logic of artworks suggests. Rather than attempting to dominate Swinburne's poetry, to subdue it to my own logic or purpose, I wish to engage in what Adorno elsewhere calls 'complete submission to the matter at hand'.[68] That is, I wish to begin with the poem, and only then ask what things I might need to know in order to appreciate it, rather than to begin by imposing a question which bears on the work.

From this reading of Adorno's *Aesthetic Theory* come three initial proposals for this experiment in verse history. Firstly, this book proposes that we understand reading as an activity located within an actual encounter with an artwork, though as I shall suggest, reading may occur many times, and one's encounter with a poem may develop as a result. Throughout, I treat content not as something which we need to defend in Swinburne's poetry against the Eliotean contention that it 'does not exist', but as what happens within an encounter with the poem. Secondly, this book seeks to understand Swinburne's style by means of his form, beginning with the question of how he arranged his materials: how did he make use of what was available to him? This is, as I have noted, an intimidating prospect in Swinburne's case. However, as Michel de Montaigne notes, difficulty increases desire. The enormity of the task is no reason to shirk the question of how we might understand Swinburne's verse practice in relation to his historical moment. Thirdly, this study wishes to stay with the understanding of mediation proposed by Adorno by arguing that Swinburne's poetry offers a critique of the mid to late nineteenth century by means of its form. As a result, this enquiry is not principally driven by the quest to discover what Swinburne explicitly said or did in relation to his poetry, although knowledge of this kind will prove important to our understanding of his choice and arrangement of materials. Distinguishing between the outward thinking about poetry and the thinking which poetry might engage becomes especially tricky once we encounter his later, supposedly more didactic poems, in which the distinction between what a poem is for and the kinds of attention it demands is especially hard to maintain. However, Adorno's ban on the philistine division of works of art into form and content should help to retain a focus on Swinburne's materials. It is what happens in my encounter with Swinburne's poetry as a result of his form, a form born of the arrangement of materials in response to a specific historical moment, that remains at the forefront of my study.

In drawing attention to my debt to Adorno's aesthetics, it is perhaps also worth exploring the difference between this understanding of form and another sense of what is meant by form which has proved influential, both in the study of Swinburne's poetry, and in Victorian poetry studies more generally. This has been called, variously, the new formalism, neo-formalism, and historical poetics. While it is not my intention to reduce the work of these critics to a single school, we might note a common concern with how the historical conditions in which poems are made bear on formal questions. This return to form has instigated much original research into the cultural inflections of prosody and a welcome focus on the resourcefulness and ambition of Victorian poetry. For example, in Meredith Martin's book *The Rise and Fall of Meter*, we have cause to think again about Hopkins's diacritical marks and the marking the body of Christ; in Yopie Prins's work, Swinburne's own connection between the experience of being disciplined at public school with the experience of being taken over by the rhythm of poetry is set before us anew. Likewise, in Kirstie Blair's ground-breaking study, *Form and Faith in Victorian Poetry and Religion*, her identification of a contemporary desire for steadying rhythms in the face of a seemingly unsteady faith has made the need to question the role of poetry in nineteenth-century religious life even more urgent.[69] Yet for all their scholarship and rigour, there is a pattern of thought in many of these studies which cannot answer to Adorno's ban on the indifference of form and content: the form of the poem is first linked to relevant historical contexts, which are then brought to bear on a relevant poem, altering our reading in such a way as to assume the analogous relation of form (how a poem is made) and content (what it is about). In such accounts, powerfully suggestive historical contingencies –such as the fact that Swinburne, in his letters, frequently likens metre to being whipped — cause critics to focus on particular aspects of poetic form, after which form is made legible in terms of those historical contexts. To put this another way: rather than encountering a poem in which the poem's form mediates the world, here historical context mediates form, and in doing so sidesteps the reader's encounter with the poem.

In order to explain where my understanding of mediation in relation to Swinburne's poetry differs, we might briefly consider Yopie Prins's seminal treatment of Swinburne's analogy between poetic metre and flagellation in *Victorian Sappho*. If I single Prins out, this is because her work still presents one of the earliest and best examples of this kind of criticism, and is candid about its assumptions.[70] Prins's intervention in the field of Victorian poetry combines classical reception, deconstructive theory, and a wide reading in the period to consider

> the cultural formations that cluster around [...] the construction of nineteenth-century female authorship on a Sapphic model [in the hope that this] will reveal what is uniquely Victorian about Victorian Sappho.'[71]

In doing so, she convincingly establishes the existence of what one might call a collective fantasy, reflected in 'a long tradition of reading Sappho as if she were a metrical body' (*Victorian Sappho*, 114), made cogent in her account of the reception of Sappho, Hephaiston and Longinus in relation to Victorian experiments with quantitative metre (*Victorian Sappho*, p. 120). Swinburne proves an important test case for Prins, since he 'learns the fine art of suffering meter from Sappho, in a sublime scenario that [she calls] "the Sapphic scene of instruction"':

> The beating of the body is internalised as the rhythm of poetry and transposed into the formal abstraction of meter: a written notation. The hyperbolic performance of this violent inscription can be understood as a perverse response to Victorian metrical theory, enabling Swinburne to constitute his own poetic corpus as a body of writing that materializes through and as meter (*Victorian Sappho*, p. 17).

The case for this peculiarly Victorian way of thinking having been made, Prins next considers how this might bear on Swinburne's poetry. Throughout, it is assumed that this knowledge of 'cultural formations' has now become part of our reading. So, for example, 'In the eclogue entitled "Algernon's flogging" we see how a body materializes through meter, like the "visible song" of Sappho' (p. 153). Here historical knowledge about what metre meant mediates the form, and it is only then that the form of the poem re-enters our reading.

This last observation may appear pedantic, a quibble about how Prins organises her argument. However, the decision to mediate reading in terms of this newly acquired historical information does risk confusion. I must admit that I do struggle to 'scan the five syllables of "Anactoria" in English to correspond to the number of syllables in the final line of the Sapphic stanza', as she suggests (*Victorian Sappho*, p. 128). And while I remain open, as Swinburne did, to the possibility that English might be able to create a kind of prosodic hospitality, to adapt a phrase of Paul Ricœur's, for Greek metres in English, it is hard to see what relevance this connection, suggestive thought it is, has to the performance of Swinburne's heroic couplets, which are an indisputably English form. And yet, in a sense to insist on asking about the performance of this or that line is to ask the wrong question. Prins's reading of Swinburne is entirely consistent, but it is not checked by an encounter with the poem. Within the metaphor which she explores, in which metre, like the lash, disciplines the body, it is perfectly cogent to claim that: 'the closer Swinburne comes to perfecting the Sapphic stanza, the less audible it becomes, for Sappho's song can only be made "visible" by the conversion of rhythm into a metrical pattern' (*Victorian Sappho*, p. 145). However, the limits placed on the investigation begin to show in her conclusion, in which she argues that we actually do not really need to read Swinburne's poetry at all, since

> if, as I have suggested, Swinburne disappears and reappears like Sappho in self-scattering rhythm, then we need not recollect the poet nor remember the poetic corpus in order to read Swinburne's poetry: his limbs can be loosened, again (*Victorian Sappho*, p. 153).

But how can we read a poet, without actually reading him? It is here that we can see two very different understandings of what it means to read at work.

For myself, any poem is already historical simply because of its form, by which I mean that it had an historical truth content. And since we, as readers of English and as readers of poetry written in English, can perform this poem, can undergo it, encounter it, allow it to unfold within us, we remain part of this tradition. The poem is not lost to us, nor in need of recovery by means of the cultural formations, even where such formations remain an undeniable part of its contemporary conception, composition and performance. I am not proposing that we abandon the Sapphic scene of instruction. But equally, we cannot abandon the poem. It is for these reasons, and for the reasons outlined above, that I prefer to think of this study as an alternative experiment in verse history.

No study of a poet who wrote and published as much as Swinburne did could pretend to be comprehensive. Accordingly, my reading takes, as test cases, four aspects of Swinburne's style that have proved least assimilable to subsequent criticism: the powerful sway of his rhythms, his repetition, his lyricization of narrative forms and — at the boundary of what is usually considered 'Swinburnean' — his more rhetorical political poetry. Accordingly, chapters focus on *Atalanta in Calydon* (1865), 'The Triumph of Time' (1866), *Tristram of Lyonesse* (1882) and Swinburne's occasional odes up to and including the choral odes of *Erechtheus* (1850–1876), although many other poems are also important to my investigation.

Even if the curious nature of aesthetic judgements were otherwise, this study cherishes no ambitions for a conversion of readers to Swinburne's poetry. There can be no going back after Swinburne. Yet it is impossible to answer the question of what poetry is without first attending to what it was, and impossible to pose the question of what poetry can become, without first questioning the truth of what it is: 'The definition of art is at every point indicated by what art once was, but it is legitimate only by what art became with regard to what it wants to, and perhaps can, become' (*Aesthetic Theory*, p. 3). The hope for this study will be achieved if, as a result, we might enter more deeply into what the late Victorian critic George Saintsbury calls the 'life-history of English verse'.[72]

Notes to the Introduction

1. Veronica Forrest-Thomson, 'Conversation on a Benin Head' in *Collected Poems and Translations* (London: Allardyce, 1990), p. 75.
2. T. S. Eliot, *Inventions of the March Hare* (London: Faber, 1996), p. 388.
3. This poem has been dated 1908, but remained uncollected until 1976. See *Collected Early Poems of Ezra Pound* (London: Faber, 1977), p. 261.
4. A. E. Housman, 'Swinburne', *Cornhill Magazine* (Autumn 1969), 397. All subsequent references will be to the page numbers of this publication and will be given in the text.
5. Ezra Pound, 'Swinburne versus Biographers', *Poetry*, 11.6 (1918), p. 325. All subsequent references are to the page numbers of this article and will be given in the text.
6. T. S. Eliot, *Selected Essays* (London Faber & Faber, 1932), pp. 323–24. All subsequent references are to the page numbers of this edition and will be given in the text, unless otherwise specified. The quotation is from J. H. Prynne's 'The Wound, Day and Night', *Poems* (Freemantle: Bloodaxe, 1995), p. 64.
7. Curiously, many of the complaints levelled against Milton which Ricks explores are also made against Swinburne by the same critics. See *Milton's Grand Style* (Oxford: Clarendon Press, 1963), pp. 1–21.
8. A note on the dust jacket of *The Whole Music of Passion* (Aldershot: Scolar Press, 1993) announces the essayists' 'shared concern [...] to challenge T. S. Eliot's subtle damnation of Swinburne whereby his writings were consigned to a particular realm of semantic nullity'. Yisrael Levin in *A. C. Swinburne and the Singing Word* (Farnham: Routledge, 2010) refers to Eliot as 'the big, bad wolf' of Swinburne criticism' (p. 1).
9. Rikky Rooksby argues that 'the recovery of a hearing for Swinburne is indispensable' (*The Whole Music of Passion*, p.xii). Terry Meyers's introduction to the 2009 special issue of *Victorian Poetry* hopes 'that these essays [...] will challenge and convert those who may still feel but somehow escape Swinburne's magic tone' (*Victorian Poetry*, 47.4 (2009), 614). Yisrael Levin claims that: 'After all, despite general scholarly acknowledgement of his abilities as a poet and critic, Swinburne remains, for the most part, a rather marginal figure' (*A. C. Swinburne and the Singing Word*, p. 1).
10. John D. Rosenberg was one of the first to argue that 'T. S. Eliot did not look closely enough' when he claimed that Swinburne, in the second chorus of *Atalanta in Calydon*, pairs

abstract nouns and their symbolic counterparts indiscriminately. The conclusion he reaches is different, but the terms remain the same. See *Victorian Studies*, 11.2 (December 1967), 133. This same movement is also evident in Forrest-Thomson's posthumously published essay. Her 'reconsideration' of Swinburne working out of Eliot's gripes creates difficulties as soon as she begins to make an Eliotan distinction between 'meaningful' and 'non-meaningful' levels of language. (See 'Swinburne as Poet: A Reconsideration', *Journal of Pre-Raphaelite Studies* (Autumn 2006), 64.) Lacey Rumsey suggests that an Eliotean aesthetic is in part responsible for 'la réticence contemporaine face à certains effets de variation rythmique chers à Swinburne' [the contemporary reluctance regarding certain effects of rhythmic variation favoured by Swinburne] ('Swinburne et la variation rhythmique', *Études Anglaises*, 62.2 (2009), 188).

11. Theodor W. Adorno, *Aesthetic Theory*, trans. and ed. by Robert Hullot-Kentor (London: Continuum, 1997), p. 4. All other references are to the page numbers of this edition and will be given in the text.
12. Pater summarises: 'I have been speaking of certain conditions of the literary art arising out of the medium or material in or upon which it works, the essential qualities of language and its aptitudes for contingent ornamentation, matters which define scholarship as science and good taste respectively' (p. 21). See *Appreciations* (London: Macmillan, 1910), pp. 17–21. For the demise of aesthetic criticism, Eliot's essay 'The Perfect Critic' might be taken as representative. See *The Sacred Wood* (London: Methuen & Co., 1920), pp. 1–14.
13. *The Poems of Algernon Charles Swinburne* (London: Chatto &Windus, 1905), I, pp. 54–56. All subsequent references are to the page numbers of this edition and will be given in the text.
14. Adorno, *Quasi Una Fantasia: Essays on Modern Music* (London: Verso, 2011), p. 3.
15. However, one could argue to the contrary for virtuosity as an attempt to harness objective intentions, as Pierre Bourdieu suggests at one point in his *Outline of a Theory of Practice*, trans. by Richard Nice (Cambridge: Cambridge University Press, 1977), p. 79. For further discussion of this question, see my conclusion.
16. *The Letters of Gerard Manley Hopkins to Robert Bridges*, ed. C. C. Abbot (London: Oxford University Press, 1935), p. 79.
17. Letter to Georgina Burne-Jones, quoted in *A. C. Swinburne: The Critical Heritage*, ed. C. K. Hyder (Padstow: Routledge, 1995), p. 123.
18. Housman, though he forgets Swinburne's political poems, argues that Swinburne's one real theme is literature, responding that 'well it's very sad to be spiritually dead, blind and half-brained: but what can we do except consider his claim in more depth?' See 'Swinburne', p. 386.
19. This is certainly implied in Dylan Thomas's throwaway remark when writing to the novelist John Sommerfield: 'Glad you liked my winter verses, very quickly produced from my tame Swinburne machine.' See 'John Sommerfield: Archive' (personal website of Andrew Whitehead, 2013) <http://www.andrewwhitehead.net/john-sommerfield-archive.html> [accessed 12 November 2014]. My thanks to Leo Mellor for discussing Thomas's interest in Swinburne with me.
20. See Derek Attridge, 'The Case for the English Dolnik, or, How Not to Introduce Prosody', *Poetics Today*, 33.1 (Spring 2012): 1–26.
21. Pound was apparently unfamiliar with the note that precedes Swinburne's translation of the 'Grand Chorus of Birds' in which Swinburne discovers that Aristophanes' 'marvelous metrical invention of the anapestic heptameter was almost exactly reproducible in a language to which all variations and combinations of anapestic, iambic or trochaic metre are as natural and pliable as all dactylic and spondaic forms of verse are unnatural and abhorrent' (V, p. 42).
22. D. S. W. Harding, *Words into Rhythm* (Cambridge: Cambridge University Press, 1982), p. 42.
23. This perhaps explains why, on the subject of Swinburne's 'marvellously good' blank verse, Saintsbury is so reticent: this 'needs the least notice' (*History*, p. 349). However, limiting our description of Swinburnean rhythm to the metrical feats of *Poems and Ballads* risks ignoring the resourcefulness of Swinburne's work in less rhythmically insistent verse forms. The influence of Swinburne's blank verse, particularly as it develops in his verse-dramas, has received little attention.
24. D. S. Carne-Ross, 'Jocasta's Divine Head' in *Classics and Translation: Essays* (Lewisburg: Bucknell University Press, 2010), p. 41.

25. As I argue below, and particularly in Chapter 4, verbal mimesis is something Swinburne's verse proves resistant to. Saintsbury praises this poem as having 'attained the furthest point yet secured' in the *karole* form, a word that indicates Saintsbury's intimation of the *dol'nik* a hundred years before Derek Attridge set out the case for this rhythm as a separate genre in its own right. See Saintsbury's *History*, III, p. 347; Derek Attridge, 'The Case for the English Dol'nik; Or, How Not to Introduce Prosody' and Chapter 1 below.
26. Donald Davie, *Purity of Diction in English Verse and Articulate Energy* (Manchester, 2006: first published 1952), p. 254.
27. A. C. Swinburne, *A Study of Shakespeare* (London: Chatto & Windus. 1880), p. 92.
28. William Wordsworth, 'The Tables Turned; An Evening Scene on the Same Subject', *The Poems*, ed. John O. Hayden, (Harmondsworth: Penguin, 1982) I, p. 356.
29. We might take, as one test case, 'The Poet to the Woodlouse', a third paeonic and particularly virtuosic in its handling of polysyllabic words within the demands of the rhythm.
30. Timothy Steele, *Missing Measures: Modern Poetry and the Revolt against Meter* (Fayetteville and London: University of Arkansas Press, 1990), p. 65.
31. See Yuri Tynianov and Ann Shukman, 'The Ode as an Oratorical Genre', *New Literary History*, 34.3 (Summer 2003), 565–96 (p. 580).
32. 'On Lyric Poetry and Society', *Notes to Literature*, I, p. 43.
33. Edward Thomas, *Algernon Charles Swinburne: A Critical Study* (London: Martin Secker, 1912), p. 93.
34. 'Cease smiling, Dear! A little while be sad', *The Poetry of Ernest Dowson*, ed. Desmond Flower (Cranbury: Associated University Presses, 1970), p. 84; 'Javanese Dancers', *The Collected Works of Arthur Symons* (London: M. Secker, 1924), I, p. 125.
35. Clive James, 'Loves in a Life', *TLS*, 5798, 14 May 2014, p. 14.
36. D. G. Rossetti, *Ballads and Sonnets* (London: Ellis and White,1881), p. 240.
37. A. C. Swinburne, *Essays and Studies* (London, Chatto & Windus, 1875), p. 162.
38. The reader may not hear the difference on first reading. Yet there is enough in this passage that seems familiar enough to make one flick backwards: Swinburne's antiphonal passages answer each other in other ways, making use of the same verse textures and syntax, unfolding, re-inscribed and altered on the tip of the tongue.
39. Donald Davie, *Purity of Diction in English Verse and Articulate Energy* (London: Penguin, 1992), p. 121.
40. Rikky Rooksby, *A. C. Swinburne: A Poet's Life* (Aldershot: Scolar, 1997), p. 31.
41. Letter to Joseph Knight, 8 July 1883, quoted in Sara Lyons, *Algernon Swinburne and Walter Pater: Victorian Aestheticism, Doubt and Secularisation* (London: Legenda, 2015), p. 90.
42. Ibid., p. 91.
43. Simon Jarvis, 'Swinburne: The Insuperable Sea', in *The Oxford Handbook of Victorian Poetry*, ed. Matthew Bevis (Oxford: Oxford University Press, 2013), pp. 521–35, p. 530.
44. See 'The Insuperable Sea', pp. 532–34 for a previous discussion of this aspect of Swinburne's poetry.
45. A. C. Swinburne, *Lesbia Brandon*, ed. Randolph Hughes (London: Falcon Press, 1952), p. 148.
46. J. H. Prynne, 'Stars, Tigers and the Shape of Words' (London: Birkbeck College, 1993), p. 22.
47. Ibid., p. 31.
48. A. C. Swinburne, *The Swinburne Letters*, ed. Cecil Y. Lang (New Haven: Yale University Press, 1959–62), I, p. 129.
49. Ruskin wrote to Swinburne in 1866: 'It is of no use to tell you what you, like all good artists, know perfectly well [...] from my own manner of later work you know also very well that I can understand yours, and think of it as I ought, which is all that needs to be said between us [...] as to the art of the book. For the matter of it — I consent to much — I regret much — I blame, or reject nothing.' (*The Swinburne Letters*, I, p. 182).
50. See 'Victorian Prosody: Measuring the Field', *Victorian Poetry*, 49.2 (Summer 2011), p. 150.
51. *The Works of John Ruskin*, ed. by E. T. Cook and Alexander Wedderburn (London: George Allen, 1903–1912), VI, p. 42.
52. Nick Freeman, 'Swinburne's *Shakespeare*: Verbal Whirlwind?' in *A. C. Swinburne and the Singing Word*, p. 92.

53. A. C. Swinburne, *William Blake: A Critical Essay* (London: John Camden Hotten, 1868), p. 87.
54. Douglas Oliver, *Poetry and Narrative in Performance* (Basingstoke: Macmillan, 1989), p. 112.
55. Clive Scott, *The Poetics of French Verse* (Oxford: Clarendon Press, 1998), p. 98.
56. Baxandall's subtle allusion to the section on the 'Fetish of the Commodity and Its Secret' in Marx's *Capital* is suggestive of how the subjective may come to seem objective by the mediating power of the social; see *Capital*, trans. Ben Fowkes (London, 1976: Penguin), I, p. 165). Compare de Bolla's argument that it is the communal aspect of aesthetic experience that produces the 'particular amalgam' of a claim at once subjective and objective in nature in *Art Matters,* p. 10.
57. *Painting and Experience in Fifteenth-Century Italy* (Oxford: Oxford University Press, 1988), p. 29.
58. Pierre Bourdieu, *Outline of a Theory of Practice,* trans. by Richard Nice (Cambridge: Cambridge University Press, 1977), p. 9.
59. Derek Attridge, *The Rhythms of English Poetry* (London: Longman, 1982).
60. For two recent attempts to think about the specifically cultural inflections of prosodic theory see Yopie Prins, 'Voice Inverse', *Victorian Poetry*, 42, 1 (2004): 43–59, and Meredith Martin, *The Rise and Fall of Meter: Poetry and English National Culture, 1860–1930* (Princeton: Princeton University Press, 2012).
61. George Saintsbury, *Corrected Impressions: Essays on Victorian Writers* (New York: Dood, Mead and Company, 1895), p. 73.
62. Oliver, *Poetry and Narrative in Performance,* pp. 114–15.
63. Simon Jarvis, 'An Undeleter for Criticism', *Diacritics*, 32.1 (2002), p. 5.
64. The term as I use it is a translation of the term used by the Russian critic Marina Tarlinskaja to indicate the critic's concern with the unspoken rules that govern verse at a given historical moment. However, my approach differs in the extent to which we rely on statistical analysis for our conclusions. For comparison, see her *English Verse* (The Hague: Mouton, 1976).
65. Adorno, *Quasi Una Fantasia,* p. 3.
66. Adorno, *Aesthetic Theory,* p. 194. Insertion mine, from Immanuel Kant, *Critique of Pure Reason,* trans. and ed. Paul Guyer and Allen W. Wood (Cambridge: Cambridge University Press, 2006), pp. 193–94.
67. Adorno, 'Lyric Poetry and Society', *Notes to Literature*, ed. Ralph Tiedemann and trans. Shierry Weber Nicholsen, 1 (New York: Columbia University Press, 1991), p. 40.
68. Ibid., p. 39.
69. See Yopie Prins, *Victorian Sappho* (Princeton: Princeton University Press, 1999); Meredith Martin, *The Rise and Fall of Meter: Poetry and English National Culture, 1860–1930* (Princeton: Princeton University Press, 2012); Kirstie Blair, *Form and Faith in Victorian Poetry and Religion* (Oxford: Oxford University Press, 2013).
70. Prins is indebted to both Jacques Derrida's 'Signature, Event, Context' (*Victorian Sappho*, 15), and Amittai F. Aviram's provocation that rhythm might be considered as: 'an interpretation or representation — an allegory — of the bodily rhythmic energy of poetic form.' For Derrida, the fallacy of presence must always turn performance into mere play, or repetition. Likewise, for Aviram, poetic rhythm is understood as a 'representation' or 'allegory' and not initially considered as part of the phenomena of bodily experience, as one might find in more phenomenological approaches to poetry.
71. Yopie Prins, *Victorian Sappho*, p. 15. All future references are to the page numbers of this edition and will be given in the text.
72. George Saintsbury, *A History of English Prosody from the Twelfth Century to the Present Day* (London: Macmillan, 1910) III, p. 513.

CHAPTER 1

'A *Renouveau* of English Prosody': Metrical Set and Rhythmic Tension in *Atalanta in Calydon*

> Germans are tourists and Frenchmen are tourists but Englishmen are Greeks.
> Virginia Woolf, 'A Dialogue upon Mount Pentelicus'

If Jerome McGann is right that 'the great prosodic scholar George Saintsbury was one of the last to have a clear grasp of what Swinburne's work involved and how it was announced' then we might do well to reconsider his estimate of 'that epoch-making book' *Atalanta in Calydon*.¹ As Saintsbury reminds us, 'Those who read *Atalanta* when it came out had no lack of "aged" horses of the very first class to try it by':

> They had just been reading Tennyson's *Enoch Arden*, with 'The Voyage' and 'In the Valley of Cauteretz' [...] and Browning's *Dramatis Personae* [...] But in the *Atalanta* choruses there was nothing in the least imitative of either of these poets, and there was a quality which Tennyson had seldom displayed, and which Browning [...] did not often employ in his best lyrics — the quality of speed [...] 'When the hounds of Spring are on Winter's traces' made an actual *renouveau* of English prosody, and sent a fresh pack of verse-hounds, bounding and doubling [...] through wood and over field of the poetic country. (Saintsbury, *History*, III, 335)

Reading the chorus of *Atalanta*, Saintsbury is able to take in the whole of the English prosodic tradition. Swinburne, 'indisputably at the head of the choir of the poets of our days', is cast as the pupil turned maestro (334). His second book, a 'Greek' play in English in the tradition of Shelley's *Prometheus Unbound*, constitutes a pivotal moment in the history of English poetry. The word *renouveau* which Saintsbury uses to describe the movement of the first choral song puns on this 'terme encore usité [...] mais qui vieillit' for 'La saison nouvelle, le printemps'.² However, the word can also mean 'renaissance' in the sense of a spiritual or artistic renewal.

Critics have since found other ways of accounting for the significance of *Atalanta*. Few take the perspective of verse history. While no reader can pass over its prosodic power, since Saintsbury there has been almost no sustained enquiry into how Swinburne's poem achieves its peculiar forcefulness. The challenge of doing so was set out by Harold Nicolson in 1926; it is 'impossible' to explain the final 'effect' of Swinburne's play by analysis or quotation, since the poem is 'cumulative' and 'organic':

> each part is dependent on the whole, and in the final *kommos* the harmonies and rhythms which have crossed and re-crossed each other in a subtle interchange throughout the poem are gathered together in the vast symphonic summary, and the whole purport and beauty of the drama is disclosed.[3]

Given the complexity of Swinburne's poem, it is perhaps understandable that critics have preferred to remake the case for *Atalanta* on the basis of its imitation — successful or not — of Greek models, or its particular take on the human situation. Nicolson himself provides a technical analysis of the play to show that, structurally at least, *Atalanta* conforms to the model of Greek tragedy, an argument that is also made by Marion Weir, C. M Bowra and Alan P. Barr.[4] George Lafourcade's attempt to analyse the chorus of *Atalanta* represents the only attempt at large-scale metrical analysis, a direction that is abandoned after 1928.[5] Since then responses to Swinburne's poem have been mainly concerned with what this play demonstrates about Swinburne's universe.

No other poem by Swinburne with the exception, perhaps, of 'The Triumph of Time' has provoked such soul-searching. For Herbert Tucker, *Atalanta* reveals Swinburne's 'creed': 'Ever since the first great chorus of *Atalanta in Calydon*, for Swinburne one thing has not just followed another but has hunted it down and preyed on it'.[6] Thomas Wymer finds in *Atalanta* 'an unorthodox affirmation of life'.[7] For Robert Mathews it 'depicts the yearning of the human soul for unity through love'.[8] Katie Paterson prefers to read *Atalanta* 'through the bleakness of Schopenhauer'.[9] Further readings reinterpret the story through the lens of mythic, semiotic, feminist and psychoanalytical theory. In many accounts the declamation in the fourth choral ode against 'The supreme evil, God' becomes a point of departure or return.

This passage, which occurs at the end of the sixth strophe of the fourth choral ode, presents one of the most complex pieces of theological reasoning in the play and is worth quoting at length here, if only to give the reader a sense of how it has been read:

> For now we know not of them; but one saith
> The gods are gracious, praising God; and one,
> When hast thou seen? or hast thou felt his breath
> Touch, nor consume thine eyelids as the sun,
> Nor fill thee to the lips with fiery death?
> None hath beheld him, none
> Seen above other gods and shapes of things,
> Swift without feet and flying without wings,
> Intolerable, not clad with death or life,
> Insatiable, not known of night or day,
> The lord of love and loathing and of strife
> Who gives a star and takes a sun away;
> Who shapes the soul, and makes her a barren wife
> To the earthly body and grievous growth of clay;
> Who turns the large limbs to a little flame
> And binds the great sea with a little sand;

> Who makes desire, and slays desire with shame;
> Who shakes the heaven as ashes in his hand;
> Who, seeing the light and shadow for the same,
> Bids day waste night as fire devours a brand,
> Smites without sword, and scourges without rod;
> The supreme evil, God. (287)

Commenting on this passage, the contemporary reviewer for *The Spectator* speaks of 'Titanic bursts of mingled despair and wrath'.[10] Samuel Chew refers to it as an 'extremity of defiance'.[11] Douglas Bush called it 'that tremendous climax of blasphemy'.[12] Hargreaves, who takes this line as the title for his article, recognises a 'jarring element' in the argument.[13] Alan P. Barr summarises over a century and a half of readers' reactions when he describes this as 'the best-known and perhaps most startling verse in the poem'. Yet despite an almost unanimous agreement as to the force cumulating in this half-line, and the efforts of many critics to explain its power by making the case for the unique nature of Swinburne's anti-theism, none have so far connected this concern with the form of the poem.

Edward Thomas, appearing as a character in Jerome McGann's dialogue, *Swinburne: An Experiment in Criticism*, interrupts these plot-driven and thematic interpretations to re-put the question of Swinburne's technique: 'You talk about this work as if it were a play and not fundamentally a poem. But surely it exerts its greatest force at the lyrical level [...]?'[14] However, despite this attempt to re-orientate critical discussion, McGann offers no real alternative inquiry. 'Thomas' quotes the opening chorus to 'illustrate how Swinburne works his language', and observes its 'exquisite pace'. Yet *Atalanta* is ultimately valued for its triumphant vision of how, 'Turned upon the wheel of change, men yet achieve a nobility beyond the reach, perhaps beyond even the conception [...] of the changeless gods'.[15]

I have read and discussed *Atalanta in Calydon* many times. Despite the different occasions for those readings, three aspects of my encounter remain constant: first, my sense of an enormous cumulative rhythmic power, working between and across two very different — might I say — modes? Second, a punctum — to borrow Roland Barthes' term in his *Camera Lucida* for that detail in a photograph which arrests the eye — around that notorious half-line in the fourth chorus just quoted. Third, a sense that the play's denouement regarding the unjust, unfair and indifferent gods resides less in what the chorus say about the divinity, or what the story shows us, than in the sense of an ineluctable force, coursing through the words of the play, which gradually overcomes each of the speakers, so much so that Swinburne's rhythm comes to figure, on reflection, as a kind of fate.

Is this encounter with *Atalanta* singular to myself? The reading record suggests not. Though Swinburne's prosody must remain a mystery for Harold Nicolson, I recognise something in his description of

> rhythm in the meticulous balance and correlation of each part, in the cadenced transitions from the major to the minor key, in the continuous processional movement of the main choruses. And music, passionate, unrestrained, and haunting, in every line and lyric, as if the whole action were accompanied by the throb of hidden flutes — as if, in truth, the essential unity of the drama were a lyric unity, a latent and continuous hymn to Dionysus.[16]

Nicolson's sense of 'balance' and 'correlation' in construction, the analogy with shifting keys and the intimation of a 'hidden' yet insistent rhythmic element further explains his sense of the cumulative or symphonic effect of Swinburne's poem. Likewise, Samuel Chew's admission that 'Under the hypnotic spell of the swift bright choruses and surging blank verse some readers have confessed their inability to follow the story' sums up my own experience of listening to Swinburne's first few choruses.[17] Richard Mathews and Margot K. Louis both suggest that there are two styles in *Atalanta*, one that Louis calls 'soothing' and 'rational', and a second that 'expresses hostility, division, and pain more frankly, with a frightening lyrical view'.[18] This view is perhaps too schematic, yet I recognise it as an apt response to the range and associated effects of Swinburne's style — from lyrical to rhetorical. Orla Polten has recently written of her encounter with *Atalanta* as a kind of sublimation.[19] And yet, while it seems that few readers can pass over its prosodic power, there has,, since Saintsbury, been almost no sustained enquiry into how Swinburne's poem achieves such a powerful effect.

Further hints into how or why Swinburne's poem achieves this force might be gleaned from studies with one ear following something other than Swinburne's poem. For example, D. W. Harding draws attention to the ease with which Swinburne's verse works to establish a metrical set, within which any variation is all the more striking.[20] D. S. Carne-Ross's essay on the classics in translation argues against the critical consensus that Swinburne did not seek to imitate Greek metre, but sought a 'comparable beauty in English'.[21] Kenneth Haynes grasps the subversive nature of Swinburne's play when he describes how *Atalanta* works against the imported German ideal which reinterpreted ancient Greece as a period in which humankind and the gods lived in unity: 'The style of *Atalanta*', he writes, 'agglutinative, rapidly shifting — is Swinburne's greatest achievement because it embodies the central themes and emotional pattern of his work: division and oblivion'.[22] However, Swinburne's style, and in particular, his rhythmic style, is not the principle focus of these studies.

Considered against subsequent accounts, then, Saintsbury's estimate of *Atalanta* remains fresh in three respects: firstly, his description of *Atalanta* as an English poem, the full significance of which will only be grasped by taking the long view on English poetry, appears to sidestep the established debate as to how close Swinburne's poem comes to its classical models. Secondly, unlike subsequent criticism, it is exclusively interested in 'talk[ing] about the work as if it were fundamentally a poem and not a play' — as McGann's 'Thomas' puts it — to the detriment of any other concern. Finally, there is his sheer pleasure in the work, something that appears less important to subsequent critics. Nicolson found his experience of *Atalanta* ineffable. Saintsbury's approach is closer to that of Charles Baudelaire, who, overcome by hearing in Wagner 'mysterious intentions and a method that were unknown to me', next 'resolved to discover the why and the wherefore and to transform my pleasure into knowledge'.[23] It is a hypothesis of this chapter, and indeed of this study, that there is more to Saintsbury's estimate of *Atalanta* than has been allowed, and much in it that still remains to be demonstrated.

It is with Saintsbury's pleasure, therefore, that this enquiry into the 'why and the wherefore' of Swinburne's rhythm begins in earnest.

Critical Philology

Saintsbury's argument that *Atalanta* is an English poem and must be valued as such runs contrary, not only to the established debate surrounding Swinburne's 'Greekness', but also to Swinburne's description of his work in an early letter to Lady Trevelyan. Here he explains the thought and form of his poem, largely composed during the period of his sister Edith's illness and death:[24]

> In spite of the funereal circumstances which I suspect have a little deepened the natural colours of Greek fatalism here and there, so as to have already incurred a charge of 'rebellious antagonism' and such-like things, I never enjoyed anything more in my life than the composition of this poem, which though a work done by intervals, was very rapid and pleasant [...] I think it is pure Greek, and the first poem of the sort in modern times, combining lyric and dramatic work on the old principle. Shelley's *Prometheus* is magnificent and un-Hellenic, spoilt too in my mind by the infusion of philanthropic doctrinaire views and 'progress of the species'; and by what I gather from Lewes' life of Goethe the *Iphigenia in Tauris* must be also impregnated with modern morals and feelings. As for Professor Arnold's *Merope*, the clothes are well enough, but where has the body gone? So I thought and still think the field was clear for me.[25]

Swinburne's assertion that his tragedy is 'pure Greek' is difficult to construe. He admits that he may have 'deepened the natural colours of Greek fatalism', yet his conscious distancing of his 'views' from Shelley and Goethe claims to be closer to the Greek. As his use of the Carlylean analogy between thought and form as body and clothes suggests, this 'Greek' attitude cannot be divorced from style. Shelley's play is 'unhellenic' and the verse of *Merope*, though acceptable, has lost touch with antique 'morals and feelings'. Swinburne's desire to 'combine lyric and dramatic work on the old principle' might be taken as a claim to similarity with classical drama. Yet he also claims this poem to be 'the first poem of the sort in modern times'. By his own account, then, the alleged 'Greekness' of *Atalanta* is complex.

This complexity is registered in the critical reaction; for every attempt to establish Swinburne's play as 'profoundly and inescapably Greek'[26], to quote the classical scholar C. M. Bowra, there is another critic to provide thematic or structural evidence to the contrary. However, if we consider Swinburne's remarks in more detail, it becomes apparent that he is not claiming to have written a 'Greek' poem in such a way as to invite arguments for and against. Instead, I want to suggest, his insistence that his play is 'pure Greek' might be better understood as originating in the same humour in which Friedrich Nietzsche, in an early lecture, wryly remarked, 'I fear that we do not understand these Greeks in a sufficiently Greek way'.[27]

Consider Swinburne's exchange with his friend, Lord Houghton, which followed the latter's review of *Atalanta* in *The Edinburgh Review*. Full of praise for Swinburne's prosodic achievement, Houghton cannot finally accept the thought of the play as 'Greek'. Commenting on the first chorus, the same that Saintsbury singles out for special praise, he considers how

> the festivity of this imagery and the gaiety of the metre are evidently intended to contrast with the coming of Althæa, the impersonation of the sad and terrible destiny of Mankind. Now all early legend abounds with the pathos of the willing victim, but the poor human creature, as Mr. Swinburne with all the vigour of his genius portrays him, is nothing more than the sport of the caprice and malice of the gods, which, however, by some incomprehensible energy of his own, he is able to denounce and defy to the last.[28]

Even the *Prometheus* of Aeschylus, Houghton argues, will not provide an acceptable example for man's defiance of the gods, since Prometheus is a god and not a man. It is crucial to place Swinburne's response against Houghton's criticism, as it demonstrates the idiosyncrasies of Swinburne's view of 'Greekness'. His reply is written, as is typical of his correspondence with Houghton, in the character of a petulant schoolboy to his flagellant master:

> One birch-twig I hereby pull out of the bloody bundle. As to my quantities and metre and rule of rhythm and rhyme, I defy castigation. The head master has sent me up for good on that score. Mr. Tennyson tells me in a note that he 'envies me' my gift that way [...] The moral and religious question I give up at once. I let down my breeches, pull up my shirt, and kneel down [...] Only don't say with my old friend of the Spectator that it isn't Greek — because it is.[29]

Swinburne's riposte suggests that he is using the adjective 'Greek' in a particular, qualified way. His insistence on the quality of his verse argues that any attempt to understand this assumed heritage must begin with his style. At the same time, his admission that he has not been entirely faithful to the 'moral and religious' aspects of Greek tragic drama suggests that his claim for the Greekness of *Atalanta* cannot be taken as a factual claim.

Swinburne never read Nietzsche. William Rutland affirms that as to 'German [...] he knew not a word, and was consequently inclined rather to belittle all things Teutonic, and even all things Germanic'.[30] However, this has not discouraged critics from making this connection. Yisrael Levin, in his recent study of Swinburne's mythography, finds reason enough in Swinburne's comparative interest in the figure of Pan.[31] His argument demonstrates a wider acceptance that, although Nietzsche and Swinburne wrote in different genres and languages, they underwent a similar education and worked with common materials. Their interest in the music of Wagner, for example, and their passionate dislike of the plays of Euripides, for which Swinburne claimed he had Benjamin Jowett's approval, suggest similar tastes.[32] But criticism has yet to compare Swinburne's description of *Atalanta* as 'pure Greek' with Nietzsche's early arguments about the value of the classics. As he argues in *Untimely Meditations*:

> It is only to the extent that I am a pupil of earlier times, especially the Hellenic, that though a child of the present time I was able to acquire such untimely experiences. That much, however, I must concede to myself on account of my profession as a classicist: for I do not know what meaning classical philology could have for our time if it was not untimely — that is to say, acting counter

to our time and thereby acting on our time and, let us hope, for the benefit of time to come.[33]

This statement about the uses of history is continuous with Nietzsche's project for philology in his early notebooks and his first publication *The Birth of Tragedy*: 'modernity can in effect afford to be ahistorical so long as philology, with its false memory of the past and its actual place in the present, does the work of historical remembrance for it. A critical philology can undo some of this work'.[34] For Nietzsche, then, a 'pure[ly] Greek' idea was the result, not of philological excavation, but of a critical philology, which understood the thought and rhythm of classical texts in untimely ways. To put this another way, what drives Nietzsche is not just the question of how the Greeks thought about the divine and made their poems, but also how we might think about the divine and make poems now. It is in this untimely sense that I understand Swinburne's claim that the prosody of *Atalanta* is 'pure Greek'. Taken in this way, Saintsbury's claim for *Atalanta* as a *renouveau*, or rebirth, is exactly right. So much for the sense — as Swinburne refers to the content of lines set for composition–but what of the sound? Might this qualified, 'untimely' sense of 'Greekness' also extend to his verse-craft?

Critical Prosody

If Saintsbury is right, then Swinburne's 'quantities and metre and rule of rhythm and rhyme...' must be understood, not in relation to Greek tragedy, but to English prosody. There are three arguments that support this view: first, Swinburne's critical writings indicate that he had a working knowledge of the discontinuities between the prosodic systems of Greek and English which makes metrical comparison between the two specious at best. Secondly, the resistance of Swinburne's prosody to the imposition of classical scansion is suggested by the confusion which attends previous attempts to explain Swinburne's prosody using classical feet. Lastly, if we reconsider Swinburne's critique of Shelley and Arnold's Greek plays in English– in the same paragraph of his letter to Lady Trevelyan in which he talks about 'lyric and dramatic work on an old principle' — it becomes clear that he has in mind here not Greek tragedy, but a native English tension, frequent enough within the tradition of Greek plays in English to be generic. Since this last connection has escaped the sustained attention of previous critics, it might therefore be valid to ask what we might need to know, in a practical sense, in order to appreciate the place that Swinburne's play has in this genre. Before I consider the play in detail, then, I wish to take each of these arguments in turn.

A 'Renouveau' of English Prosody

Saintsbury would have understood that Swinburne's insistence that his poem was 'pure Greek' was not to be taken literally. 'No metre', he argues in his discussion of Richard Dixon's *Mano*, 'is the same in any two languages: most, if not all, metres are absolutely different in any two languages' (*History*, 362–63). It is for this reason that he has

> paid very little attention in this book to the tracing of foreign 'origins'. They say that the experiment of sowing tobacco ground in Manila with Havana seed has been tried over and over again, and that sooner or later the quality of the leaf is purely Philippine. In prosody it is not the case sooner or later: it happens almost at once. (*History*, 363)

However, it is Swinburne's preface to his translation of the Grand Chorus from Aristophanes' *The Birds* that confirms Saintsbury's conviction of the nigh-impossibility of rendering Greek metre in English. Swinburne's comments on this point were enthusiastically supported by Saintsbury, who dedicates a considerable amount of attention in his *History* to this 'very rare and specially precious vouchsafing of a directly prosodic note':

> This contains one particular sentence, which shows that he knew, and knew consciously, more about preceptist prosody than nine out of ten, if not ninety-nine out of a hundred, of the preceptists whom we have discussed and shall discuss in this book. 'His (Aristophanes') marvelous metrical invention of the anapaestic heptameter is almost exactly reproducible in a language to which all variations and combinations of anapaestic, iambic or trochaic metre are as natural and as pliable as all dactylic and spondaic forms of verse are unnatural and abhorrent.' The excommunication is indeed put with that hearty hyperbole which was Mr. Swinburne's natural mode. But it is only a hyperbole of the truth, the whole truth and nothing but the truth. Neglect it, and you will fumble in vain with English prosody; observe it, and you will be in no danger of Poor Peter Bell's sad fate when he made experiments on nature. (*History*, 352)

The truth about English prosody which Swinburne has hit upon is in fact a very basic one: since English prosody is characterised by both the principle of stress-timing and the principle of syllable-timing, the distribution of the ictus across syllables is flexible.[35] Stress can be distributed alternately across syllables, as in duple verse. However, it can also be distributed after every second unstressed syllable, as in triple verse, and even, very rarely, after every third syllable, as in a third paeonic (for an example of which see Swinburne's parody 'The Poet to the Woodlouse'.). Attridge, following Uldall, suggests that a run of four unstressed syllables seems to be the limit-point of English isochrony, since after this a mediate stress will be employed to ensure the rhythm continues to be perceptible.[36] This is why English prosody will accommodate what Swinburne, working with an inherited humanist terminology, calls iambic, trochaic and anapaestic metre, but not the spondaic or dactylic feet.

Swinburne's prefatory note was enough to convince Saintsbury that Swinburne knew more about the limits of English prosody than most 'preceptists'. Yet far from being a cause for dismay, this brings with it a renewed sense of the capacities and limits of the English language. In fact, Swinburne's sense of the difference between English and Greek prosodic systems originates, not from precepts, but from his own training, reading and practice, the fruits of which can be seen from the discussions of the Old Mortality Society — the Balliol College debating group of which Swinburne was an early member — was concerned with towards the late 1850s.

In an undergraduate review of Matthew Arnold's Greek tragedy *Merope*, published in the group's magazine 'Undergraduate Papers', Swinburne's friend John Nichol criticises Matthew Arnold for his failure to write sufficiently 'English' choruses:

> whatever be the place of lyrical effusions on the stage, there is one requisite which attaches to them above all other sorts of composition; they must be natural. To be so they must be written, said, or sung in the verse natural to the language in which they are expressed. Translation is not the mere transference of words from one tongue to another: a good translation is one which produces the same effect on the reader as that which is produced by the original. Measures as well as words are in so far matters of language, and vary in their effect according as they are married to Greek, Latin or English verse [...] Iambics and the more irregular Hellenic metres do not exist in our tongue. Mr. Arnold has done well to adopt blank verse both in 'Balder' and 'Merope' as his heroic line; he has failed in his adaptations of the chorus.[37]

Here we recognise Swinburne's argument that there are certain metres in Greek that cannot be accommodated in English and an argument for English prosody as its own resource for creating similar effects on the reader. Of course, Arnold's own view is not so different from that of Nichol. As he explained in his preface to *Merope*, 'what I have done is to try to follow rhythms which produced on my own feeling a similar impression to that produced on it by the rhythms of Greek choric poetry'. The difference, then, is not so much in theory as in the execution. For Arnold, since no equivalent English metres exist, 'he [...] is drawn to invent new measures, whether he will or no'.[38] For Nichol, Arnold has taken a wrong step, since native metres already exist. If, he argues, 'we compare the most musical of those choruses [from *Merope*] with Shelley's "Arethusa", the chants in "Hellas", or even with the songs in Byron's worst plays we are struck with the contrast between forced adaptations from a foreign literature and the natural melodies of our own tongue'.[39] Faced with the impossibility of translating from the Greek into English, the poet must find a native English equivalent. To have been tried against 'Byron's worst plays' and to have come up short is criticism indeed.

It seems impossible that Swinburne would not have had both Nichol's views on Arnold and his own verse practice in mind when writing 'Matthew Arnold's New Poems', an essay published nine years after *Merope* and two years after the success of *Atalanta*. His comments offer further insights for thinking about what might have been at stake in his own critical prosody. Here Swinburne argues that the chorus of *Merope* is 'noble in form and colour' but hardly fixes itself in the memory like the song of Callicles in *Empedocles at Etna*. Swinburne's praise stems from the importance of rhyme, 'the native condition of lyric verse in English', as he puts it. Reflecting on *Merope* that 'A rhymeless lyric is a maimed thing', he remakes Nichol's and Arnold's arguments about the impossibility of translating Greek metre into English:

> It is hard to realise and hopeless to reproduce the musical force of classic metres so recondite and exquisite as the choral parts of a Greek play. Even Milton could not; though with his godlike instinct and his godlike might of hand he made a kind of strange and enormous harmony by intermixture of assonance

and rhyme with irregular blank verse, as in that last Titanic chorus of *Samson* which utters over the fallen Philistines the trumpet-blast and thunder of its triumph. But Milton, it may be said, even if he knew them, did not obey the laws of the choral scheme, and so forfeited the legitimate condition of its music. Who has observed those laws and obtained that success which he did not? I scarcely think that Mr. Arnold has; and if ever man was qualified for the work it is he only.[40]

In two respects, Swinburne agrees with Nichol and Arnold: absolute translation is a 'hopeless' task and 'realis[ing]' the musical force of Greek tragedy is 'hard'. Yet 'the laws of the choral scheme' must still be obeyed. It would be a contradiction, having just declared absolute translation to be an impossibility, to mean by 'laws' the actual metrical schema of Greek choruses. Therefore, we must conclude that Swinburne is responding to the musicality of Greek choral metre in general.

What Swinburne criticizes in Arnold has further implications for our understanding of what he thought achieved in *Atalanta*. Having asserted again that 'Rhymeless choral metre' is pure 'prose', he next considers Arnold's 'patron[age] of the English hexameter'. Arnold's experiments simply cannot be scanned:

they look like nothing on earth, and sound like anapaests broken up and driven wrong [...] some of them begin with a pure and absolute anapaest; and how a hexameter can do this it passes my power to conceive. And at best what ugly bastards of verse are these self-styled hexameters![41]

While to Swinburne's ear the experiments of Arnold, along with Clough and Kingsley, are a failure, this provides an occasion to remind his reader of the strengths of an authentically English prosody:

Nothing but loose rhymeless anapaests can be made of the language in that way; and we hardly want these, having infinite command and resource of metre without them, and rhyme thrown in to turn the overweighted scale. I am unwilling to set my face against any doctrine or practice of a poet such as Mr. Arnold, but on this matter of metre I was moved to deliver my soul.[42]

For Swinburne, English prosody is its own resource. Though his decision not to state his convictions in a preface to *Atalanta,* as Arnold did for *Merope,* means that we are working by implication, Swinburne's critical writing supports Saintsbury's sense of *Atalanta* as a *renouveau* of English prosody. That his efforts did not go unappreciated is suggested by the reviewer in *The Times,* who wrote that this 'musical rhyming metre'

seems better adapted to convey to an unlearned Englishman the exceeding beauty of the Greek choric poems (which have been compared in their melody to the sound of singing birds) than the somewhat rugged blank verse, with metres equally foreign to Greek and to English, which Mr. Matthew Arnold employed in his tragedy of *Merope*.[43]

Oliver Elton goes further, arguing that:

charged as these poems are with reminiscences of Greek tragedy, and carefully as they are laid out on the Greek convention, their predominantly lyric tone, overflowing even into dialogue and monologue, keeps them from being Greek in essence, and leaves them only the more original. They are, in soul and spirit, not so near even to the more decorative kind of ancient drama as *Samson Agonistes* is to the plays of Sophocles. It is less the thought than the sure mastery of swift-footed and magnificent cadence that remains upon the memory — a cadence new and young that has not yet spent itself in myriad self-echoes [...] no poems leave a surer conviction that the untouched musical resources of the language are infinite; that no measure is so old as to be dead, and that when the right player comes the long burden of the metrical past is as nothing.[44]

This understanding that *Atalanta* presents a renewal of English poetry, and should be read as such, receives further confirmation once we consider the resistance of Swinburne's prosody to a system of scansion designed for another language.

Karole

Despite having gone to the effort of providing the most lengthy metrical analysis of *Atalanta* to date, Georges Lafourcade is forced to conclude that 'les chœurs de Swinburne sont d'une irrégularité complète, ou se bornent à répèter plusieurs fois la même forme en une série de strophes identiques, comme il arrive parfois chez les Grecs dans certains chants d'acteurs, mais jamais dans les chœurs véritables.'[the choruses of Swinburne are completely irregular, or merely repeat several times the same shape in a series of identical stanzas, as sometimes happens with the Greeks in some songs of actors, but never in the actual chorus]. While the perception of a mixture of feet suggests that Lafourcade also recognises the pliability that elicited such praise from Saintsbury, this variety can only be seen as a fault once viewed through the prism of classical scansion.[45] Compared to the chorus of *The Libation Bearers*, Swinburne's chorus is 'd'une 'asymétrie' barbare, ou d'une répétition monotone' [a barbarous asymmetry, or a monotonous repetition].[46]

Further attempts to make sense of the prosody of *Atalanta* through the prism of classical scansion remain incomplete or unconvincing. D. S. Carne-Ross, full of praise for Swinburne's Greek translations and poems, remakes the case for an English equivalent to Greek quantity, arguing that stress and quantity 'coincide', but provides no examples to test this.[47] Harding finds his description of Swinburne's 'familiar swing' in terms derived from classical scansion will only get him so far, and gives up: to 'speak of a mixed iambic-anapaestic metre may specify the ingredients of the mixture but not their proportions nor the order in which they come'.[48] Orla Polten suggests a link between Swinburne's epigraph, Euripides' *Andromache* and Swinburne's final *kommos*. However, the lack of direct link between elegiac couplets and the *kommos* itself (which actually bears more of a resemblance to the final chorus of Arnold's *Empedocles at Etna,* which — as I shall suggest — Swinburne admired), combined with Swinburne's sense that English poetry cannot support spondees (as her scansion suggests it must) and his dislike of Euripides means that this argument remains speculative at best.[49]

However, perhaps the most compelling case for reading *Atalanta* as an English poem comes in a single moment in which Saintsbury, despite being an influential advocate for classical foot-scansion for English verse, has to seek another name to describe what he was hearing in Swinburne's verse:

> I have commented, in more places than one or two of this prosodic history, on instances of *karole* — of the continuous dancing measure that picks up the movement from stanza to stanza in a sort of endless chain, and maintains this movement, of dance not of pace, throughout. [...] Schematically it is nothing more than 'long measure' with the odd lines double-rhymed hypercatalectically. But, by working on the fact that this additional syllable gives a trochaic 'throw-back' throughout the line, and by marvellous management of the occasional substitution of anapaests, the poet actually keeps the three balls of iambic, trochaic, and anapaestic rhythm in the air all at the same time. (*History*, 347)

This analysis of 'At a Month's End', from *Poems and Ballads: Third Series* is the closest we ever get to Saintsbury's definition of *karole*. However, the epigraph to his *History*, '*Ainsi karoloient illecques*' [and so they foot it lustily], taken from the *Roman de la Rose,* suggests the importance of this form in his work. The line suggests a metre that originates in dance, repetition, coordinated movement. Elsewhere in his *History* Saintsbury offers an example from Chaucer's *The Knight's Tale*, which conforms to his description here of a four-beat line ('long measure'), in which 'substitution' or 'catalexis' at the end of lines can affect prosodic contour, creating a ripple back through the line, so as to make it seem rising or falling.[50] Saintsbury uses terminology taken from classical foot scansion to describe this form. Yet this system, which assumes the separate nature of rhythmic units, is utterly undone by the effect he is describing, since the overwhelming magic of this rhythm is the way in which it seems to be composed of iambic, trochaic and anapaestic feet, all at once.

That Saintsbury had this particular 'measure' in mind when writing about the chorus of *Atalanta* is suggested by his footnotes, but also by his description of how Swinburne's verse-hounds go 'bounding and doubling'.[51] This identification of the *Atalanta* chorus with the *karole* measure has consequences for how we choose to read. As Saintsbury warns us, if we

> insist merely on the 'four-stress' character; rein up the iambs into unbroken sequence as such; slur the anapaests into iambs themselves; miss the under-suggestion of trochaic rhythm; and the whole beauty of the thing has vanished. Allow the fountain of song, within its limited-unlimited powers, to rise in liquid mazes; let iamb, trochee, anapaest, perform their wondrous *chassé-croisé* as it is their nature to do; and you get a choreographic and harmonic effect absolutely unparalleled. (347)

As an aside, it is worth pausing here to note that Saintsbury's attempt to find an adequate term to describe Swinburne's rhythm further justifies the appropriateness of Attridgean beat scansion to this study. As I argued in my introduction, a system of scansion — like all critical terminology — requires that we use the most accurate vocabulary available to describe our encounter with a poem. However, in the case of what Saintsbury calls the *karole*, to talk of feet belies both the basic rhythmic principle of the form and its execution in performance. Take the first verse of the chorus from which Saintsbury quotes:

> When the hounds of spring are on winter's traces,
>   The mother of months in meadow or plain
> Fills the shadow and windy places
>   With lisp of leaves and ripple of rain;
> And the brown bright nightingale amorous
> Is half assuaged for Itylus,
> For the Thracian ships and the foreign faces,
>   The tongueless vigil, and all the pain. (249)

Here it is not the repetition of individual feet — trochees, iambs and anapaests — but the number of unstressed syllables between each of the beats in the four-beat line (between one and two) which is the determining aspect of my experience of how the line leaps and moves, eddies and springs. This identification of the *Atalanta* chorus with the *karole* measure has consequences for how we choose to read, since, in identifying how the chorus of *Atalanta* exceeds foot scansion, Saintsbury appears to have anticipated Derek Attridge's more recent description of the English *dol'nik* by a century and a half.

Saintsbury's classical training meant that it would take until 2012 — forty years after Attridge pioneered beat scansion as a system for describing prosodic effects — for this to be fully formulated, as follows:

> 1) the number of syllables varies from line to line; the number of beats per line — four — is unchanging; (2) there is some freedom in the disposition of stressed and unstressed syllables, in contrast to stricter forms that control the number of syllables as well as beats; (3) the large majority of stressed syllables are felt as beats, and the large majority of unstressed syllables are felt as offbeats (or elements in offbeats); (4) if a syllable that normally does not carry a strong emphasis, like the first syllable of under, is treated as a beat, the forceful rhythm encourages the reader to give it some additional weight; (5) beats can be omitted and experienced silently under very particular conditions; offbeats between beats can be omitted with slightly more freedom (neither of these omissions occurs in this poem); (6) only rarely do more than two syllables make up the offbeat between the beats — the norm is to vary between one and two, to produce single and double offbeats; (7) lines can begin and end on a beat or an offbeat; (8) the disposition of the different types of offbeat is such as to enhance the strength of the rhythm; (9) there are no feet...'[52]

Returning with this description in mind to the stanza quoted above, you might insist on attending to feet in the scansion of your encounter, and that can certainly be done, for example, by carving up the first line into an anapaest, followed by an iamb, followed by another anapaest and another iamb and so on. But I run into difficulties once I realise that the second syllable of the word 'winter's', which should surely be scanned as the unstressed syllable of the aforementioned iamb, does not add up once I factor in the way the line then dips to end on what seems like a trochee (beginning on 'trace-'). Scanning the whole poem like this will involve numerous substitutions, leading to an incoherent metrical and rhythmical characterisation which would justify Lafourcade's phrase 'irrégularité complète'.

While poetry in English does exist in which the perception of repeating rhythmical units is the foremost aspect of our encounter with the poem's rhythm, here feet can only be spoken of as what Douglas Oliver calls a secondary order perception when compared to my primary perception of variant intervals of unstressed syllables between sounded syllables.[53] Classical scansion may be appropriate to certain kinds of poetry. However, in this case and in the case of the native English song rhythms which Swinburne specialised in early, attending to feet remains an abstraction which overlooks what makes the *karole* so powerful: its principle of flexibility. To miss this is to belie the strong rhythmical pull of the poem, in which — to use an analogy with dance — the reader must be ready to leap through either one or two steps in order to come down again on the beat. Following Attridge and Saintsbury, but more importantly my own sense of the need for an accurate vocabulary to describe Swinburne's innovation, it makes more sense to talk of duple and triple rhythm, than to refer to 'anapests', 'iambs' and 'trochees'.

Lyric and Dramatic Work on an Old Principle

Saintsbury's remarks about the *karole* gesture towards something larger about the structure of *Atalanta*, which is the stark difference in tone which I experience between the two alternating parts of the poem. In fact, this play alternates between two metrical sets: the five-beat heroic line for the drama and dialogue, and the four-beat line (or *karole*) of the chorus. Now, shifts between metrical sets will always produce a strong impression. However, in placing these two particular metrical sets side by side, Swinburne has tapped a particularly English metrical tension, perhaps best captured by Attridge's description of five-beat duple verse as an 'evasion' of the 'stronger, and probably more fundamental, rhythmic principle' he associates with four-beat triple verse. As Attridge notes:

> the ease with which the four-beat pattern is established means that it is sometimes experienced as a kind of sub-rhythm in the pentameter, imparting a little of its rhythmic insistence to the gentler line [...] But this is not to say that the four-beat rhythm is part of the pentameter's structure, as has sometimes been claimed (most influentially by Frye, 1957); it is precisely because the writer is free to make use of it as he wishes, or to avoid all suggestions of it, that it is a valuable rhythmic resource in five-beat verse.[54]

A better description of the basic prosodic principle of *Atalanta* could not be found. From the opening five-beat line, 'Maiden, and mistress of the months and stars' — a five-beat line with fewer than five stresses — to the shifting between duple and triple rhythms in the exodus — readers of *Atalanta* are caught in a struggle between the four-beat, triple, insistent, catatonic obscurity of the chorus, which appears to be forever threatening to overwhelm the five-beat, duple, gentle, speech-like rhythms of the dialogue.

Carne-Ross is right when he writes that Swinburne '*heard* Greek poetry, found what he heard most beautiful, and, without troubling to come up with a formal defense, set about composing a comparable beauty in English' (Carne-Ross, p. 40):

> What Swinburne heard in Greek poetry was 'the music that Aeschylus set to verse, the music that made mad, the upper notes of the psalm strong and shrill

as a sea-wind, the "bull-voiced" bellowing undersong of those dread choristers from somewhere out of sight, the tempest of tambourines giving back thunder to the thunder, the fury of divine lust that thickened with human blood the hill-streams of Cithaeron.

This characterisation of music as an 'undersong [...] set to verse', finds its technical expression in Swinburne's expert handling of a native English tension between four-beat and five-beat lines. By 'metrical set' I mean the set of expectations which a reader may reasonably have, including the variations which are possible within that form, which exert a continuing influence over their encounter with a poem as those expectations are fulfilled, disappointed or tested. This definition follows Attridge in its borrowing from the idea of a psychological set, which he defines as 'an expectation which involves a predisposition to interpret stimuli in a particular way'.[55] It is further useful, if the reader is to follow my argument about the structure of *Atalanta*, to make a distinction between metrical set and rhythmic set. Following Attridge again:

> [Metrical set] is the widespread disposition to perceive rhythmic structures in sound stimuli; an example noted earlier is the perception of alternating patterns in objectively undifferentiated sounds like the ticks of a clock. When a simple underlying rhythm is directly embodied in language (in a chanted nursery rhyme, for instance), the hearer's rhythmic set enables him to perceive the regular form, whether or not he knows the English language. But as the underlying rhythm grows more complex, its embodiment in language is less direct, and the element of convention more significant, the role of metrical set increases. Through experience, the reader grows familiar with this or that metrical form in his language, until he responds readily to the rhythms it creates. He can then be said to have acquired a set for that metre; if one were using a linguistic analogy, one would say he had internalised its rules. Moreover, any given poem in a regular metre will establish its own highly specific metrical set, which in most cases will be a more sharply-defined version of a common metrical set. It should be obvious that any metrical set is built on, and embodies, a more fundamental rhythmic set, and that the two kinds of set correspond roughly to the underlying rhythm on the one hand, and on the other hand to the metrical pattern together with the principles by which it may be realised in a sequence of stressed and unstressed syllables.[56]

I quote Attridge's definition of metrical and rhythmical set at some length here, because it is important to be clear about what it is that I am and am not claiming about Swinburne's rhythmical style and his handling of rhythmic tension at this early point in his career. I am not suggesting that Swinburne has fused two distinct metrical sets — the four-beat and the five-beat line — in his poem, or created a new kind of metre, only that he has developed the rhythmical set of each individual metrical set so as to make them seem — in certain lines, and sometimes for a few lines at a time — almost alike. This creates a tension which, as Attridge defines it, comes very close to the edge of collapse:

> there are other directions in which a line can travel only a very short distance before it plunges into metrical chaos, or, what is sometimes worse, a totally different rhythm. It is these sharp distinctions which prove the existence of a

subtle but firm sense of metrical structure shared by poets and readers, and it is on this basis that any adequate account of metrical form must be built.[57]

As I aim to show in detail here, it is the way in which Swinburne's verse courts the collapse of blank verse, or the collapse of the *karole*, without losing control of either, which accounts for the particular rhythmical force of this poem.

Once we connect this metrical tension to Swinburne's claim for *Atalanta* as the 'first poem of the sort in modern times, combining lyric and dramatic work on the old principle', then it becomes clear how *Atalanta* is placed in an established English tradition. For as Swinburne well knew, the construction of Greek plays in English on the basis of a tension between four-beat lyrical sets and blank verse is in evidence in Milton's *Samson Agonistes*, Landor's *Dramatic Sketches*, Arnold's *Empedocles at Etna*, and, to an extent, in Shelley's *Prometheus Unbound*.

To demonstrate how this peculiar kind of metrical tension works, we might here consider the last verse of another choral poem by Shelley, the 'Song of Pan', which was originally intended to sit within a longer play not unlike Swinburne's *Atalanta*:

> I sang of the dancing stars,
>   I sang of the daedal Earth,
> And of Heaven — and the giant wars,
>   And Love, and Death, and Birth, —
> And then I changed my pipings, —
>   Singing how down the vale of Maenalus
>   I pursued a maiden and clasped a reed.
>   Gods and men, we are all deluded thus!
>   It breaks on our bosom and then we bleed:
>   They wept, as I think both ye now would,
> If envy or age had not frozen your blood,
>   At the sorrow of my sweet pipings.[58]

The character of the first four lines is initially uncertain. They could be read as a hemistich, a shortened five-beat line, or as a four-beat line with a final unrealised final offbeat, as in Swinburne's chorus 'Before the Beginning of Years'; either would explain the strong sense we have of a predominantly triple rhythm followed by a pause. At the fifth line quoted we experience a shift into duple rhythm, then an even greater shift in the next, which undeniably comprises five beats. Shelley, as he often does, gives us a clue to the rhythmical shift in the content of the line: 'And then I changed my pipings'. The four five-beat lines that follow firmly establish the five-beat set, this time in duple rhythm, which approaches blank verse. This allows the 'moral' of the poem — the equivalence of men and gods — good voice. Shelley reinforces this shift in metrical set by interrupting his rhyme scheme, letting the *abab* scheme include an as yet unrhymed element, 'pipings'. This scheme, as Attridge notes, tends to reinforce the four-line, four-beat stanza.[59] At the introduction of 'pipings', it seems, song is interrupted by speech.

The shift back towards the four-beat line is hinted at in the tenth line quoted, when a nine-syllable line offers an apt demonstration of Attridge's sense that 'To omit the final syllable of the five-beat pentameter is to deliver it over to the four-beat pattern which is always waiting for an opportunity to gain dominance'.[60] The achievement of this takeover in the next line suggests the final triumph of the triple rhythm, of song, until we experience the dropping-off of triple rhythm towards duple in the last line. This experience is coincident with the repetition (not rhyme) of 'pipings' at the end of the line. This echo recalls Pan's first reference to his songs, and asks that we reconsider the triple rhythm again. Shelley's switching rhythm emerges as the counterpoint to an argument about the powerlessness of song in the face of some higher force than gods and men, with the result that the return of triple rhythm feels like a muted triumph.

Carne-Ross argues for this stanza — which 'falls into a number of metrically distinct units, with much variation of rhythm and pace' — as a 'Greek' achievement: 'in this seemingly modest form we have an English equivalent of the jewel of Greece's metrical crown, the choric ode of attic tragedy'.[61] The same basic principle of variation between song and dialogue is also the root of the rhythmic energies that Shelley employs in *Prometheus Unbound*, a poem which, we recall, Swinburne called 'magnificent' though 'unhellenic' in spirit. We might expect to see Swinburne following Shelley in the construction of his choral odes. However, Swinburne's choral song rarely allows for shifts at a range of four to five lines within a single strophe. Instead, his innovation is to take this tension, distil it, and use it to stage powerful effects.

However, in dividing the four-beat and five-beat lines into two discrete functions, Swinburne is perhaps following the example of Walter Savage Landor, to whom *Atalanta* was dedicated. In Landor's short dramatic sketch 'Agamemnon and Iphigenia' — 'the first poem [...]', Swinburne confesses to Eliza Lynn Linton, 'I ever read of his, and fell in love with at the age of twelve' (*Letters*, IV, p. 188) — the song of the chorus comprises a four-beat line, creating a contrast with the five-beat line of the dialogue. The sketch allows the two metrical sets time to become established as independent, before they are combined in the final chorus of Argive elders:

> Blessed art thou who hast repelled
> Battle's wild fury, Ocean's whelming foam;
> Blessed o'er all, to have beheld
> Wife, children, house, avenged, and peaceful home![62]

Here five-beat lines are clearly distinguishable from the four-beat, and are experienced as a slowing of the pace. Although they are combined in the same stanza, what Landor never does is to allow the integrity of the blank verse line, and of speech, to be threatened by the rhythmic pull of the four-beat line. In fact, Landor's four-beat line, Saintsbury's 'long measure', is never as insistent as Swinburne's: it contains hardly any runs of unstressed syllables, with the consequence that it never allows a potential triple rhythm to emerge. Likewise, the 'stiff' manner of the blank verse — to borrow an adjective from the German prosodist much maligned by Saintsbury, Dr. Brandes — is more resistant to runs of five-beat lines with fewer than five stresses.

Swinburne's innovation really emerges when we consider the structure of his two metrical sets, and their arrangement against the other poets in this tradition.

Attridge suggests that 'the distinction between duple and triple rhythms [in four-beat metre] occurs not as a structural principle, but in the surface realisation; it is for this reason that there is no clear dividing line between the two (100). While this might be true of the triple rhythms which occur in the most lyrical passages of Shelley's *Prometheus Unbound*, Browning's translation of *Agamemnon* and Arnold's *Empedocles on Etna*, in Swinburne's chorus the frequent repetition of two unstressed syllables as an offbeat — the frequency which sets triple rhythm in motion — is so regular as to promote it to the level of constituting a metrical expectation in itself. This especially true of this stanza, in which the chorus longs for the goddess of spring:

> Where shall we find her, how shall we sing to her,
> Fold our hands round her knees, and cling?
> O that man's heart were as fire and could spring to her,
> Fire, or the strength of the streams that spring!
> For the stars and the winds are unto her
> As raiment, as songs of the harp-player;
> For the risen stars and the fallen cling to her,
> And the southwest-wind and the west-wind sing. (249)

Harding, as I have noted, draws attention to this chorus in the course of making a larger argument about the perception of metrical set, noticing how 'Swinburne's manipulation in many poems of a two unstressed syllables as an offbeat at least once in each line rapidly establishes a perceptual set which makes a strictly duple line seem out of place, even though a full triple rhythm is never established.'[63] The natural result of this is speed, as the reader moves swiftly over the non-stressed syllables to reach the end of the line. This quality, we recall, is what Saintsbury claims differentiates Swinburne from Browning and Tennyson. However, Swinburne's own comments in his essay on Arnold suggest *Empedocles at Etna* might be a more apt comparison when trying to explain the peculiar force of Swinburne's lyric choruses. If we compare this stanza with the last section of the song of Callicles we can understand the peculiar 'swing' of Swinburne's chorus:

> Through the black, rushing smoke-bursts,
> Thick breaks the red flame;
> All Etna heaves fiercely
> Her forest-clothed frame.
>
> Not here, O Apollo!
> Are haunts meet for thee.
> But, where Helicon breaks down
> In cliff to the sea,
>
> Where the moon-silver'd inlets
> Send far their light voice
> Up the still vale of Thisbe,
> O speed, and rejoice![64]

The four-beat line may be split in two here; however, this is still the essential four-beat structure which characterises Swinburne's first two choruses. The triple rhythm is undeniably present; however, duple lines, like the second quoted, are still possible, even within Callicles' grand musical finale. In addition, the splitting of the line into shorter units provides less of an opportunity for the offbeat as two unstressed syllables to become established at the ends of lines or to interact with syntax within the stanza. We might offer as a further point of comparison this stanza from Shelley's *Prometheus Unbound*, which might well be an ancestor of those lines in the penultimate verse of the first choral ode, 'And Pan by day and Bacchus by night,/ Fleeter of foot than the fleet-foot kid,':

> Whence come ye, so wild and so fleet,
> For sandals of lightning are on your feet,
> And your wings are soft and swift as thought,
> And your eyes are as love which is veiled not?[65]

Though the line is not split in two, this is the same four-beat line and rhyme scheme as Arnold. It too shows a marked tendency towards triple rhythm. However, as with Arnold, the triple rhythm does not exhibit so tight a hold of the rhythm or syntax. While the triple rhythm is heard in the first two lines, this falls back into duple rhythm in the third line. It would have been so easy for Shelley to have kept this up, for example, by the addition of an extra syllable or two: 'And your wings are [as] soft and [as] swift as thought'. It is curious that, to my ear at least, increasing the number of unstressed syllables between beats instantly makes this line sound somehow more 'Swinburnean' —a fact which confirms my suspicion that a regular triple rhythm is more characteristic of Swinburne's lyric choruses.

Attridge writes of how the four-beat line appears to lend itself to four-line stanzas, or stanzas which combine in multiples of four.[66] This allows for a quick establishment of metrical set, usually by the end of the second line, which also tends to be reinforced by rhyme. If we bring Attridge's observations to bear on the stanza of Swinburne's chorus just quoted, we note how Swinburne has built on this tendency even further, first by not simply rhyming, but also repeating the word 'her', and secondly by a string of three *a*-rhymes together. The result is a highly lyrical rhyming stanza, in which the reader is always straining ahead to the next but one line, instead of a more measured opening and closing of couplets, as in the *aabb* stanzas of Shelley and Arnold discussed above. If this were not enough to convince of the very precise and regular set of expectations which attend Swinburne's establishment of the 'lyrical' metrical set, we might consider, as a negative comparison, the 'monostrophe' of Milton's *Samson Agonistes*, which is only very loosely rhymed, and a strophe from the chorus of *Merope*, which is rhymeless:

> Just are the ways of God,
> And justifiable to Men;
> Unless there be who think not God at all,
> If any be, they walk obscure;
> For of such Doctrine never was there School,
> But the heart of the Fool,
> And no man therein Doctor but himself.[67]

> Truly I hear of a Maid
> Of that stock born, who bestow'd
> Her blood that so she might make
> Victory sure to her race,
> When the fight hung in doubt! but she now,
> Honour'd and sung of by all,
> Far on Marathon plain,
> Gives her name to the spring
> Macaria, blessed Child.[68]

In Milton the length of lines varies between two and five beats, meaning that metrical set is never fully established. If we have expectations, it is that the five-beat line — our blank verse norm — will return. Rhyme does not 'weight' the strophe or aid the perception of metrical set by sounding the boundary between regular lines. Something of what Swinburne says about Milton's forfeiture of 'the laws of choral music' rings true here — though, as he argues, this is compensated for by the undeniable splendour of Milton's blank verse.

Arnold's chorus from *Merope*, by contrast, is the same four-beat line with an unrealised last beat as we encounter in the second chorus of *Atalanta*, 'Before the Beginning of Years'. However, the realisation of the offbeat as two unstressed syllables never becomes established to the same extent as in *Atalanta*. Partly this is to do with the awkwardness of the syntactical constructions, for example, in third line quoted. After the skipping of Callicles' song, the rhymelessness of the chorus of *Merope* feels flat. No rhyme here serves to act as a bass drum to the 'continuous dancing measure' which caused Saintsbury to look for an analogue in the sixteenth-century *quadrille* or *karole*.

If Swinburne's chorus establishes strong expectations, the same is true of his other metrical set, blank verse. Though the reviewer in *The Times* found it 'a little mannered and stiff, reminding one of Landor'[69], Swinburne's five-beat line was not without its admirers: 'It is in our truly national measure, blank verse, that Mr. Swinburne has achieved his most undoubted success' writes the reviewer in *The Fortnightly Review*.[70] This is an occasion for much back-patting, since 'Our blank verse of the nineteenth century [...] seems, at any rate in mere verbal rhythm and movement, superior to that of all preceding English poetry.' It is the 'fluency' of Swinburne's English that this reader most responds to. However, as we shall see, it would be wrong to connect this quality with that very different kind of fluency which we meet in the chorus. If blank verse is supposed to achieve its effects because of its proximity to, yet marked difference from, everyday speech (Attridge 126), then Swinburne's blank verse seems to embrace the principle of alteration across syllables to a preternatural degree. This is especially so in the stichomythic exchanges, in which Swinburne's verse becomes monosyllabic, pushing us to distribute stress alternately across syllables, realising five beats in ten movements of the mouth. As a result, a resolutely duple rhythm is quickly established, which when realised in Althæa's last line, 'I did this and I say this and I die' (316), can be emphatic, crystalline and lucid all at once. Though Lafourcade persists in his attention to the syllable, rather than beat, his observations on this aspect of Swinburne's blank verse and its interaction with diction are acute:

> Le rythme est toujours énergique et clair, parfois dur. Ceci tient en grande partie à l'emploi continuel de mots brefs et sans syllabes longues; Swinburne a été plus loin dans ce sens dans *Atalanta* que dans *Chastelard* : on y trouve des groupes de vers purement monosyllabiques. [The rhythm is always energetic and clear, sometimes hard. This is due in large part to the continuous use of short words without long syllables; Swinburne has gone further in this direction in *Atalanta* than in *Chastelard*: there are groups of purely monosyllabic verses.][71]

As an example, he offers these lines from *Atalanta*, remarkable not simply because they are almost entirely monosyllabic, but also because they come — not from the stichomythic exchanges, but in the course of the chorus's later blank verse speech:

> Nay, for the son lies close about thine heart,
> Full of thy milk, warm from thy womb, and drains
> Life and the blood of life and all thy fruit,
> Eats thee and drinks thee as who breaks bread and eats,
> Treads wine and drinks, thyself, a sect of thee;
> And if he feed not, shall not thy flesh faint?
> Or drink not, are not thy lips dead for thirst? (307)

Emphatic, '*dur*', lines like these make the 'tight rhyming anapests' of the earlier choral songs seem very far off indeed. It is probable that Swinburne was following the stichomythic exchanges of *Merope* in which there is a high incidence of monosyllabic words:

POLYPHONTES:	To chance impute their deaths, then, not to me.
MEROPE:	Such chance as kill'd the father, kill'd the sons.
POLYPHONTES:	One son at least I spared, for still he lives.
MEROPE:	Tyrants think him they murder not they spare.
POLYPHONTES:	Not much a tyrant thy free speech displays me.
MEROPE:	Thy shame secures my freedom, not thy will.[72]

The sheer blankness of these necessarily discrete lines comes to have an almost repetitive quality by virtue of their isochrony. Such lines have an eloquence, even a rhetorical edge, but in a different way to the pathos which we experience reading the Chorus's plea to Althæa to spare her son. For pathos, we have to go — as the reviewer in *The Fortnightly* suggests — to Walter Savage Landor.

Though Landor's blank verse can be 'stiff' and 'mannered', this also allows for the full effects of enjambment to be felt. This is combined with a high incidence of monosyllables in an imaginary conversation between Iphigenia and Agamemnon in the underworld. Iphigenia, who does not know of her father's murder, forgets for a moment that they are 'shades', and wonders why he will not embrace her:

> Look on me; smile with me at my illusion.
> You are so like what you have ever been
> (Except in sorrow!) I might well forget
> I could not win you as I used to do.
> It was the first embrace since my descent
> I ever aim'd at: those who love me live,
> Save one, who loves me most, and now would chide me.[73]

Here it is the 'stiff' monosyllabic lines which have the most clarity, and, as a result, the most emotional force. To demonstrate this, we might put this preternatural speech alongside three lines from Browning's translation of Aeschylus's *Agamemnon*, which, though it has its merits when taken on its own terms, 'violates English while only occasionally managing to sound Greek', as Carne-Ross puts it (Carne-Ross 32):

> But speak thou, herald! Meneleos I ask of:
> If he, returning, back in safety also
> Will come with you — this land's beloved chieftain?[74]

This sense of a violation of natural speech is even more acute in his blank stichomythic lines:

> CHOROS: How sayest? The word, from want of faith, escaped me.
> KLUT.: Troia the Achaioi hold: do I speak plainly?
> CHOROS: Joy overcreeps me, calling forth the tear-drop.
> KLUT: Right! for, that glad thou art, thine eye convicts thee.
> CHOROS: For — what to thee, of all this, trusty token?[75]

Nothing could be further from the stichomythic exchanges in *Atalanta*, which, at their most 'blank' — that is to say, when the five-beat, duple, rhythm of English dramatic verse is taken in the direction of stark, unadorned, monosyllabic lines like those I have been considering — realise the expectation of a very different metrical set from that which we have just been exploring in the 'lyric' set. And yet, remarkably and as we shall see, Swinburne's blank verse can also accommodate the occurrence of fewer than five stresses within the five-beat line, a rhythmic variation which, when used precisely, troubles the integrity of the five-beat line, creating tension, and making it seem as if the rhythm of the chorus is interfering with the blank verse. The secret of Swinburne's innovation is his control of exactly when and where this happens.

Saintsbury's pleasure has led us to talk about the work as a poem, and from the poem to a consideration of its place the history of English prosody. We have grasped the why, but not the wherefore. It is high time that we turned to the poem.

Metrical Set and Rhythmic Tension

Having argued that Swinburne's play must be understood as an English poem, making use of a native English tension, occurring naturally between two metrical sets, I can now begin to understand Swinburne's innovation in *Atalanta*. Although, as I have argued, it is meaningless to consider the structure of *Atalanta* in the abstract — Nicolson is right that it is something that the reader must undergo — some kind of a map might be useful before I attempt to recount my own encounter with the poem.

Swinburne's innovation is two-fold. First, he divides the two metrical sets, four-beat and five-beat lines, which we saw in the other Greek plays in English into two discrete functions: song and dialogue. He then develops the potentialities of each metrical set to such an extent that the former may seem as if it is interfering with the latter at precise moments. However, crucially, this split is also linked to two forms of attention — we 'hear' some things loud and clear, other things less so. There is a gathering sense of unease surrounding the half-heard content of the choral song, which becomes gradually more audible as the play goes on. Having established a distinction between obscure, choral lyric, and clear blank verse dialogue, Swinburne experiments with triple rhythm (which we associate with the four-beat metrical set of the choral song) in the five-beat line in the third choral ode. He lets go of this distinction between choral ode and dialogue at the fourth choral ode, pitching the reader into confusion. To talk, as Attridge does, of a sub-rhythm imparting rhythmic insistence in the pentameter is a flawed yet useful way to talk about what I encounter in the fourth choral ode; by combining frequent runs of five-beat lines with fewer than five stresses with a tendency towards fewer than ten syllables per line, he pushes the five-beat line so far towards song rhythm that the chorus's song appears to be active within the pentameter. In this lies the secret of one of the most charged moments in the poem. However, in order to understand the force of this moment, we first need to understand the way in which, as Nicholson puts it, the two distinct metrical sets 'cross and re-cross each other'.

The First Two Odes

Swinburne's combination of 'lyric and dramatic work on an old principle' is initially navigable in terms of a division between four-beat lines for the chorus, and five-beat lines for the dialogue. This split in metrical set is also experienced as a split in modes of attention. We hear the chief huntsman's prayer to Artemis, the immortal goddess, to grant success to the hunting of the boar ravaging Calydon; but it takes serious effort to offer a summary of the first choral song, which celebrates the elapse of seasons and the ceaseless cycles of violence. We grasp the debate between Althæa and the chorus concerning the unjust nature of the gods, but we do not register the chorus's apparent celebration of Althæa's vision in the following song 'Before the Beginning of Years', which seems an outworking of Althæa's previous argument of the futility of prayer:

> Night a black hound, follows the white fawn day,
> Swifter then dreams the white flown feet of sleep;
> Will ye pray back the night with any prayers? (251)

If Swinburne's poem could be said to have characters, in the sense of private individuals with an internal life, we might argue that there is something amiss here. The chorus affirms the power of prayer in their dialogue, and yet, in their song, sing of the inevitability of grief, suffering, and death. We might take the fact that this contradiction initially fails to register as evidence of the relative obscurity of Swinburne's first two choruses:

> When the hounds of spring are on winter's traces,
>   The mother of months in meadow or plain
> Fills the shadows and windy places
>   With lisp of leaves and ripple of rain;

And the brown bright nightingale amorous
Is half assuaged for Itylus,
For the Thracian ships and the foreign faces,
    The tongueless vigil, and all the pain.

Come with bows bent and with emptying of quivers,
    Maiden most perfect, lady of light,
With a noise of winds and many rivers,
    With a clamour of water, and with might;
Bind on thy sandals, O thou most fleet,
Over the splendour and speed of they feet;
For the faint east quickens, the wan west shivers
    Round the feet of the day and the feet of the night.

Where shall we find her, how shall we sing to her,
    Fold our hands round her knees and cling?
O that man's heart were as fire and could spring to her,
    Fire, or the strength of the streams that spring!
For the stars and the winds are unto her
As raiment, as songs for the harp-player;
For the risen stars and the fallen cling to her,
    And the southwest-wind and the west-wind sing.

For winter's rains and ruins are over,
    And all the season of snows and sins;
The days dividing lover and lover,
    The light that loses, the night that wins;
And time remembered is grief forgotten,
And frosts are slain and flowers begotten,
And in green underwood and cover
    Blossom by blossom the spring begins.

The full streams feed on flower of rushes,
    Ripe grasses trammel a travelling foot
The faint fresh flame of the young year flushes
    From leaf to flower and flower to fruit;
And fruit and leaf are as gold and fire,
And the oat is heard above the lyre,
And the hoofed heel of a satyr crushes
    The chestnut-husk at the chestnut-root.

And Pan by day and Bacchus by night,
    Fleeter of foot than the fleet-foot kid,
Follows with dancing and fills with delight
    The Mænad and the Bassarid;
And soft as lips that laugh and hide
The laughing leaves of the trees divide,
And screen from seeing and leave in sight
    The God pursuing, the maiden hid.

The ivy falls with the Bacchanal's hair
    Over her eyebrows hiding her eyes;
The wild wine slipping down leaves bare
    Her bright breast shortening into sighs;

> The wild wine slips with the weight of its leaves,
> But the berried ivy catches and cleaves
> To the limbs that glitter, the feet that scare
>   The wolf that follows, the fawn that flies. (249–50)

Reading this chorus, my overall impression is of an extremely strong rhythmical pull. Yet it is never monotonous. Pushed to account for this, we can look to the schema. There are, with one or two exceptions, four beats per line with a variant number of unstressed syllables in between, from one to two. This is perhaps what Saintsbury meant when he described these verse-hounds as 'bounding and doubling'. Since stress is being distributed across syllables on the basis of rhythmic isochrony, and not alternation, considerations of natural word stress or emphasis in performance, are put off in favour of the rhythm. The natural result of this is a tendency to downplay the semantic and grammatical aspects of language. As Saintsbury notes, from this emerges the 'quality of speed'.

The overall effect of this set of metrical co-ordinates is an experience akin to day-dreaming, moments of 'zone-out' in which words fail to register entirely as words. There are few readings which do not attest to the curious effect of Swinburne's chorus. For some it is the dominant or final impression. Robert Browning called *Atalanta* a 'fuzz of words'. Ruskin writes of the poet 'foam[ing] at the mouth.' Edward Burne-Jones was more sensitive, describing how the rhythm 'goes on with such a rush that it is enough to carry the world away.'[76] This effect continues to trouble readers of Swinburne. Maurice Bowra writes that 'When we first read *Atalanta*, we may hardly notice the plot or the thought behind it, so overwhelming is the effect of the words, so strange the impression which they make.'[77] Edward Thomas was far more candid: *Atalanta*, on first reading, 'can hardly have been interesting, though it contains an interesting story which is probably revealed to the majority of readers by the foregoing argument alone.' However, Thomas qualifies this quip with an observation: 'This story is obliterated by the form of a Greek drama, by abundant lyrics [...] by an exuberance and individuality of language which could not always transmit instantaneously a definite meaning. But the obscurity is not one of incompetence...'[78]

Thomas's appreciation for Swinburne's 'obscurity', added to Saintsbury's perception of variety, might prompt us to look a little closer. Despite its firm grip on the words, this rhythmic energy actually originates in a fairly flexible set of metrical co-ordinates. The syllable-count of the lines varies from eight to twelve so that the schema can accommodate, within a single stanza, a line of eight syllables, 'Bind on thy sandals, O thou most fleet,' and twelve syllables, 'Round the feet of the day and the feet of the night', without either of them sounding unmetrical. An alternation between polysyllabic and monosyllabic words at the ends of lines means that the cadence of the lines appears to switch between falling and rising. All of this goes to prevent Swinburne's strong triple rhythm from descending into dull monotony.

Yet there are also variations in the metrical schema which do have an effect far beyond simply preventing us from switching off, including variations which cause us to re-attend. We might note the three stressed syllables, instead of the expected four, in the fifth and six lines of the first stanza. The lack of the last stressed syllable appears to be compensated for by realising the missing beat by a pause at the end of both lines, checking the previously free- flow of rhythm from line to line. Saintsbury's sense of how stanzas 'hide' but never 'falsify' their norm seems prescient here. These two lines may seem a large deviation — almost like a shorter line in the centre of the stanza. However, they are the same four-beat structure, realised in a different manner. The effect is that we are pulled up short for a moment, and the coincidence of these rhythmic stops with the *cc* rhyme underpins this sense of a break. However, given the gravity of the chorus's allusion — the story of Philomena — this pause in the music seems entirely appropriate. A further example might be the line 'The wild vine slipping down leaves bare'. Here the rhythm is oddly duple, as if Swinburne's hounds have, for a line, only one leg on the ground at any one moment. The result is an oddly 'blank' moment: the rhythmic spell slips, allowing the meaning of the words forward, letting the image of exposed skin come to the fore. Evidently Swinburne is able to adjust the 'obscurity' of his verse when he pleases. At other times the rhythm holds absolute sway. The last two lines might be read as duple rhythm. However, within the context of the choral song, the strong four-beat structure joins forces with the rhetorical and syntactical organisation of the line — two beats on either side of the caesura — to jump over the caesura, over the line break, skipping far too quickly past a body in pieces, a wolf pursuing and a hind pursued. These last four images of violence are heard as if through a veil, obscured by the effects of the metre. Some readers will take an about-turn. Others will flick back to this moment at a later point in the poem. Thomas is right that Swinburne's 'obscurity... is not incompetent'. In fact, it varies — and it is expertly handled. As William Empson notes:

> When Swinburne comes off he is a very full and direct writer; it is no use saying these verses show interest in mere sound, or pattern of verbal cadence. It would be true, perhaps, to say that he feels it more important to keep up his texture than that, in any particular case, the meanings, the chord of associations should come through. But in a literary, not perhaps in a stage sense, this hypnotised detachment is a powerful dramatic weapon...[79]

Not many critics agree. T. S. Eliot, as we have seen, took issue with the second choral song 'Before the Beginning of Years', a poem which is constructed (like the fifth and sixth lines of the first chorus) from a four-beat line with an unrealised final offbeat leading to a pause at the end of lines; a fact which made it so very suitable for chanting, as the 'The Swinburne Stomp' (1965) by avant-rock band The Fugs makes clear (though the kazoos and penny-whistles are their own).[80] Again, I note an immense flexibility in the number of unstressed syllables between beats:

> Before the beginning of years
>   There came to the making of man
> Time, with a gift of tears;
>   Grief, with a glass that ran;
> Pleasure, with pain for leaven;
>   Summer, with flowers that fell;
> Remembrance fallen from heaven,
>   And madness risen from hell;

>   Strength without hands to smite;
>   Love that endures for a breath:
>   Night, the shadow of light,
>   And life, the shadow of death.
>   And the high gods took in hand
>   Fire, and the falling of tears,
>   And a measure of sliding sand
>   From under the feet of the years
>   And froth and drift of the sea;
>   And dust of the labouring earth;
>   And bodies of things to be
>   In the houses of death and of birth;
>   And wrought with weeping and laughter,
>   And fashioned with loathing and love
>   With life before and after
>   And death beneath and above,
>   For a day and a night and a morrow,
>   That his strength might endure for a span
>   With travail and heavy sorrow
>   The holy spirit of Man. (258–59)

'This is not merely "music";' Eliot writes, 'it is effective because it appears to be a tremendous statement, like statements made in our dreams; when we wake up we find that the "glass that ran" would do better for time than for grief, and that the gift of tears would be as appropriately bestowed by grief as by time.'[81] Eliot's sense of having entered another mind-state when reading the poem, only to wake up at the end of it, aptly describes the way in which Swinburne's poem courts one mode of attention — the rhythmic — at the expense of another kind of attention — common sense.[82] Subsequent responses to Eliot's opposition by C. M. Bowra, John D. Rosenberg and Veronica Forrest-Thomson have responded that Swinburne's choice is defensible, since the yoking of 'grief' and the 'glass' is unexpected and therefore more powerful. However, these responses tend to adopt Eliot's criteria, and argue with it on its own terms.

A more powerful defence of Swinburne's verse-craft might, I think, be to understand his verse as operating in a different way to the kind of poetry which Eliot was trying to write. Eliot gives us a clue to this in his conclusion to the essay, where he declares his preference for the prose of Joyce or Conrad, but not before he has given us an explanation of what seems most problematic about Swinburne's songs:

> [...] There is no reason why verse intended to be sung should not present a sharp visual image or convey an important intellectual meaning, for it supplements the music by another means of affecting the feelings. What we get in Swinburne is an expression by sound, which could not possibly associate itself with music. For what he gives is not images and ideas and music, it is one thing with a curious mixture of suggestions of all three.[83]

What Eliot seems to be striving for at this point in his essay is an identifiable relation between images, ideas and music. Not this 'curious mixture' that we get in Swinburne, and not this 'expression by sound'. Criticism has tended to agree with Eliot. Following the advent of free verse, certain aspects of the Swinburnean technique, including insistent rhythm like that of the first choral ode, became defunct in the repertoire of Anglophone poetry. This dislike of what Eliot called 'expression by sound' has acquired the status of a truism, appearing in the most unlikely places. For example, seeking an explanation for the rhythmical power of the triple rhythm that I encounter in Swinburne's first chorus, I discover the following remarks:

> Duple verse coincides with the two rhythmic principles in English: stress-timing and syllable-timing, because one syllable answers a rhythmic peak and one for a trough [...] triple verse, on the other hand, favours stress-timing, both in its implied equivalence of one strong to two weak syllables, and in its overriding of the alternations of the language. This alliance with the stronger, and probably more fundamental, rhythmic principle produces a prominent rhythm that tends to simplify the contours of speech [...] A strong triple rhythm will often force a bad poet (or even tempt a good one) to subordinate semantic and syntactic choices to metrical choices, producing verse which is more gesture than expression [...] which lodge in the mind less for what they say than the rhythm in which they say it.[84]

Attridge's description of the way in which a 'strong triple rhythm', leads to 'a simplification of the contours of speech' aptly describes our experience of reading the first choral ode. However, to characterise this style as a 'temptation', implying weakness, or as mere 'gesture', is problematic. Anyone, Eliot included, who has read *Atalanta* knows that this aspect of Swinburne's poem has a power not easily dismissed as mere 'gesture'. In fact, the obscurity is a crucial part of this poem's unfolding.

Waking from the second choral song, 'Before the Beginning of Years', we are again able to follow the debate between Meleager and his mother Althæa, on the nature of law — whether god-given, or customary — and the affront to custom which Atalanta, as a maiden huntress who rejects love and motherhood, presents. Throughout the first half of Swinburne's play, the 'obscurity' associated with the four-beat, triple rhythm of the choruses is 'enchased' — to borrow Swinburne's description of the choruses of *Empedocles at Etna* — within the blank verse. The result is a perception of two styles: the song metre associated with the chorus and the blank verse associated with the dialogue. Yet there is also a gradual, gathering sense of unease surrounding the half-heard content of the choral song.

The Triple Pentameter

This unease begins to register around the third choral ode. The theme of the chorus's song is appropriately, given Meleager's admiration for Atalanta and his mother's warning against 'following strange loves', love. However, this is no celebratory song, for in the allegory 'Love' is accompanied by a young married couple called 'fate' and 'death'. The reader who has been fighting to attend to the content of the chorus's songs might well feel a sense of foreboding. However, the queasiness which we feel on reading these lines has as much to do with the way the chorus sing it:

> We have seen thee, O Love, thou art fair ; thou art goodly, O Love;
> Thy wings make light in the air as the wings of a dove.
> Thy feet are as winds that divide the stream of the sea;
> Earth is thy covering to hide thee, the garment of thee.
> Thou art swift and subtle and blind as a flame of fire;
> Before thee the laughter, behind thee the tears of desire;
> And twain go forth beside thee, a man with a maid;
> Her eyes are the eyes of a bride whom delight makes afraid;
> As the breath in the buds that stir is her bridal breath:
> But fate is the name of her ; and his name is Death.
>   For an evil blossom was born
>   Of sea-foam and the frothing of blood,
>   Blood-red and bitter of fruit,
>   And the seed of it laughter and tears,
>   And the leaves of it madness and scorn;
>   A bitter flower from the bud,
>   Sprung of a sea without root,
>   Sprung without graft from the years [...] (273–74)

The design of this choral ode falls into two stages. Following on from the blank verse exchange between Meleager and his parents, who counsel him not to follow Atalanta, we encounter ten extremely regular triple five-beat lines. This rhythm is odd. Following this, the four-beat line takes over and we slip back into the much faster, insistent and familiar rhythm of 'Before the Beginning of Years', in which there are four beats per line, the last unrealised, and a strong tendency towards triple rhythm. We move from a rational discussion of the laws of Zeus, to a song in which the pain and pleasure of love is celebrated, yet which is never allowed to be completely transparent because of the insistence of the rhythm. Attridge's sense of the different ways in which duple and triple metre elicit our attention proves elucidating on this point. But not before the oddness of the triple pentameter has chance to register.

If we were initially unsure as to whether what we were hearing was a five-beat line with triple rhythm and not, for example, a combination of two four-beat lines, syntax will right us: there is no tendency to mark a central caesura with an offbeat, and the punctuation, especially in the first line, encourages regular runs of unstressed syllables. The four-beat line more usually associated with triple rhythm does eventually take back over. However, this does not cancel my sense that for the first ten lines of the choral ode we are pitched between two modes of attention.

It is here that I realise, retrospectively, that my perception of two metrical sets was dependent on a third condition: that they should remain separate. By forcing the five-beat line towards triple rhythm, while simultaneously holding open the line long enough for the swift four-beat line to become saddled with an extra beat, Swinburne pitches us between chorus and dialogue modes. And yet this breach of local expectations is only a part-explanation for the effect of these lines.

John Ruskin, in his *Elements of English Prosody*, notes that while four-beat lines in English naturally accommodate both duple and triple rhythms, this is not true of the five-beat line. He describes a most notable phenomenon, significant of much more than I can at present understand — how much less explain; [...] the historical fact being quite indubitable and unalterable, that no poet has ever attempted to write pentameter in any foot but the iamb, and that the addition of another choreus to a choreic tetrameter — or of another dactyl to a dactylic one, will instantly make them prosaic and unreadable.[85]

Ruskin's sense of the incapacity of the English pentameter to accommodate 'any foot but the iamb' as a 'liberty of choice refused' appears significant when it comes to *Atalanta*. This suggests that in going against 'historical fact' and taste, Swinburne was attempting something very rare in English verse and, indeed, Attridge notes only two other examples, Browning's *Saul*, and 'one or two examples in Lawrence's *Rhyming Poems*'.[86] To Attridge's observation, I must add that this kind of line is not confined to the chorus, but reasserts itself at two later moments in *Atalanta*. Rarity alone cannot account for our sense of the oddness of this line. Indeed, both Ruskin and Attridge understand the rarity of triple five-beat lines in English to spring from deep phonological structures rather than custom, which suggests that the triple five-beat line might sound strange in any context.

Yet Swinburne's chorus proves far from 'unreadable' within the context of *Atalanta*. It is at this point that the different forms of attention that I began to explore in the last section come into play at a conscious level. At the same time that I feel the clarity of blank verse slipping away, the chorus begins to sing a chant that explores the idea of love as pain. Since it follows Althæa's speech to Meleager in which she counsels him against Atalanta, the chorus's connection of love with fate and death constitutes a warning. We might therefore expect a little more clarity in the delivery. However, the metre now snaps back towards the more rhythmically insistent four-beat line, like the sound of waters closing around one's head. And yet, for a brief moment, the triple five-beat line does achieve a counterpointing of these two previously opposite modes of attention. By allowing the more song-like triple rhythm, which we half associate with violence, to appear in the five-beat line, which we associate with speech and dialogue, Swinburne succeeds in producing a new expectation: that the two different metrical modes experienced might not be so incommensurable. Viewed retrospectively, the third choral ode can appear pivotal.

The strangeness of the triple pentameter is also felt in the answering chorus to this — the sixth choral ode beginning 'Not as with sundering of the Earth' (312–13) — in which the opposite movement from four-beat lines (on the model of 'Before the Beginning of Years'), to triple-pentameter, and back to blank verse occurs. If the third choral ode feels like the chorus's song was beginning to be heard for the first time before we slip back into the obscurities of song, the movement in the sixth ode from the insistent choral song, through the triple pentameter, towards Althæa's blank verse, feels a little like waking from a nightmare to discover oneself in a similar situation. In the next blank-verse speech Althæa will choose to become an instrument of fate and return to the fire the brand that will kill her son, since 'Fate's are we/ Yet fate is ours a breathing-space' (314). The tragic pattern in the universe which the chorus has for so long being singing of has, by the sixth choral ode, become a reality at the level of conscious action, which is to say: at the level of blank verse dialogue. However, there is a difference between our encounter with this 'unreadable metre' in the sixth ode and our previous encounter in the third choral ode, since by the time the reader encounters the sixth choral ode, the interweaving of metrical sets to produce moments of tension has succeeded in confirming a suspicion, already at work, about the role of the choral rhythm. In order to explore this perception, I want to consider two intervening moments of rhythmic tension: the fourth choral ode, and the Herald's description of Atalanta's success in the hunt.

The Fourth Choral Ode

The third choral ode awakens us to two possibilities. First, it causes us to rethink our previous expectation that the dialogue and chorus are marked by two different and discrete metrical sets. Second, it indicates that the content of the chorus's song, half-heard till now, is beginning to break through. In the intervening third episode the hunters prepare to leave. Althæa's brothers, Toxeus and Plexippus, debate the transgressiveness of Atalanta, joining them in pursuit of the boar ravaging Calydon — a charge to which she responds eloquently. Oeneus, Meleager's father, again plays the role of arbiter, and urges the hunters to depart 'In peace and reverence, each with blameless eye / Following his fate' (284). The fourth choral ode takes up where Oeneus leaves off, with a song that explores the origins and the dangers of speech. However, in a certain sense, to focus on the plot is to miss the main event. The metrical and rhythmical shift that we experience here from dialogue to choral song marks a radical departure from anything encountered previously in the play:

> Who hath given man speech? or who has set therein
> A thorn for peril and a snare for sin?
> For in the word his life is and his breath,
> And in the word his death,
> That madness and the infatuate heart may breed
> From the word's womb the deed
> And life bring one thing forth ere all pass by,
> Even one thing which is ours yet cannot die —
> Death. Hast thou seen him ever anywhere,
> Time's twin-born brother, imperishable as he
> Is perishable and plaintive, clothed with care
> And mutable as sand,
> But death is strong and full of blood and fair
> And perdurable and like a lord of land (284)

The first line of the choral ode contains six stressed syllables, three on either side of the caesura, promoting the expectation of a new line to the chorus's repertoire, perhaps composed of two four-beat lines, the last beat realised as a pause, strung together. Yet the slip-back experienced in the second, shorter line disappoints this. A third five-foot line troubles us, but is completed by a fourth shorter line again. The sense of disorientation as we move from a line with six stresses, to a line with four, then to five, then to three is underpinned by the couplet-rhyme, which forges a sense of similarity in difference and emphasises the see-sawing between short and long lines. The alternation between pentameter lines culminating in duple lines of shorter length continues for another couplet, before lines seven and eight, in which the full five-beat line is established. This receives tentative confirmation at the tenth line quoted, when the speech-like clarity of the question, 'Hast thou seen him ever anywhere?' affirms the reader's suspicion that this is duple, five-beat verse.

However, it is not until the tenth line quoted that the reader begins to realise that a reversal of expectations has taken place. Instead of the four-beat line, which had dominated the choral songs until the third choral ode, the fourth choral ode is delivered in five-beat. Yet the foregoing confusion, the to-ing and fro-ing between the full line and the hemistich, has also awoken us to the possibility that this five-beat line might contain within it shorter units. This is demonstrated by the syntactical construction of the ninth line quoted. Though the word 'Death' is metrically part of the ninth line, the unusual caesura, occurring after the first position, means that the question with which the next sentence begins gives the impression of an independent line, or a line of four stresses.

Attridge has suggested that the four-beat rhythm is sometimes experienced as a kind of 'sub-rhythm' in the pentameter. The technique of Swinburne's choral ode promotes that experience by shuttling between short and long lines, through syntax, but also by means of alliteration and monosyllabic diction. Though the tenth and eleventh lines quoted are indisputably pentametric in character, the combination of alliteration which, as we will see in 'The Triumph of Time', often coincides with stress, and the central caesura means that we read four stresses, two each on either side of the caesura, on 'time', 'broth-', '-per'sh-', 'he' / 'per'sh-', 'plain-', 'cloth-', 'care'. To experience the four-beat rhythm 'as a kind of sub-rhythm' is not in itself shocking. William Keach, writing of lines like this in Shelley, calls these 'expedient' lines — an example would be 'Speed in the van and blindness in the rear...' from *The Triumph of Life* — while Attridge dubs this occurrence of fewer than five stresses in a five-beat line in Pope's verse a 'sprung pentameter.'[87] Swinburne's blank verse exhibits this tendency from the opening *parode*. Yet within the context of the rhythmic schema of *Atalanta*, the disorientation that I feel on encountering it in the fourth choral ode is palpable. Pushed to discover why, I find two reasons.

Firstly, there is the shock of reading a choral ode in duple rhythm. Previously the choral odes were experienced as shift away from speech towards song. However, this ode witnesses the falling away of obscurity as the iambic line becomes gradually established. The moment at which this happens feels pivotal. Somewhere around the question 'Hast thou seen him ever anywhere?' I hear the chorus for the very first time, and their theme is terrible. Secondly, the way this line is constructed to recall the four-beat line within a five-beat line reminds me of the four-beat rhythm previously associated with choral song, and its undersong of violence. Previously the chorus spoke obscurely, and the rhythm which caused that obscurity reigned absolute. Now the chorus speaks clearly, and the rhythm associated with that obscurity appears as part of that song, as if we were able to step outside the embodied experience of the first choral ode and stare ourselves in the face. The veil of rhythm has been lifted; the undersong has broken through. Now we can finally hear it singing of the ceaseless cycle of the seasons, of inevitable violence, of the sorrow of death.

The critical metaphor of the four-beat line as an undersong is a useful one when trying to describe the reversal of expectations that the fourth choral ode presents. The separation of lyric and dramatic elements is no longer tenable. Instead the lyric rhythm appears to register in the pentameter, but in such a way and at such a point in the action as to suggest that it has always been there, hidden within even the most speech-like sections. This fact also registers in the experience of past commentators. This is the only ode that Lafourcade characterises as being comprised of 'iambes et anapestes' instead of 'anapestes et iambes'.[88] Saintsbury calls this fourth choral section 'a "greater Ode" of the best and most serious kind' (336). Though his appeal to the English Pindaric, an ode characterised by eccentric changes and switch-backs in metre and rhyme scheme, is apt, Saintsbury's description of this ode as 'mainly iambic' requires expansion. Though it does display a great number of duple, five-beat lines, Swinburne's poem is so resolutely various that at times the experience of the sub-rhythm within the pentameter holds sway long enough to seem almost established. This experience of a more rhythmically insistent, fundamental rhythm erupting within the pentameter — the line that comes closest to everyday speech — would be powerfully effective in any setting. However, it is especially so within the cumulative, symphonic schema of *Atalanta,* a fact that is demonstrated by one of the most charged moments in the poem.

Rhythmic Anagnorisis

However they choose to account for the significance of *Atalanta*, readers and critics have always found that the line which rails against 'the supreme evil, God' a particularly forceful moment. Yet, as I have suggested, the force of this line cannot be explained with reference to the theological argument alone. Instead the associational attributes that have been allowed to build up, combined with the fact that I am able to hear the chorus's song loud and clear for the first time, mean that I am primed to interpret this line in a particular way:

> For now we know not of them; but one saith
> The gods are gracious, praising God; and one,
> When hast thou seen? or hast thou felt his breath
> Touch, nor consume thine eyelids as the sun,
> Nor fill thee to the lips with fiery death?
> None hath beheld him, none
> Seen above other gods and shapes of things,
> Swift without feet and flying without wings,
> Intolerable, not clad with death or life,
> Insatiable, not known of night or day,
> The lord of love and loathing and of strife
> Who gives a star and takes a sun away;
> Who shapes the soul, and makes her a barren wife
> To the earthly body and grievous growth of clay;

> Who turns the large limbs to a little flame
> And binds the great sea with a little sand;
> Who makes desire, and slays desire with shame;
> Who shakes the heaven as ashes in his hand;
> Who, seeing the light and shadow for the same,
> Bids day waste night as fire devours a brand,
> Smites without sword, and scourges without rod;
> The supreme evil, God. (287)

Up until now this choral ode has shown a high incidence of lines containing fewer than five stresses. The re-establishment of five beats per line at the beginning of this strophe is therefore somewhat unusual. However, this strophe proves very much more than a metrical exercise: at 'Swift without feet...' I am again tipped into a line in which only four stresses sound. For ten lines we hear the chorus denouncing the cruelty of the gods, but although we know this is supposed to be a five-beat line (a pattern which reasserts itself around the line 'The lord of love...'), the frequent compulsion to perform only four stresses per line pushes the pentameter a long way towards song rhythm. This pull towards four stresses is partly enforced by the syntax and repetition. 'Who gives a star and takes a sun away;' is a pentameter, but its monosyllabic character, and the repetition of the syntax in the lines which precede it, asks that we attend to those objects in the utterance which the gods control, emphasising the verb and the direct object, which number four.

It is as if I am half choosing, half giving way to, the 'underlying' four-beat rhythm that we associate with the choral song. My sense of a gathering tension peaks at the line 'Smites without sword, and scourges without rod' which is syntactically and alliteratively arranged so as to tip us towards the utterance of four, and not five, stresses. This in itself would not be enough to suggest the impulsive, dancing measure associated with the first choral ode — there are many lines in this ode which sound nothing like 'When the hounds of spring are on winter's traces'. However, Swinburne was not called a 'prosodist magician' by Saintsbury for nothing.

Here, in the penultimate line 'Smites without sword, and scourges without rod', by means of an expert arrangement set in motion by the strong syllable falling on the verb in the first position, and encouraged by the central caesura, Swinburne is able to create two runs of two or more unstressed syllables. The result is a line containing four stresses again, but with a distinct swing to it, which we can trace to the recurrence of two or more unstressed syllables at the beginning of these lines. This line is still recognisable as a line of iambic pentameter. Yet, read within the context of Swinburne's play, it appears as if this pentameter has been overtaken by the song-measure of the chorus.

This rising penultimate line speeds the reader up and over the line break and rises, via two unstressed syllables, moving towards the first beat — sounded on '-preme' — here seeming to introduce the triple rhythm; yet this is cut short, swiftly and dramatically, by the downward shift into a duple rhythm, brought about by the first stress on 'ev-'. We see again here the impossibility of accounting for Swinburne's line in the terms that classical scansion has left us: this 'trochee' next metamorphoses into an 'iamb' at the mid-point, the last ictus finally falling to terminate the couplet in an emphatic rhythmical upthrust, underpinned by the termination of the couplet rhyme: 'The supreme evil, God'. Saintsbury was right to note how 'the poet actually keeps the three balls of iambic, trochaic, and anapaestic rhythm in the air all at the same time' (Saintsbury, 347) — yet, Saintsbury, when he made this admiring comment, was referring to the *karole* of the chorus. Here, the line shifts from rhythmical lilt, into crystal clear, emphatic, duple verse, right at the moment at which the chorus identify the cause of the tragic action. To call this hemistich in the fourth choral ode a flourish would be an understatement: rhythmically, this is one of the most metrically tense moments in the entire play.

The effect of this concurrence of expectations, associations, and of sheer technical finesse is a curious one. What we appear to be undergoing here is a kind of rhythmic *anagnorisis*. The painful truth of the matter — the futility of prayer against the whims of the gods — is explicable without the rhythmic schema of the play, while simultaneously appearing to gain everything from it. From this point on the experience of speed, and of lines with fewer than five stresses– song-like, daydream-inducing, jubilantly violent — will be connected with the will of the unjust gods. And yet, since this painful revelation is entirely dependent upon the build-up and confirmation of previous rhythmic expectations and associations, the line confirms something I have suspected all along.

Nietzsche, in his discussion of the dithyramb, speaks of an analogous moment in Greek tragedy in which the 'living wall' of the chorus is broken down through the stimulation of the 'symbolic faculties', through movement, dance and rhythm:

> In order to grasp this complete unleashing of all symbolic forces, man must already have reached that height of self-abandonment which seeks to express itself symbolically through those forces: so the dithyrambic servant of Dionysus will only be understood by those like him! With what astonishment the Apollonian Greek must have regarded him! With an astonishment which was all the greater for being accompanied by the horror that all this was really not so unfamiliar to him after all, even that his Apollonian consciousness did no more than cast a veil over this Dionysian world before him.[89]

Nietzsche's view of the role of the chorus comes very close to describing how Swinburne's rhythm is working here. Though we might disagree with Nietzsche's characterisation of metre as 'symbolic' (if so, scholarship should be able to offer an account of the symbolic meaning of certain metres, and this has so far proved impossible) this term indicates how rhythm depends, for its effectiveness, on recognition.[90] Yet Nietzsche's sense of the role that 'self-abandonment' might play in relation to such music is also an apt description of what feels so dangerous about Swinburne's chorus. Previously I had given myself over to the pleasure of the choral rhythms, without attending to the wisdom it contained. It is only in the fourth choral ode, when the Dionysian rhythm reappears, contained within the Apollonian line, that are we able to understand both the force of that rhythm, and to hear for ourselves the wisdom of Silenus. This realisation is astonishing, searching, but also full of horror. For this hint of an irresistible force behind speech has been with us in *Atalanta* from the end of the first choral song.

'What do ye singing? what is this ye sing?' Following the first choral ode, the chorus respond to Althæa's question with a curious explanation: 'Flowers bring we, and pure lips that please the gods,/ And raiment meet for service: lest the day/ Turn sharp with all its honey on our lips' (251). The idea of speech as a sweet yet dangerous power is established early on in the play. The chorus's argument that libations and prayers might only provide a partial protection against future events is figured differently by Althæa first and Meleager, a little later, when watching the approach of Althæa's brothers:

> Speech too bears fruit, being worthy; and air blows down
> Things poisonous, and high-seated violences,
> And with charmed words and songs have men put out
> Wild evil, and the fire of tyrannies. (263)

Althæa here defends language and her brother Plexippus against Meleager's charge that he is 'fruitful' in hand but 'ignorant' in mouth. Notably, this passage is one of the few major alterations between extant manuscripts and publication. Althæa's response to Meleager originally ran:

> Speech too bears fruit, being sound; but who treads next
> I ask not, knowing, nor praise a woman born
> Unwomanlike, a loathing to the loves
> And loathing them and all desires of men.[91]

In the later, altered lines, the introduction of Atalanta in the procession of arriving hunters is cancelled and moved to a later moment in the dialogue. In the first version the reader is allowed to connect fruits of speech with 'who treads next' — Atalanta — with the debate concerning the distance between speaking and acting, willing and being able to do — the space, in other words, within which the gods consistently thwart the desires of humans. Evidently the power to speak and the power to act were part of a question that Swinburne was still pursuing in the penultimate stages of his composition. Curiously, in the later, published version the power of speech is given the greater weight. The alteration of 'sound' for 'worthy' also reflects on this poem's economy of words. It is this 'sharp lust of praise' that will eventually cause Althæa's brothers, shamed by the skill of a female huntress, to rob Atalanta of the spoils, thereby provoking Meleager to avenge her dishonour and bringing the tragedy to its sad conclusion. The poem hints that to speak is to make oneself vulnerable. This perhaps explains why the chorus's enquiry in the fourth choral ode into 'Who hath given men speech? Or who hath set therein/ A thorn for peril and a snare for sin?' concludes by recognising that as 'words divide and rend…/ […] silence is most noble till the end'.

Since it is within this ode that the violence which we half hear in the first choral ode becomes audible for the first time, such advice seems laudable. And yet it is revealed to have come too late. 'What new thing wolf-like lurks behind thy words?' — the chorus's question is put to the second messenger, who brings news that Meleager is dying, just at the moment when the deliverance of Calydon seemed assured. And yet, this figuration of speech merely confirms everything we have suspected about speech in this play: again and again the speech of characters is overtaken by forces beyond its control, just as the dialogue appears to be overtaken by an irresistible rhythm.

However at this moment in the fourth choral ode, at which what I have been calling a rhythmic *anagnorisis* occurs, the speakers in Swinburne's play are not yet aware of this. The reappearance of the four-stress line as a kind of microclimate within the pentameter at several later points in the poem therefore has the quality of irony. Alan P. Barr has recently discussed this aspect of *Atalanta in Calydon* in an article which investigates the play's 'classical sense of the pervasively, ineluctably ironic human condition'.[92] Barr's surprise that 'there has been stunningly little discussion of this pivotal, controlling element in the play' is both right and wrong, since it names the symptom of Swinburne's irony but not the cause. In order to demonstrate how this 'pivotal, controlling element' of Swinburne's rhythm works, I want to consider several later moments which show Swinburne's style at its most effective, beginning with this description of the hunt reported by the Herald:

> And seeing, he shuddered with sharp lust of praise
> Through all his limbs, and launched a double dart,
> And missed; for much desire divided him,
> Too hot of spirit and feebler than his will,
> That his hand failed, though fervent; and the shaft,
> Sundering the rushes, in a tamarisk stem
> Shook, and stuck fast; then all abode save one,
> The Arcadian Atalanta; from her side
> Sprang her hounds, labouring at the leash, and slipped,
> And plashed ear-deep with plunging feet; but she
> Saying, Speed it as I send it for thy sake,
> Goddess, drew bow and loosed, the sudden string
> Rang, and sprang inward, and the waterish air
> Hissed, and the moist plumes of the songless reeds
> Moved as a wave which the wind moves no more.
> But the boar heaved half out of ooze and slime
> His tense flank trembling round the barbèd wound,
> Hateful, and fiery with invasive eyes
> And bristling with intolerable hair
> Plunged, and the hounds clung, and green flowers and white
> Reddened and broke all round them where they came. (292–93)

'Sundering the rushes, in a tamarisk stem' marks a point of departure from the previous run of five stresses per line, reawakening certain rhythmic expectations. However, although the late caesura in the tenth line quoted makes the phrase 'And plashed ear-deep with plunging feet' sound like an independent line of just four stresses, the apparent eruption of the song rhythm within the pentameter line is not fully realised until the line 'Rang, and sprang inward, and the waterish air'. Here internal rhyme speeds the line, a velocity that tips our well-trained ear into recognising runs of two unstressed syllables, reminiscent of choral song. This rhythm begins to dominate around the line 'Moved as a wave which the wind moves no more', a line that is indisputably pentameter, yet which could be performed as having four stresses, each interspersed with intervals of two unstressed syllables, leading to the perception of something uncannily like similar to the insistent rhythm we encountered in the earlier choral songs.[93]

It appears that the song-rhythm has overcome the Herald's speech, bringing with it all the same associations of violence, suffering and death. And yet, since such associations are born of the tension between the apparent sub-rhythm and the metre, to allow this rhythm full sway would be to risk losing the metrical tension that accompanies the flight of Atalanta's arrow, and which makes it seem so willed. As if he knows this, Swinburne allows five stresses to sound at the line that describes 'His tense flank trembling round the barbèd wound'. The temporary confirmation of the design is, as the accent on 'barbèd' indicates, a tight-run thing and is only just achieved. However, it is enough to maintain tension. By returning to the base character of the line, Swinburne effectively belays the verse to leap magnificently forward, in a run of four four-stress lines which, combined with internal rhyme, speed us over the line breaks.[94] Of course, many blank verse poems contain lines with fewer than five stresses such as this. However, to combine several of these lines in which there are fewer than five stresses together, and to reinforce our perception of a four-stress character through syntax, so as to create a kind of micro-climate within the pentameter within which song-rhythm thrives, is unusual. A brief comparison with the passage in Arnold's '*Merope*' which describes the faked death of Ægyptus while hunting and which Swinburne must have had in mind when writing his hunt scene (note, for example, the use of some similar vocabulary, such as 'plunged'), will demonstrate Swinburne's stylistic achievement:

> We cheer'd him; but, that moment, from the copse
> By the lake-edge, broke the sharp cry of hounds;
> The prickers shouted that the stag was gone.
> We sprang upon our feet, we snatch'd our spears,
> We bounded down the swarded slope, we plunged
> Through the dense ilex-thickets to the dogs.
> Far in the woods ahead their music rang;
> And many times that morn we coursed in ring
> The forests round that belt Cyllenê's side;
> Till I, thrown out and tired, came to halt
> On that same spur where we had sate at morn.[95]

Though fluid and enjambed, Arnold's description has nothing like the powerful sense of movement I experience in Swinburne's verse, which stems from the tendency towards the sprung pentameter and triple rhythm. Unlike Arnold's duple rhythms, Swinburne's verse-paragraph terminates triumphantly, in a last line in which the temptation to stress 'where' — which would make the end of this line duple, realising each of the five beats,- is never felt. Oeneus's wish that each character depart 'Following his fate' is here proved true. There is an unshakeable sense that fate has been following Atalanta's arrow.

My sense that rhythm is working as a figure for fate receives further retrospective confirmation at several later points in the play. Althæa's declaration to the chorus that she has brought about the death of her son in revenge for her brothers — 'I did this and I say this and I die' — is a curiously double line: it might be performed by even alternation of stress across the syllables (duple rhythm), or it might take on a familiar rhythmical swing if one chooses to perform this line so as to stress the verbs. In the same way, the effect of the final *kommos*, which Nicolson likened to a symphony, is traceable to its stanza-form, which is based on the four-beat line, and comprises four two-beat lines rhyming *abab*. This is followed by a longer *b* line comprising two four-beat lines with an unrealised final offbeat run together, performed as six stressed syllables divided by a central caesura. A very similar stanza also occurs in Arnold's *Empedocles at Etna*. However, in the context of Swinburne's play, the four-beat nature of this stanza supports runs of unstressed syllables that add towards the by now notorious triple rhythm. While the *kommos* presents a last musical interlude, any unity that might be achieved by bringing the characters and the chorus into conformity through having them speak in a uniform stanza is plainly at odds with the sinister associations of this rhythm. Our pleasure is no longer unqualified. Instead, the *kommos* feels like a triumph of the triple rhythm, a veritable dance of death.

The Melodic Knot

From the time the second messenger arrives with news that Meleager is dying, and our sense of foreboding is confirmed, triple rhythm merely confirms our sense that this rhythm has come to mean ineluctable fate. Yet this phrase 'come to mean' seems inadequate to describe the curious immediacy of my encounter with Swinburne's tragedy. To suggest that rhythm and will might be close associates is to rationalise an aesthetic encounter — Kenneth Haynes's description of Swinburne's style as in some sense 'embodied' might be more apt. Yet it is, nonetheless, a connection that we are frequently led to make. In this sense Swinburne's rhythmic style succeeds in turning the expectation that Victorian poetry might argue for a new autonomous individualism on its head. As Matthew Campbell has shown, poetry was the 'strenuously argued medium' in this period, in which we encounter 'a concern with sounding a sense of self or character through the experience of that character's volitional abilities or failings.'[96] Though poets' working exploration of will was often ambivalent, what we encounter in Swinburne's verse is a long way from the 'multitude of autonomous individuals' (8) which Campbell identifies with Victorian liberalism. Instead, Swinburne's subtle manipulation of metrical set results in a different attitude to the will, one which emphasises, not responsibility and autonomy, but the total insufficiency of human action in the face of a cruel, indifferent and irresistible divine force.

Of course, the peculiar way in which Swinburne's rhythm asks us to attend to it has not escaped Swinburne's readers. Nicolson, as I have noted, suggests that it is 'by such perfection of technique [that] Swinburne is able from the first to create full emotional sympathy between himself and the reader', concluding that '*Atalanta* is an event in the mind'.[97] Bowra also comments on how Swinburne's 'instinctive flair taught him to look for those indefinable effects which lie behind meaning and beyond emotion in the essential and authentic delight which comes from inspired words'.[98] However, in the absence of any sustained analysis into Swinburne's style, the curious way in which rhythm functions in this play has been constrained to hunches and impressions.

Jerome McGann offers the fullest account of this aspect of Swinburne's style so far. In a recent article he suggests the importance of Baudelaire's 1861 article, 'Richard Wagner et Tannhäuser à Paris', for Swinburne's early development as a poet. Baudelaire sent Swinburne a presentation copy of this essay in 1863, partly in thanks for Swinburne's 1862 review in *The Spectator* of *Les Fleurs du Mal*. McGann notes how Baudelaire and Wagner

> stressed the importance of dramatic form (in particular the form of Greek drama), of mythic content, and of an inner musical structure based on the melodic transformation of key motifs. These ideas all emerge as major features of Swinburne's writings in the key works of late 1863 [...] [among these] *Atalanta in Calydon* is not only a pastiche Greek drama, its manuscript, as we shall see, connects itself to the Wagnerian prosodics of 'Anactoria'.[99]

McGann argues that 'Anactoria' was 'the first poem Swinburne consciously constructed on his new prosodic scheme'. However, when one reconsiders the extracts from Liszt's book on Wagner which Baudelaire quotes, these seem more relevant to a reading of *Atalanta* than to Swinburne's first mature attempt to write heroic couplets — though, as I shall show in a later chapter, the couplets of *Tristram of Lyonesse* are not un-Wagnerian:

> The spectator, forewarned and willing to forego *those unrelated passages which, cogged to each other along the thread of some plot, form the substance of our usual operas,* will find it strangely interesting to follow throughout three acts the profoundly studied, astonishingly skilful and poetically intelligible arrangement with which Wagner, *by means of several leading musical phrases,* has tightened the *melodic knot* which constitutes his whole drama. The turns that these phrases make, clinging to and intertwined with the words of the poem, create an effect that is deeply moving.[100]

> By this method, which complicates the facile enjoyment obtained by *a series of songs rarely related to each other,* he demands an unusual amount of attention from the audience; but at the same time he prepares more perfect emotions for those who know how to enjoy them. His melodies are, in a sense, *personifications of ideas;* their return signals the particular feelings which the words do not explicitly indicate [...] The important situations and characters are all described musically by a melody which becomes their constant symbol.[101]

These extracts, quoted and italicised by Baudelaire, are taken from Liszt's book on Wagner. However, they might have been written about *Atalanta*. Liszt's sense of the way in which Wagner's opera is driven by something other than character or plot, the 'strangely interesting' way in which rhythmic movements come to be associated with a theme or feeling, the construction of the play around this 'melodic knot', and the unusual amount of attention required to puzzle it out — all these aspects of Wagner's drama ring true of our experience of reading Swinburne.

Swinburne's copy of Baudelaire's essay, sold at auction in 1916 to Arthur Symons, is not now extant. However, were we able to show Swinburne underlining and commenting on these passages, it is unlikely that we would be any closer to proving that a causal link exists between Wagner's principle of musical construction and Swinburne's first attempt at a Greek tragedy in English. What remains most suggestive in McGann's account is the analogy it provides us with for thinking about what we might undergo when reading *Atalanta*. Baudelaire's description of the intensity of Wagner might contain all we need: 'Everything that is implied in the words: *will, desire, concentration, nervous intensity, explosion*, is felt and is sensed in his works'.[102]

Swinburne recognised a similar quality in the poets he most admired. In his essay on William Blake (1868) he famously rejected the idea that art must have a moral, arguing that:

> the shape or style of workmanship each artist is bound to look to, whether or no he may choose to trouble himself about the moral or other bearings of his work. This principle, *which makes the manner of doing a thing the essence of the thing done,* the purpose or result of it the accident, thus reversing the principle of moral or material duty, must inevitably expose art to the condemnation of the other party.[103]

The reader in search of an example to demonstrate this need look no further than the exode of *Atalanta*:

> Who shall contend with his lords
> Or cross them and do them wrong?
> Who shall bind them as with cords?
> Who shall tame them as with song?
> Who shall smite them as with swords?
> For the hands of their kingdom are strong. (333)

A four-beat line, we have learnt, can support many rhythms. Here the trip of the first two lines recalls all the associations attached to the triple rhythm, from choral song, to daydream, to will, to death-dance. In the lines that follow we switch rhythm, though the metrical set remains unchanged. For three lines, monosyllables, parallel syntax and anaphora build within the line to allow the duple rhythm, speech-like and clear, to offer a final warning — or is that a temptation? — to those who would resist the will of the gods. And yet the return of the triple rhythm in the last line of the play has more power than any moral — for it trips from the tongue in three triple skips. The 'principle' on which Swinburne's poem works is witnessed in this last line, in which the meaning of the music of poetry has come to exceed the meaning of words. Once we appreciate this we can begin to understand how profoundly powerful Swinburne's rhythmical gift was. No wonder, then, that Eliot would prefer to have this dangerous 'expression by sound' confined within the bounds of an intelligible meaning.

Atalanta, like Wagner's *Tannhäuser*, convinces us of the power of music to mean. In this way Swinburne's poem also achieves a reversal of the Socratic expectation which Nietzsche criticises in *The Birth of Tragedy*, that in order to be beautiful, a thing must be intelligible. It is in this sense that we should finally understand Saintsbury's understanding of *Atalanta* as a *renouveau* of English prosody. Saintsbury knew, better than anybody, how much English poetry needed *Atalanta*. Swinburne's poem might be judged as the first and last poem of its kind: in its heroic effort to move and think and feel through a genre fast becoming traditional it is truly untimely. Swinburne's experiments with the four-beat line, and particularly his development of triple rhythm as one of its potentials, did not end with *Atalanta* — we shall see a very different use of the *karole* form in 'The Triumph of Time'. But his rhythms were never again so innovative, nor his tension so carefully cumulative; the power of *Erechtheus*, his second attempt at a Greek play in English, is confined almost entirely to the choral odes. In pushing the affective capacities of rhythm and metre further, he also put the question that later generations would answer. It is impossible to understand how much Pound and Eliot owe to Swinburne, or indeed how impossible a poem like *The Waste Land* would be without *Atalanta*, without first understanding the lengths to which Swinburne pushed English poetry in his pursuit of the question: how can rhythm mean?

Notes to Chapter 1

1. Jerome McGann, 'Wagner, Baudelaire, Swinburne: Poetry in the Condition of Music', *Victorian Poetry*, 47,4 (2009), p. 619; see George Saintsbury, *A History of English Prosody from the Twelfth Century to the Present Day* (London: Macmillan, 1910). All subsequent references are to the page numbers of this edition and will be given in the text.
2. [A term still used, but becoming archaic [...] [for] the new season, spring.] *Dictionnaire de la langue française*, ed. Emile Littré (1872–1877) made searchable by the ARTFL Project, maintained by the University of Chicago <https://artfl-project.uchicago.edu/content/dictionnaires-dautrefois> [last accessed 25 April 2018].
3. Harold Nicolson, *Swinburne* (London: Macmillan, 1926), p. 86.
4. Marion Weir, *The Influence of Aeschylus and Euripides on the Structure and Content of Swinburne's Atalanta in Calydon and Erechtheus* (Ann Arbor, MI: George Wahr, 1920), *passim*; C. M. Bowra *The Romantic Imagination* (Oxford: Oxford University Press, 1961, repr. 1995), pp. 221–44; Alan P. Barr, 'The Irony of Swinburne's Atalanta in Calydon', *Victorian Poetry*, 51,1 (2013), 1–13.
5. Georges Lafourcade, *La Jeunesse de Swinburne (1837–1867)*, 2 vols (Paris: Les Belles Lettres, 1928) II, pp. 408–10.
6. Herbert Tucker, *Epic: Britain's Heroic Muse 1790–1910* (Oxford: Oxford University Press, 2008), p. 556.
7. Thomas L. Wymer, 'Swinburne's Tragic Vision in "Atalanta in Calydon"', *Victorian Poetry*, 9,1/2 (1971), p. 1.
8. Richard Mathews, 'Heart's Love and Heart's Division: The Quest for Unity in "Atalanta in Calydon"', in *Victorian Poetry*, 9, 1/2 (1971), p. 35.
9. Katie Paterson, '"Much Regrafted Pain": Schopenhauerian Love and the Fecundity of Pain in "Atalanta in Calydon"', *Victorian Poetry*, 47, 4 (2009), p. 717.
10. "Atalanta in Calydon", *The Spectator*, 15 April 1865, p. 16.
11. Samuel C. Chew, *Swinburne* (London: John Murray, 1929), p. 62.
12. Douglas Bush, *Mythology and the Romantic Tradition in English Poetry* (Cambridge, MA: Harvard University Press, 1937), p. 340.
13. Hargreaves, 'Swinburne's Greek Plays and God, "The Supreme Evil"' *Modern Language Notes*, 76 (1961), p. 607.
14. Jerome J. McGann, *Swinburne: an Experiment in Criticism* (Chicago: University of Chicago Press, 1972), p. 104.
15. More recently, McGann has described *Atalanta* as one of a number of poems that present a 'major shift' in Swinburne's work after reading Baudelaire's essay 'Richard Wagner et Tannhäuser à Paris' in 1863. However, though his exploration of Swinburne's ideas of 'harmony' in relation to those of Wagner remains suggestive, this essay is only tangentially concerned with *Atalanta*. See McGann, 'Wagner, Baudelaire, Swinburne: Poetry in the Condition of Music', 619–32.

16. Nicolson, *Swinburne*, pp. 91–92.
17. Chew, *Swinburne*, p. 59.
18. M. K. Louis, 'Wise Words and Wild Words: The Problem of Language in Swinburne's "Atalanta"', *Victorian Poetry* 25.1 (1987), p. 45; Mathews, 'Heart's Love and Heart's Division: The Quest for Unity in "Atalanta in Calydon"', *Victorian Poetry*, 9, 1/2 (Spring 1971), p. 46.
19. Orla Polten, 'Swinburne's *Atalanta in Calydon*: Prosody as Sublimation in Victorian 'Greek' tragedy', *Classical Receptions Journal* 9.3 (2017), 331–49.
20. Denys Harding, *Words into Rhythm: English Speech Rhythm in Verse and Prose* (Cambridge: Cambridge University Press, 1976), p. 41.
21. D. S. Carne-Ross, 'Jocasta's Divine Head' in D. S. Carne-Ross, *Classics and Translation: Essays*, ed. by Kenneth Haynes (Lewisburg: Bucknell University Press 2010), p. 40.
22. Kenneth Haynes, *English Literature and Ancient Languages* (New York: Oxford University Press, 2003), p. 167.
23. 'Richard Wagner et Tannhäuser à Paris', in *Baudelaire as a Literary Critic*, intro. and trans. by Lois Boe Hyslop and Francis E. Hyslop Jr. (University Park: Pennsylvania State University Press, 1964), p. 201.
24. Rikky Rooksby, *A. C. Swinburne: A Poet's Life* (Aldershot: Scolar, 1997), p. 111.
25. *The Letters of Algernon Charles Swinburne*, ed. Edmund Gosse and Thomas James Wise (London: Heinemann, 1918), I, pp. 30–31.
26. Bowra, *The Romantic Imagination*, p. 225.
27. Quoted in James I. Porter, *Nietzsche and the Philology of the Future* (Stanford: Stanford University Press, 2000), p. 28.
28. Richard Monckton Milnes [1st Baron Houghton], 'Atalanta in Calydon: a Tragedy', *Edinburgh Review*, July 1865, p. 205.
29. *The Swinburne Letters*, ed. Cecil Y. Lang (New Haven: Yale University Press, 1959–1962), p. 21.
30. William Rutland, *Swinburne: A Nineteenth-Century Hellene* (Oxford: B. Blackwell, 1931), p. 2.
31. Yisrael Levin, *Swinburne's Apollo: Myth, Faith and Victorian Spirituality* (Surrey: Ashgate, 2013), p. 133.
32. *Letters*, ed. by Gosse and Wise, I, p. 248.
33. Friedrich Nietzsche, *Untimely Meditations*, trans. by R. J. Hollingdale, ed. by Daniel Breazeale (Cambridge: Cambridge University Press, 1997), p. 60.
34. Porter, *Nietzsche and the Philology of the Future*, p. 10.
35. Derek Attridge, *The Rhythms of English Poetry* (London: Longman, 1982), pp. 72–74.
36. Ibid., p. 73.
37. A. C. Swinburne, *Undergraduate Papers; an Oxford Journal (1857–1858)*, ed. Thomas Hill Green, John Nichol, Algernon Charles Swinburne and others. Facsimile reproduction with an introduction by Francis Jacques Sypher (Delmar, NY.: Scholars' Facsimiles and Reprints, 1974), p. 175.
38. Matthew Arnold, *Complete Prose Works*, I, ed. R. H. Super, (Ann Arbor: University of Michigan Press, 1960–77)
39. A. C. Swinburne, *Undergraduate Papers*, p. 173.
40. A. C. Swinburne, 'Matthew Arnold's New Poems', *Essays and Studies* (London: Chatto & Windus, 1875), p. 162.
41. *Essays and Studies*, pp. 163–64.
42. Ibid., p. 164.
43. Unsigned Review, 'Atalanta in Calydon', *The Times*, 6 June 1865, p. 6.
44. Clyde K. Hyder, *Algernon Charles Swinburne: The Critical Heritage* (London: Routledge, 1995), p. 229.
45. Lafourcade, *La Jeunesse de Swinburne*, II, p. 408.
46. Ibid., II, p. 408.
47. Carne-Ross, *Classics and Translation*, p. 40.
48. Harding, *Words into Rhythm*, p. 41.
49. Polten, 'Swinburne's Atalanta in Calydon: Prosody as Sublimation in Victorian 'Greek' tragedy', 340. For Arnold's *kommos*, see *Poems of Matthew Arnold*, ed. by Kenneth Allott (London: Longman, 1965), pp. 159–72.

50. *History of English Prosody*, I, 158.
51. Commenting on the second chorus 'Before the Beginning of Years', Saintsbury appends a note in which he refutes the comments of a German prosodist: 'It is very interesting to find a critic like Dr Brandes complaining of "stiffness," "sameness," of too "classical" an effect, etc. [...] The fact is that there is a sort of loose sloppiness in the German or Germanised ear, which cannot understand elasticity combined with form' (*History of English Prosody*, III, p. 336).
52. See Derek Attridge, 'The Case for the English Dolnik: Or, How Not to Introduce Prosody', *Poetics Today*, 33,1 (2012), p. 7, and *passim*.
53. Douglas Oliver, *Poetry and Narrative in Performance* (Basingstoke: Macmillan, 1989), pp. 114–15.
54. Attridge, *Rhythms of English Poetry*, p. 143.
55. Ibid., p. 78; 153.
56. Ibid., p. 153
57. Ibid., p. 213.
58. *The Poems of Shelley*, ed. by Kelvin Everest and Geoffrey Matthews (Padstow: Longman, 2000), III, pp. 354–55, ll. 25–36.
59. Attridge, *Rhythms of English Poetry*, p. 82.
60. Ibid., p. 127.
61. Carne-Ross, *Classics and Translation*, p. 37.
62. Walter Savage Landor, *Poems, Dialogues in Verse and Epigrams*, I (London: J. M. Dent, 1892), p. 83.
63. Harding, *Words into Rhythm*, pp. 41–43.
64. *Poems of Matthew Arnold*, ed. by Kenneth Allott (London: Longman, 1965), p. 192, ll. 417–28.
65. Percy Bysshe Shelley, *Prometheus Unbound*, in *The Poems of Shelley*, ed. by Everest and Matthews, II, p. 617, ll. 89–92.
66. Attridge, *Rhythms of English Poetry*, p. 82.
67. John Milton, *Samson Agonistes, Complete Shorter Poems*, ed. John Carey (New York: Longman, 1971), pp. 368–69, ll. 293–99.
68. *Poems of Matthew Arnold*, ed. by Allott, pp. 410–11, ll. 425–33.
69. Unsigned Review, 'Atalanta in Calydon', *The Times*, 6 June 1865, p. 6.
70. J. Leicester Warren, 'Atalanta in Calydon', *Fortnightly Review*, May 15, 1865, p. 76.
71. Lafourcade, *La Jeunesse de Swinburne*, II, p. 412.
72. *Poems of Matthew Arnold*, ed. by Allott, p. 409, ll. 347–51.
73. Walter Savage Landor, *Poems, Dialogues in Verse and Epigrams*, I (London: Dent, 1892), p. 81, ll. 118–24.
74. Robert Browning, *The Agamemnon of Aeschylus* (London: Smith, Elder and Co., 1877), p. 152.
75. Ibid., pp. 23–24.
76. *Quoted in Edward Thomas*, (London: Secker, 1912), p. 23.
77. Bowra, *The Romantic Imagination*, p. 235.
78. *Thomas*, , p. 12.
79. William Empson, *Seven Types of Ambiguity* (London: Pimlico, 2004), p. 164.
80. My thanks are due to Alice Notley for directing my attention to this singular performance.
81. T. S. Eliot 'Swinburne as Poet', *The Sacred Wood* (New York: Methuen, 1921), p. 135.
82. I must here add that I remain unconvinced by Empson's far too commonsensical attempt to undo Eliot's criticism by identifying the objects to which Swinburne is supposedly referring: 'This pretends to be two elements of a list with their attributes muddled, but is in fact a mutual comparison between the waterclock and the tearbottle.' See Empson, *Seven Types of Ambiguity*, 164–65.
83. 'Swinburne as Poet', p. 133.
84. Attridge, *The Rhythms of English Poetry*, p. 101.
85. John Ruskin, *Elements of English Prosody* (Orpington: George Allen, 1880), p. 56.
86. Attridge, *The Rhythms of English Poetry*, p. 130.
87. See William Keach, *Shelley's Style* (New York and London: Methuen, 1984), p. 162; Attridge, *The Rhythms of English Poetry*, pp. 353–55.
88. Lafourcade, *La Jeunesse de Swinburne*, II, p. 409.

89. Friedrich Nietzsche, *The Birth of Tragedy*, trans. by Douglas Smith (Oxford: Oxford University Press, 2000), p. 26.
90. For an attempt to do so, which runs quickly into difficulties, see Chapter 9 of Attridge's *The Rhythms of English Poetry, passim*.
91. Lafourcade, *La Jeunesse de Swinburne*, II, p. 406.
92. Barr, 'The Irony of Swinburne's *Atalanta in Calydon*', *Victorian Poetry*, 51.1 (2013), p. 3.
93. Of course, one could also choose to place a secondary stress on the verb 'moves', yet the previous run of lines with four stresses, which is reinforced by parallel syntax, makes this less likely.
94. I cannot help but read four, not five stresses, in the line 'Plunged and the hounds clung and green flowers and white' — the fifth syllable is demoted next to 'hounds' for me, and realised in performance by a drop in pitch on 'clung'. Though this reading does not go against Tarlinskaia's evidence as regards the distribution of stress in monosyllabic lines (after nouns, autonomous verbs have the second highest metrical index in such cases: see her *English Verse*, pp. 66–70), this may disappoint those readers who would prefer to stress the tenacity of the hounds and, perhaps, fate, delaying the stress until the verb 'clung'.
95. *Poems of Matthew Arnold*, ed. by Allott, pp. 418–19, ll. 786–96.
96. Matthew Campbell, *Rhythm and Will in Victorian Poetry* (Cambridge: Cambridge University Press, 1999), pp. 4–5.
97. Nicolson, *Swinburne*, p. 92.
98. Bowra, *The Romantic Imagination*, p. 242.
99. Jerome McGann, 'Wagner, Baudelaire, Swinburne: Poetry in the Condition of Music', p. 626.
100. 'Richard Wagner et Tannhäuser à Paris, p. 217.
101. Ibid., p. 218.
102. Ibid., p. 223.
103. A. C. Swinburne, *William Blake: A Critical Essay* (London: John Camden Hotten, 1868), pp. 88–89.

CHAPTER 2

'Reverberate Words': Repetition in *Poems and Ballads*

The young man's problem is, *whether repetition is possible*.
CONSTANTINE CONSTANTIUS

'In a culture that has been resurrected on a false basis, one's relation to the cultural past is poisoned' — this is how Theodor Adorno, writing 'In Memory of Eichendorff', begins his description of a break in the continuity of historical consciousness.[1] For Adorno this rupture results in a choice: either one loves the past and laments the present, or one chooses to focus on the present to the extent that the past might have never existed. This polarisation of attitudes finds expression in two kinds of cultural consumer — the antiquarian and the modernist. However, Adorno does not limit his argument to the aesthetic realm. The same break that reduces taste to a function of distorted temporality also affects the person's experience. 'The rhythm of time has become distorted', Adorno argues:

> While the streets of philosophy are echoing with the metaphysics of time, time itself, once measured by the steady course of a person's life, has become alienated from human beings; this is probably why it is being discussed so feverishly' (p. 56).

This presents a radical departure from the usual paradox involved in talking about time, as summarised by St Augustine: 'Provided that no one asks me ["what, then, is time?"], I know. If I want to explain it to an enquirer, I do not know'.[2] Writing for a different society, Adorno makes the case for modernity as a temporal situation in which everybody asks and nobody knows.

It is the task of 'advanced consciousness' to correct this 'distortion', not by 'glossing over the breach' between past and present, but 'by wresting what is contemporary away from what is transient in the past and granting no tradition authority' (p. 56). It is because Joseph von Eichendorff 'resists such efforts' that Adorno is so interested in his poetry. Having identified in the poet's 'all too unbroken tones' a homesickness that registers this temporal 'distortion', his essay offers a description of Eichendorff's poetry which neither attacks nor defends it. Instead: 'rescuing Eichendorff from both friends and foes by understanding him is the opposite of a sullen apology' (p. 57).

Adorno's dismissal of Swinburne, whose 'remoteness from true musicality' he elsewhere connects with an 'indulgence' in 'incipient intentions' in musical language rather than a harnessing of them, is a missed opportunity for a reader dedicated to the question of how the crisis of modernity registers in art.[3] His description of Eichendorff's poetry as a 'rambling erotic utopia' bears an uncanny resemblance to Swinburne's *Poems and Ballads* (1866).[4] In particular, his sense that the poet cannot countenance 'any particular woman', since this would destroy the possibility of 'boundless fulfilment', puts one in mind of the uniform description of female figures in Swinburne's poetry and the longing that drives the valedictions, leave-takings and elegies that recur through his work. Of one of his more notorious female addressees, Alan Young-Bryant notes, perceptively, that: 'To say "Félise" is less an act of address than a ciphered invocation that calls forth charm or spell...' so much so that "Félise" is predominately a sound with particular acoustic properties, one that the poem calls "the sweetest name that ever love / grew weary of."[5] This expression of yearning in Eichendorff Adorno identifies as 'Romanticism at the threshold of modernity':

> It is genuinely anti-conservative: a renunciation of the aristocratic, a renunciation even of the dominion of one's own ego over one's psyche [...] His poetry is not subjectivistic in the way one tends to think of Romanticism as being [...] this poetry never knows where 'I' am, because the ego squanders itself on what it is whispering about (p. 65).

A similar renunciation of the ego runs throughout Swinburne's early dramatic poetry.[6] Rikky Rooksby argues that this 'need to worship and to achieve an ecstatic loss of self' was Swinburne's 'central emotional drive'.[7] However, even without what we know of Swinburne's near-death experiences from drowning, climbing Culver Cliff without ropes, or his continual attempt to lose himself first, as a child, through religious ecstasy and later, as an anti-theist, through alcohol, flagellation, and the recitation of poetry, to read *Poems and Ballads* is to encounter the speaking 'I' 'squandering' itself.[8]

A Strange Longing

Writing in 1916, the poet Arthur Symons recognised this desire and its symbol, drawing on their connection to evoke an encounter with Swinburne's poetry:

> Reading [...] Swinburne on a high rock around which the sea is washing, one is struck by the way in which these cadences, in their unending, ever-varying flow, seem to harmonise with the rhythm of the sea [...] A mean, or merely bookish, rhythm is rebuked by the sea, as a trivial or insincere thought is rebuked by the stars [...] the whole essence of Swinburne seems to be made by the rush and soft flowing impetus of the sea. The sea has passed into his blood like a passion and into his verse like a transfiguring element. It is actually the last word of many of his poems, and it is the first and last word of his poetry.[9]

Symons's description of the sea 'passing' through Swinburne, filling his verse suggests the achievement of self-annihilation. This prompts a half-fantasy around the recurrence of the word 'sea'. While the claim that this is the first and last word of his poetry is too large a claim, Symons's statement captures the way Swinburne's poetry becomes fixated on individual words — of which 'sea' is one — which he uses for their accumulative, almost symbolic, effect.[10] Each word that repeats falls anew. Yet each word that repeats falls again, like all previous waves, and like all waves to come. The sea, with its regular waves, its seasonal ebb and flow, seems the natural symbol for these two different yet connected modes of attention, just as the word 'tide' ('tyd' in Old English, also meaning 'time') appears to be the natural word for it.[11] Between these two forms of attention the present emerges. However, with repetition comes a risk — one often experienced when listening to the sea — of redundancy, *ennui*, trance-like states.

It seems unlikely that Symons was not aware of Swinburne's consistent use of this figure when describing poetic rhythm. Seeking for a way to explain his encounter with the second book of William Blake's *Milton* (1810–11), Swinburne searches first for poetic analogues, comparing this section with the 'symphony of flowers' in Tennyson's *Maud* (1855), before turning to consider the sea. This 'glorious passage', he argues,

> was not cast at random into the poem, but has also a 'soul' or meaning in it though the ways of seeing and understanding are somewhat too closely guarded by 'Og and Anak'. Heading it as an excerpt indeed one need hardly wish to see beyond the form or material figure. That 'innumerable dance' of tree and flower and herb is not unfit for comparison with the old ἀνήριθμον and γέλασμα of the waves of the sea.[12]

Swinburne's impression of the scene in the garden from *Maud* draws on several points of similarity between verse and the sea. The rhythmical regularity and lexical repetition (by which I mean repetition of individual words) seem an apt description of one of the most iterative passages in Tennyson's work — and beg the question of the limits of critical perception: the poem has hidden depths. His use of the Greek words ἀνήριθμον ('countless', 'without number'), and γέλασμα ('smiling', 'laughing'), alludes to the speech in Aeschylus's *Prometheus Bound*, in which the protagonist requests that all nature witness his suffering, and adds a further dimension.[13]

Here the antiquity and irrefutable presence of the ocean seems to act as an analogy for the tradition of poetry, which has, since Greek tragedy, sought to describe it: 'Sophocles long ago / Heard it on the Ægæan', Matthew Arnold writes in 'Dover Beach', 'we / Find also in the sound a thought'.[14] 'I have a strange longing for the great simple primeval things, such as the sea' writes Oscar Wilde, in one of the most Hellenistic passages of his curious christological letter *De Profundis*.[15] A similar longing is present throughout Swinburne's work, in poems as different in subject as 'Les Noyades' and 'On the Cliffs', and as chronologically distant as 'Anactoria' and *Tristram of Lyonesse*. Yet the desire is acute in Swinburne's case: this longing is not simply for the sea, but to lose oneself in union with that past time, to become one with the tradition that the sea represents. If this sounds suspiciously like the 'all too unbroken tones' that Adorno identifies in Eichendorff, this may be because their poetry registers — albeit in different languages, and in different ways — the temporal 'distortion' that Adorno's essay seeks to comprehend. Evidently Swinburne, like Eichendorff, is in need of further understanding.

Romanticism at the Threshold of Modernity

Swinburne is a poet given to repetition, and 'The Triumph of Time' is Swinburne's most repetitive poem. Between the forbidden valediction in the first mournful stanza — 'I will say no word that a man might say' — and the remaking of that resolution forty-seven verses later, in lines that again resolve on silence — 'Come life, come death, not a word be said' — this poem breaks without ceasing against the common-sense logic of saying things once. Instead the poem iterates, its recursive elements accumulating, shifting and shedding meaning.

Though this aspect of Swinburne's style has not gone unnoticed, critics have tended to narrativise repetition, rather than stay with it, moving quickly from the technique to explain a theme or world view. For example, Jerome McGann's study addresses repetition in relation to Swinburne's 'doublets', or tautological imagery, which he counts among 'Swinburne's most elementary techniques for suggesting the unity of existence, no matter what its transformations, which are always many'.[16] This tendency to interpret, rather than to follow the kinds of attention that repetition elicits, is also evident in Margaret K. Louis's interpretation of the repeated words 'time' and 'change' as an aspect of Swinburne's agnosticism. In 'The Triumph of Time' and 'The Garden of Proserpine' she argues: 'metaphors and images evolved, or dissolved, one into another; but this shifting surface was itself the focus of attention. It embodied an acute sense of transience; it evoked no unifying principle within the process of change.'[17] Locating the zenith of 'The Triumph of Time' in lines 257–88 since 'all of the recurrent images in the poem here reach their height and perfection of felicity', she argues that the poem 'descends steadily', ending in an involuntary celebration of change. While Louis's response is apt — this passage is rich in lexical and phonemic repetition — her thematic interpretation means that she does not stay to consider the development of recursive elements as they contribute towards the poem's crisis in the penultimate stanza. Catherine Maxwell likewise notes that 'love, time and transience are keynotes in *Poems and Ballads* that echo in a substantial number of the volume's sixty-two poems'. However, her discussion of recursivity remains thematic.[18].

Though Swinburne's repetitiveness has never been out of view, no critic has taken this as their point of departure. As Alan Young-Bryant argues: 'Swinburne has been taken to be so much a poet of frustrating obscurity and empty musicality that his techniques and purposes are often avoided for the sake of confirming the patently ostentatious.'[19] Yet as Symons's analogy between hearing Swinburne and hearing the sea suggests, this poem's repetitious technique is not just representative or symbolic, it is also something that we experience: a mode of attention.

John Hollander has written of the refrain:

> The dialectic of memory and anticipation enacted by the scheme of poetic refrain can become prominent when the scheme has become most fully troped, or, to put it another way, when the formal occasion of redeploying the conventional lyric device [...] enters the allegory of the poem's own making.[20]

His description captures the way in which all kinds of repetition in poetry, because they must be conspicuous in order to be recognised, lean towards self-reflexivity.

However, his subsequent description of how the reader is moved between *ennui* — a rap on the knuckles — and the question 'what does it mean this time?' does not quite capture the urgency that I encounter in Swinburne's most repetitive poetry. Take the following lines from 'The Triumph of Time':

> But who now on earth need care how I live?
> Have the high gods anything left to give,
> Save dust and laurels and gold and sand?
> Which gifts are goodly; but I will none.[21]

The four-beat rhythm is especially prominent in the third line quoted, in which the poet ticks off the stock stuff of poetic reward. Stock stuff indeed, because each of these words, with the exception of 'laurels', repeats a minimum of four times over the course of the poem. This grouping might be construed as arbitrary, were it not for the fact that all the objects listed are inert (laurels, as Petrarch thought, were traditionally believed to provide protection from lightning). Repetition here appears indistinguishable from a speaking consciousness which shrugs its shoulders, accepting the equivalence of all things. This is one reason why Swinburne's repetition exceeds the bounds of Hollander's definition. It is his adjective 'troped' that sits awkwardly here. For Hollander, it is as if the 'self-reflexivity' which repetition courts has come to stand in for the experience I have while reading, as if the dialectic between recognition and boredom which occurs when we encounter a repeating element only registers at the level of theme, topos and narrative. A better model for Swinburne's poem might be found in Eric Griffiths's advocacy of the 'dramatized lyric'. Here the link between literary style and thinking is understood as one of the genre's defining assumptions:

> the dramatized lyric presents imaginative activity as a form of conduct, so that, for example, literary conventions appear as answers to needs or impulses, and those values which might narrowly be thought 'aesthetic', such as prolongation of melody or spinning a yarn or vowel-music, resound in imagined contexts where they are judged as behaviour.[22]

It is this genre which allows Griffiths, writing about the question of personal immortality, in Tennyson's poetry to advance further thoughts on the difference between the 'conceptual hygiene' of some ways of doing philosophy, and 'realism about what and how people think':

> Desirable as timeless truths rid of contradiction are, an exclusive devotion to them may hinder right understanding of some styles people speak and think in — styles that answer to the contradictions of desire, and the thoughts desire prompts. We live in time and so we need the truths of time as well as timeless truths.[23]

This quiet manifesto for the importance of Victorian poetry seems especially pertinent to Swinburne's *Poems and Ballads*, in which the 'truths of time' involve a style of repetitive thinking which is always at risk of collapsing into *ennui*, even forgetfulness. To extend Hollander's insights on the refrain to Swinburne, it seems we must countenance, not a dialectic between boredom and the question 'what does it mean this time?', but a third possibility: redundancy — can it mean this time?

Swinburne's repetition presents a special case in the history of anglophone poetry. That this aspect of his style presents not just a 'truth in time', but also a truth of his time, is suggested once we compare it to earlier accounts of poetic repetition. Wordsworth's defence of repetition, in his appended note to 'The Thorn', proves significant as a point of comparison to which subsequent critics would return in attempting to account for the effects of Swinburne's verse:

> There is a numerous class of readers who imagine that the same words cannot be repeated without tautology: this is a great error: virtual tautology is much oftener produced by using different words when the meaning is exactly the same. Words, a Poet's words more particularly, ought to be weighed in the balance of feeling and not measured by the space which they occupy upon paper. For the Reader cannot be too often reminded that Poetry is passion: it is the history or science of feelings: now every man must know that an attempt is rarely made to communicate impassioned feelings without something of an accompanying consciousness of the inadequateness of our own powers, or the deficiencies of language. During such efforts there will be a craving in the mind, and as long as it is unsatisfied the Speaker will cling to the same words, or words of the same character.[24]

Swinburne's repeated non-valediction in 'The Triumph of Time' appears Wordsworthian to the letter. The grounds for poetic repetition — 'an accompanying consciousness of the inadequateness of our own powers, or the deficiencies of language' — might well serve as a summary of both the topos and the style of thinking of 'The Triumph of Time'. Yet Swinburne's peculiar stylisation of repetitive thinking is working out of a different time, and in different circumstances. While Wordsworth is prepared to contemplate 'inadequacies' and 'deficiencies' of consciousness, this experience lasts only 'as long as' the 'craving in the mind' remains. In Swinburne's poetry repetition manifests as a 'literary convention', resonating within an imaginative context in which its 'need' or 'impulse' remains unsatisfied:

> My thoughts are as dead things, wrecked and whirled
> Round and round in a gulf of the sea (p. 40)

Instead of Wordsworth's assumption that 'satisfaction' is a possibility, the speaker in 'The Triumph of Time' cannot foresee such an event. Stylistically, as well as thematically, the continuation of repetition bears witness to a break, one that calls to mind Nietzsche's analogy between the student's freedom from history and falling in love:

> All his valuations are altered and disvalued; there are so many things he is no longer capable of evaluating at all because he can hardly feel them anymore: he asks himself why he was for so long the fool of the phrases and opinions of others; he is amazed that his memory revolves unweariedly in a circle and yet is too weak and weary to take even a single leap out of this circle.[25]

It is in this sense that I think that we might understand Swinburne's poetry, in Adorno's phrase, as 'Romanticism at the threshold of modernity'. However, rather than concentrating on the narrative of leave-taking and longing which runs throughout *Poems and Ballads,* this chapter will attempt to grasp the singular quality of Swinburne's repetitive style, with a particular focus on 'The Triumph of Time'.

There is evidence that Swinburne thought of this poem as having a central or pivotal role in his collection. Shortly after the first edition of the book was withdrawn from circulation, Swinburne responded to William Michael Rossetti's suggestion that he reorder the poems for the later edition, a response which suggests that he had strong views about the order in which the collection is encountered:

> P. P. S I add a word or two to show that I have read and weighed what you say about my poems. I should not like to bracket 'Dolores' and the two following as you propose. I ought (if I did) to couple with them in front harness with 'The Triumph of Time' etc. as they express that state of feeling the reaction from which is expressed in 'Dolores'. Were I to rechristen these three as a trilogy, I should have to rename many earlier poems as acts in the same play.[26]

The 'two following poems' which Swinburne refers to here are 'The Garden of Proserpine' and 'Hesperia', poems that also explore the desire to be out of, or at one with all, time. Rossetti suggests that he make the thematic relation more explicit: 'labelling them as to entitle them (suppose) A Trilogy (or perhaps "The Passionate Trilogy" or "A Trilogy of Desire")' — a comment which has since become something of a sticking point for critics of Swinburne.[27] Despite being happy to acknowledge this connection in *Notes on Poems and Reviews*, Swinburne's decision not to reorder the poems asks us to consider how we read this collection.

Swinburne is a poet who thinks in terms of versions and re-versions, often returning to a theme or form at a later date. Consider his earlier attempt to tell the legend of Jaufré Rudel in 'The Death of Rudel', or the reuse of the 'Dolores' stanza to open *Songs before Sunrise*.[28] Within *Poems and Ballads* the poems 'In the Orchard', 'Félise', 'A Leave-Taking', 'Before Dawn' and 'Before Parting' might be considered versions of the *razo* — the Provençal term for narrative situation — of the failed valediction explored in 'The Triumph of Time'. Yet none of these poems has been consistently talked of as Swinburne's *cri de cœur*, nor prompted so much biographical speculation.[29] While critics have always been quick to note the thematic centrality of 'The Triumph of Time' to the collection's interest in desire for impossible things, none have recognised that much of the power of this poem has to do with its technical exemplarity. In a sense, it is the set-piece of the collection, and this is especially true in the case of his repetition.

Take the iteration of the word 'sweet'. Before we come to 'The Triumph of Time' the reader has already encountered the repetition of this word locally in the first twinned poems 'A Ballad of Life' and 'A Ballad of Death':

> I found in dreams a place of wind and flowers
> Full of sweet trees and colour of glad grass
> In midst whereof there was
> A lady clothed like summer with sweet hours... ('A Ballad of Life', I, 1)

> Then I behold, and lo on the other side
> My lady's likeness crowned and robed and dead.
> Sweet still, but now not red,
> Was the shut mouth whereby men lived and died.
> And sweet, but emptied of the blood's blue shade,
> The great curled eyelids that withheld her eyes.

> And sweet, but like spoilt gold,
> The weight of colour in her tresses weighed.
> And sweet, but as a vesture with new dyes,
> The body that was clothed with love of old. ('A Ballad of Death', I, 6)

In the first poem the word 'sweet' is used as an epithet to round all phenomena, whether hours or trees, into one dream-like, unified quality. By the time we reach the companion poem, 'sweet' has come to seem more suspect: decay has set in, and the iterated adjective, already made prominent by the speaker's riddling in the lines in between, is accompanied by a sequence of qualifying statements.

Yet this iterant 'sweet' will not stay still. Having recognised the comparative role played by the repeated word 'sweet' across both poems, the reader now has cause to recognise the capacity of repetition to facilitate complex ideas, as 'sweet' moves between epithet to being an abstract quality in 'Laus Veneris':

> Let me think yet a little; I do know
> These things were sweet, but sweet such years ago,
> Their savour is all turned now into tears (I, p. 19)
> I think now, as the heavy hours decease
> One after one, and bitter thoughts increase
> One upon one, of all sweet finished things; (I, p. 21)

In the first stanza quoted repetition of 'sweet' in two half-clauses on either side of a caesura works to enforce a contrast between now and 'years ago'. In the second stanza, which occurs towards the end of the poem, 'sweet' no longer appears to be playing a comparative role, but has actually become representative of a class of experiences which exist in the past — here courtly romance, passionate emotional and physical love.

When the reader next encounters this word — if they notice it at all — they may be struck by the only use of 'sweet' which does not appear to act as an iterant in the collection. In the dramatic monologue 'Phaedra' the temporary relief provided by Swinburne's unornamented blank verse and the lack of repetition mean that 'sweet' feels less insistent:

> He will have nought of altar and altar-song
> And from him only of all Lords in heaven
> Persuasion turns a sweet averted mouth (I, 30)

However, the potential of repeated elements to play a role in generating meaning which exceeds the word's local and situated use is, by the time the reader turns to 'The Triumph of Time', a foregone conclusion. If the reader already feels led to read in a certain way, 'The Triumph of Time' presents the reader's apprenticeship in this form of attention. This way of attending might not be so familiar nor so effective were the poem to be encountered earlier or later in the collection, and may be one reason behind Swinburne's decision not to follow William Michael Rossetti's advice.

Repetition in the Triumph Stanza

Yet what is it about 'The Triumph of Time' that makes it seem so exemplary of Swinburne's iterative style? Its topic and its position within *Poems and Ballads* cannot entirely account for its apparent centrality. One aspect that critics have not yet fully explored is the way in which the poem's stanza form actually invites repetition. Consider the second stanza in which the speaker continues his or her initial refusal to say goodbye to the beloved and which is fairly typical in structure:

> Is it worth a tear, is it worth an hour,
>   To think of things that are well outworn?
> Of fruitless husk and fugitive flower,
>   The dream foregone and the deed forborne?
> Though joy be done with and grief be vain,
> Time shall not sever us wholly in twain;
> Earth is not spoilt for a single shower;
>   But the rain has ruined the ungrown corn. (I, p. 34)

Saintsbury describes how 'the intricate and massive stanza of "The Triumph of Time" swells and swings like a wave'.[30] At first this stanza form appears to defeat all metrical analysis. The line does not keep to a particular number of syllables, which range from eight to twelve, and the alternate masculine and feminine endings leave one undecided as to whether the rhythm of the poem is rising or falling. This malaise is at odds with the experience of an extremely regular, compelling rhythm, which proves relatively easy to perform and maintain — in fact, it is almost too easy, because it is almost too repetitive. Trusting to my ears, I acknowledge the regular presence of four strong beats, which can be interspersed with one to two unstressed syllables. Though it is still possible to carve these units up and argue for iambs, trochees or anapaests, I think we are once again dealing with the English *dol'nik* — that four-beat line with a flexible number of unstressed syllables (between one and two) between stressed syllables which we encountered in the chorus of *Atalanta*. However, this version is quite different: the regular alternation of 'masculine' and 'feminine' end-rhymes means that the rhythm alternates between falling and rising on a line-by-line basis — one can see here why both Saintsbury and Symons likened this rhythm to the rising and falling of the tide — and the poem appears much slower than 'When the Hounds of Spring Are on Winter's Traces'.

Might this perceived lack of speed in the Triumph stanza have something to do with the poem's repetition? In addition to the incantatory quality which Saintsbury hints at, the most tangible opportunity allowed by the four-stress *dol'nik* is the division of the line into two halves. This medial break can take the form of a caesura or a conjunction — in fact the difference does not often register, as the precise meaning of the conjunctions become blunted by the repetition of the break. This medial divide allows for parallelism between separate halves of the line, producing a close interaction between syntax and rhythm. Working with four nodes in the rhythm and allowing these to infiltrate or be infiltrated by the poem's grammar means that Swinburne's stanza encourages a mode of attention in which the reader looks for repetition or difference between syntagms on either side of a medial break. In the first line quoted above, for example, the repetition of 'worth' in the same syntactic and rhythmical position on both sides of the line enforces a connection between 'tear' and 'hour', the equivalence of which betrays the lover's despair as beyond measurable: neither water shed, nor minutes counted, will equate to his loss. Though there is no medial break in the second line which completes this clause, the habit of mind remains, enforcing an even closer sense of the equivalence between 'things' — a euphemism, if ever there was one — and the adjective 'outworn'. Though parallelism is sometimes interrupted by individual lines that do not divide into two halves — a variation that explains the jolt experienced when, around line 41, the stanza form opens its arms to enjambment, making us realise, retrospectively, the high coincidence of line-end and grammatical unit in this poem — this stanza's capacity to stage comparison between and across lines is high.

The trace-like effect of 'The Triumph of Time' results from the poem's particular structure — a fact suggested by the fact that we do not encounter the same level of iteration in other poems written on the same theme, which also make use of lexical repetition. 'In The Orchard', surtitled 'Provençal burden', is much more explicit than *The Triumph* about its links to old French poetry and the topos of unhappy love. However, though it makes use of parallelism and repetition, it does not require quite the same effort to attend to repeated elements, or bait a knowledge of their gradually accruing significance:

> Nay, I will sleep then only; nay, but go.
> Ah sweet, too sweet to me, my sweet,
> I know Love, sleep, and death go to the sweet same tune;
> Hold my hair fast, and kiss me through it so.
> Ah God, ah God, that day should be so soon. (I, p. 103)

This poem varies in line lengths, but it is largely in five-beat, without the strong four-beat pull or the medial caesura. For example, the third line quoted above is surely extra-metrical. As a result, the stanza lacks the accretion of iteration, and the play of substitutions which we encounter in 'The Triumph of Time'. By the time we reach the last stanza 'sweet' has come to hold a rhetorical importance in the argument as to whether it is sweeter to experience love upon earth, or to die virtuously in the hope of experiencing heavenly sweetness. However, it never attains to the kind of autonomy which recursive words gain in 'The Triumph of Time'. This is also true of 'Erotion' (I, p. 132), where the recurrence of 'sweet' has, by the end of the poem, not an iterative significance, but continues to play a more straightforwardly comparative role. We tend to read instances of syntactical repetition in 'In The Orchard' less as parallelism, than as forming subsequent and separate units. For example, take the line which describes how Love acts 'dividing my delight and my desire...' and consider it against a similar repetition of the pivotal word 'my' in 'The Triumph of Time':

> Love, till dawn sunder night from day with fire,
> Dividing my delight and my desire, [...] (I, p. 103)

> I shall go my ways, tread out my measure,
> Fill the days of my daily breath [...] (I, p. 46)

In 'The Triumph of Time' the habit of mind which seeks to create multiple referents for things will read the line 'I shall go my ways, tread out my measure' as drawing a comparison between treading and going, between the 'ways' of the speaker and his limitations or 'measure'. In 'In The Orchard' this analogizing habit is not present, hence 'my delight' and 'my desire' are read as subsequent, non-synonymous units, which are related, but by the syntax of the sentence as it unfolds, rather than parallel structures.

Unusually for Swinburne, end-rhyme in 'The Triumph of Time' is probably the least prevalent of all of Swinburne's techniques for enforcing extra-semantic links between words. Throughout the poem syntactical repetition — by turns *anaphora*, *epistrophe* and *symploce* — adds to create a general feeling that each phrase is in some way related to each other. This can be exploited locally, as at lines 148–52 which underline the conditional past in a hyperbolic statement of grief and longing:

> Not time, that sayeth and gainsayeth,
> Nor all strong things had severed us then;
> Not wrath of gods, nor wisdom of men,
> Not all things earthly, nor all divine,
> Nor joy nor sorrow, nor life nor death. (pp. 38–39)

Here the repetition of the negative, re-repeated in the last three lines when it comes to be repeated after the caesura, succeeds in rounding all the adversaries of the lover and beloved into a single if only. The effect may be local, but the building texture of Swinburne's parallelism also has general consequences for the reader's attention.

That this tendency for iterated elements to accrue significance is a particular capacity of the four-beat Triumph stanza is further suggested by comparison with one possible ancestor of the 'Triumph' stanza, Jaufré Rudel's '*Pro ai del chan essenhadors*'. While Swinburne's interest in the legend of the troubadour poet is attested by his early poems 'The Death of Rudel' and 'The Golden House', which predate 'The Triumph of Time', the precise extent of Swinburne's familiarity with the songs of Rudel is uncertain. However, it is no large stretch of the imagination to think that he might have come across Rudel's work while reading in the library of his uncle, the Earl of Ashburnham, who had a considerable collection of antiquarian books and manuscripts in a variety of European languages.[31] Swinburne claimed to be familiar enough with the influence of medieval French literature on Chaucer to speak on this topic in public. His critical writing also suggests a working knowledge of French poetry of the Albigensian period:

> Pro ai del chan essenhadors
> En torn mi *et* esenhairitz:
> Pratz e vergiers, albres e flors
> Voutas d'auzelhs e lays e critz,
> Per lo dous termini suau;
> Qu'en un petit de joy m'estau
> Don nuhls deportz no *m* pot jauzir
> Tan cum solatz d'amor valen.

[I have masculine indicators (teachers) of song / around me and feminine indicators (teachers): / fields and bowers, trees and flowers, / songs of birds and lays and cries, / throughout the sweet, soft season, / wherein I find myself with little joy;/ and from this no pleasure can make me rejoice / so much as solace from worthy love.][32]

Rudel's song is built on syntactical parallelism around a medial break, often using anaphora or conjunctions between lines to forge contrast, repeating words in a rhetorical gesture known as *amplificatio* — what I am calling lexical repetition — that expands upon a theme. The stanzas unfold like a set of gestures which we experience again and again, yet differently each time. Phonemic and lexical repetitions run in parallel with syntactic units, so that the reader is led to attend not only to the syntax of his verse, but also of his syntagms. These often coincide with points of rhythmical stress, meaning that emphasis falls on the repeating or replacing elements of speech. The rhyme scheme here folds a couplet in the latter half of the stanza into the fifth and sixth lines in what Dante called *bacciata* or 'kissed' rhyme, in a series of otherwise alternating rhymes: *ababccde*.[33] So far, the stanza works in a similar way to Swinburne's 'Triumph' stanza. Yet Swinburne's innovation is to take the rhyme-repetition one stage further, choosing not to introduce a fourth *d* rhyme to the poem, but to repeat the *ab* alternation after the couplet: *ababccab*, taking us back to the beginning of the stanza, as if the compulsion to repeat proved irresistible. From this arrangement all his other effects come and to it all things return.

Though critics have often noted Swinburne's recursivity, none have taken this as their point of departure, perhaps with good reason. Repetition requires that we bring past experience to bear on the present, yet is always threatening to fall into redundancy. It is a way of knowing which is highly personal, temporal and contingent. It cannot be codified or made to stand still. Yet it also, by risking redundancy, puts that knowledge at risk. Since repetition has meaning in a way which is not dependent on the semantic significance of the word being repeated, it challenges and exceeds semantic meaning. It consistently transports us beyond the narrative situation into the grey area of meaning which is the proper domain of poetics and prosody. It is difficult. Yet such difficulties also offer the opportunity to consider what is unique and even valuable about Swinburne's verse.

Hunting the Same Word To Death

T. S. Eliot's observation in his 1920 essay 'Swinburne as Poet' that it seems impossible to criticise Swinburne because our 'words of condemnation' are the same words that express his 'qualities' is especially true of his tendency to repeat: some of the fullest engagements with this aspect of Swinburne's style come from his detractors.[34] It is worth considering these previous encounters with *Poems and Ballads* at some length, because of the clues they offer as to the nature of Swinburne's repetition, now unacceptable in the contemporary repertoire, except perhaps in the anaphoric protest song. Among the more sophisticated objections to *Poems and Ballads*, John Morley, writing in the *Saturday Review*, suspects a 'trick' in this 'hunting of letters

[...] of the same word to death', leading him to conclude that

> of enlarged meditation, the note of the highest poetry there is not a trace, and there are too many signs that Mr. Swinburne is without any faculty in that direction. Never have such bountifulness of imagination, such mastery of the music of verse, been yoked with such thinness of contemplation and such poverty of genuinely impassioned thought.[35]

While the metaphor of 'hunting' might suggest *Atalanta in Calydon*, Morley's description aptly captures the mode of attention created by Swinburne's repetitiveness. Having entered a zone of recurring words, the reader's ears are pricked. Connecting alliteration with repetition, Morley draws attention to the all-encompassing reach of Swinburne's iteration, which also operates at the phonemic level in the frequent use of alliteration and assonance. Yet despite its pervasiveness, repetition is held to be inadequate to 'contemplation'. While it may pass as a kind of verbal music, Swinburne's collection fails to meet Morley's more Wordsworthian requirement of 'impassioned thought'. This connection between the repetitive style and an unhealthy mental state is a theme that recurs throughout the early critical reception of *Poems and Ballads*.

Henry Morley (no relation, but writing in the same vein) diagnosed Swinburne's 'repeated iteration' in the *London Review* as a strain of poetic blepharospasmodism: 'the effect of the incessant flash of eyelids has to our mind the effect of conversation with a man who is perpetually twitching and winking':

> There is the same indication of crudity in Mr. Swinburne's yet more eager enjoyment of the word bite. Smoke 'biting the eyelids' must have seemed a very fine phrase to him because there he contrived to set his two favourite words in juxtaposition. Of 'sweet' — 'sweet' — 'sweet', he has the iteration of a canary bird. There are 'sweets' enough in these two little volumes to set up a wholesale grocer for his lifetime. No matter. Our eyelids are not blind to the defects of these volumes, and we even recognise in many pages of them an artificial diction that is not poetry, but may be taken for it because it is not prose, a diction that sometimes breeds in Mr. Swinburne's verse obscurity in which there is neither depth of thought nor superficial beauty of expression.[36]

Unlike other critics who interpret repetition as a kind of poverty of linguistic resources or automatism, 'repeated iteration' suggests a repetition of a repetition, a willed compulsion.[37] Although Morley begins by taking this aspect of Swinburne's verse seriously, this only serves to increase the force of his rejection: repetition, understood as a kind of thinking, is not just a distraction from what the speaker is saying, it is also 'crude' and not even 'superficially beautiful'. The swipe about the poet's hawking of stockpiled verbal riches as a species of middle-class acquisitiveness is especially provocative. Yet it captures that supersaturation, a sense we have of being external to language, which we undergo when a word is repeated, leading us to rethink the economy implicit in the phrase 'verbal riches'. The idea that Swinburne's diction is 'artificial', and produces a kind of 'obscurity' inimical to 'deep thought', again presents the stylistic gesture of repetition as a disreputable form of thinking, or even un-thinking.

Even William Michael Rossetti, writing in defence of *Poems and Ballads*, found these poems 'too uneasily iterative'. Here he seeks to excuse Swinburne by means of a sick-note explaining the symptoms of poetic rapture:

> A minor form of this monotony is the frequent, and indeed continual, iteration of certain words, phrases, or images. Curious statistics might be compiled, out of Mr. Swinburne's four volumes, of the number of recurrences of the idea of fire, with its correlatives, fiery, flame, flaming etc. — of kissing, with its correlatives of lips, breasts, breast-flowers, stinging, bruising, biting, etc. — of wine, with spilling, draining, filling, pouring, etc. — of flowers, with flowery, flowering, bud, blossom, etc. (not very frequently the names of particular flowers [...] — of blood, with staining, tingling, bloody, red, crimson, dark, hot, etc. — of the sea, with images and epithets as inexhaustible as itself, and only less noble, for the sea-passion surges through the personal and poetic identity of Mr. Swinburne; and several other of these typical or verbal revenants might with ease be picked out for enumeration. This [...] would only deserve a passing glance from us, were not that particular detail, as we have intimated, a symptom of the comparative monotony of poetic excitation acting upon our author, — of his being somewhat unduly rapt in his own individual mental world, and not so open in sympathy (which lies at the root of most poetic debates) as to be freely and continually receptive, a fresh eye and mind to whatsoever of fresh appeals to either.[38]

Rossetti's treatment of Swinburne's 'repeated iteration' — the latter word recurs again and again in contemporary reviews — is qualified by the anxiety that it might be 'too *uneasily* iterative', a qualification which may give us cause to wonder whether this was an acceptable poetic technique here taken to the extreme. For William Michael, reading for repetition is not so much a case of hunting as of tracking, as his division of repeated words into genus and species indicates. That these groups are made up of 'epithets' that sum towards an 'idea' points to the curious way in which Swinburne's repetition often focuses, not on objects, but more abstract qualities. His description of recurring words as 'revenants' is especially provocative: it captures the haunting character of these words, their uncanny quality, returning from earlier usage within the poem, or beyond it, resulting in a strange sub-species of allusion. This critic's subsequent volte-face, in which repetition is described as a 'passing detail', is curious. Having opened the complex problem of the interrelation between the verbal construct and mind, and begun to consider what this might mean, his investigation is cut short by the conclusion that Swinburne's poetry is not solipsistic but rapt, though this argument did nothing to prevent subsequent readers — most famously T. S. Eliot — from coming to the former conclusion.[39]

I find a similar about-turn in one of our most modern poets' attempt to account for changes in the ambitions of the meditative poem from late Romantic to Victorian poetry. Though J. H. Prynne's early article does not mention Swinburne, repetition is central to its investigation of the relation between the poem and mind-state, in which what Prynne terms 'the meditative poem' is understood — like Griffiths's 'dramatized lyric' — as 'the image of an awareness in action'. Prynne argues for the subsequent failure of the meditative poem by considering the figure of Penelope in Wallace Stevens's poem 'The World as Meditation'. Made to stand for the 'elegiac' consciousness which Prynne also locates in Arnold and Tennyson, Penelope repeats her husband's name over and over, tremulously expectant, yet wilfully ignorant of the world going on without her. Prynne concludes: 'Like Penelope in Stevens's poem, the poet would hardly recognise a contingent event if he saw one, and least of all if he had been expecting it'. Repetition here signs a historical decline in poetic ambition, a 'force of circumstance', which he associates with the post-Wordsworthian generation:

> Meditative poetry at some point after Wordsworth's last contact with the Augustan tradition abandoned the ambition to present the reflecting mind as part of an experiential context and withdrew into a self-generating ambiance of regret [...] with this went an amazing degree of control over incantatory techniques.[40]

Having identified repetition and its associated techniques with the withdrawal of meditative poetry from the world, and recognised these procedures as a kind of thinking, this style is dismissed as too 'crass' and 'sentimental' — and certainly too apolitical — to serve as a model for twentieth-century poetic practice. Like Rossetti, Prynne's investigation stops short just before it begins to engage with the problem of repetition.[41]

If Prynne's gloss on Stevens's Penelope has a back history, one version of it might be the sense that Eliot and Pound have regarding the risk of redundancy that repetition always courts. Though both poets acknowledge the power of 'The Triumph of Time', Eliot and Pound sidestep recursivity, choosing to focus instead on one of its results: Swinburne's diction. As noted in my introduction, Pound claims that the 'word-selecting, word-castigating faculty was nearly absent' in Swinburne: 'Unusual and gorgeous words attracted him [...] he uses the same adjectives to depict either a woman or a sunset'.[42] The result of this poetic profile is 'verbal confusion', a phrase echoed in Eliot's sense that what we experience in Swinburne's poetry is a 'hallucination of meaning'.

However, when it comes to Swinburne's repetition, Eliot takes Pound's argument further, claiming that Swinburne prefers the 'general word' to the particular. Where Pound acknowledged the poet's revelling in the 'gorgeousness' of words, Eliot is less enthusiastic about the 'vague associations' which Swinburne allegedly hunts. Clearly what Rossetti called the 'fragrance [...] of classic reminiscence' — that allusive quality which we might experience when encountering a word such as 'tamarisk' or 'spikenard' — is no longer a valid element of poetic repertoire for Eliot. For Swinburne, he argues, it is the word and not the object that 'gives him the thrill', a phrase that betrays just as much about Eliot's own failure to be titillated as it does about Swinburne's style. However, for a poet who placed 'unrepeatability' at the centre of his theory of how individual writers orientate themselves with regard to tradition, this is hardly surprising (Eliot, *The Sacred Wood*, p. 44). It is no coincidence that the word which he lights upon to demonstrate the way in which Swinburne 'works the word's meaning (a wonderful description of one of the ways in which repetition functions) is the word 'weary' itself — not, as I suggest in my introduction, the most recognisably Swinburnean word (it is much more

Tennysonian to 'wax weary', in fact) — but one which captures Eliot's exhaustion with this technique.

The most sustained investigation into Swinburne's repetition is Veronica Forrest-Thomson's posthumously published essay 'Swinburne and Eliot: A Reconsideration'. This essay sets out to test the assumptions of Eliot's 1920 essay, meaning that she remains limited by the terms of his investigation. However, the contradictions that result prove revealing. In particular, her close attention to the 'snowball quality' of certain repeated words in 'The Triumph of Time' leads her to focus on repeated 'topic words', which she argues must be connected in line with the poem's 'theme', leading her to postulate two different kinds of 'meaning' in Swinburne's poem:

> The extreme condensation of 'Give thanks for life O brother, and death' is only possible to understand if the snowball quality of these words is noted. It sounds paradoxical but in the system of alliance and opposition the poem has built up life is not exclusive of death; they complete each other in a happy love. The line does not strike a discordant note, then, as it would if the poem were really diffuse; it is rather a climactic point for which the previous stanzas have been preparing.[43]

Forrest-Thomson moves from effect to cause, noting how the 'meaning' of words — which can no longer be 'known' or 'assumed' in advance — is transformed through repetition, building towards a point of intensity.[44] However, at this point a contradiction emerges. Since the richness of meaning which she identifies in her reading is achieved through sustained attention to those aspects of language that were earlier designated as 'non-meaningful', 'meaning' undergoes a kind of nervous collapse, as she is forced to recognise:

> The words whose meaning we must think about in greater precision perform a highlighting function opposite to that of the 'topic' words. While the latter indicate an attenuation of meaning and dominance of formal structuring requirements the former represent dominance of meaning. The opposition is not complete, however, for none of the words is meaningless and none is without its part in the formal pattern. (p. 64)

Forrest-Thomson's 'working' — to borrow Eliot's word — of the word 'meaning' captures the way in which Swinburne's verse can, paradoxically, seem most meaningful at the point at which words are almost meaningless. Yet this paradox only holds in so far as our concept of 'meaning' remains circumscribed within the Eliotean paradigm. Nothing in Eliot's phrase 'the hallucination of meaning', or Pound's sense of 'verbal confusion', proposes that Swinburne's poetry is entirely meaningless. It is simply that its procedures do not produce the kinds of effect that tally with their hopes and fears for poetry.

As with Prynne, Rossetti, Morley and Morley, at this point Forrest-Thomson's interest in Swinburne's repetition wanes and the investigation draws to a close. To reopen the question of Swinburne's poetry at the point where they broke off will require us rethink the 'hallucinatory' or 'confusing' effects of Swinburne's verse, beginning with the question as to how Swinburne's poetry courts these modes of attention. These previous readers have already given us some direction in their attention to phonemic and lexical repetition (this 'hunting of letters [...] of the same word to death'), collocation and the way that certain parts of speech appear to gain prominence (those 'epithets [...] inexhaustible'), parallelism ('the system of alliance and opposition the poem has built up') and allusion ('revenants'). To build on their insights will involve us in a more sustained investigation into the forms of attention which Swinburne's style courts, within the confines of this poem and in comparison to other poets.

Phonemic Repetition

Two side-effects — or perhaps we might later think of them as opportunities — of the *dol'nik* rhythm include the emphasis laid on prefixes, and the prevalence of repeated monosyllabic words. In Attridge's definition of the *dol'nik*, explored in Chapter 1, he notes how a word that would not usually receive stress on the first syllable can be made to bear one. This has a particular relevance for 'The Triumph of Time', in which the compound stems of words that describe processes are often allowed to take a stress: 'ungrown' l.16, 'unclean' l.44, 'unshed' l.215, 'undone' l.216, 'undo' l.235, 'unwound' l.282, 'unforgotten' l.316, 'foregone [...] forborne' l.13, 'forgotten' l.231, 'unforgotten' l.236. The emphasis on prefixes that indicate undoing and redoing emphasise the problem of repetition at a thematic or narrative level, while also contributing to the 'hallucinatory' or 'incantatory' effect of this poem.

A much less obvious consequence of the Triumph stanza is the opportunity it creates for the repetition of single, monosyllabic words. The flexibility which the *dol'nik* calls for in the number of unstressed syllables between beats is easily solved in composition by the use of short, monosyllabic words, often adjectives. Many of the repeated elements or 'topic words' that Forrest-Thomson identifies are monosyllabic, for example the adjectives 'sure', 'fast', 'one', 'sweet'; and the nouns 'time', 'change', 'love', 'life', 'death'. Swinburne turns this into an opportunity, 'working' the words so that they come to exceed their original rhythmical or epithetical function, a fact that explains Forrest-Thomson's sense of the grammatical oddities of Swinburne's verse:

> I do not mean that nouns and verbs are not stressed in Swinburne's poetry; most commonly they are the words which take the strongest metrical stress [...] [However] the fact of there being so many adjectives and prepositions and adverbs endemic to the construction of the stanza, rhythm, and metre makes us more aware of them than we normally are' (p. 62).

As we shall see, it is oddities in the grammar such as these which also help to explain the peculiar effects of words that repeat across the poem, such as 'sweet'.

The multiplication of links between words in 'The Triumph of Time' is, of course, encouraged by repetition at the phonemic level. Morley's sense of the way in which Swinburne 'hunts' letters is best corroborated in lines like these, in which even the strong presence of four stresses per line cannot keep us from stuttering:

> I wish we were dead together to-day,
> Lost sight of, hidden away out of sight,
> Clasped and clothed in the cloven clay, (p. 37)

This last line is particularly indicative of the verbal confusion or hallucinatory effects that Pound and Eliot detected. However, far from ornamenting the basic rhythmic structure, the interaction between rhythm and phoneme is dynamic. Through phonemic alliteration of 'cl-', teamed with assonance, we are pushed beyond the differential semantic meanings of what it is to be 'clasped' and 'clothed', or what it means to be 'cloven', to view these adverbs as much of a muchness of non-being. A similar effect is also discernible in Swinburne's placement of homoeleuetic words (words with similar endings) in parallel such as 'clamour' and 'rumour', and of words with a similar stem: 'foregone', 'forborne' — both of which refer to the lost object, 'the life to come', 'the dream' and 'the deed'. Sounding together, they add to create the impression of irrecoverable, all-consuming loss. In time this particular stylistic tendency pushes us to rethink the appropriateness of the term 'parallelism'. Rather than drawing attention to the process of analogising, what emerges when reading 'The Triumph of Time' is the impossibility of analogising, because of the interconnectedness, the possible equivalence of all things. Our sense that this 'verbal confusion' is not a fault, but a mode of attention, is confirmed by lines like these, which invite us to connect the style of the poem with a mode of thought:

> There is not room under all the sky
> For me that know not of worst or best,
> Dream or desire of the days before,
> Sweet things or bitterness, any more (p. 45)

When I go back and re-read those lines, I realise that the exploded synecdoche connecting 'room' and 'sky' has hardly registered. Instead, I have merely made a connection between 'room' and 'sky' as second and fourth syntagyms in the line, realising the second and fourth beats. And it goes on, in a seemingly endless list of fours, in which atonyms — 'worst' and 'best'; 'sweet things' and 'bitterness'; and synonyms — 'dream' and 'desire' — pass by in equal numbers towards the neat completion of the kissed couplet. I am not arguing that the grammar of Swinburne's verse has failed to function, or, as some critics would argue, that what is said is poorly expressed or does not make sense. Only that the structure of the four-by-four unit on which Swinburne's stanza is based, a unit which Attridge notes is self-reinforcing, asks us to attend to this pattern, in competition with semantic meaning, a pattern which maintains sway even in spite of the rare enjambment between the first and second line. It is the way in which this rhythmic pattern gets the upper hand over argument which contributes towards this 'hallucination' of meaning.[45] The fact that lexical repetition and, for that matter, parallelism can still register, despite the extent of this 'hallucination' is one of the remarkable things about this poem.

Parallelism

Laury Magnus argues that 'parallelism is a mode of constructing language so as to call attention to the very process of analogizing'.[46] This 'habit of mind', as James Kugel calls it in his study of biblical parallelism, is as old as poetry itself.[47] However, the peculiarity of Swinburne's contribution lies in the way his verse pushes us to analogise to such a degree that each word seems to reverberate on every other word, every line to echo another, each stanza to vibrate as if in tune with the others. Consider the opening of 'The Triumph of Time':

> Before our lives divide for ever,
> While time is with us and hands are free,
> (Time, swift to fasten and swift to sever
> Hand from hand, as we stand by the sea)   (I, p. 34)

In the first four lines the repetition of 'time' shifts from an everyday construction into a personification. The unfolding subject of the poem — time's triumph — is transfigured even before its first octave has come to a close. This is also the case with the two hands, which undergo the opposite transformation, moving from the general idea of freedom towards the two specific pairs of hands of the speaker and beloved immobilised on the strand. Despite the fact that the same words repeat, neither hands nor time are the same by the end of the four lines. However, this mode of attention, in which the same word acquires a set of gradually different meanings (*anastasis*) is met by an inverse form of attention, in which one is pushed to notice similitude between different words. Here the infinitive verbs 'to fasten' and 'to sever' become mediated by the pivotal adverb 'swift'. Though antonyms, the grammar of Swinburne's third line requires that the essential difference between both actions is blunted by the attenuation of the adverb. We can see here the seed of Forrest-Thomson's gathering sense that by a certain point in the poem, the word 'life' might come to achieve a kind of equivalence with 'death'.

This meaning is underpinned by the syntactical and metrical arrangement of the line, which means that 'fasten' and 'sever' are made to seem both metrically and syntactically interchangeable because of their position on either side of the conjunction 'and'. Syntactical repetition and difference, in which syntagms repeat or shift, also contribute to the effect of line 14: 'Time shall not sever us wholly in twain', in which 'time' comes back — stressed, and in prime position as at line 3 — once again with feeling, sounding a boldness and fluency not present at the third line. The phrase 'shall not sever' jumps into the same syntactical and metrical space previously occupied by 'swift to fasten' in an upsurge of feeling which has as much to do with the reader's sense that the line is a partial, formal revision as it has to do with what the line asserts. From the very beginning of the poem, therefore, Swinburne's repetition fosters an awareness of the links between words in ways that exceed, and in some cases disturb, the semantic meaning of the words in question.

My sense that this trait is peculiar to Swinburne's style, and to 'The Triumph of Time' in particular, receives further confirmation once I consider Swinburne's parallelism against that of his near-contemporary, Gerard Manley Hopkins. For Hopkins, as Maria Lichtmann notes, parallelism was 'the fundamental principle and controlling device of poetry':[48]

> In [...] Hebrew poetry, Hopkins found a way to unite verse's disparate effects so that sound correspondences of alliteration and rhyme work to create correspondences in word meanings. Those correspondences in turn create parallelism of thought in the reader's response to the poem.'[49]

There is a similar union of verse's disparate effects observable in Swinburne's parallelism, which, as I have suggested, often gains much from poetic stress and alliteration. Swinburne would, I think, have agreed to a certain extent with Hopkins as to the centrality of parallelism for poetry, though he might well have used another name for it: 'analogy':

> Of true analogy we may take two kinds as heads of the division: Poetic and Scientific analogy. To the first we may suppose that Metaphor & such like forms are separable; the perception of likeness & aptitude, of relation & community which give to poetry the powers of comprehension & exposition through which he becomes interpreter & prophet of things unapparent to ordinary men & this we may perhaps define as the special aim of poetry, to which the subordinate analogies of metaphor & rhythm serve as attendants; & rhyme itself thus assumes meaning & reason, if we accept it as a musical balance & relation of sound or responding to the analogy of sense expressed 'thro it; in short, as a material & outward analogy of words comprehensible by all as the type or countersign of an inward analogy of perception; which is in fact the use & explanation of Verse — so much for poetic analogy ...[50]

So much for poetic analogy! Swinburne's brevity in this unpublished undergraduate essay 'Of Analogy' — and his undergraduate essays are often brief — after such a breathless sentence is somewhat at odds with the claims that he makes for analogy as the basis of perception and the defining technique and purpose of poetry. However, where Swinburne's understanding of analogy differs from Hopkins's parallelism (as described by Lichtmann) is in the importance of the temporal order of verse. It is not the links between disparate things, the similarity in difference, which Hopkins identifies with the divine force pervading nature, but 'a musical balance & relation of sound' which Swinburne offers as his main example of analogy. In addition, unlike Lichtmann's stricter understanding of parallelism as a formal characteristic which may unite with other aspects of Hopkins's technique, for Swinburne poetic techniques such as rhyme and rhythm count *as* analogy. The crucial difference is that whereas for Hopkins, parallelism is conceptual, and involves thinking through a logical sequence, for Swinburne, analogy is also temporal — it need not depend upon a logical sequence, only the fact of contiguity. This is perhaps what Forrest-Thomson means when she argues that words, just as much as objects, constitute events in Swinburne's poetry. This finds its practical expression in the way in which Swinburne's verse seems to multiply the occasions for linking things, at the conscious level, through simile and metaphor, in his lexical repetition, and even in what Basil Bunting calls 'the thud of the ictus'.

Consider Swinburne's parallelism in the eleventh stanza of 'The Triumph of Time', which considers the natural decay of all things, against the second section of Hopkins's late sonnet 'That Nature is a Heraclitean Fire, and of the comfort of the Resurrection'. There 'Nature's bonfire', symbolic of all creation's paradoxically glorious decay, burns on:

> But quench her bonniest, dearest | to her, her clearest-selvèd spark
> Man, how fast his firedint, | his mark on mind, is gone!
> Both are in an unfathomable, all is in an enormous dark

> Drowned. O pity and indig | nation! Manshape, that shone
> Sheer off, disseveral, a star, | death blots black out; nor mark
>   Is any of him at all so stark
> But vastness blurs and time | beats level. Enough! the Resurrection,
> A heart's-clarion! Away grief's gasping, | joyless days, dejection.
>   Across my foundering deck shone
> A beacon, an eternal beam.[51]

> It is not much that a man can save
>   On the sands of life, in the straits of time,
> Who swims in sight of the great third wave
>   That never a swimmer shall cross or climb.
> Some waif washed up with the strays and spars
> That ebb-tide shows to the shore and the stars;
> Weed from the water, grass from a grave,
>   A broken blossom, a ruined rhyme.

We can see here just how much Swinburne's parallelism gains from the structure of his stanza. Though the parallelism is mainly felt in the last two lines quoted, the foregoing lines build towards it, as the grammatical structure 'a... and/ or b' is set up across the medial break from the second line quoted. Again the conjunction does not really matter; the emphasis is on the futility of issue, or belatedness, as the fruitless origin of 'weed [s]' from 'water' and 'grass' from a 'grave' suggest — images held in parallel and followed by the further image of a blossom that will not come to fruit, or a rhyme-word left hanging. However, here the sense of parallelism does not only arise from the logical sequence of these images, but from their succession in two-beat units, in which syntax and rhythm work together to give a sense of successive, parallel items. The parallelism works logically, but what draws them together are the phonic linkages, or, as the undergraduate Swinburne put it: 'musical balance & relation of sound'. A similar situation might also be detected operating in those much-debated lines from the chorus of *Atalanta* which describe how the creation of man involved 'Time, with a gift of tears;/ Grief, with a glass that ran ;' and which Eliot found so illogical.

   The fact that this situation does not arise in Hopkins can only partly be attributed to the fact that his sprung rhythm, and his ode, formed of competing line lengths, do not easily lend themselves to parallelism as the four-by-four structure of the Triumph stanza does. There is also a much more logical, even conceptual use of alliteration and rhyme to bind and support parallelism at work here: 'how fast his firedint, | his mark on mind, is gone!' Here, I encounter two related images on either side of a pause — a 'foot', in Hopkins's parlance — but there is no temptation to blur them, or to attend to the formal pattern at the expense of the logical. Instead alliteration binds the first image, and next the other image, while assonance through the phrase serves to underline a sense of progression, of difference in similarity. Likewise Hopkins's use of rhyme in this daring rhyming couplet, which serves not to blur the conceptual parallelism, but enforce it:

> [...] Enough! the Resurrection,
> A heart's-clarion! Away grief's gasping, | joyless days, dejection.

Commenting on these lines, Lichtmann writes:

> For Hopkins, who so treasured the distinctiveness and individuality of the human and natural worlds, this blurring vastness and extinction are the ultimate cruelty. Death seems to be the only stable condition, until it too succumbs at the pivotal caesura... Hopkins rhymes the opposites, 'dejection' and 'Resurrection'; it was his intention with rhyme, as with every other form of parallelism, to let similarity in sound and form be joined to difference in meaning. The 'beacon' of the first coda contrasts with the night that has gone before and overcomes the fading flesh and ashes that follow... [and in doing so] brings Hopkins' mature poetic corpus full circle.[52]

Ultimately, it is the fact that Hopkins's conceptual parallelism — here the overcoming of death by life — can be shown to map so easily onto his technical parallelism — which suggests his essential difference from Swinburne. Though both poets use alliteration, syntactical parallelism, rhythm and rhyme, it is a difference of the degree to which the poet creates links between words, and the use to which those linkages are put. In Hopkins's verse all nature is discovered, in each unique instance of its 'Haecceity', to be one. Reading Swinburne's verse, on the other hand, one is more tempted to declare, with the speaker of the Triumph of Time, that 'it's all one to me'. We see again how right Forrest-Thomson was when she claimed that, by a certain point in the poem the word 'life' might come to achieve a kind of equivalence with 'death'. This is perhaps why Hopkins, in a letter to Bridges, warns against Swinburne's 'self-drawing web':

> [he] does not see nature at all or else he overlays the landscape with such phantasmata, secondary images and what-not of delirious-tremendous imagination that the result is a kind of bloody broth [...] At any rate there is no picture.[53]

However, while for Hopkins, that 'self-drawing web' proved a temptation, for some it has proved a strength. As Jerome McGann argues, it is precisely this anti-visual, more temporal understanding of analogy which is Swinburne's contribution:

> When Swinburne forces the reader to negotiate language through its tactility and sound, he is moving to enlarge our perceptual resources. To speak of his verse as 'Pure Sound' is to register Swinburne's critique of the dominance that visual imagination had gained in poetic theory and practice. That critique, along with the reforming practices entailed by it, is perhaps Swinburne's greatest legacy to poetic tradition.[54]

McGann's sense of the analogical, even alogical, thrust of Swinburne's verse as 'reforming practices' is extremely useful, inviting us to see this impetus in his style, not as a weakness, but as a mode of attention. This is especially true of the way in which his verse seeks to reform already established links between words.

Collocation

From a 'habit of mind' which looks for differences between syntagms held in parallel comes the breaking or re-establishment of links which achieve a symbolic — and perhaps an anti-symbolic — status. Here Swinburne's anti-theistic strain (more fully explicit in the 'Hymn to Proserpine' and 'A Litany') seeks to break up the collocations 'bread' and 'wine', and 'bread' and 'honey'. These are linked naturally in the biblical imagination and, I would contend, in the period ear. However, Swinburne's repetition of these symbols from the imaginative zone of sacrifice and ritual seeks to extend and recombine their meanings:

> Had you eaten and drunken and found it sweet,
> This wild new growth of the corn and vine,
> This wine and bread without lees or leaven (p. 35)
>
> I had grown pure as the dawn and the dew,
> You had grown strong as the sun or the sea (p. 39)

Swinburne's collocations disturb the usual patterns of association, to the extent that the question which usually attends repetition — 'what does this mean this time?' — gathers a new urgency. A similar technique is also in evidence in the rhyme-work of Félise, often leading to the total breakdown of simile, as Young-Bryant has argued:

> The sounding of 'Félise' enumerates a series of objects and properties of objects — colours in the sea, flowers, a cat's eyes — introduced with a hanging, assimilative 'like' (l. 91) that repeats differently across the two stanzas. In the first instance, 'like' (l. 91) lacks the second element of comparison, and we are seemingly meant to supply the elided object, 'your name,' to the beginning of the stanza, the qualities and objects listed in the enumeration being somehow 'like' the name 'Félise.' The effect of suppressing the first member of the comparison is to give the stanza a riddling, enigmatic character in the sense that the figure of enigma tends to resemble a 'closed simile' in which the typical formula of simile, 'X is like Y,' is reorganized or deranged in the form of a question, 'What is X like?'... The language of the comparison itself generates an interpretive problem posed by 'only' in the comparison, 'only like...' (l. 96). Are the objects mentioned the only items that are like the name 'Félise,' as if to suggest that the list of colours, the sea, etc., exhausts the set of things similar to the name, or are the objects only *like* the name, shadowed approximations that fall short of the thing itself? This difference, the ambiguously restrictive difference of 'only like,' may explain why 'Félise' is 'the sweetest name,' a question the Poem begs by predicating 'sweetness' to 'Félise.'[55]

I quote Young-Bryant at some length because his exploration of Swinburne's rhyme-work and simile identifies a similar tendency in Swinburne's style to attach and to break up the expected associations between words and to a similar end. However, whereas in 'Félise', the name of the beloved works as a catch-all rhyme word, binding its rhymes into a sought-for 'sweetness', the disorder that I experience in 'The Triumph of Time' is more radical, dismantling not just simile and likeness, but also the natural collocations and connections between words in the English language. Swinburne would later exploit the links between accepted symbols towards satire, parody, and surprisingly — as M. K. Louis has shown — sacramental theology. Here, however, the pathos of the reallocation of collocations throughout 'The Triumph of Time' comes with the recognition that this desire to recombine old symbols into new meanings ultimately fails: the beloved has not tasted the new wine and therefore she has not found it 'sweet'.

Lexical repetition

Unlike phonemic repetition, parallelism and collocation, lexical repetition invites a different form of attention, especially when operating over longer distances. Forrest-Thomson detected an 'attenuation' of meaning as a result of continual repetition. However, the 'meaning' of these long-range revenants is actually double-edged. The time that elapses between repetitions — what Magnus calls the 'intersentential context' — means these words can also achieve echolalic effects. That this mode of attention is peculiar to Swinburne can be seen from further comparison with two poems which we know Swinburne admired, and which 'The Triumph of Time' puts me constantly in mind of. Both Shelley's *Epipsychidion*, and Tennyson's *Maud* received criticism for their iteration, and yet neither of these poems seems to have provoked the 'unease' which Swinburne's poem elicits in his readers.

This may be because they are both longer poems, hence repetition is not so intensive. Nor do they have the Triumph stanza structure which, as I have argued, promotes this peculiarly hallucinatory mode of attention. In contrast, Shelley's poem repeats the word 'sweet' fifteen times over 600 lines of iambics, while the metrical experimentation and range of Tennyson's multi-part monodrama, which was an inspiration and a challenge to Swinburne, means that the reader's attention cannot be caught and drilled continuously, as in Swinburne's poem. As with Hopkins, however, the mode of attention which Swinburne's lexical repetition courts is very much a difference in degree and usage.

'I know/ That Love makes all things equal', Shelley's speaker declares, rhyming the worm in the 'sod' with 'god' in a way which recalls William Blake's exploration of the interconnectivity of things in *The Book of Thel*. However, unlike Blake — for whom this statement forms the problem, rather than the solution, to perception — in Shelley's poem the repetition of 'sweet' works thematically to enforce the union of all things, a union which is the revelation that love secures. In order to express this, or perhaps because of this, 'sweet' is always in an adjectival position, even when it takes the form of an apostrophe to the beloved. Reiteration of 'sweet' unites similes of union across the poem, making them present at a higher structure of thinking. So Shelley is able to argue that the 'sweetest sounds' come from souls which sound as 'two different notes', and for 'sweetness' at the heart of all meaning, where 'all other sounds 'were penetrated/ By the small, still, sweet spirit of that sound...' Since this 'sweetness' is discovered, not so much as a result of, but at the origin of all union, it poses questions about the nature of experience. 'Sweetness' is thus understood, through frequent repetition, to be a quality of experience which begs questions about experience, often lying just beyond the bounds of ordinary comprehension and language: 'sweet as stops/ Of planetary music heard in trance' (ll. 85–86); 'And we will talk, until thought's melody/ Become too sweet for utterance.' (ll. 560–61; 358–60) 'And all their many-mingled influence blend,/ If equal, yet unlike, to one sweet end.'

Despite this range of meanings 'sweet' is made to bear, throughout Shelley's poem the adjective remains faithful to its nouns. In fact, its regularity is what makes that faithfulness seem possible to Emily, or the spheres, from its first utterance as the first word of the poem proper — 'Sweet spirit' (1), 'seeking her 'sweet kisses', to the poem's envoy in which the speaker asks the poem to call on its 'sister verses' to reinforce the message: 'Love's very pain is sweet,/ But its reward is in the world divine/ Which, if not here, it builds beyond the grave'. The ambiguity of this final statement, which translates and paraphrases the reported words of Emilia herself, is crucial, and must have seemed terribly so for Swinburne. For whether the adjective divine attaches itself to the world here, or a reward elsewhere, will determine the speaker's entire spiritual outlook. Whether love, experienced as 'sweetness', can be experienced on earth — therefore assuming a divine presence on earth, and life after death in some form — or whether it must be deferred to another world, officially known and bounded as 'The World Divine' goes right to the heart of the lover's dilemma in Swinburne's poem:

> There are fairer women, I hear; that may be;
> But I, that I love you and find you fair,
> Who are more than fair in my eyes if they be,
> Do the high gods know or the great gods care?
> Though the swords in my heart for one were seven,
> Would the iron hollow of doubtful heaven,
> That knows not itself whether night-time or day be,
> Reverberate words and a foolish prayer? (p. 42)

In contrast with the repetition of 'sweet' in Shelley's poem, which is argumentative, logical, even rhetorical, Swinburne's own usage is much more restless and unresolved. In 'The Triumph of Time' 'sweet' occurs as an abstract noun denoting an experience not undergone by the lover or the beloved, as an epithet (most often with the sea as its object), but also as an adjective describing the beloved, life, dreams undone, the feet of the lady of Tripoli, music, words themselves, before finally coming to act as an apostrophe to the beloved. Unlike the one word refrain in Edgar Allan Poe's 'The Raven', it does not have 'the precision and rigid consequence of a mathematical problem', nor is it 'some pivot on which the whole structure might turn'.[56] In its range of uses and situations — sometimes recurring in collocation, sometimes alone, sometimes in a prominent metrical position, sometimes not — it forms the greatest challenge to the reader who, encouraged to seek out the similarities between words, might well come to face the recurrence of 'sweet' with a certain degree of apprehension.

That the unease surrounding repetition voiced by contemporary reviewers pertains to Swinburne's verse in particular is suggested by reviews which address Tennyson's repetition. In his 1830 review of *Poems Chiefly Lyrical* W. J. Fox praises 'the felicitous effect often produced by the iteration of a word or sentence so posited that it conveys a different meaning or shade of meaning, and is involuntarily uttered in a different tone. There are many beautiful instances of this kind…'[57] That this technique still found appreciative ears in 1856, seven years before the publication of Swinburne's first collection, is confirmed by R. J. Mann, who, in his review of *Maud,* speaks of the 'excited ear' of the lover.[58] And the reader of Maud still discovers much to excite her ears: the poem is strewn with instances of lexical repetition. That this technique is self-conscious is suggested when Tennyson comes close to quoting that most iterative of poems *The Song of Solomon* word for word.⁵⁹

However, unlike Swinburne's poem, the allusion to the biblical love poem works without that long-range attention prompted by recurring words in Swinburne's poem. The passage which begins 'Dark cedar, tho' thy limbs have here increased, / Upon a pastoral slope as fair... (ll. 616–17) ' might draw on the biblical language and situation: 'As the apple tree among the trees of the wood, so is my beloved among the sons. I sat down under his shadow with great delight, and his fruit was sweet to my taste'.⁶⁰ However, this is a different kind of allusion to the one made available through the repetition of the word 'cover' in the near redundant image which Swinburne writes into 'The Triumph Of Time': 'We, drinking love at the furthest springs,/ Covered with love as a covering tree' (p. 35), a further indication of that paradox in which Swinburne's poem in fact appears to be most meaningful at precisely those points where his verse repeats to the point of redundancy.

In contrast to Swinburne's repetition of the word, 'sweet' in Tennyson is always appropriate, for example when we see Tennyson using the word 'sweet', to reinforce the links between lovers — where — in two lines separated by one line, but parallel in structure Maud 'suddenly, sweetly' blushes, and the speaker's heart 'suddenly, sweetly' beats stronger (p. 536–37). In *Maud* the adjective 'sweet' comes to gather a particular association with the beloved, whose presence it becomes indistinguishable from: 'the meadow your walks have left so sweet' (p. 562). This peculiar set of associations explains the force of the speaker's naming of his beloved as 'sweet', almost as if to conjure her into presence: 'She is coming, my own, my sweet;' (p. 563) which Mann quotes. In time 'sweet' becomes unavoidably collated with Maud, and this collocation signs the speaker's — one might very well use the word 'morbid' — obsession, a small but recognisable structure in the larger question of whether the speaker might presume to hold 'dominion sweet', or, more philosophically, suspend judgement on 'our low world, where yet 'tis sweet to live'. Yet, despite the constant collocation of 'sweet' with Maud and all the meaning in the world, the word is never allowed to cross into equivalence with any of its collated objects. Even when we witness the speaker at his most iterative, the iteration of 'sweet' remains rhetorical:

> And Maud is as true as Maud is sweet:
> Tho' I fancy her sweetness only due
> To the sweeter blood by the other side;
> Her mother has been a thing complete... (pp. 545–46).

Four strong beats, and a continuous 'working' of the word 'sweet' are also two of the conditions behind the 'verbal confusion' in Swinburne's poem. Yet this fantastic argument for Maud's genealogy involves none of the riddling, nor the redundancy which are my consistent experience of similar passages in Swinburne. Instead parallelism in the first line compares Maud's qualities without attempting to fuse them; it is a different kind of gesture from that advanced in Keats's equation of beauty and truth, or Swinburne's use of repeated words as pivots to forge a link between dissimilar qualities or ideas. 'Sweet' is varied in the line which follows, naming an abstract quality, before it next appears as a comparative adjective. Though the word 'sweet' repeats, it is always accurate, always appropriate, it does not seek to gather yet more referents. When 'sweet' is placed in a position of rhythmic and syntactical prominence, at the end of the line, it rhymes with 'complete' in a way which seems entirely logical, given the argument about *Maud* and her mother. That Tennyson chooses to do so here, despite the fact that he could create these kind of extra-semantic connections between words, is demonstrated by another poem in *Maud*: 'Go not, happy day,/ From the shining fields...' (XVII):

> Go not, happy day,
> Till the maiden yields.
> Rosy is the West,
> Rosy is the South,
> Roses are her cheeks,
> And a rose her mouth
>
> [...] Blush from West to East,
> Blush from East to West,
> Till the West is East,
> Blush it thro' the West.
> Rosy is the West,
> Rosy is the South,
> Roses are her cheeks,
> And a rose her mouth.

Parallelism and a strong diatonic beat join forces in a poem in which the reader is led towards a rhythmic blending of words, in the wilful effort to round every aspect of experience into the beloved, whose presence blends with all the created world. This litany is much more Swinburnean. However, the structure of Tennyson's monodrama means that this episode remains discrete, a single isolated metrical interlude, or 'litany of flowers', as Swinburne puts it, in the speaker's long and varied performance. Though Tennyson, like Swinburne, could turn the redundancy which repetition always risks into a stylistic opportunity, he falters with a word such as 'sweet'. Nothing could be more different than Swinburne's iteration. By the penultimate stanza of 'The Triumph of Time' 'sweet' has come to seem, simultaneously, the most important word in the book, and the most meaningless word in the world. It has also acquired a kind of detachment from the immediate context, a kind of independence that approaches the allusive.

Repetition and Allusion

This allusive quality partly explains my tendency to detect in Swinburne's poem allusions which, on reflection, cannot be substantially proven to be allusions (in the strict sense that one might offer chapter and verse in a footnote). William Empson was perhaps right to identify in Swinburne a wider variety of the fifth type of ambiguity ['when the author is discovering his idea in the act of writing, or not holding it in his mind at once...'] [61] Though Empson is writing of *Laus Veneris,* these remarks might equally have been made about the allusive nature of 'The Triumph of Time':

> In the next verse, *air might wash,* like water, and *leaves might cover,* like the sea or the grave; then by direct implication *grass* and *flowers* are compared to waves; then the *wind's feet shining along the sea,* whitening the tops of the waves, is compared, the other way round, to *grass* and *flowers,* and, as a fainter implication, to grassy mounds with white tombstones on them. The sea, in Swinburne, shares with the earth the position of great sweet mother, is cleaner, fresher, and more definitely dead. Nor must one forget the feet, so beautiful upon the mountains, of him that brings good tidings of the Lord.[62]

To take one example: in 'The Triumph of Time' we encounter the homophone 'strait' repeated three times. In each case the use of the word is relatively straightforward — at line 82 'strait' is used as a noun in a figuration of time as a sea; in the second instance, at line 168, 'strait' is the adjective used to describe the closed entrance which imagines the lover's projected absence being discovered by the beloved: 'The gate is strait; I shall not be there'. The last recurrence of 'strait', as a synonym for waters, is non-figurative, yet the fact that it is a revenant leads the reader to seek for the meaning of this word outside the poem and in other poems, and other usages from other periods. Margaret K. Louis depends on this when she argues for these lines as an echo of St Luke's gospel, in which Christ talks of the difficulty of entering heaven: 'Strive to enter in at the strait gate: for many, I say unto you, will seek to enter in, and shall not be able' (Luke 13. 24). However, other echoes might also be heard returning: 'He brought him through a darksom narrow strayt, To a broad gate', or, closer to Swinburne in time and in mood, lines that describe 'Mine own [spirit] [...] hovering o'er the dolorous strait / To the other shore'.[63] There is no way of proving conclusively any one of these allusions to be more really present than the others. What is evident is the way that Swinburne's verse calls up other lines in my mind, provoking me to turn to the bookshelves seeking other poems.

Repetition and Attention

The form of attention that I have been describing here might be thought of as analogous to the cumulative acquisition of a foreign language, were it not for the fact that this analogy does not capture the way in which Swinburne's poetry asks us to attend to those aspects of a language rarely found in any dictionary. They are, for the most part, circumstantial, situated and associative. A more sensitive analogy would be to a re-acquisition of one's own language, built upon those aspects of a language that cannot be learnt from a book, but instead arise out of 'being there'; the precise gesture, or prosodic contour that accompanies a word or phrase. In the same way that this language competence is the result of multiple conversations, the knowledge that Swinburne's poetry stirs in his reader requires participation in hundreds of poems, stretched across many languages.

Charles Baudelaire, writing on Victor Hugo, recalls reading 'in the Bible about a prophet who was asked by God to devour a book':

> I do not know in what world Victor Hugo has previously consumed the dictionary of the language which he was called upon to speak, but I see that

> the French lexicon, as he uses it, has become a world [...] from it come those frequent repetitions of words, all destined to express the captivating shadows or the enigmatic countenance of mystery.[64]

The same observation could have been made about Swinburne's *Poems and Ballads*. However, rather than appearing mysterious, Swinburne's repetition involves the reader in a double risk. 'Sweet' is a word that operates in non-poetical speech, to mean, in various ways, a satisfaction. It cannot be altogether dismissed as 'artificial'. However, as a repetition of previous repetitions, this word is also recognisably poetic. Not only does he repeat words to the point where they risk shedding sense for pure sound, but he also chooses to repeat words such as 'life', 'death', 'love' and 'sweet', which — though they might not be ostentatious enough to approach, say, the poetical diction of the Augustan period — are nevertheless the 'stock' stuff of poetry. Adorno writes of the way in which 'Eichendorff achieves the most extraordinary effects with a stock of images that must have been threadbare even in his day':

> The castle that forms the object of Eichendorff's longing is spoken of only as the castle; the obligatory stock of moonlight, hunting horns, nightingales and mandolins is provided, but without doing much harm to Eichendorff's poetry. The fact that Eichendorff was probably the first to discover the expressive power in fragments of the *lingua morta* contributes to this (p. 66)

Adorno's term to describe Eichendorff's diction, *lingua morta*, seems an apt description of Swinburne's use of the word 'sweet'. Eliot voices a similar incredulity, arguing that Swinburne's words are not 'dead', as in the case of 'bad' poetry, but alive 'with this singular life of [their] own' ('Swinburne as Poet', p. 136). This relegation of Swinburne's poetry to the realm of life-in-death is suggestive, as it captures the double risk involved in Swinburne's iteration. Reusing words, tropes or figures that are consciously literary makes for a curious relation between the literary past and the present. To read 'The Triumph of Time' as a 'dramatized lyric' is not just to encounter a style of thinking, the 'truths of time', in Griffiths's phrase; we also encounter 'truths of time', which are timely. Swinburne's iteration presents an especially complex kind of dramatic monologue because at the same time that his repeated iteration presents a habit of mind which is always just about to discover the impossibility of repetition, the allusive aspect of his verse-practice draws attention to repetition as a stock poetic gesture. Hence the book which Baudelaire imagined Victor Hugo to have swallowed becomes, in Swinburne's case, a peculiarly iterative anthology. Repetition becomes triply complex here, to include, not just the repetition of key words in the poem, but the repetition of repeated words and their associated forms of experience present in other poems. To put this another way: reading Swinburne one gets the sense that one is not only dealing with a style of thinking but a stylization of thinking.

The Repetitive Style

It is this aspect of Swinburne's style which leads Peter Nicholls to argue for Swinburne as a 'nexus' linking late nineteenth-century French poetry and the new poetic:

> I think that what both Pound and Eliot, in their different ways, took ultimately from Swinburne was his recognition that metre and rhythm might have a kind of signifying function, or, to put it in more clearly Mallarméan terms, that poetic musicality might be a kind of writing.⁶⁵

Nicholl's characterisation is especially pertinent to 'The Triumph of Time', in which the speaker consistently draws on the figure of music and rhyme as provoking memory. They are 'a kind of writing', with a 'signifying function'. This interaction between the thematic and technical aspects of repetition is demonstrated in the first of two musical analogies. This occurs at the end of his apostrophe to the sea (the second of two fantasies of self-renunciation) and is experienced as something like a key change:

> And grief shall endure not for ever, I know.
> As things that are not shall these things be;
> We shall live through seasons of sun and of snow,
> And none be grievous as this to me.
> We shall hear, as one in a trance that hears,
> The sound of time, the rhyme of the years;
> Wrecked hope and passionate pain will grow
> As tender things of a spring-tide sea.
>
> Sea-fruit that swings in the waves that hiss,
> Drowned gold and purple and royal rings.
> And all time past, was it all for this?
> Times unforgotten, and treasures of things?
> Swift years of liking and sweet long laughter,
> That wist not well of the years thereafter
> Till love woke, smitten at heart by a kiss,
> With lips that trembled and trailing wings? (p. 44)

This is the first time that the conjunction 'And' has been used at the beginning of a line, a variation that registers as a surprise for me, and promises development. However, what looks set to be a moment of reflection soon emerges as a further phase in the repetitive style: we have entered an allegory of the poem's own making. Onomatopoeic words are rare in Swinburne and the use of 'hiss' here to describe the roll and crash of waves is startling yet evocative of the many repetitive stanzas which seem to endlessly empty themselves. No doubt Eliot would find the euphemisms 'these things' and 'treasures of things' 'vague', yet the ambiguity here is entirely appropriate, allowing the reader to connect the 'sea-fruit' with 'The sound of time, the rhyme of the years;'. The 'trance' the speaker names — which we feel ourselves at risk of slipping into again, as the swing of the *dol'nik* regains dominance — can only hold so far, as it is broken by the jamming together of a run of three monosyllables: 'Till love woke' — breaking with expectation — 'smitten at heart by a kiss'. The use of the ambiguous word 'smitten' here, to mean both joined in love and dealt a violent blow is brilliantly double and anticipates the last 'kissed' couplet in the penultimate stanza of the poem.

In this verse 'kiss' answers 'hiss', breaking the spell. Yet the rhyme also looks back to the question 'Was it all for this?' In doing so the speaker puts Wordsworth's question about poetic vocation, 'Was it for this?', again, but with a curious variation. For by 'it', I am led to understand not just the speaker's personal development, but 'all' passionate experience. No wonder Swinburne took as his *Erbe* not the Wordsworthian river heard in early childhood, nor the Tennysonian 'rivulet', but the infinitely more capacious and more ancient sea.

The reader is being invited to approach poetry in a curious way here. More than any other poem by Swinburne — except, perhaps, his roundels, which as Herbert Tucker and Francis O'Gorman both show, are highly self-reflective— the thematic and technical aspects of the poem consistently tempt comparison. What these stanzas on music prepare us for is a fuller exploration of the theme of repetition, when the poem moves to consider the fate of the poet Jaufré Rudel, who died happy in the arms of the Lady of Tripoli.

Repetition and Experience

Forrest-Thomson calls these stanzas an 'episode', while Eliot remarks, somewhat more cynically, that 'Provence is the merest point of diffusion here'. Both answer to the way in which in this poem — in which each new stanza is thematically or linguistically epaneleptic — the line 'There lived a singer in France of old' seemingly comes out of nowhere. However, this sudden shift is effective, requiring the reader to modify their attention to the work of repetition, again from technique to theme:

> There lived a singer in France of old
> By the tideless dolorous midland sea.
> In a land of sand and ruin and gold
> There shone one woman, and none but she.
> And finding life for her love's sake fail,
> Being fain to see her, he bade set sail,
> Touched land, and saw her as life grew cold,
> And praised God, seeing; and so died he.
>
> Died, praising God for his gift and grace:
> For she bowed down to him weeping, and said
> 'Live;' and her tears were shed on his face
> Or ever the life in his face was shed... (pp. 44–45)

The movement in these stanzas is unlike any other point in the poem. Instead of unfolding via repeating words, symbols, images, patterns, the story unfolds logically: it has a narrative. As the variation of the verb 'saw her [...] seeing' in the first stanza demonstrates, language ranges around this single, vital moment of recognition in ways that seem to leave the 'verbal confusion' of the preceding stanzas far behind. And it continues:

> The sharp tears fell through her hair, and stung
> Once, and her close lips touched him and clung
> Once, and grew one with his lips for a space;
> And so drew back, and the man was dead. (p. 45)

The catharsis involved in these lines may have to do with rhythmical variation. Swinburne's stanza usually varies the last syllable of lines alternately, so a rising line is followed by a line that terminates with a falling rhythm — hence Saintsbury's sense of how the stanza 'swells and swings like a wave' from line to line. Unusually here though the iambic upthrust wins twice, and the result of placing two monosyllabic words on either side of an enjambed line creates the double emphasis laid on the repeated word 'once', a set of circumstances that would cause the reader to pause after the word, irrespective of the comma. This notion is repeated, but not exhausted, in the mirror-like syntax that echoes how the lady's lips 'grew one' with the poet's — an image he would reuse in *Tristram* to describe the lovers' fatal union ('and their four lips became one burning mouth'). Swinburne's rhetorical repetition of 'once', combined with his handling of the rhythm, works to emphasise this finality: the once-upon-a-time union of Rudel with his beloved brings rest. However, this moment cannot be allowed to stand alone as an isolated event. As the presence of verbal revenants throughout these stanzas makes us aware, the requited love of Rudel and the experience of the lover in 'The Triumph of Time' are described using the same words– a similarity in difference that emphasises their irreconcilable positions:

> Give thanks for life, and the loves and lures;
> Give thanks for life, O brother, and death,
> For the sweet last sound of her feet, her breath,
> For gifts she gave you, gracious and few,
> Tears and kisses, that lady of yours. (p. 45)

Forrest-Thomson writes of the 'extreme condensation of "Give thanks for life, O brother, and death"', and attributes this to the number of 'topic words' within the line (p. 61). However, while the revenants 'life' and 'death' may have acquired a 'snowball-like' importance by this stage in the poem, their particular effect at this point in the poem is to demonstrate the failure of the speaker's allusion to Rudel. Since theme and technique have been brought into alliance, the failure of the speaker to bring about a repeat of Rudel's happy demise appears not just a cruel fate, but also tantamount to linguistic failure:

> Rest, and be glad of the gods; but I,
> How shall I praise them, or how take rest? (p. 45)

'Rest, and be glad of the gods;' is another epanaleptic line, which looks set to continue this theme indefinitely, but the late caesura proves pivotal, directing attention back towards the speaker. The chiastic repetition of 'rest' in a prominent position at the opposite end of the clause underlines the difference. The same word might be in use, but instead of securing continuity with the past, the speaker can only note his own exceptional status. The revenant 'love', which occurs a few lines later, prompts a similar thought: 'Love will not come to me now though I die, / As love came close to you, breast to breast'. In contrast to successful repetition, in which the lovers meet 'breast to breast', or even both 'blush' in Tennyson's lines, the word 'love' has, in some sense, failed in the later instance. The interaction of theme and technique here means that, far from being a personal plight, the failure to repeat comes to seem, first linguistic, then, by extension, epistemological:

> There is not room under all the sky
> For me that know not of worst or best,
> Dream or desire of the days before,
> Sweet things or bitterness, any more. (p. 45)

These lines recall a previous four-line unit, earlier in the poem, in which the speaker connects the endless repetition, the endless reverberation of words, with a spiritual crisis (p. 42). However, unlike Petrarch's system in his 'Triumph of Time', or Augustine's faith, 'The Triumph of Time' assumes no continuity elsewhere. There is no eternal triumph. Nor is there any meeting of lovers in paradise, as in Dante's *Paradiso*. In this sense, it is appropriate that, in the second musical analogy in the poem, music appears — not as a trance-like state, but interrupted:

> I shall never be friends again with roses;
> I shall loathe sweet tunes, where a note grown strong
> Relents and recoils, and climbs and closes,
> As a wave of the sea turned back by song. (p. 45)

Anaphora enforces the particular insistency with which the 'I' rejects the variation of 'sweet' music. Likewise, relentless polysyndeton in these lines serves to render all objects and actions equivalent and equally worthless. However, the past imagined in the previous musical analogy as a kind of flotsam now appears, not as a vision in a 'trance', but as a lost possibility:

> There are sounds where the soul's delight takes fire,
> Face to face with its own desire;
> A delight that rebels, a desire that reposes;
> I shall hate sweet music my whole life long. (pp. 45–46)

What Eliot calls 'vague associations' are everywhere in force here. Yet what in fact repeats here on the thematic level is failure, and it repeats indefinitely. Here, the 'craving in the mind' that Wordsworth spoke of can find no satisfaction:

> The pulse of war and passion of wonder,
> The heavens that murmur, the sounds that shine,
> The stars that sing and the loves that thunder,
> The music burning at heart like wine,
> [...]
> These things are over, and no more mine. (p. 46)

In technique and in theme, then, Swinburne's poem elicits an attitude to language, and, by extension, to poetry, as temporally situated, an attitude which Benjamin, in his analysis of Baudelaire, would later identify with a break in the continuity of consciousness:

> There is something odd about speaking of a *raison d'état* in the case of a poet; there is something remarkable about it: the emancipation from experiences. Baudelaire's poetic output is assigned a mission. He envisioned blank spaces which he filled with his poems. His work cannot merely be categorised as historical, like anyone else's, but it intended to be so and understood itself as such.[66]

For Benjamin, the self-conscious nature of Baudelaire's art registers as a break in the continuity of historical consciousness, leading to a definition of its opposite:

> Where there is experience in the strict sense of the word, certain contents of the individual past combine with material of the collective past. The rituals with their ceremonies, their festivals [...] kept producing the amalgamation of these two elements of memory over and over again. They triggered recollection at certain times and remained handles of memory for a lifetime. In this way, voluntary and involuntary recollection lose their mutual exclusiveness.[67]

This understanding of memory and consciousness is immensely suggestive for my reading of Swinburne's repetition. The recurrence of the revenant 'sweet', for example, might be understood within the frame of 'dramatic lyric' as a movement towards 'experience', part of an attempt to overcome the division between voluntary and involuntary memory by reaching after continuity in the form of pure repetition. However, while for Benjamin this definition remains static, for the reader of Swinburne it is something encountered. Indeed, this might be seen as the motivating factor in all Swinburne's early work — whether his aim was a version of Scots border ballad which could be taken for an original, or to be able to write 'sweet' just as Keats might have done. Yet his work is shot through with doubt: what if it can no longer be done? What if 'sweet' cannot *mean* this time?

Poetry, Griffiths suggests, may have the edge on the 'timeless truths' of philosophy. However, Swinburne's 'truth in time' has also escaped previous. What neither Nicholls's description of poetic musicality as 'a kind of writing', nor Hollander's understanding of repetition as a dialectic between interest and boredom, nor Kugel's description of parallelism as 'a habit of mind' capture is the agony of the repetitive style:

> Poetry, the workings of genius itself, which in all times, with one or another meaning, has been called Inspiration [...] is no longer without its scientific exposition. The building of the lofty rhyme is like any other masonry or bricklaying: we have theories of its rise, height, decline and fall — which latter, it would seem, is now near, among all people. Of our 'Theories of Taste,' [...] wherein the deep, infinite, unspeakable Love of Wisdom and Beauty [...] is 'explained,' made mechanically visible, from 'Association' and the like, why should we say anything?[68]

If, Thomas Carlyle argues, all that can be considered 'deep, infinite, unspeakable' is assumed to be reduced to 'taste' or association, then there will be nothing more to say. The poet might be reduced to using a mechanised language in which only the 'vague associations' attached to certain words are possible. Words thus become detached from experience, and thus from pleasure, fulfilment, the end of longing. That class of experiences which 'sweet' names will have become impossible.

If Carlyle understood the risk which capitalism in its industrial form posed to experience, then no Victorian poet knew the risk of the mechanisation of verse like Swinburne, and no poet feared this mechanisation more. It is in this uneasy tension between repetition and redundancy, this uneasy disordering of voluntary and involuntary memory, and this nowhere place between the ever-distant past and a newly historicised present, that we can understand the complexity of Swinburne's repetition. However, rather than having to do with 'timeless truths', or 'truths in time', the repetition we encounter in Swinburne's poetry must be understood as a 'truth in time' unfolding at a certain moment in history — or so lyric poetry would have us read.

The Ruined Rhyme

For myself, this is what I encounter in the penultimate stanza of 'The Triumph of Time', in which the reappearance of the revenant 'sweet', dancing with 'feet' in the second to last 'kissed' rhyme of the poem, hits with the cumulative force of a verbal avalanche:

> But if we had loved each other — O sweet,
> Had you felt, lying under the palms of your feet,
> The heart of my heart, beating harder with pleasure
> To feel you tread it to dust and death — (p. 46)

I read aloud as I type these lines from memory, suppressing my desire to capitalise 'sweet', and stop, pausing a moment to check the full stanza in *Poetical Works*. Surprised by the comma enforcing a caesura after 'heart' — so quick are these lines to me — I remember that 'pleasure' recalls the word 'measure' in a not-so-far-away stanza. In the *same* stanza, I realise, correcting myself and, in doing so, I recognise that these lines have worked themselves free, forming a four-line unit that appears independent of the eight-line stanza.

The rest of the penultimate and last stanza of 'The Triumph of Time' dies away; it is with the fourth and fifth lines of the penultimate stanza that I am concerned, compelled, to voice these lines as 'I', 'I' — irresistibly 'I' — for the sake of a 'we' that ranges widely, above and beyond 'thee', the 'sea', seeking: 'you', a particular 'you' in all your sweetness, close and closing, undeniably there. That doubt of doubt, that 'but' returning, which comes out of nowhere, out of everywhere, pauses and jumps, rising to reach, not pitch, but another kind of intensity ringing on 'feet':

> I shall go my ways, tread out my measure,
> Fill the days of my daily breath
> With fugitive things not good to treasure,
> Do as the world doth, say as it saith;
> But if we had loved each other — O sweet,
> Had you felt, lying under the palms of your feet,
> The heart of my heart, beating harder with pleasure
> To feel you tread it to dust and death — (p. 46)

This stanza begins like a version of 'And grief shall endure not forever I know', tracing the embroidery on the tablecloth, laying plans towards a half-willed resolution: if fulfilment is denied, we will 'fill' our days with something, if not 'bread' then 'breath', if not 'treasure' then 'fugitive things' — any of 'these things' will do. The first four lines iterate, emptily restating the facts as the speaker attempts to resolve himself into a perfect rhyme with what Wallace Stevens calls, not at all prosaically, 'things as they are': to do as the world 'doth', say as it 'saith'. These lines sound the base-line of the returning rhythm, the amnesiac's trance.

However, at that 'but' the speaker changes tack. The rhythm, disturbed, hesitates and surges forwards. Up until this moment in the poem 'sweet' — the most repeated, clichéd, overused and empty of all of Swinburne's verbal revenants — has been forever at risk of falling into meaninglessness. Yet here, at the end of the poem, at the end of the line, four and three-quarter lines towards an unwanted resolution, it appears again, in the most prominent metrical position in the line-end, lashed to the mast of this penultimate 'kissed' couplet, calling on its rhyme-twin 'feet', resurrecting his poet-ancestor Rudel, hectoring back to the possibility: of address, of speaking out, of risking everything, while at the same time courageously, unswervingly looking forward: to uncertain fulfilment, self-annihilation, dust, death. This hope against hope takes hold before I can recognise it for what it is. The rhythm of the fifth line shows no sign of deviating until the last late pivot at the caesura when enjambment and the couplet hurry us on and over into the final stanza. The ambiguity of 'sweet' here, the strangest case of diaphora in the poem yet, is crushing. It names at once the beloved, from whom all sweet things come; yet it cannot name the beloved, who appears beyond address.

Wordsworth assumed that repetition would come to an end when the 'craving in the mind' was satisfied. In Søren Kierkegaard's psychological allegory, *Repetition,* the failure to repeat is a cause for jubilation. As the ironic frame of Constantius's narration implies, the 'young man' mistakes one kind of repetition — continuance in his old mode of life as a bachelor — for another kind of repetition, the kind which faith or marriage requires.[69] The young poet, released from his engagement, interprets the news that his lady has become engaged to another as a kind of return of his life to himself, mistaking his old rhythm for the real thing:

> The beaker of inebriation is again offered to me, and already I am inhaling its fragrance, already I am aware of its bubbling music-for first a libation to her who saved a soul who sat in the solitude of despair: Praised be feminine generosity! Three cheers for the flight of thought, three cheers for the perils of life in service of the idea, three cheers for the hardships of battle, three cheers for the festive jubilation of victory, three cheers for the dance in the vortex of the infinite, three cheers for the cresting waves that hide me in the abyss, three cheers for the cresting waves that fling me above the stars![70]

By contrast, the speaker in Swinburne's poem can conceive of no end to that craving:

> It is not much that a man can save
> On the sands of life, in the straits of time,
> Who swims in sight of the great third wave
> That never a swimmer shall cross or climb.
> Some waif washed up with the strays and spars
> That ebb-tide shows to the shore and the stars;
> Weed from the water, grass from a grave,
> A broken blossom, a ruined rhyme.

Here the revenant 'sweet', both personal and impersonal, so particular yet so general, falls like the myrrh before the door in *The Song of Solomon*, which opens on the beloved's absence, or the amputated epithet 'Dear' in Walter Savage Landor's poem 'Memory':

> To these, when I have written and besought
> Remembrance of me, the word *Dear* alone
> Hangs on the upper verge, and waits in vain.[71]

What remains of 'The Triumph of Time' dies away, a less insistent version of the stanzas that previously described the 'music burning at heart like wine'. The speaker's sacrifice of 'the wine and honey, the balm and leaven' add to make a kind of reprise, a last attempt to wring some meaning from these elements before they are relegated along with their rhythmical ancestors: 'dust and laurels and gold and sand'. Yet the poem repeats its decision not to speak. And it is this, rather than any kind of narrative, which might allow us to talk of development in the poem, the real secret of its repetition: what emerges between the first and the forty-seventh stanza of 'The Triumph of Time' is the failure of words to repeat, that necessary condition of experience. Yet for a single imagined moment it was almost here. Perhaps this is why the poem ends on a question:

> Come life, come death, not a word be said;
> Should I lose you living, and vex you dead?
> I never shall tell you on earth; and in heaven,
> If I cry to you then, will you hear or know? (p. 47)

Notes to Chapter 2

1. Theodor W. Adorno, "In Memory of Eichendorff', in *Notes to Literature*, ed. Ralph Tiedemann, trans. Shierry Weber Nicholsen (New York: Columbia University Press, 1991) I, p. 54. All subsequent references will be to this edition, and will be given in the text.
2. Augustine, *Confessions*, ed. and trans. by Henry Chadwick (Oxford: Oxford University Press, 2008), p. 230.
3. Adorno, *Quasi Una Fantasia*, trans. Rodney Livingstone (London: Verso, 1998), p. 3. I take up Adorno's critique in my introduction, and again in my conclusion.
4. Much of what Adorno has to say about the later readership of Eichendorff finds its parallel in Swinburne's reception. According to Adorno, Eichendorff appeals to cultural conservatives who identify with his regionalism and religiosity, mistaking his 'homesickness' for home: the beauty of his verse is perceived but not questioned. This 'humble irrationalism' translates into 'a lazy unwillingness to muster up the energetic receptivity the poem requires [...] a readiness to go on admiring what has already found approval'. We can put this estimate beside those of Swinburne that claim him as a poet of nationalist, revolutionary or feminist sympathies, yet continue to reverence his verse as, to borrow Adorno's phrase, 'a mystery one must respect' (p. 57). Swinburne's poems are often read opportunistically — their precise stylistic procedures becoming harnessed to concepts or ideas — or not at all, admiration for his musical effects instead being celebrated or denigrated *ad infinitum*.
5. Alan Young-Bryant, 'Swinburne: "The Sweetest Name"', *Victorian Poetry*, 49, 3 (2011), 308–09.
6. The term is Swinburne's: 'I desire that one thing should be remembered: the book [*Poems and Ballads*] is dramatic, many-faced, multifarious; and no utterance of enjoyment or despair, belief or unbelief, can properly be assumed as the assertion of its author's personal feeling or faith'. See *Notes on Poems and Reviews* (London: John Camden Hotten, 1866), p. 6.
7. Rikky Rooksby, *A. C. Swinburne: A Poet's Life* (Aldershot: Scolar, 1997), p. 5.

8. For a critical account of Swinburne's climbing of Culver Cliff which makes suggestive parallels with *Poems and Ballads,* see Francis O'Gorman, 'Swinburne and Cowardice: Running Away From *Poems and Ballads', Journal of Pre-Raphaelite Studies* 26 (2017), 61–80.
9. Arthur Symons, *Figures of Several Centuries* (London: Constable, 1916), p. 161.
10. For an account of Swinburne's verse which also explores Swinburne's rhyming of the word 'sea' see Simon Jarvis, 'Swinburne: The Insuperable Sea', in *The Oxford Handbook of Victorian Poetry*, ed. Matthew Bevis (Oxford: Oxford University Press, 2013), pp. 521–35.
11. 'Tyd' in *An Anglo-Saxon Dictionary*, ed. Joseph Bosworth and T. Northcote Toller (London: Oxford University Press, 1972), p. 1028.
12. A. C. Swinburne, *William Blake: A Critical Essay* (London: John Camden Hotten, 1868), pp. 274–75.
13. *Greek-English Lexicon*, ed. Henry George Liddell and Robert Scott et al. (Oxford, 1996), p. 118; p. 341; 'Prometheus Bound', *Aeschylus*, ed. and trans. Alan H. Sommerstein, Loeb Classical Library Series: 145 (Cambridge, MA: Harvard University Press, 2008), I, p. 454, l.90.
14. *Poems of Matthew Arnold,* ed. by Kenneth Allott (London: Longman, 1965) , p. 255.
15. Wilde, Oscar, *The Complete Works*, ed. Russell Jackson and Ian Small, (Oxford: Oxford University Press, 2005), II, p. 151.
16. McGann, *Swinburne: An Experiment in Criticism* (Chicago: University of Chicago Press, 1972), p. 156.
17. M. K. Louis, *Swinburne and His Gods* (Montreal: McGill-Queen's University Press, 1990) , p. 116.
18. Catherine Maxwell, *Swinburne* (Tavistock: Northcote House, 2006), p. 27.
19. Alan Young-Bryant, 'Swinburne: "The Sweetest Name"', p. 302.
20. John Hollander, 'Breaking into Song: *Some Notes on Refrain',* in *Lyric Poetry: Beyond New Criticism*, ed. Chaviva Hošek and Patricia Parker (Ithaca: Cornell University Press, 1985), pp. 78–79.
21. *The Poems of Algernon Charles Swinburne* (London: Chatto & Windus, 1905) I, p. 39. All subsequent references will be to the page numbers of this edition and will be given in the text.
22. Eric Griffiths, *The Printed Voice of Victorian Poetry* (Oxford: Clarendon Press, 1989), p. 142.
23. Ibid., p. 115.
24. Samuel Coleridge and William Wordsworth, *Lyrical Ballads* (London: Routledge, 2013), p. 332.
25. Friedrich Nietzsche, *Untimely Meditations,* trans. by R. J. Hollingdale, ed. by Daniel Breazeale (Cambridge: Cambridge University Press, 1997), p. 64.
26. See Swinburne's letter dated 9th October 1866 in *The Swinburne Letters,* ed. Cecil Y. Lang, 6 vols (New Haven: Yale University Press, 1959–1962), I, p. 195.
27. See Jerome McGann, *Swinburne: An Experiment in Criticism* (Chicago: University of Chicago Press, 1972), pp. 207–08; David G. Riede in 'Swinburne and Romantic Authority' in *The Whole Music of Passion: New Essays on Swinburne* (Aldershot: Scolar, 1993), pp. 57–58.
28. George Saintsbury, *A History of English Prosody from the Twelfth Century to the Present Day* (London: Macmillan, 1910), III, p. 347.
29. The argument for this poem as autobiographical lyric first appears to have been made by W. H. Mallock in his *Memoirs of Life and Literature* (London: Chapman & Hall, 1920), p. 75.
30. George Saintsbury, *Corrected Impressions: Essays on Victorian Writers* (London: W. Heinemann, 1895), pp. 66–67.
31. Rikky Rooksby, *A. C. Swinburne: A Poet's Life*, p. 19.
32. *The Songs of Jaufré Rudel,* ed. Rupert T. Pickens, Studies and Texts Series: 41 (Toronto: Pontifical Institute of Mediaeval Studies, 1978), p. 138.
33. For a discussion of *bacciata* rhyme see Giorgio Agamben, *The End of the Poem*, trans. by Daniel Heller-Roazen (Stanford: Stanford University Press, 1999), p. 115.
34. T. S. Eliot, *The Sacred Wood* (New York: Methuen, 1921), p. 132. All future references will be to the page numbers of this edition, and will be given in the text.
35. C. K. Hyder, ed., *A. C. Swinburne: The Critical Heritage* (London: Routledge, 1995: first published 1970 as *Swinburne: The Critical Heritage*), p. 29.
36. Ibid., p. 44.

37. A. E. Housman, 'Swinburne', *Cornhill Magazine*, 177 (1969, written 1910), 380–400.
38. C. K. Hyder, ed., *A. C. Swinburne: The Critical Heritage* (London: Routledge, 1995), pp. 57–58.
39. See, for example, Harold Nicolson, *Swinburne* (London: Macmillan, 1926), p. 13.
40. 'The Elegiac World in Victorian Poetry' [transcript of BBC broadcast talk], *The Listener* (14 February 1963), 290–91.
41. For an alternative interpretation of 'virtuosic effects' via Adorno's aesthetics see Simon Jarvis, 'Why Rhyme Pleases', *Thinking Verse*, 1, (2011), p. 25, available at <www.thinkingverse.com>[last accessed 26 April 2018].
42. Ezra Pound, 'Swinburne versus Biographers', *Poetry*, 11, 6 (1918), p. 328.
43. Veronica Forrest-Thomson, 'Swinburne as Poet: A Reconsideration', *Journal of Pre-Raphaelite Studies*, 15 (2006), 51–71, p. 61. All subsequent references are to this version and will be given in the text.
44. The influence of Empson's thinking in *The Structure of Complex Words* around 'appreciative and depreciative pregnancy [...] a process that makes the meaning of the word warmer and fuller or contrariwise less so' is apparent here. (See William Empson, *The Structure of Complex Words* (London: Chatto & Windus, 1951), p. 16.) Forrest-Thomson constructs a similar sliding scale in her attempt to understand the powerful effects brought about by repetition.
45. Attridge, *The Rhythms of English Poetry* (London: Longman, 1982), pp. 81–82.
46. Laury Magnus, *The Track of the Repetend* (New York: AMS Press, 1989), p. 16.
47. James Kugel, *The Idea of Biblical Poetry* (New Haven: Yale University Press, 1981), p. 42.
48. Maria R. Lichtmann, *The Contemplative Poetry of Gerard Manley Hopkins* (Princeton: Princeton University Press, 1989), p. 4.
49. Ibid., p. 4
50. Algernon Charles Swinburne, 'Of Analogy', College Essays [1856–58] London, British Library, Ashley MS.4349, pp. 11–13.
51. *Hopkins: The Major Works,* ed. Catherine Phillips (Oxford: Oxford University Press, 2002), p. 181
52. Lichtmann, *The Contemplative Poetry of Gerard Manley Hopkins*, p. 217.
53. *The Letters of Gerard Manley Hopkins to Robert Bridges*, ed. by Claude Colleer Abbott (London: Oxford University Press, 1935), p. 209.
54. *Algernon Charles Swinburne: Major Poems and Selected Prose*, ed. by Jerome McGann and Charles Sligh (New Haven: Yale University Press, 2004), p. xxv.
55. Alan Young-Bryant, 'Swinburne: "The Sweetest Name"', pp. 311–12.
56. Edgar Allan Poe, 'The Philosophy of Composition', *Literary Criticism of Edgar Allan Poe,* ed. by Robert L. Hough (Lincoln: University of Nebraska Press, 1965), pp. 22, 24.
57. *Lord Alfred Tennyson: The Critical Heritage*, ed. John Jump (London: Routledge, 1995), p. 31.
58. Ibid., p. 202.
59. *Tennyson: A Selected Edition*, ed. Christopher Ricks (Harlow: Longman, 1989), p. 552.All subsequent references are to the page numbers of this edition, and will be given in the text.
60. *The Bible, Authorised King James Version*, ed. Steven Prickett (Oxford: Oxford University Press, 2008) I, p. 761
61. William Empson, *Seven Types of Ambiguity* (London: Pimlico, 2004), p. 155
62. Ibid., p. 164.
63. Edmund Spenser, *The Faerie Queene*, ed. A. C. Hamilton, text ed. by Hiroshi Yamashita and Toshiyuki Suzuki (Harlow: Pearson Education, 2001), p. 219, ll.352–53; Tennyson 'In Memoriam', in *Tennyson: A Selected Edition*, ed. by Christopher Ricks (Harlow: Longman, 2007), p. 422.
64. 'Victor Hugo', in *Baudelaire as Literary Critic*, trans. Lois Boe Hyslop and Francis E. Hyslop Jr. (University Park: Pennsylvania State University Press, 1964), p. 239.
65. Peter Nicholls, 'The Swinburne Nexus', *Parataxis*, 10 (2001), 33–53, p. 42.
66. Walter Benjamin, *Charles Baudelaire: A Lyric Poet in the Era of High Capitalism*, trans. Harry Zohn (London: NLB, 1973), p. 113.
67. Ibid., p. 116.
68. Thomas Carlyle, 'Signs of the Times', *Critical and Miscellaneous Essays* (London: J. Fraser, 1840), II, p. 286.

69. Of course, it took a woman to bring this thought to birth: for criticism of both Kierkegaard and Adorno's reading of this scenario, see Gillian Rose, *The Broken Middle: Out of Our Ancient Society* (Oxford: Blackwell, 1992), Chapter 2, *passim*.
70. Søren Kierkegaard, *Repetition, A Venture in Experimental Psychology, by Constantin Constantius*, ed. and trans. by Howard V. Hong and Edna H. Hong (Princeton: Princeton University Press, 1983), pp. 221–22.
71. Walter Savage Landor, *Poems, Dialogues in Verse and Epigrams* (London: Dent, 1892), II, p. 274.

CHAPTER 3

'Faithless Faith':
Outrunning the Couplet in
Tristram of Lyonesse

> There's nothing metaphysical about it. Unless, of course, you flatter
> yourself into thinking that what you're experiencing is 'yearning'.
> FRANK O'HARA

Perhaps the fullest statement of Swinburne's religious belief comes in a letter he wrote to the American critic Edmund Clarence Stedman in 1875. Stedman's anonymous article on Swinburne's poetry was published in *Scribner's Monthly*, a magazine to which Swinburne did not subscribe, but which reached him via the poet Paul Hamilton Hayne.[1] Swinburne must have found Stedman a sympathetic correspondent, for he took the ensuing correspondence as an opportunity to set the record straight: 'As my antitheism has been so much babbled about perhaps I may here say what I really do think on religious matters'.[2] Swinburne recalls how he was 'brought up quasi-catholic', yet 'always felt by instinct and perceived by reason that no man could conceive of a personal God except by brute Calibanic superstition or else by true supernatural revelation [...] because no man could [...] conceive of any sort of divine person than man with a difference'. Swinburne offers various cultural examples of this 'absurdest of figments'. Yet this section of his letter concludes with a curious avowal:

> Therefore I might call myself if I wanted a kind of Christian (of the Church of
> Blake and Shelley), but assuredly in no sense a Theist. Perhaps you will think
> this is only a clarified nihilism, but at least it is no longer turbid.[3]

While a second baptism into a radical political tradition is not unheard of, Swinburne's peculiar credo, combining Christianity, antitheism, and poetry, is not so easily dismissed as the kind of hyperbolic inversion readers of his critical prose usually delight in. Neither can it be dismissed as a throwaway remark (the letter is self-consciously autobiographical), or taken as evidence of later apostasy in Putney; on matters of faith and politics — synonyms for Swinburne — he proves remarkably consistent.[4]

Yet it is curious that a poet who became a byword for atheism within his own lifetime — who prompted Christina Rossetti to paste paper strips over the anti-religious parts of *Atalanta*, whom Carlyle allegedly dismissed as 'a man standing up to his neck in a cesspool and adding to its contents' and who lies behind the saddest lines in Thomas Hardy's elegy 'A Singer Asleep' — should risk this affiliation with Christianity.[5] How should we understand this statement? Can one reject theism and yet profess membership of a poetic *ecclesia*? What does poetry have to do with faith? This chapter focuses on Swinburne's response to these questions, and to those who may be tempted to assume that, given his avowed antitheism, Swinburne's poetry has nothing to do with 'religious matters', or what Swinburne, in his later epic *Tristram of Lyonesse*, calls 'faithless faith'.

This paradoxical phrase appears first in the Prelude to *Tristram* as 'The faithless faith that lives without belief / Its light life through, the griefless ghost of grief' (IV, p. 7).[6] However, the full implications of this paradox are not explored until the ninth canto, in lines that describe the beatific vision of the faithless-faithful. Throughout this passage the thinking is inextricable from the movement of its couplets. Here, enjambment lets the thought overrun the bounds of the couplet, giving these subsequent lines the speed and force that hurries us towards the chancel floor:

> Truth, stablished and made sure by strong desire
> Fountain of all things living, source and seed,
> Force that perforce transfigures dream to deed
> God that begets on time, the body of death,
> Eternity: nor may man's darkening breath,
> Albeit it stain, disfigure or destroy
> The glass wherein the soul sees life and joy
> Only, with strength renewed and spirit of youth,
> And brighter than the sun's the body of Truth
> Eternal, unimaginable of man,
> Whose very face not Thought's own eyes may scan,
> But see far off his radiant feet at least, (IV, 135)

Swinburne delays the subject of the clause for seven lines while cosmic similes and analogies are allowed to build. 'Truth', when it arrives, therefore comes as something of a relief. This strong-stressed syllable, jamming with the first syllable of 'stablished', breaks the unfolding of the previous lines, fixing 'truth' as a pivot between these souls and the desire the singer describes. The body of truth — 'unimaginable' — is seen 'far off', trampling the source of fear and subjugation: God. In this connection, the echo of Pope's 'Essay on Man' in his working-out of the rhyme-pair 'man' and 'scan' is hard to miss:

> Know, then, thyself, presume not God to scan;
> The proper study of mankind is man.
> Placed on this isthmus of a middle state,
> A being darkly wise, and rudely great:
> With too much knowledge for the sceptic side,
> With too much weakness for the stoic's pride,
> He hangs between; in doubt to act, or rest;
> In doubt to deem himself a god, or beast;[7]

Swinburne's allusion reverses the order of 'man' and 'scan' rhetorically and philosophically, overthrowing the idea of the ordered middle state so persuasively facilitated by the balance of Pope's heroic couplets. Against the idea that man is too knowing to be sceptical about the presence of the divine order, yet too weak to attain to the stoic detachment of *ataraxia*, Swinburne poses the sceptical view of a higher truth that can be subject to no power.[8] This truth lies so far beyond the grasp of the god-making tendencies of man as to be unimaginable. It cannot be 'scanned', but we see its feet. And where those feet tread they overthrow authoritative power:

> Trampling the head of Fear, the false high priest,
> Whose broken chalice foams with blood no more,
> And prostrate on that high priest's chancel floor,
> Bruised, overthrown, blind, maimed, with bloodless rod,
> The miscreation of his miscreant God. (IV, 135)

The reader must double back to keep up with the repetition of 'God' here, which, once we replay our steps, is understood not to name a second, false god, opposed to 'truth', but to demonstrate a false appellation. What is at stake here is the entire process of knowing God. The couplet beginning 'Bruised, overthrown' stretches wide before snapping back in the cramped last line, culminating in a pun and a prayer. This tongue-twister depends upon our multiplying out the alliterative terms. 'Miscreation' suggests the idolatry of the high priest who worships false gods instead of truth. 'Miscreant' complicates this further, since the word can mean both something that bodes ill and an unbeliever. A false yet nevertheless valid etymology, which mistakes the Latin *credere* for *creare*, allows for a final sense of 'miscreant' as an aberration: this false God is a monster.[9] By means of a rhetorically and phonically dense verse-paragraph, the narrator invites us to imagine the overthrow, not simply of the high priest of religion, but God himself as a misbeliever in 'truth'.

Yet more is happening here than an isolated reading of these lines will allow. Rhyme is also working allusively within Swinburne's own poem, and beyond it. The lines quoted above follow the much commented upon 'antiphonal' opening, in which Swinburne reuses the same couplet rhymes as he did in the Prelude, with one significant exception.[10] Though these lines from the ninth canto come after the answering antiphonal passage has ended, we still have one ear harking back towards the Prelude in which 'faithless faith' is first described. Yet Swinburne's verse is also working allusively across his own work. The reader may, for example, recall the rhyme-pair in the 'greater ode' of *Atalanta*. In those lines 'the supreme evil, God' 'smites without sword and scourges without rod'. Here 'a bloodless rod' has become dissociated from the God, who has been overthrown.

It is no coincidence that the same rhyme-pair also appears in Swinburne's 'For the Feast of Giordano Bruno' (1878), which commemorates this 'philosopher and martyr' who, after Lucretius and Shelley, completes Swinburne's triumvirate of poets who fought and died in the cause of free thought (*Poetical Works*, III, p. 48). Of this poem, Martin Priestman comments that 'Swinburne's loud reaffirmation of the atheism that lay at the heart of Victorian nervousness about [*De Rerum Natura*] will serve [...] as a reminder that the robust Lucretius of late Enlightenment

Romanticism was not entirely buried'.[11] However, although Swinburne's 'faithless faith' might well prove paraphrasable along Lucretian lines, his verse far outruns any 'babble' about 'religious matters'. Swinburne's couplets hark simultaneously, and in a moment, back to *Atalanta*, back further still to Pope, back to Giordano Bruno, and through *Tristram*. Reading the poems, Swinburne's claim to be a member of 'the church of Blake and Shelley' proves more complex than his letter to Stedman implies. Evidently to do justice to that complexity the question 'what is the relation between poetry and faith?' will require further thinking. Swinburne's poetry may even offer a vital test case for the question of how poetry and faith are related in this period, and an opportunity to reconsider how we connect his explicit thinking about poetry to the way his poems actually think.

Simon Jarvis makes a valuable distinction between the explicit thinking about poetry that poets engage in and the kinds of thinking that poems involve. Of course, it would be a mistake to call the latter kind of thinking 'implicit' since nothing can be said to be implicit to itself:

> All is not representation. Gossip, correspondence, manuscripts, printing, editing, reviews, metrical theories: all these represent essential evidence about the historical meaning of verse-thinking. Yet they remain liable to be exceeded or corrected by what happens in that verse-thinking itself.[12]

Jarvis's distinction proves provocative for a poet such as Swinburne. Even on a first reading, his verse promises to be far more complex than any 'babble' about 'religious matters'.

However, the problem of how explicit thinking and verse-thinking are connected is further complicated in the case of religious poetry, because of the antagonistic relation between art and religion which develops through the nineteenth century. Adorno, in a short essay that has implications for the study of this period, sets out both the challenge of reading beyond the 'rationalisation' of art in religious terms and the difficulty of doing so. He begins by criticising the idea that art fulfils the same function in society as religion once did. Against established narratives that read this period as a pivotal moment in the history of disenchantment, Adorno's conclusion that 'the notion that art has broken away from religion only during a late stage of enlightenment and secularisation is erroneous' challenges that particular privilege of Victorian poetry studies to comment on their interrelation.[13] Adorno's check goes further than recent reconsiderations of the secularisation narrative.[14] Rather than debating the truth or falsity of a presumed juncture between poetry and religion, he requires us to attend instead to the conditions that make this particular way of thinking about art and religion possible. Following Adorno, criticism can no longer regard the relationship between art and religion as mutually exclusive, or even neutral. Instead the two appear locked in antagonism.[15]

That the presumed unity or disunity of art and religion has proved to be the more legible narrative for cultural critics is suggested by its currency. A recent monograph takes this rationale as given:

> This study started from a very simple and obvious premiss: when Victorian poetry speaks of faith, it tends to do so in steady and regular rhythms; when it

speaks of doubt, it is correspondingly more likely to deploy irregular, unsteady, unbalanced rhythms [...] This may seem self-evident. It certainly did so to Victorian poets and critics.[16]

In Kirstie Blair's comprehensive study of the topic, faith is understood to be manifest in poetic technique through a correspondence between religious and poetic orderliness. However, only poems that submit their form to the principles of those 'Victorian poets and critics' Blair presents can count as having 'faith'. As a history of what poets have said about form and faith, Blair's study is unrivalled. However, quite apart from the difficulty of determining systematically what is meant by a 'steady and regular rhythm' (as we shall see, Swinburne's couplets can at moments rival Pope in their 'balance'), attending only to the explicit thinking around the poetry of this period risks drawing conclusions before a reading of the poem can properly be said to have begun.

'Against this sort of thing', Adorno writes, 'art can keep faith to its true affinity with religion, the relationship with truth, only by an almost ascetic abstinence from any religious claim or any touching upon religious subject matter. Religious art today is nothing but blasphemy' (Adorno, *Theses*, 678–79). This last sentence is directed against the 'religious novels' of the 1940s, yet its hyperbolic inversion of the sacral and heretical might have come from Swinburne.

The challenge for readers of Swinburne's poetry is twofold: first, to allow that explicit thinking may 'be exceeded or corrected by what happens in that verse thinking itself', and secondly, to remain open to Adorno's suggestion that poetry may in fact be most truthful when it appears most resistant being rationalised in religious terms. This chapter will try Swinburne's explicit thinking about poetry and faith against how his verse actually thinks, before turning to consider how this might be related to the 'faithless faith' expressed in *Tristram of Lyonesse*.

The Church of Blake and Shelley

While Swinburne might protest to Stedman that he is 'in no sense a Theist', he continued to use the idea of belonging to a certain denomination when expressing the kind of poetry he was writing. This is especially so in the case of *Tristram of Lyonesse*. In a letter to Richard Monckton Milnes, Swinburne makes the following throwaway remark:

> Not that I am disloyal to Tennyson, into whose church we were all in my time born and baptised as far back as we can remember at all; but he is not a greek nor a heathen; and I imagine does not want to be; and I greatly fear believes it possible to be something better: an absurdity which should be left to the Brownings and other blatant creatures begotten on the slime of the modern chaos.[17]

Here Swinburne, a convert to the church of Blake and Shelley, finds himself in an uneasy relation to the congregation of Tennyson and the Brownings. It is a curious question to ask in which tradition he would have placed Matthew Arnold. As far as his version of the legend of *Tristram* is concerned, Arnold is clearly on the wrong side. As Swinburne wrote in a letter to the poet and critic R. H. Horne: 'I do not forget that two eminent contemporaries have been before me in the field, but Arnold has transformed and recast the old legend, and Tennyson — as usual, if I may be permitted to say so — has degraded and debased it'.[18] The competitive spirit we witness here is everywhere apparent in the correspondence which surrounds the writing of this poem.

Of course, Swinburne is more tactful when he comes to explain this to Arnold himself in a letter:

> the old legend was so radically altered in its main points by your conception and treatment of that subject, and especially of the circumstances which bring about the catastrophe in all the old French forms of romance, that the field was really open to a new writer who might wish to work on the old lines.[19]

Swinburne will defer so far to Arnold, but on the question of the amorality of the lovers, which follows from their being at the mercy of Fate, and the pre-Christian setting, he remains absolute.

Sara Lyons, in her brilliant recent study of Swinburne and Pater, considers Swinburne's letter in relation to Tennyson and Arnold, rightly identifying the fact that Swinburne gives us a Tristram who, far from being a 'debased empiricist' experiences 'ecstatic submission to the laws of nature'. 'In his version of the story', she notes,

> Swinburne does not entirely ignore the problem of suffering, nor abolish the sense of the tragic, but he clearly presses his sado-masochistic imagination into the service of a grand cosmic 'yes' [....] His lovers experience only 'honeyhearted pain' [...]. That is, a pain which gives texture to their pleasure and makes their endorsements of life a form of heroism.[20]

This is an apt description of the ways in which Swinburne sought to take his reader's hearts, reorientating the debate about Swinburne's materialism. To her detailed reading of Swinburne's 'cosmic yes', we must also note that Swinburne's overt discussion of this poem is inextricably also tied up with the form the poem is to take.

On 4 November 1869, he writes of his need for 'orthodoxy' to the truth of the legend in a letter to Edward Burne-Jones. On 21 December, he writes, again to Burne-Jones, of reading Tennyson, whose Arthurian romance spurs to his ambition 'to lick the morte d'albert'. The next day finds him more reflective, commenting to Dante Gabriel Rossetti on his choice of metre:

> As you see, my verse (though the British buffer may say I am following Topsy [William Morris] in the choice of metre for romantic narrative) is modelled not after the Chaucerian cadence of *Jason* but after my own scheme of movement and modulation in Anactoria, which I consider original in structure and combination.[21]

Throughout his correspondence Swinburne consistently invites comparison between his predecessors' treatment of the legend and his own. He searches after the 'facts' of the story, ordering Francisque Michel's collection of the fragments and requesting Mathilde Blind's translations of Gottfried von Strassburg (Lang,

Letters, I, 131–32). However, when it comes to technique Swinburne appears apparently unruffled. William ('Topsy') Morris enters his discussion as an obvious but misplaced point of comparison, rather than a contender.

Herbert Tucker recognises this 'flat-footedness' in Swinburne's Prelude to the poem, arguing that: 'Among epic *proemata* Swinburne's remains remarkable for the indiscriminateness with which it lavishes praise on other makers and for the *sangfroid* with which it goes about joining them'.[22] He reads Swinburne's drive towards self-obliteration in tradition as analogous with the drives of his protagonists. Yet Swinburne's remarks about the kind of couplets he is writing are far from indiscriminate. The fact that he was writing in this form may have been enough to invite comparisons between him and other writers.[23] Given the super-historical consciousness of couplet poems, perhaps another explanation for Swinburne's 'flat-footedness' is required. Rather than seeking to compete with Arnold or Tennyson, might Swinburne have regarded himself as existing in another tradition, one that maintained what Walter Pater refers to as a 'theological' understanding of poetry's capacity to move us, but believed, instead, in an antitheistic universe?[24] If so, how might this belief be connected to the style of his couplets? Swinburne's comments have got us so far, but to consider this last question we must bring the explicit thinking of Swinburne and others towards 'the scheme of movement and modulation' in *Tristram of Lyonesse*.

The Period Ear

Swinburne could count on Rossetti's knowledge of the cadences of Chaucer and Morris. Today these cadences, along with Swinburne's couplets, are harder to hear. The demise of a trans-historical kind of listening epitomised by Walter Pater's scholar-reader and practised by critics such as Saintsbury, Symons, and by Swinburne, is registered in the gathering dissatisfaction with aesthetic criticism around 1920.[25] At the same time, the break with tradition on which the development of free verse is understood to depend means that much of the knowledge which we can suppose present at a hearing of *Tristram* in 1882 has been suppressed.

In order to understand what Swinburne meant when he claimed that his metre was 'original in structure and modulation' we might attempt a reconstruction of the period ear in the spirit of Michael Baxandall's *Painting and Experience in Fifteenth-Century Italy*. His argument for style as the proper subject of art historical research is provocative for literary studies. Following Marx, he describes how light reflected from the art object enters the eye, falls on the retina and is conveyed by a series of nerves to our brains.[26] After this, what the eye sees is no longer uniform. Instead, 'That which we tend toward will depend on many things [...] but not least on the interpreting skills one happens to possess [...] what we may call one's *cognitive style*'.[27] There are 'three variable and indeed culturally relative kinds of thing the mind brings to interpreting the pattern of light [...]: a stock of patterns, categories and methods of inference; training in a range of representational conventions; and experience, drawn from the environment, in what are plausible ways of seeing what we have incomplete information about' (pp. 31–32). Baxandall attends to each in his attempt to reconstruct how a *quattrocento* person saw. He does this in two ways: through selection and comparison of a range of paintings in the same genre and through attention to contemporary accounts of seeing, including letters and documents written by painters, patrons, and people who encountered these artworks.

Translating the concept of 'the period eye' as 'the period ear' for our investigation cannot avoid the difficulties already present in Baxandall's art historical method. The 'stock of patterns', 'training in conventions', and 'experience' or 'plausible ways of seeing' — translated here as 'plausible ways of hearing' — which he ranges as aspects of 'cognitive style' are difficult to separate. Baxandall admits: 'In practice they do not work serially, as they are described here, but together; the process is indescribably complex and still obscure in its physiological detail' (p. 32). Yet his example remains valuable precisely because it does not sidestep the complexity of artworks.

The difference between a 'stock of patterns' and 'training in conventions' is particularly hard to define in the case of poetry written before the emancipation of verse, since to our ears convention often functions as shorthand for that unfreedom from which free verse sought to extricate itself. Traditional verse-form might be understood as 'conventional' to the extent that critical encounters with poems that fit this category are often based on a model of recognition rather than cognition. Our sense of differentiation may be blunted: a couplet poem might be read as a couplet poem, rather than a couplet poem in the style of Dryden or a couplet poem in the style of Shelley. If 'a stock of patterns' and 'training in conventions' are not to be thought of as synonymous, thereby reducing their complexity, then we must begin by reawakening our capacity to engage in the range of effects which the couplet form involves. To do so, we might begin by revisiting contemporary accounts of reading *Tristram*.

Lyricising the Heroic Couplet

Tristram of Lyonesse and Other Poems elicited strong reactions. While *The Athenæum* welcomed the publication of Swinburne's 'most varied' and 'important' book, *The Spectator* reassured its readers that although the principal poem was 'Repellent [...] to all pure taste', it was thankfully 'so repellent as to be comparatively harmless'.[28] However, despite these divisions, there appears to have been a remarkable degree of consensus as to what reviewers were hearing. In order to understand Swinburne's claim that his couplets were 'original in structure and combination', I will consider four aspects of Swinburne's couplet style which reviewers drew on in their responses: speed, structure, monotony and innovation.

'Although "Anactoria" is a fine poem', George Saintsbury writes, 'I cannot be unreservedly enthusiastic over Mr. Swinburne's heroics (with due exception for *Tristram*, to be developed later)'. Swinburne's couplets in the earlier poem are, he explains, too fast:

> The stopped form is not quite in his way, and the enjambed encourages, rather too much, his tendency to be *Isaeo torrentior*. Many, very many, single couplets rise up and smite me in the face for this utterance, as —

> Take thy limbs living, and new mould with these
> A lyre of many faultless agonies;
>
> wherein one may discover capabilities of a new Drydenian model, very admirable. But on the whole I have written; and I turn with ineffable relief to the 'Hymn to Proserpine', ...[29]

Saintsbury's comments draw attention to the shifts that occur between stopped and enjambed couplets in 'Anactoria'. We might consider these lines, in which Sappho anticipates the accusation that she is 'cruel', a thought that builds from the analogy of being beloved, to being beloved of the gods, taking in the entire cosmic order. Here the tension and variation between stopped and enjambed couplets are made to yield powerful effects:

> Cruel? but love makes all that love him well
> As wise as heaven and crueller than hell.
> Me hath love made more bitter toward thee
> Than death toward man; but were I made as he
> Who hath made all things to break them one by one, (I, pp. 61–62)

Though the first line of the first couplet quoted here is open, it is demonstrative of Swinburne's use of the couplet for rhetorical effects: to be above heaven and worse than hell in your servitude to love is a powerful state. The following enjambed lines make full use of the couplet's capacity for extended simile: 'me' rhymes internally with 'thee', naming the relation, compared in the next line with 'death' and man. The caesura breaks this, allowing for a shift into the conditional, extending the simile which began at 'me' all the way to 'he': not death, we learn, travelling over the ensuing enjambed lines, but whoever it is who 'hath made all things to break them one by one'.

The monosyllabic line stretches out here, but snaps back at the simile: 'If I' (we might paraphrase) behaved like this unnamed person, treading down the highest and most unreachable things, and — the enjambed line throws in the souls of men too — then: 'God knows'. Swinburne's switching of 'he' for 'God' here, at the end of these syntactically complex lines, is an arch move. The full line thus performs another 'Me [...] thee' analogy, only this time through repetition. Through his manipulation of the couplet as a verse-unit ripe for rhetorical invention, Swinburne builds an argument for Sappho's cruelty which depends for its irony on the reader being complicit in the intuition of God's cruelty.

What follows is a couplet which is both epigrammatic, yet distinctly unDrydenian in its thinking:

> For who shall change with prayers or thanksgivings
> The mystery of the cruelty of things? (I, p. 62)

It is lines like these which threaten to change Saintsbury's mind about Swinburne's heroics. Though unpointed, the syntax of the first line terminates with the rhyme and the end of the line, and the meaning stops at the completing rhyme and question mark. It is a little looser than the Drydenian couplet, but just as epigrammatic, pithy, succinct. Part of this is due to the elision in the second line, which contains only three stresses. However, this couplet is not so different from those we encounter in a series of rhetorical questions in 'Religio Laici':

> Who knows what reasons may his mercy lead,
> Or ignorance invincible may plead?[30]

Large chunks of Dryden's couplets are, like Swinburne's, hard to extract, a fact which testifies to his similar ability to build an argument or narrative from many couplet-units. However, though we can follow the syntax beyond the single couplet, the boundary of the individual unit is always respected. This causes us to read more slowly than we do when reading Swinburne's enjambed couplets, occasionally coming to a standstill at an appropriate point:

> Most righteous doom! because a rule revealed
> Is none to those from whom it was concealed.[31]

The argument in this passage for the importance of interpretation of God's law by religious authority closes with a summative statement: the rhyme word 'revealed', set off by the alliteration, becomes an adjective only in retrospect as we pass from the first to the second line. Revelation is set in opposition to the idea of concealment by means of rhyme. The argument is so straightforwardly put as to be verging on the blindingly obvious: yet it is the couplet-rhyme, terminating with the end of the line, which pushes us to consider the absurdity of believing otherwise. The expectation, hinted at by the pointing but denied by the continuation of syntax, that the couplet will end is fulfilled.

If Dryden's argument takes place in couplets that build under the constant risk of epigrammatic closure, Swinburne's couplets have the opposite urge:

> Or say what God above all gods and years
> With offering and blood-sacrifice of tears,
> With lamentation from strange lands, from graves
> Where the snake pastures, from scarred mouths of slaves,
> From prison, and from plunging prows of ships
> Through flamelike foam of the sea's closing lips —
> With thwartings of strange signs, and wind-blown hair
> Of comets, desolating the dim air [...] (I, p. 62)

After the introduction of a comparison at 'or', Sappho's argument stretches out, overrunning the just-established couplet-unit, to fill two units. However, respect for the integrity of the couplet is maintained, in the co-termination of syntax and line breaks. One is still navigable in terms of the other. That relation threatens to break down at the enjambed line which places the noun 'graves' in a rhyme position, and its modifier 'where the snake pastures' after the line break. The reader, following the syntax, is hurled forward into the next line, but recovers — just — at the termination of syntax at 'slaves'. However, after this, all is lost.

In the lines that follow, the nominal phrase 'wind blown hair' has separated from its source 'of comets', a move that tempts mimetic readings, as if the asteroid has passed us by and we are left looking at its trail.[32] Yet Swinburne's meaning is more subtle than that; these lines put forward a vision of a disordered, 'desolate' universe, which nevertheless cannot, for all its suffering, appease God nor love. Rhymes in the lines that follow seem to pass by like lights in the sky that gleam and are gone. The splitting of the syntax across the couplet 'And life yield up her flower to violent fate? / Him would I reach, him smite, him desecrate,' marks the final undoing of the couplet as a tangible unit. In just twenty lines Swinburne has tipped the relation between syntax and rhyme, so constant in the Drydenic couplet, into reverse.

The result of this undecidability is speed. If rhyme, and particularly couplet-rhyme, begets more rhyme, and enjambment that interrupts the correspondence between syntax and line-end causes the reader to look quickly over to the next line for completion, then Swinburne draws on both processes to produce metrical momentum.[33] It is his ability to do both that makes his heroics so undecidable to Saintsbury, whose reservations are only partially allayed by the overture to *Tristram*:

> To the somewhat similar but less decided doubt hinted already about his couplet, the opening of *Tristram of Lyonesse* may, of course, be objected. That astonishing overture — which, for nearly fifty lines at a breath, as it were, and with few breathing spaces through its nearly three hundred, transforms the decasyllabic pairs into one billowing volume of lyrical outrush, [...] But if you take the poem as a whole — and, after all, a 'long poem' *does* hold itself out to be taken as a whole — I do not think the measure justifies itself fully. I do not think it justifies itself nearly as well as the couplet of Morris. Perhaps this was much more because the poet had not 'the narrative head' than because he could not manage the metre; but the fact remains.[34]

It follows that Saintsbury should prefer the Prelude to *Tristram*. Though these lines are not consistently end-stopped, the opening section tends towards the co-termination of syntax and rhyme which, unlike certain torrential moments in 'Anactoria', respect the bounds of the couplet:

> Love, that is first and last of all things made,
> The light that has the living world for shade,
> The spirit that for temporal veil has on
> The souls of all men woven in unison, (p. 5)

In the opening lines of Swinburne's poem, 'love' — as the first word, governing subject and the point to which all similes and processes return — appears as the origin for each subsequent line. Line adds to line, and couplet adds to couplet, reaching towards a 'lyrical outrush'. Yet this style of couplet does not continue through the poem as a whole. Saintsbury's question as to whether the flexibility of Swinburne's metre — strung between the enjambed Drydenian couplet and the tendency to be *Isaeo Torrentior* — 'justifies itself', pushes us to consider how speed, experienced at the local level, relates to the overall structure of the narrative.

His contemporary, scholar and translator Oliver Elton, also notes the rapidity of Swinburne's couplets, but interprets this as a tension between narrative and speed. The difficulty of Swinburne's task, he perceives, consists of trying 'in a narrative metre, to sing and tell a story at the same time':

> The verse goes apace, but the manner is so expansive and diffusive that the tale goes slowly [...] the old regular way, the spacious, tardy and not less beautiful way of romancing, as it is seen in Chaucer's *Troilus and Creseide* [sic]. or in Morris' 'Story of Rhodope', is used in *Tristram of Lyonesse*: but here the movement is vehement and quick, there it is gentle and leisurely [...] Our old heroic couplet has never been so hastened by the devices of overflowing line and trisyllabic bar and by the lightening of accent. Yet all such comparisons, which try to convey the impression of rapid tempo, are really out of place. For *Tristram* is a true romance, where the conception of time is abolished altogether [...] the real persons are only two or three, and the active world is a far-off murmur [...] For time can only be measured in such a story by the interruptions of the world, and these are never suffered to happen.[35]

The tension that Elton identifies between telling and singing strikes a chord with Tucker's sense of the challenge that Swinburne took on in writing *Tristram*: 'How might a poetics of momentariness be dilated to epic proportions, or conversely how might a verse narrative of book length be maintained at the pitch of intensity to which his imagination resonated?'[36] Taking these two insights, we see how Swinburne's speed must be linked to the lyrical quality of *Tristram*. For Elton, 'manner' refers not to the style of the couplets, but the story itself, which should be slow, but the quickness of the verse works against this: the poet has adapted the heroic couplet in the interests of speed. Some clues as to how he does this include the use of elision previously noted, and 'trisyllabic bars', Elton's term for double offbeats. The varying speed of Swinburne's couplet and its relationship to the overall structure of the poem are key to an understanding of how Swinburne's couplet prioritises the individual moment at the expense of the narrative. In order to gauge the way in which the couplet in *Tristram* is set apart from 'the old regular way [...] of romancing' we might consider these lines from Morris's *The Life and Death of Jason* in which the hero is first brought into the king's hall:

> Lords of the World, fair let our bliss abide
> This hour at least, nor let our dear delight
> Be marred by aught, until the silent night
> Has come, and turned to day again, and we
> Wake up once more to joy or misery,
> Or death itself, if so it pleaseth you:
> Is this thing, then, so great a thing to do?[37]

The syntax of these open couplets frequently overruns the line break, yet we experience nothing approaching the violation of the couplet, nor the speed which we encountered in 'Anactoria'. The narrative proceeds in stages, one movement per line, or one movement strung between caesura and caesura. This corpuscular movement draws attention to the fact that, although syntax and couplet-rhyme exist in counterpoint to each other (the syntax terminating, not at the end, but in the middle of a line) they do not work against each other, but exist in an easy tension. Once we realise this, it becomes clear that Swinburne's couplets show a different relation between the couplet-unit and grammar.

In 'Anactoria', in contrast, we witness a frequent separation of nouns and modifiers, or subjects from verbs. In *Jason* verbs occur at line endings, yet the object always follows in the first half of the next line; this never disorientates us. Occasionally we can see Morris's prioritisation of the couplet over syntax, which leads him to reverse syntax as Keats had done before him: 'where right royally / Was Jason clad'. Rather than separate noun and verb, the verb is moved to the next line, introducing a slightly archaic — one might well say Chaucerian — note. Swinburne, were he to write these lines, might have kept to regular word order and ignored the break, or even seen an opportunity to use alliteration as a spur to movement: 'where Jason was / Right royally clad'. Morris deviates from the 'Drydenic model' to let syntax and verse run counterpoint to each other, but he does not seek to break it. His verse will not allow it, since to break the bounds of the couplet-unit depends on our consciousness of it as a unit, and Morris's heroics are rarely epigrammatic in the same way that Dryden's are. The splitting of the couplet at the end of verse-paragraphs, marked on the page by a dividing line, does not result in the inversion of the couplet, as it did in 'Anactoria', but seems to naturally move the reader on; a linking note provides the cue for the next verse in a round. Morris's 'narrative head' has no interest in prolonging certain moments through the mechanism of his verse. If his tale does sing, it gains its richness from the precise diction, or rich imagery.

Read against Morris, we can see why the tension between singing and telling in Swinburne's poem was interpreted as a lack of skill or consistency. *The Spectator* would prefer selections, while *The Saturday Review* locates a lack of 'keeping', a term borrowed from art criticism, to imply a consistent loss of perspective:

> the whole effect is not great, in spite of the surpassing splendour of individual parts [...] there is a profusion of wonderful gems distributed in the poem [...] Against these qualities [...] we must set [...] the unsympathetic nature of the subject and of many incidents; the rhetorical overloading of ornament; the want of clearness, which compels one to read passage after passage several times over before the meaning becomes distinct; and the want of keeping (as we think it) in a long philosophical soliloquy of Tristram's.[38]

Writing in a similar vein, *The Westminster Review* notes a disjunction between narrative and 'a certain amplification of striking thoughts or situations':

> which begets undue lengthiness, degenerating sometimes into downright tediousness. When a fine idea has been sufficiently and happily expressed [...] it is taken for the theme of complex and endless variations, tortured and twisted, enlarged upon and reiterated, in language always melodious, often eloquent, but also often obscured and forced, till at last it looks so small, amid the sea of sounding words whereon it floats.[39]

While the criticism that *Tristram* is 'obscure' and 'reiterative' might be explained as a failure to see the value of 'singing and telling a story at the same time', a further explanation might be sought in the repetitive nature of certain couplet textures.[40] Instead of subordinating the narrative to the story, the verse in this poem establishes its own patterns.

Gosse later wrote in his *Life*: 'It is perhaps the uniformity of effort in the texture of Tristram which produces a sense of fatigue':

> The Prelude [...] is a magnificent performance [...] as learned and brilliant a piece of studied versification as we meet with in the whole of English literature [...] Swinburne's achievement here can only be compared with that of Shelley in *Epipsychidion*, which as a metrical feat the Prelude surpasses [...] Again, at the close of the last canto, the final scene of the dying Tristram, perplexed with the juggle of the white sail and the black, is admirably told, and the closing lines are very striking. But between these extremities, and relieved by marvellous maritime effects, there are long stretches of monotony caused by strain and effort to make every passage a purple one. The poem is less a story than a homily on the theme that Love is 'So strong that heaven, could Love bid heaven farewell. Would turn to fruitless and unflowering hell; So sweet that hell, to hell could love be given. Would turn to splendid and sonorous heaven,' — a theme that Dryden himself could not illustrate in the redundancy of an epic.[41]

Gosse's term 'monotony' has hit upon a truth which requires that we recognise the way in which certain verse textures in *Tristram* repeat. The 'strain and effort' he identifies names the lyrical impulse and speed we have just been discussing. However, unlike those reviewers who found this impulse worked against the expectation of narrative progression, Gosse provides us with an antecedent for 'this particular kind of verse' in Shelley, one precedent for the speed of Swinburne's couplets. We will return to the question of what Swinburne took from Shelley in a moment. However, before this, we must attend to the question of how innovative the couplets of *Tristram* actually were.

Swinburne's anticipation of comparison with Morris in his letter to Rossetti shows how acute his ear was. For a less pitch-perfect, yet still well-practised ear, we can turn to a review published in *The Athenæum*.[42] Having considered the plot and story, the second half of the review considers the poem from 'the metrical point of view'. Swinburne's use of the 'Drydenic triplet and alexandrine' is not always successful, the reviewer concludes. Where Dryden always used the triplet to bring about climactic and cumulative effects which answer to the matter at hand, Swinburne is far less discriminate, even building triplets mid-sentence. The result is that there is 'no rest' for the ears. The reviewer identifies two possible options for a poet writing couplets in 1882 and places Swinburne in an uneasy relation to them:

> It is poets of the Keats order, and not poets having a kinship with Shelley, who have any real affinity to Dryden and his essentially epigrammatic movements. 'Lamia' gains as much as 'Tristram of Lyonesse' loses by the introduction of the triplet and the alexandrine.[43]

The same tension between the 'epigrammatic movements' of Dryden and the tendency to fluency which Saintsbury and Elton recognise, and which we saw in 'Anactoria', is reinterpreted here in relation to the triplet. At the same time, the reviewer draws our attention back towards the use of triple rhyme, whether it is used to build or release tension, whether it concludes or acts as a spur. Despite these reservations, the reviewer is clear about the innovative nature of Swinburne's couplets:

> But never before has the heroic couplet become so lyrical, never before has it allowed itself such freedom in the introduction of anapaestic bars, and never before has it been to achieve so completely the fluent continuity of blank verse. That this lovely freedom and variety is mainly achieved by skilful vowel-elision we need scarcely say.[44]

What Swinburne seems to have achieved here is the lyricisation of the couplet. This is connected to a number of aspects of Swinburne's technique. A variety in rhythm, a tendency towards anapaestic feet — what I would call double offbeats — which Elton also notes, and vowel elision combine with a shifting relation between grammar and the couplet-unit. A brief consideration of two poems by Dryden and Keats which Swinburne knew well will help to ground this description.

In Dryden's translation from Lucretius's *De Rerum Natura* we witness a tension between the epigrammatic potential of the couplet to contain and marshal an argument towards its close, and the alternative resource of the triplet to throw a final gauge. The construction of a unit such as 'Why are we then so fond of mortal life, / Beset with dangers, and maintained with strife?', poised in its end-pointing and with a navigable co-termination of syntax and metre, is familiar to us as the kind of couplet preferred by Saintsbury.[45] Dryden's triplets, though they are not enjambed, offer an alternative movement:

> Besides, we tread but a perpetual round;
> We ne'er strike out, but beat the former ground,
> And the same mawkish joys in the same track are found.
> For still we think an absent blessing best,
> Which cloys, and is no blessing when possest;
> A new arising wish expels it from the breast.[46]

In the first triplet the sense overruns the bounds of the couplet to reiterate and enlarge on the point made: stoic peace is difficult to attain when doubts continually return and resurface. Against the end of doubt, change and suffering urged by the finality of the couplet, the triplet facilitates the qualification, the difficulty of reaching this. Our suspicion is confirmed a few lines later, by a run of two triplets which defy the possibility of closure, *ataraxia*, by the introduction of 'mawkish joys' and the 'new arising' — the fear and hope which make human beings human and not god-like. The tension between couplet and triplet facilitates two kinds of argument: one that would have done with doubt, and another which gives space to joy. Dryden is therefore able to gesture, even in a translation of Lucretius, towards another kind of hope not found in Epicurean philosophy, which cannot be gained from self-sufficiency. In this his verse-thinking marks a development from Thomas Creech's translation, which uses the triplets to advance a new thought, but which sticks more closely to his source text.[47]

The tension between triplet and couplet is handled differently by Keats, as in these lines from 'Lamia':

> [...] yet in content
> Till she saw him, as once she pass'd him by,
> Where 'gainst a column he leant thoughtfully

> At Venus' temple porch, 'mid baskets heap'd
> Of amorous herbs and flowers, newly reap'd
> Late on that eve, as 'twas the night before
> The Adonian feast; whereof she saw no more,
> But wept alone those days, for why should she adore?[48]

Keats cannot draw on the same tension between couplet and triplet because his couplet is not epigrammatic as Dryden's is.[49] The detention enforced by Keats's rhymes — an experience that we do not encounter in reading Shelley — is particularly acute in the case of the triplet. Here it causes us to dwell on Lamia's inexplicable suffering, the line running to an awkward stop, which seems at odds with the onward push of the previous lines. Our experience of the first triplet that we encounter in *Tristram*, in the second canto, has a similar kind of arrest:

> And in his face a lordship of strong joy
> And height of heart no chance could curb or cloy
> Lightened, and all that warmed them at his eyes
> Loved them as larks that kindle as they rise
> Toward light they turn to music love the blue strong skies. (p. 16)

In contrast to the Prelude, Swinburne here overruns the bounds of the couplet-unit, allowing his syntax to carry the description of his hero over the line breaks, and even between couplet-units, as the number of split couplets urges the narrative on towards its looked-for object, Tristram. The couplet then pulls back, in an epigrammatic flourish, to present his hero and affirm his fame before mounting again to a lyrical description, heightened by anaphora in the lines quoted above, as if this song of praise could go on forever adding clause to clause, before outrunning the couplet in an unlooked-for triplet. The preposition 'toward' is grammatically correct, yet the line is a shock. The lack of punctuation in this grammatically crammed phrase, combined with the awkwardness of two extra syllables, leaves us with a sense that the verse has broken beyond its banks.

This, the first of Swinburne's triplets, is in many ways the least successful. However, it is demonstrative of the kind of movement that Swinburne uses to facilitate the lyrical impulse in *Tristram*. Taking the triplet's capacity to offer an extra thought from Dryden, and the use of the triplet in Keats as a chord that signs a moment of emotional intensity, Swinburne seeks to lyricise the couplet by allowing speech to outrun the couplet in an outrush of joy. This does not work by jamming together rhymes to detain the ear, as we saw in 'Lamia', because his rhymes are not, like Keats's, resourceful yet forced. Instead, at his most lyrical Swinburne's rhymes slide like the days which the lovers fail to notice passing 'over [us] like music'. In this way Swinburne's couplets are indebted, as Edmund Gosse and the reader in *The Athenæum* both attest, to Shelley, and to that aspect of Shelley's couplet poetry which pushes its reader towards rapid recitation.

Though William Keach's study *Shelley's Style* does not attend to *Epipsychidion* at length, his reading of 'To a Skylark' suggests four close correspondences between the construction of the couplet in *Tristram* and that of Shelley's ode.[50] The lines in Shelley's poem, Keach notes, are enjambed, the rhythm flowing on uninterrupted from line to line, and 'urge the reader past the separation imposed by punctuation and stanzaic division'. At the same time, enjambment often divides a verb or a verb modifier from the direct object, meaning that the reader has to read forward, leaning into the next line. Both of these techniques were seen in the extract from 'Anactoria'. A further aspect of Shelley's couplet verse is the reduction in the number of stresses per line as an 'expedient' line. That Swinburne's verse might do something similar is suggested by the reviewer in *The Athenæum* who called his 'vowel-elisions' 'impracticable'. Lastly, there is something similar in the way rhyme can, at times, pass unnoticed. Keach notes that 'We tend to assume that Shelley wrote more blank verse than he actually did, in part because rhymed decasyllabic poems such as *Mont Blanc*, *Julian and Maddalo* and *Epipsychidion* often create the impression of blank verse through their rhythm and syntax'.[51] Simon Jarvis is struck by what Donald Davie calls the 'urbane lucidity' of *Julian and Maddalo*, when considered alongside the 'rich impenetrability' — the phrasal inversion and dense vocabulary — of Keats. The extension of syntax over many lines in Shelley's poem means that we pass over rhymes 'as though these were the merest chance felicities of a turn of mind, rather than a device obligatory once committed to'.[52] That this is also a tendency in Swinburne's poem can be seen from the praise of the reviewer in *The Athenæum*: 'never before has [our heroic couplet] been able to achieve so completely the fluent continuity of blank verse'.[53]

In order to demonstrate what 'Anactoria' and *Tristram* owe to Shelley, we can return to *Epipsychidion*:

> She met me, Stranger, upon life's rough way,
> And lured me towards sweet Death; as Night by Day,
> Winter by Spring, or Sorrow by swift Hope,
> Led into light, life, peace. An antelope,
> In the suspended impulse of its lightness,
> Were less aethereally light: the brightness
> Of her divinest presence trembles through
> Her limbs, as underneath a cloud of dew
> Embodied in the windless heaven of June
> Amid the splendour-wingèd stars, the Moon
> Burns, inextinguishably beautiful[54]

In the first line quoted, four stressed syllables instead of the expected five offer an 'expedient', but the impulse to quicken is held back by the commas, which prioritise syntax. The caesura in the second line, breaking past the mid-point, as we have seen lines do in 'Anactoria', becomes the occasion for a forward-leaning that speeds us through the associated pairs of sequential events, at the same time that these lines propose a force that lures all things towards their termination. Here rhythm is interacting with allegory, and allegory with metre: each element of each pair bears a strong stress, as if to capitalise them. We barely notice the rhymes as we hurtle towards the indeterminable phrase 'light, life, peace' — not a resolution, but a pause as we attempt to distribute stress across the monosyllables. The movement of the first four lines, were we to sum it up, is one of restraint, then a jump, an outrunning of the couplet, then a termination of the sentence in such a position that the lines seem primed to go through it all again — which they then proceed to do. It is difficult to tell, given the interaction of metre with form, how far the disorientation we feel on meeting with 'An antelope' is to do with the non-germane quality of these animals to Western love-lyrics, or the placement of the caesura which tips us back into the rush.

This poem lacks the 'urbanity' of *Julian and Maddalo*, yet the rhymes go by almost unnoticed. Occasionally Shelley manages the caesura in the second line of a couplet in order to dwell for a moment's moment on a single word. Breaking syntax before 'brightness' in the sixth line quoted creates a pause, and allows this culminating couplet-rhyme to ring out, bringing about an effect not unlike some of the more enforced rhymes in *Endymion* but with the opposite consequence. Instead of the clunk in Keats's poem, 'brightness' here acquires a kind of independence, just as the 'moon', also a culminating couplet-rhyme, does four lines later. The separation of the subject 'moon' from the verb 'burns', a move that we saw in 'Anactoria' and will see in *Tristram*, results in the frequent placement of the verb in prime syntactical position with a strong stress. This encourages the reader to overpass both line break and rhyme, yet it also prioritises the idea of action: verbs come to the fore in Shelley's verse. It is Shelley's prerogative as to when syntax will be allowed to terminate, on occasion, with the line break, as he does here to great effect: 'Burns, inextinguishably beautiful'. This line completes the sense of the foregoing lines, yet the syntax ends mid-couplet. It is as if Shelley's entire manner — the rhymeless rhymes, the separation of subject and verb, the elisions for speed and the prolongation of syntax over many lines — are poised for continuation; like a pendulum, they come to a stop only to gather momentum again, poised for the next movement.

Yet prolongation is also what these lines are about. Over and against the idea of momentariness expressed by the verb 'quivers', this verb is repeated, and then extended via the adverbial phrase 'Continuously prolonged, and ending never'. All Shelley's description aims to maintain the rapture proper to the lyrical impulse, the self-obliteration and sublime revelation involved in coming across one's twin soul. This impulse to stop a moment's moment decaying to a moment's monument is in tension with the speed of his couplets, which seem to facilitate that 'lure' he describes, that downward movement of all things. Here, as throughout the poem, it is difficult to separate the experience of speed from what is at stake in the idea of quickness — the 'swift hope' — which follows from the speaker's 'sorrow'.

Keach's sense that 'Throughout Shelley's poetry the pre-eminent figurative standard for speed is the action of thought or spirit' was not lost on Swinburne. Speed is a crucial aspect of his response to *Epipsychidion*:

> then we are afloat not on a river, but on a torrent, on whose swift and flashing surface, as we move, we have scarcely time to breathe. This marks the whole poem. It is the most rapid of all his works.[55]

Swinburne's praise of quickness also tallies with his reading of Blake's 'monotony', which Swinburne uses, contra Gosse, as a term of praise. 'Here, as in all swift "inspired" writing' he discovers:

> huge various monotonies [...] By no manner of argument or analysis will one be
> made able to look back or forward with pure confidence and comprehension.
> Only there are laws, strange as it must sound.[56]

Blake's 'The Everlasting Gospel', which Swinburne comments upon here, is also a couplet poem, written in ballad metre and with lines that are almost entirely enjambed. The effect of rhyming over a shorter line in a metre that tends towards four strong stresses per line creates a metrical and syntactical isochrony which is certainly monotonous — yet it is also quick. Swinburne's critical interest in couplet poems by Blake and Shelley suggests a precedent for the speed and the 'various monotonies' that can be read in his own poem. Yet he also discovered the potential for a link between this speed and a figuration of universal processes which stems, not from a symbolic understanding of form, but from how the couplet facilitates certain styles of thinking. However, with this realization comes a risk.

The positive form of monotony that Swinburne discovered in Blake's 'laws' finds its answer in *Tristram*. However, as Gosse's use of the word implies, these textures are consistently at risk of decaying into a motif. William Morris felt this keenly when he described the unnatural literariness of Swinburne's verse. The instability surrounding Swinburne's triplets is particularly acute in *Tristram*, since what is at stake here is the capacity of the couplet to think about agency, time, and death. Yet it is testament to Swinburne's innovativeness that he manages to recombine and reuse verse textures to produce effects, without allowing these textures to decay. In the remainder of this chapter, I want to consider three moments in which Swinburne's verse works to exceed any rationalisation of his verse in terms of his faithless faith, beginning with the lovers' approach to Tintagel.

Here at the opening of the second canto, the 'new Drydenian model' that Saintsbury admired and the outrun couplet are combined to produce a dramatic tension between the lovers — newly fallen — and their situation. The canto begins in enjambed, loose couplets, not dissimilar to those found in the 'Prelude':

> Out of the night arose the second day,
> And saw the ship's bows break the shoreward spray
> As the sun's boat of gold and fire began
> To sail the sea of heaven unsailed of man, [...] (p. 39)

The co-termination of syntax and rhyme allows the narrative to progress in neat stages, facilitating comparison. The sun in the sky and the boat in the sky, threaded together by the comparative 'as', allow for simile and simultaneity at the same time, recalling Swinburne's earlier 'homily' that love can bring about heaven on earth.

Following this lyrical yet balanced advance, the split couplet which communicates the end of the journey runs up a little short. As we saw in Morris's *Jason*, this has the knack of propelling the narrative. However, what we are propelled into is not the end of the journey, as one might expect, but a backward glance which suddenly rounds on us in the form of a question: can today's sun be the same as yesterday?

> Ah, was not something seen of yester-sun,
> When the sweet light that lightened all the skies
> Saw nothing fairer than one maiden's eyes,
> That whatsoever in all time's years may be
> To-day's sun nor to-morrow's sun shall see? (p. 39)

Running four 'new Drydenic' couplets into a rhetorical question, the epigrammatic answer, with its universal, balanced caesura is almost Popeian. However, our sense of fate and fatedness, of a tremendous shift in the order of Iseult's experience, has as much to do with the force of this couplet working in contrast with the previous lines as it has to do with the narrator's interjection.

In the lines that follow the 'Drydenic' model wavers, falls away and is outrun. The first sign of this change in texture is the placement of 'Tristram and Iseult' at the beginning of the line, the strong stress on the first syllable of 'Tristram' having already become associated (three times in the first canto alone) with the strong stress that follows the breaking of syntax across a line break ('So like the morning through the morning moved / Tristram, a light to look on and be loved' (p. 16)). Our suspicion is confirmed by the longest verse-paragraph yet in the canto, in which the 'soul-satisfaction' of hero and heroine is described in ever-mounting detail, the couplet-unit disappearing, as the rhymes fail to register. From here the Shelleyan run takes over, and the Swinburnean lyrical couplet comes into its own:

> Nought else they saw nor heard but what the night
> Had left for seal upon their sense and sight,
> Sound of past pulses beating, fire of amorous light
> Enough, and overmuch, and never yet
> Enough, though love still hungering feed and fret,
> To fill the cup of night which dawn must overset. (p. 40)

Meanwhile, the reader knows nothing except the forward momentum of Swinburne's lines. The termination of syntax and couplet-rhyme at 'sight' suggests a pause, yet the line leaps over, to clinch a triplet, mid-sentence: very un-Drydenic. At the line beginning 'enough', the vacillation which follows, brilliantly executed through paratactic syntax, strings the reader between satisfaction and want. Here theme and form interact in mutually enforcing ways. The triplet overspills, the poem is full of noises, then into a second triplet which outruns the usual syllable count, as well as rhyming again in a line that leaves Tristram and Iseult totally isolated, yet intent upon the cosmos.

The triplet is still ringing in our ears after the more balanced texture again takes hold, so the arrival — this is the most like Morris that Swinburne ever gets — line by line at the walls of Tintagel almost fails to register. More than Wagner's uprising sailors' song, Swinburne's intricate layering of verse textures successfully instils in the reader that moment of panic in which, shaken out of a reverie, our attention is cruelly forced back towards the world. The end of this verse-music signals the conflict between individual experience and the *polis*, between lyric and narrative. Yet as the source of that music in the 'quiring spheres' suggests, this music also has to do with the conflict between fate and how his characters meet it.

Three Couplet Textures

It is difficult to talk about character in a poem in which the characters are less than person-like. Tucker captures this when he describes Swinburne's protagonist, not in terms of character development, but perspective: 'they become lovers by accident and because they cannot help it; they become heroes by the intensity with which they grasp in this salient absurdity an instantiation of the human condition that lies beyond regret or blame — and that is, in fact, to die for'.[57] Tristram and Iseult are as full of fate, and of love, as past epic heroes had been full of God. This has been interpreted as a form of Lucretian monism.[58] Yet Tucker's remarks are perhaps the more insightful, suggesting how the impersonality of Swinburne's hero and heroine stems, not from self-obliteration, but self-fulfilment in attuning oneself to the movement of the spheres. As one reviewer put it, comparing Swinburne's romance with Tennyson's *Idylls*, 'We shall not find in "Tristram" those sharp keen touches which in a few winged words embody a complete personality, or an entire situation'. However, '[t]hough in no one memorable phrase is Tristram's personality revealed as by a lightning flash, still by other means the result is no less surely and perfectly attained'.[59] If Swinburne's poem cannot be said to have 'characters', then he must hold his reader's interest by 'other means'. The recognisable, determined and seemingly determining variation in verse textures is one way in which he does this, and this is nowhere more apparent than in the third canto.

Selections of Swinburne's Arthurian epic tend not to quote from Tristram's long soliloquy in which he despairs at his separation from Iseult. Yet this speech is one of the most intricate passages in all his work. Here three distinct verse textures work to suggest a determining force that courses through Tristram. Yet these textures are interrelated, originating in the same lyricised couplet and triplet. We might therefore prefer to think of them as tendencies: firstly towards a fluent downward movement, secondly towards epigrammatic statement, and thirdly, the refluent texture, building towards what I will call affirmative moments, which sometimes culminate in a triplet. Somewhere between the first and third couplet textures lies Tristram and Iseult's heroism. Yes-sayers in a cruel and impersonal universe, the joy they take in nature, swimming, sex, and living is transformative. It is in this portrayal of two lovers freed from hope or fear that Swinburne's verse keeps faith to truth.

Tristram's speech begins by repeating words said aloud to Iseult, in the bower in the woods:

> As the dawn loves the sunlight I love thee;
> As men that shall be swallowed of the sea
> Love the sea's lovely beauty, as the night
> That wanes before it loves the young sweet light,
> And dies of loving; as the worn-out noon
> Loves twilight, and as twilight loves the moon
> That on its grave a silver seal shall set —
> We have loved and slain each other, and love yet. (p. 54)

In these lines, a Shelleyan, fluent movement tips the reader over the line breaks, letting term replace term, as one entity dies and is replaced by its opposite. We recall comparable descriptions of process in *Jason* and *Epipsychidion*, yet in neither extract quoted above is the 'lure' — to use Shelley's word — of one thing towards its opposite so cyclical. In *Jason*, night and day are appealed to as facts — certain enough to make an oath on — whereas in Shelley the verse will support self-obliteration but not renewal. In Swinburne's verse-thinking, terms replace terms, as rhymes replace rhymes. The ceaseless turnover of entities held in process, from 'noon' to 'moon', 'slain' to 'twain', 'set' to 'yet' supplant each other in a downward movement which proceeds with such metrical ease as to seem entirely independent. That metrical movement is allowed to interact with a particularly Lucretian cosmic vision, in which nothing comes from nothing, and nothing returns to nothing, culminating in a question:

> Each into each dies, each of each is born:
> Day past is night, shall night past not be morn?
> Out of this moonless and faint-hearted night
> That love yet lives in, shall there not be light?
> Light strong as love, that love may live in yet? (p. 55)

The downward movement of the verse, like the 'cosmic stream' which Myers also encountered reading Swinburne, is countered by a question asking for respite. Surely, Tristram asks, as all things die and go down, something may rise again? Yet this hope, once sounded, is instantly rejected. At the same time that Tristram lets go of hope, the fluent metre of these downward-moving couplets shifts towards a more Drydenic, epigrammatic verse texture:

> Ay, what of these? but, O strong sun! O sea!
> I bid not you, divine things! comfort me,
> I stand not up to match you in your sight —
> Who hath said ye have mercy toward us, ye who have might? (p. 57)

The line 'Who hath said ye have mercy towards us, ye who have might?' which seemed such a problem for the reviewer in *The Athenæum*, seems entirely natural within the context of a wavering between overflowing lines and the more Drydenic model. Though we still tip from a mid-line caesura into Shelleyan runs, these culminate in epigrammatic statements that argue against an impersonal, detached and uncaring God: 'What man would stretch forth hand on them to make / Fate mutable, God foolish, for his sake?' This question is not so different in form or sentiment from that raised in 'Anactoria'. From here the texture which we recall from the Prelude reasserts itself, and the line becomes more rhetorical, allowing Swinburne to lay example on example to prove the futility of attempting to overthrow the natural order — the 'apocalyptic means' he dismisses in his letter to Stedman. The fluent texture occasionally appears to struggle against this, yet the balanced texture reasserts itself, for example, in the lines 'how should this / die that was sown, and that not be which is'. These lines divide verb from subject across the line, yet instead of the anticipated tip towards Shelleyan speed we instead encounter verse-paragraphs that are composed of discrete lines which rhyme opposites into impossible resolution:

> And the old fruit change that came of the ancient root,
> And he that planted bid it not bear fruit,
> And he that watered smite his vine with drouth
> Because its grapes are bitter in our mouth,
> And he that kindled quench the sun with night
> Because its beams are fire against our sight,
> And he that tuned untune the sounding spheres
> Because their song is thunder in our ears? (p. 59)

This verse texture recalls the description of 'love' working through all things, while the rhyming of 'spheres' and 'ears' draws a connection between the triplet texture used to communicate the joy of the lovers approaching Tintagel. Swinburne here appears to be enforcing a connection between an experience of plenitude there, and reworking it within an Epicurean cosmic order; joy, like Tristram's suffering, comes and goes. The challenge is not to challenge it — 'How should we make the stable spirit to swerve [...] ?' (p. 58) — but to find oneself sufficient.

Tristram's soliloquy ends here, as he wanders 'a banished man', 'musing with close lips and lifted eyes / That smiled with self-contempt to live so wise'. However, part of the rhetorical power of the passage lies in its mobilisation of associations made possible by the various verse textures. The epigrammatic tendency of the couplet was, just a few verse-paragraphs before, the force driving an argument against a Christian hope of the possibility of redemption at the merciful hand of a divine being. By using the same texture as that of the Prelude in which all things stem from and return to 'love' — a texture that recurs in the antiphonal piece that describes how 'Fate' has a similar action — Swinburne offers an alternative statement of things as they are. The argument is as rooted in the movement and modulation of his verse as it is in Epicurean philosophy. Once we begin to recognise this movement, we can begin to understand Tristram's heroism:

> And the spring loved him surely, being from his birth
> One made out of the better part of earth,
> A man born as at sunrise; one that saw
> Not without reverence and sweet sense of awe
> But wholly without fear or fitful breath
> The face of life watched by the face of death;
> And living took his fill of rest and strife,
> Of love and change, and fruit and seed of life,
> And when his time to live in light was done
> With unbent head would pass out of the sun (p. 62)

In this soliloquy a fluent, then an epigrammatic, followed by a refluent verse texture facilitates the description of Tristram's changing mood: from despair, towards confirmation of the downward movement of all things, and from confirmation towards a countering affirmation mounting towards joy. Tristram's heroism lies in his decision to tie himself to the mast of this cosmic movement, and to live without fear or hope. That the same verse texture can be used to communicate, not despair, but joy, suggests the possibility of two reactions to the endless cycle of joy and suffering involved in the 'cosmic stream', to use Myers's phrase. However, this argument has as much to do with the eventual tendency of either texture to culminate in either a couplet, as we have seen, or, on certain occasions, a triplet.

In *Tristram* the epigrammatic couplet, which brings rhythm and syntax to the same end, comes to be associated with finality. In contrast, the triplet, which outruns the couplet sometimes so far as to stretch to an alexandrine, often facilitates an impulse to prolong the moment, stretching it out indefinitely. More than simply placing narrative and lyric impulses in tension, Swinburne's lyricised couplet is able to facilitate other kinds of tension: his verse can choose to 'float with the cosmic stream', to borrow Myers's phrase, or undergo an affirmative moment much like Nietzsche describes when he makes the choice to be a yes-sayer:

> If we affirm one moment, we thus affirm not only ourselves but all existence. For nothing is self-sufficient, neither in us ourselves nor in things; and if our soul has trembled with happiness and sounded like a harp string just once, all eternity was needed to produce this one event — and in this single moment of affirmation all eternity was called good, redeemed, justified, and affirmed.[60]

This is something that verse, because it works by means of the fulfilment of expectations, bringing a whole history of moments to bear on a single moment, has always known. Couplet verse, which is built on the opening and closing of a gesture, knew this especially. Swinburne's lyricised couplet works to facilitate this experience of momentariness through quick textures that can go one of two ways: decaying into a moment of finality, or outrunning themselves, stretching rhyme and verse towards an affirmation which seems, in the face of all things, simply heroic.

Outrunning the Couplet

It should come as no surprise, then, that triplets like those that we saw in the second canto return in all of the 'purple' passages of *Tristram of Lyonesse*, in the description of the love-making in the second canto (pp. 49–50) and towards the end of 'Joyous Gard' when the lovers are again reunited (pp. 95, 97). These lyrical, inward moments slow the plot, just as the triplet prolongs the moment. Swinburne's triplets are perhaps most effective in those passages in which Tristram and Iseult decide to live for the moment, above and against their circumstances. In 'The Last Pilgrimage', with Tristram again separated from Iseult, the refluent verse texture is so strong as to make triplets seem, for a space, the norm of this passage. At the mention of Iseult, the verse texture moves towards triplets, yet the shift is slow to take effect. It is not until Tristram witnesses 'love' animating the natural world that Swinburne's line finally tips to describe how he

> Beheld and heard things round her sound and shine
> From floors of foam and gold to walls of serpentine.
> For splendid as the limbs of that supreme
> Incarnate beauty through men's visions gleam,
> Whereof all fairest things are even but shadow or dream,
> And lovely like as Love's own heavenliest face,
> Gleams there and glows the presence and the grace
> Even of the mother of all, in perfect pride of place. (p. 119)

These triplets continue undiminished for over twenty lines, until the verse-paragraph terminates in a state of 'marvel[ling]' at

> The gospel graven of life's most heavenly law,
> Joy, brooding on its own still soul with awe,
> A sense of godlike rest in godlike strife,
> The sovereign conscience of the spirit of life. (p. 119)

Here, as elsewhere in the poem, Tristram's 'faithless faith', his 'godlike rest in godlike strife' has as much to do with this verse texture as it does with Swinburne's description. However, this is not the only thought which the fluent outrunning of the couplet and resulting triplet makes possible.

After the third canto, Swinburne makes use of the triplet in a way that recalls Dryden's use of the third line to add an unlooked-for third thought. The point at which the reader realises this alternative capacity of the triplet occurs relatively late in the poem, in the eighth canto. Tristram and Iseult have parted again, for the last time — though they cannot know this:

> So surely seemed the silence even to sigh
> Assurance of inveterate prophesy,
> 'Thou shalt not come again home hither ere thou die.' (p. 121)

This triplet here is neither refluent nor lyrical, but is instead more final. An epigrammatic couplet is rounded by a triplet, which here asserts an end to joy — the opposite of prolongation or affirmation. This is very different from the triplets we have previously encountered. Consider the different ways in which this double potential of the triplet is fulfilled, in the speech of Iseult of the White Hands in 'The Wife's Vigil' and Iseult in 'Joyous Gard'. Here Iseult of Brittany swears to be revenged upon her husband for marrying her, though he remains faithful to Iseult of Ireland:

> What wall so massive, or what tower so high
> Shall be thy surety that thou shouldst not die,
> If that which comes against thee be but I?
> Who shall rise up of power to take thy part,
> What skill find strength to save, what strength find art,
> If that which wars against thee be my heart? (pp. 110–11)

The texture of the verse is more epigrammatic than at any other point in the poem. Even Swinburne's Prelude, we realise, contained enjambment. Here rhetorical question builds upon rhetorical question, in an appeal to God for vengeance. The recollection that this texture, combined with questions, was also present at certain points of Tristram's soliloquy prompts comparison.

Iseult of Brittany's desire for vengeance appears mistaken, partly because her belief that she is working as an instrument of God contradicts Tristram's assertion of an impersonal universe. Yet this thought is never announced explicitly, but is part of the arrangement of verse textures across the poem.

The introduction of a triplet more in the style of Dryden or Pope is something of a surprise. In Iseult of Brittany's speeches it communicates not joy but an extra, rhetorical addition. We can place this against the earlier triplets in which Iseult of Ireland rejects the Christian idea of God's will, in favour of fate:

> Good end God send us ever — so men pray.
> But I — this end God send me, would I say,
> To die not of division and a heart
> Rent or with sword of severance cloven apart,
> But only when thou diest and only where thou art,
> O thou my soul and spirit and breath to me,
> O light, life, love! yea, let this only be,
> That dying I may praise God who gave me thee,
> Let hap what will thereafter.' (pp. 102–03)

These triplets in Iseult's speech at 'Joyous Gard' have a certain poignancy when read in retrospect. Following the 'purple' passages, Tristram's soliloquy, Iseult's vow, and the subsequent move towards the Drydenic triplet in the speech of Iseult of Brittany, triplets do not recur again until the final scene. The magnificent passage that describes Tristram's dawn swim partly derives its power from the disappointment of an expectation that the verse will break the bounds of the couplet once again, stretching to a triplet (pp. 127–28). Yet no triplet occurs. The realisation that these refluent couplets cannot stay a moment before the rising of the sun, before the rush of rhyme, thus appears proleptic.

And yet Swinburne's couplets in *Tristram* are very far from being mechanical or symbolic. Jarvis, writing in response to the couplet genre, borrows the phrase 'archaist innovators' from the Russian critic Yuri Tynianov to describe how couplet poems operate.[61] Following the decay of certain gestures towards symbolism and their renewal through an overview of the couplet form enables Jarvis to claim that 'Significant innovations in verse thinking happen just at the limit of such symbolisations — and therefore, also, at the limit of the recruitment of style to the function of operating as a political badge'. The same might be claimed of Swinburne's triplets. It is not the case that triplets mean joy, any more than his epigrammatic couplets might be said to stand for finality. Yet the consistency with which Swinburne mobilises certain gestures, made possible by the structure of his lyricised couplet, means that we are conscious of thinking with, as well as thinking in, certain sub-styles in his verse. By the penultimate deathbed scene these ways and means have gained such power that Swinburne is able to use them to bring about almost immediate effects. Under Swinburne's handling, that old tension within the couplet genre between opening and closing, prolongation and ending, sounds forth in couplets rarely heard before, and certainly not since:

> 'Iseult, my life that wast and art my death,
> My life in life that hast been, and that art
> Death in my death, sole wound that cleaves mine heart,
> Mine heart that else, how spent soe'er, were whole,
> Breath of my spirit and anguish of my soul,
> How can this be that hence thou canst not hear,
> Being but by space divided? One is here,
> But one of twain I looked at once to see;

> Shall death keep time and thou not keep with me?'
> And the white married maiden laughed at heart,
> Hearing, and scarce with lips at all apart
> Spake, and as fire between them was her breath;
> 'Yea, now thou liest not: yea, for I am death.' (p. 145)

Extracting these lines proves to be a somewhat artificial exercise, because much of the force of Tristram's speech draws on the cumulative associations and potential of different verse textures. Here the placement of 'Iseult' at the beginning of the line recalls previous lines in which the narrator presents Iseult of Ireland or Tristram as heroes; but she is not here. The couplet pair which rhymes 'art' and 'heart' also looks back to the triplet we have just been considering, in which Iseult of Brittany swears she will be revenged. The reuse of this rhyme at this point therefore brings two views of the universe into conflict: a world in which a vengeful God is at work, and an alternative view which supersedes this, which the protagonists have achieved.

In the lines quoted above, the refluent texture builds, but there is no looked-for triplet that might recall the prolonged moments of joy, redeeming the speaker on his deathbed. The finality which accompanies the termination of syntax and rhyme with that surest word, 'for I am death', falls like the sealing of Tristram's fate. Lastly, splitting sentences across the couplet tends to speed the narrative, and what Tristram needs is time. The completion of Tristram's speech mid-couplet by Iseult of Brittany is therefore triply ominous.

In the lines that follow two views of the universe are pitched against each other: Tristram's 'faithless faith', and Iseult of Brittany's conviction that she acts as a divine agent. However, the sense of these two world views being in tension owes less to what is said than it does to the gestures of the verse:

> 'Iseult?' and like a death-bell faint and clear
> The virgin voice rang answer — 'I am here.'
> And his heart sprang, and sank again: and she
> Spake, saying, 'What would my knightly lord with me?' (pp. 145–46)

In this passage, Tristram's refluent couplets are continually wrested and completed by Iseult's balanced and final couplets. The line that begins 'And his heart sprang' is testament to this. The verb has been continually associated with Tristram, though it is usually split from its subject via the line break, tipping the reader into mounting song, as in the following lines:

> And sighing, she looked from wave to cloud about,
> And even with that full-grown feet of day
> Sprang upright on the quivering water-way, [...] (IV, p. 25)

> [...] And the day
> Sprang: and afar along the wild waste way
> They heard the pulse and press of hurrying horse hoofs play (IV, p. 46)

> Then the heart in him
> Sprang, seeing the low cliff clear to leap, and swim
> Right out by the old blithe way the sea-mew takes [...] (IV, p. 70)

Three times previously, this verb occur within refluent textures, which mount towards a triplet. However, this time Tristram's heart 'sprang, and sank again', culminating, not in a triplet expressing joy, but in a couplet delivered by his mortal enemy. Iseult of Brittany is not someone to trust one's life with. Yet this is what Tristram does in asking her to watch the horizon for the white sail which will signal his lover's arrival, or the black sail which signifies that she cannot come:

> For seeing he had found at these her hands this grace,
> It could not be but yet some breathing-space
> Might leave him life to look again on love's own face. (p. 147)

The reappearance of the triplet, so long expected and so long denied, appears to offer some form of hope. As the rhymes build and prolong the moment, so too does Tristram hope for a few more hours in which he might be reunited with Iseult of Ireland. The cumulative association of the triplet with joy, affirmation, lyrical moment, and delay, answers perfectly to Tristram's interpretation of his keeper's 'grace'. It is as if Tristram drops into hope. Yet the triplets remain closed, more like longer epigrammatic couplets, rather than achieving the full cut and run, the outrunning of the couplet-unit, terminating in the alexandrine, which we saw earlier in the poem.

In the lines which follow, Swinburne mobilises our expectations of the two different triplet textures, pitching them against each other directly, to tragic effect:

> And high from heaven suddenly rang the lark,
> Triumphant; and the far first refluent ray
> Filled all the hollow darkness full with day.
> And on the deep sky's verge a fluctuant light
> Gleamed, grew, shone, strengthened into perfect sight,
> As bowed and dipped and rose again the sail's clear white. (p. 147)

The verse-paragraph pitches forward into the narrative by means of a split couplet, which takes its cue from Tristram's rhetorical question. 'Lark' answers 'dark', as the ray answers darkness. The replacement of term by term recalls the fluent downward movement of all things. This texture would have us believe that all is lost: Tristram, the verse, the narrative are all hurtling downwards towards the certain end, signalled by the pointing of the first triplet quoted. Yet immediately following, there after the line break, comes the now familiar enjambment, which splits noun and verb across the line break, and which pitches the rhythm towards the refluent, mounting song we have come to associate with Tristram, dawn, spring, joy, sex, and love: 'the light / Gleamed'. The reader's ears strain, as Tristram, whose sight is dark now, strains out towards the horizon of the line. And there, returning, at the end of a perfect, rising, English alexandrine is the sign of Iseult's return.

Anaphora carries us over another enjambed couplet, nearing as the sail nears, ending on a split couplet. The movement of this couplet seems positively poised for completion in Iseult's step, heard upon the stair. Yet at the introduction of the pointed line all is lost:

> And swift and steadfast as a sea-mew's wing
> It neared before the wind, as fain to bring

> Comfort, and shorten yet its narrowing track.
> And she that saw looked hardly toward him back,
> Saying, 'Ah, the ship comes surely; but her sail is black.' (p. 147)

The refluent texture of the triplet turned alexandrine ends here.

Following the third line of Iseult of Brittany's speech, the narration speeds, with no pause or hope of respite. The finality of Tristram's death is undersigned and blotted by the repetition of the couplet-rhyme which recalls their initial union:

> [...] and her head
> Bowed, as to reach the spring that slakes all drouth;
> And their four lips became one silent mouth. (pp. 147–48)

That a tiny modulation in the execution of the couplets and triplets of this poem can feel so devastating is testament to Swinburne's innovative handling of couplet verse. The difference in construction between the triplet that describes the white sail, and the triplet in which Iseult of Brittany has her revenge is minimal. It is the execution of the two, in contrast with each other, and in relation to the way in which Swinburne's couplets have us think, which is so effective.

Tristram's tragedy stems from his choice to hope for one last affirmative moment, a choice that goes against his former detachment. Iseult of Brittany, acting under the belief that she is working for God, is neither free nor tragic. Yet Swinburne's 'faithless faith' is not satisfactorily paraphrasable. The triplets that we encounter in *Tristram* do not preach an antitheistic universe: they invite us to think it. His verse-thinking cannot be reduced to a formula in which his belief can be adequately explained in terms of style, or style in terms of belief. Instead this 'faithless faith' hangs in the balance between tradition and innovation, in the unfolding moment of Swinburne's poem.

Notes to Chapter 3

1. Claude K. Hyder, *Swinburne's Literary Career and Fame* (Durham, NC: Duke University Press, 1933), p. 161.
2. Letter dated 21 February 1875, reprinted in A. C. Swinburne, *Major Poems and Selected Prose*, ed. Jerome McGann and Charles Sligh (New Haven, 2004: Yale), pp. 470–72.
3. *The Swinburne Letters*, ed. Cecil Y. Lang, 6 vols (New Haven: Yale University Press, 1959–1962) III, pp. 13–15.
4. Ezra Pound concludes his 1918 article on Swinburne: 'His unbelief did not desert him; no, not even in Putney'. See 'Swinburne Versus Biographers', *Poetry*, 11, 6 (1918), p. 326. Francis O'Gorman has recently made the argument for the consistency of Swinburne's politics in 'Swinburne and Ireland', *Review of English Studies*, 64, 265 (2013), 454–74.
5. William Michael Rossetti, *Some Reminisces* (London: Brown, Langham, 1906), p. 292; Clyde K. Hyder ed., *A. C. Swinburne: The Critical Heritage*, (London: Routledge, 1995: first published 1970 as *Swinburne: The Critical Heritage*) p. 118; *The Complete Poetical Works of Thomas Hardy*, ed. S. Hynes, (Oxford: Clarendon Press, 1984) II, p. 33.
6. This phrase also appears in Shelley's *Prometheus Unbound*, III. iii. 130. Earth describes how a temple, built close to the place where her 'spirit came forth', leads to 'mutual war [...] And faithless faith, such as Jove kept with thee' (see *Prometheus Unbound: A Variorum Edition*, ed. by Lawrence John Zillman (Seattle: University of Washington Press, 1959), p. 245). The phrase 'faithless faith' suggests a double deception, capturing the seriousness of covenant-breaking. Swinburne appears to be using this phrase in a positive sense, to indicate the legitimacy of heretical belief.

7. Alexander Pope, 'An Essay on Man', II, *The Poems of Alexander Pope*, ed. John Butt (London: Routledge, 1965), p. 516.
8. Swinburne's later sonnet 'Hope and Fear', published in *A Century of Roundels* (1883), is a neat meditation on this theme, ending with the recommendation 'Hope thou not much, and fear thou not at all' (Swinburne, *Poetical Works*, V, p. 227).
9. See 'miscreant', adj. and n., in *The Oxford English Dictionary* (online edition) <http://www.oed.com/view/Entry/119394?redirectedFrom=miscreant#eid> [accessed 27 April 2018].
10. The couplet 'Love that is fire within thee and light above, / And lives by grace of nothing but of love' (IV, p. 6) is answered by an alternative rhyme-pair in the later canto: 'Fate, that is pure of love and clean of hate, / Being equal-eyed as nought may be but fate;' (p. 134). The jarring note in an otherwise perfect antiphony, where rhyme-pair answers rhyme-pair thousands of lines apart, underpins the overtaking of 'love' — the sustaining force in the universe — by fate, which is indifferent to both love and hate.
11. Martin Priestman, 'Lucretius in Romantic and Victorian Britain', in *The Cambridge Companion to Lucretius*, ed. by Stuart Gillespie and Philip Hardie (Cambridge: Cambridge University Press, 2007), p. 304.
12. Simon Jarvis, 'What is Historical Poetics?' in *Theory Aside*, ed. by Jason Potts and Daniel Stout (Durham, NC: Duke University Press, 2014), p. 101.
13. Theodor W. Adorno, 'Theses upon Art and Religion Today', *Kenyon Review*, 7, 4 (1945), p. 677.
14. For a recent overview see Charles LaPorte, 'Victorian Literature, Religion, and Secularization' in *Literature Compass*, 10 (2013), pp. 277–87.
15. 'Hence there is reason for the suspicion that wherever the battle cry is raised that art should go back to its religious sources there also prevails the wish that art should exercise a disciplinary, repressive function' (Adorno, 'Theses Upon Art and Religion Today', p. 678).
16. Kirstie Blair, *Form and Faith in Victorian Poetry and Religion* (Oxford: Oxford University Press, 2013), p. 1.
17. *The Swinburne Letters*, I, pp. 97–98.
18. Ibid., IV, p. 260.
19. Ibid., IV, p. 286.
20. Sara Lyons, *Algernon Swinburne and Walter Pater* (London: Legenda, 2015) pp. 78, 116 and 128.
21. *The Swinburne Letters*, IV, p. 174.
22. Herbert Tucker, *Epic: Britain's Heroic Muse 1790–1910* (Oxford: Oxford University Press, 2008), p. 531.
23. Simon Jarvis argues that 'Couplet-poems so often included passages about writing couplets that the whole mode was infused with a metatechnical force in potential, a potential which could readily be awoken at the slightest allusion, marking or reference'. See 'Archaist-Innovators: The Couplet from Churchill to Browning', in *A Companion to Romantic Poetry*, ed. Charles Mahoney (Oxford: Wiley-Blackwell, 2011), p. 28.
24. Walter Pater, in his 'Essay on Style' comments 'The way in which theological interests sometimes avail themselves of language is perhaps the best illustration of the force I mean to indicate generally in literature, by the word soul'. See *Appreciations* (London: Macmillan, 1901), pp. 25–26.
25. Pater summarises: 'I have been speaking of certain conditions of the literary art arising out of the medium or material in or upon which it works, the essential qualities of language and its aptitudes for contingent ornamentation, matters which define scholarship as science and good taste respectively' (p. 21). See *Appreciations* (London: Macmillan, 1901), pp. 17–21.
26. Baxandall's subtle allusion to the section on the 'Fetish of the Commodity and Its Secret' in *Capital* is suggestive of how the subjective may come to seem objective. Marx writes: 'Through this substitution, the products of labour become commodities, sensuous things which are at the same time suprasensible or social. In the same way, the impression made by a thing on the optic nerve is perceived not as a subjective excitation of that nerve but as the objective form of a thing outside the eye'. See *Capital*, trans. by Ben Fowkes (London: Penguin, 1976), I, p. 165.
27. Michael Baxandall, *Painting and Experience in Fifteenth-Century Italy* (Oxford: Oxford University Press, 1988), p. 29.

28. Unsigned Review, *Spectator*, 12 August 1882, pp. 1055–57; Unsigned Review, *Athenæum*, 22 July 1882, pp. 103–05.
29. George Saintsbury, *A History of English Prosody from the Twelfth Century to the Present Day* (London: Macmillan, 1906–10), III, p. 341. Saintsbury's allusion to Juvenal's third satire, directed against 'A Rome of Greeks' connects quick speech and Greekness, perhaps appropriate given Swinburne's reputation as a 'Greek' thinker. Lines 73–75 caricature Isaeus, an orator: 'ingenium velox, audacia perdita, sermo / promptus et Isaeo torrentior: ede quid illum/ esse putes?' [Quick of wit and of unbounded impudence, they are as ready of speech as Isaeus, and more torrential] See trans. by G. G. Ramsay, Loeb Classical Library (unnumbered) (London: Heinemann, 1918), p. 37.
30. John Dryden, 'Religio Laici', *Selected Poems*, ed. Steven N. Zwicker and David Bywaters (London: Penguin, 2001), pp. 178–79.
31. Ibid., pp. 178–79.
32. These lines perhaps lie behind T. E. Hulme's remarks, refuting causal links between historical events and efflorescence in verse, that: 'The discovery of America had about as much effect on the Courtier poets at that time as the discovery of a new asteroid would have had on the poetic activity of Swinburne'. See *The Collected Writings of T. E. Hulme*, ed. Karen Csengeri (Oxford: Clarendon Press, 1996), p. 60.
33. For an investigation into Swinburne's verse's momentum, partly provoked by Tucker's comments on *Tristram*, see Orla Polten, 'Setting sea-serpents in verse: Momentum and meaning in Swinburne's decasyllabic couplets', *Cambridge Literary Review*, 6 (2012), pp. 157–73.
34. Sainstbury, *History of English Prosody*, III, pp. 349–50.
35. Reprinted in *A. C. Swinburne: The Critical Heritage*, (London: Routledge, 1995: first published 1970 as *Swinburne: The Critical Heritage*) p. 232.
36. Tucker, *Epic*, p. 523.
37. William Morris, *The Life and Death of Jason*, 2nd rev. edn, (London: Bell and Daldy, 1868), p. 25, ll.308–14.
38. Unsigned Review, *Spectator*, 12 August 1882, p. 1057; 'Tristram of Lyonesse', Unsigned Review, *Saturday Review*, 29 July 1882, pp. 156–57.
39. Unsigned Review, *Westminster Review*, October 1882, p. 586.
40. For this word, by which I understand the relationship between syntax and metre within the line, I am drawing on the work of Roger Fowler in his essay 'Three Blank Verse Textures', in *The Languages of Literature: Some Linguistic Contributions to Literature* (London: Routledge and Kegan Paul, 1971), pp. 184–99.
41. Edmund Gosse, *Life of Swinburne* (London: Macmillan, 1917), p. 263.
42. 'Review of '*Tristram of Lyonesse* by A. C. Swinburne', *Athenæum*, 22 July 1882, pp. 103–05.
43. *Athenæum*, 22 July 1882, p. 104. Presumably 'anapaestic bars' are what Attridge and I would call a 'double offbeat'.
44. *Athenæum* , 22 July 1882, p. 105.
45. John Dryden, *Selected Poems*, pp. 197–98.
46. Ibid., pp. 197–98.
47. Thomas Creech, *T. Lucretius Carus, the Epicurean philosopher, his six books De natura rerum: done into English verse, with notes* (Oxford: Printed by L. Lichfield for Anthony Stephens, 1682).
48. John Keats, *The Complete Poems* (Harmondsworth: Penguin, 1996), pp. 422–23, ll. 310–21.
49. Simon Jarvis describes Keats's couplets as 'opening a bottle by smashing its neck': 'the effect of such consistent crossing of metrical with syntactical limits would ordinarily be one of apparently unstoppable momentum, where syntax pushes the verse rudely over the line-ends. In couplets, of course, such onward drive is in cooperative antagonism with the echo of rhyme which detains attention just at the moment when syntax will be propelling it forward'. See 'Archaist Innovators: The Couplet Form from Churchill to Browning' in *A Companion to Romantic Poetry*, ed. Charles Mahoney (Oxford: Wiley-Blackwell, 2011), p. 36.
50. William Keach, *Shelley's Style* (New York: Methuen, 1984) p. 162.
51. Ibid., p. 157.
52. Jarvis, 'Archaist Innovators', p. 39.

53. *Athenæum*, 22 July 1882, p. 105.
54. *Shelley's Poetry and Prose*, selected and ed. by Donald H. Reiman and Neil Fraistat, 2nd edn (New York: Norton, 2002), p. 395, ll. 72–82
55. A. C. Swinburne, 'Note on The Text of Shelley', *Essays and Studies* (London: Chatto & Windus, 1875), p. 237.
56. A. C. Swinburne, *William Blake: A Critical Essay* (London: John Camden Hotten, 1868), p. 187.
57. Tucker, *Epic*, p. 523.
58. The founder of the Society for Psychical Research, F. W. H. Myers, uses the word 'impersonal' to describe the laws of nature in Swinburne's poem, before asking: 'is any effort possible to us, or must we drift helplessly with the cosmic stream?' For his speculations on Swinburne's debt to Lucretius see *A. C. Swinburne: The Critical Heritage*, ed. Clyde K. Hyder, pp. 188–97.
59. *Westminster Review*, October 1882, p. 587.
60. Friedrich Nietzsche, 'The Will to Power', *The Complete Works of Friedrich Nietzsche*, trans. by T. N. Foulis, ed. by O. Levy (London, Edinburgh, 1910), pp. 406–07.
61. Jarvis, 'Archaist Innovators', pp. 40–41.

CHAPTER 4

'Lyrics for the Crusade': Swinburne's Odes

Didactic poetry is my abhorrence.
P. B. SHELLEY

On 10 March 1867 the Italian patriot Giuseppe Mazzini, then in his thirtieth year of exile, wrote to Swinburne to thank him for his copy of *Atalanta in Calydon*. He was reminded of his omission to acknowledge the gift on reading Swinburne's 'Ode on the Insurrection in Candia' in *The Fortnightly Review*.[1] 'I cannot help writing a few words', he begins, 'to tell you how [...] hopeful I feel now; hopeful that the power wich [*sic*] is in you has found out its true direction and that, instead of compelling us merely to admire *you*, you will endeavor to transform *us*, to rouse the sleeping, to compel thought to embody itself into Action. That is the mission of Art; and yours.' Mazzini next issues a call-to-arms which would present a considerable challenge to Swinburne:

> The poet ought to be the apostle of a crusade, his word the watchword of the fighting nations and the dirge of the oppressors. Don't lull us to sleep with songs of egotistical love and idolatry of physical beauty: shake us, reproach, encourage, insult, brand the cowards, hail the martyrs, tell us all that we have a great beauty to fulfill, and that, before it is fulfilled, Love is an undeserved blessing, Happiness a blasphemy, belief in God a Lie. Give us a series of 'Lyrics for the Crusade'. Have not our praise but our blessing. You *can* if you choose.[2]

How difficult Mazzini's request would prove to be is hinted at in the correspondence surrounding *Songs before Sunrise* (1871), the collection which Swinburne, in his 'Dedication', characterises as a 'sword of song' (II, p.vi.). Writing after the publication of *Poems and Ballads*, he reflects that political poetry would involve compromises: 'After all [...] it is nice to have something to love and believe in as I do Italy [...] I know the result will be a poem more declamatory than imaginative, but I'd rather be an Italian stump-orator than an English prophet.'[3] However, later that year he writes of his repulsion for 'metrical stump-oratory', 'didactic-declamatory', arguing that 'I will have nothing of the platform in it if possible'.[4] In a letter dated 7 May he writes to reassure his mother that, regarding his 'Chief', it is poetic and not political involvement which Mazzini requires: '[A]ll he wants is that I should dedicate and consecrate my writing power to do good and serve others exclusively, which I can't. If I tried I should lose my faculty of verse even. When I can, I do'.[5]

When Swinburne could, he did. When he couldn't, he tried. This chapter will consider Swinburne's response to Mazzini, and the difficulty of writing poetry in the service of liberty through a study of his odes beginning in the 1850s, until the choral odes of *Erechtheus,* his second Greek play in English, in 1876.

Swinburne and the English Pindaric Ode

If, as Susan Stewart argues, 'odes give birth to poets', then it is natural that Swinburne, having 'something to love and believe in', should return to this form.[6] What is remarkable is the length to which he goes in his attempt to reanimate a genre that has always been at risk of becoming merely a formal exercise — a genre for laureates and prize-winners.[7] While Tennyson, Barrett Browning and Patmore throw in their lot with what Penelope Wilson has called 'one of literature's most creative mistakes [...] the popular idea of Pindar as a symbol of uncontrollable poetic fervour',[8] Swinburne innovates, not by effusive irregularity, but by going back to Pindar.[9] In contrast to poems such as Tennyson's 'Ode to Memory' and his 'Wellington Ode', Elizabeth Barrett Browning's 'Napoleon III in Italy' and Patmore's *The Unknown Eros,* this stricter regimen gives him recourse to only a handful of former examples.[10] His odes present an anomaly in the verse-historical record, challenging the accepted history of the ode, and inviting reconsideration of a stylistic mode that is largely discredited today.

However, even if they were not so unusual, Swinburne's odes are due critical attention; the reading record is remarkably out of touch with the poet's own commitments. As he recognises in his 'dedicatory epistle', written to introduce his *Collected Poems,* the ode is one of his major genres:

> Perhaps, too, my first stanzas addressed to Victor Hugo may be ranked as no less of an ode than that on the insurrection in Candia: a poem which attracted, whether or not it may have deserved, the notice and commendation of Mazzini [...] But for this happy accident I might not feel disposed to set much store by my first attempt at a regular ode of orthodox or legitimate construction: I doubt whether it quite succeeded in evading the criminal risk and the capital offence of formality [...] But in my later ode on Athens, absolutely faithful as it is in form to the strictest type and the most stringent law of Pindaric hymnology, I venture to believe that there is no more sign of this infirmity than is in the less classically regulated poem on the Armada; which, though built on a new scheme, is nevertheless in its way, I think, a legitimate ode, by right of its regularity in general arrangement of correspondent divisions. By the test of these two poems I am content that my claims should be decided and my station determined as a lyric poet in the higher sense of the term; a craftsman in the most ambitious line of his art that ever aroused or ever can arouse the emulous aspiration of his kind. (I, p.xiv).

Swinburne does discuss other single-stanza poems as odes (pp. xv–xvi). However, it is the 'Pindaric or triune ode' that I am concerned with here. To these odes which Swinburne singles out as 'of orthodox or legitimate construction' we might add his 'Ode to Mazzini' (*c.*1857), 'Ode on the Proclamation of the French Republic'

(1870), 'Christmas Antiphones' (1871), 'England: An Ode' (1894), 'The Altar of Righteousness' (1904), 'Music: An Ode' (1904) and the nine choral odes of *Erechtheus* (1876). However, despite Swinburne's evident dedication to the regular ode, the three most recent anthologies of Swinburne's poetry focus on other aspects of his verse.[11] Of course, there is no requirement that we should honour Swinburne's request that we try him as 'a lyric poet in the higher sense of the term'. Yet to fail to do so risks simplifying both the complexities of Swinburne's style and his significance as a poet who struggled to 'never assert, [but] suggest', an aesthetic credo which he held to even when writing consciously political poetry.[12] It is partly because *Erechtheus* is so often overlooked that Swinburne's fidelity to this aspect of his 'faith' has come to seem so questionable.[13]

If anthologies overlook Swinburne's odes, critical readings tend to go around them. Julia F. Saville argues that Swinburne's poems 'illustrate the kinds of complications that individual passions and pleasures often introduce into negotiations of democratic freedom'. However, her exploration focuses on 'Les Noyades' and 'Before a Crucifix', rather than Swinburne's odes — the genre in which individuality is ranged against the collective, or on *Erechtheus* — a play that pivots on the sacrifices which democracy requires.[14] Stephanie Kuduk-Weiner proposes that 'As the genre most closely associated with the inner life of the individual, lyric poetry bore a close relation to the advanced thinkers' ambitions of renewing minds' and that 'Swinburne, too, believed in the power of poetry to rouse a sleeping people'.[15] However, her reading concentrates on Swinburne's *William Blake*, his 'Dedication' to Mazzini, and the 'Hymn of Man'. Marion Thain, in her account of Swinburne's resistance to what she terms 'lyric crisis', quotes Swinburne's discussion of the ode at some length, but goes on to concentrate on 'Anactoria', a poem in heroic couplets, not among the poems that Swinburne counts as a Pindaric ode (although, as I argue in Chapter 3, it contains some lyrical elements).[16] Where critics do attend to the specific nature of Swinburne's odes, this tends to be descriptive, rather than evaluative. Linda K. Hughes connects Swinburne's odes with Pindar in style and theme, arguing that 'Swinburne's formal choice evokes an ancient pagan democracy suited to republican hostility to state religion [...] Pindar's choral odes, moreover, call for lyric rhapsody, Swinburne's special province' and that Tennyson's well-known 'Wellington Ode' contextualized the odes of Barret Browning and Swinburne 'enabling their very different politics to be enunciated more clearly'.[17] However, the introductory nature of this study means their different ode styles are not explored in any depth. Charlotte Ribeyrol notes that 'The choruses of Swinburne's play *Erechtheus* follow the same triadic structure as his Pindaric "Ode on the Insurrection in Candia", alternating strophe, antistrophe and epode, a poetic pattern which he believed to be perfect'. However, the precise qualities and motivations involved in Swinburne's odes are not her aim in this survey.[18]

The critical neglect of Swinburne's odes is connected to another pressing difficulty in the reception of Swinburne: there was, until very recently, little consensus regarding Swinburne's politics. As Francis O'Gorman argues, the myth dies hard that Swinburne, *enfant terrible* of the 1860s, hardened into conservatism in later life.[19] However, another more widespread critical shift, difficult to track and harder to point to, may also be at work here, which requires us to acknowledge that by the middle of the twentieth century Swinburne's odic lyricism had come to seem intensely suspicious. E. M. W. Tillyard's suspicions of 'Hertha', published in *Songs before Sunrise*, might be taken as representative:

> I do not suggest that Swinburne consciously reached this decision, but *Hertha* does indeed suggest the climate in which such totalitarian ideas can flourish. The intoxication of these ideas is well known. To surrender the individual will and the painful business of making choices to what a leader, guiding the group mind, dictates may bring with it a wonderful sense of release and happiness. And the intoxicating quality of Swinburne's verse represents such a process only too well.[20]

Here the failure to value the individual becomes connected with a particular poetic style. This may be, as Herbert Tucker comments, just another species of 'post-war vigilance'.[21] Yet there is something troubling in Tillyard's connection between Swinburne and fascism which merits further investigation. Of course, fear of this peculiar capacity of poetry to cause the poet or reader to be 'beside himself', in Benjamin Jowett's translation, stretches as far back as Plato.[22] However, contemporary reviewers of *Erechtheus* appear much more comfortable with the lyricism of Swinburne's political poetry. It is this suspicion which perhaps allows Matthew Reynolds to argue that Swinburne's 'Dedication to Joseph Mazzini', 'Like much else in *Songs Before Sunrise* [...] enthusiastically amalgamates inspiration, motherhood and the Italian state in a rhetoric that was later to be echoed by Mussolini'.[23] That this association could be seamlessly incorporated into Reynolds's critical introduction suggests the challenge facing readers of Swinburne's political poetry today.

However, in focusing on Swinburne's odes, I also wish to make a small contribution towards lyric theory. I have suggested that Swinburne's odes are unusual because of their recourse to Pindar's strict form. However, Swinburne's odes are also remarkable for the challenge they pose to the widely held critical view that the romantic lyric was superseded in the nineteenth century by other hybrid forms, principally the dramatic monologue.[24]

Isobel Armstrong, Jonathan Culler, Herbert Tucker and, more recently, Virginia Jackson and Yopie Prins all situate their understanding of lyric in relation to the dramatic monologue and in doing so they each draw on J. S. Mill's axiom that 'Eloquence is heard; poetry is overhead'. However, Mill's hopes for lyric are often interpreted as counter-factual, absurd and even ideal.[25] In such accounts, the appeal of poetry to drama, the bracketing of lyrical techniques within a narrative frame, and the uncertain testimony of the speaker, all of which Tucker convincingly identifies (pp. 233–36) as the technical characteristics of dramatic monologue, may come to seem inevitable. However, in returning to read Swinburne's odes via Mill, I hope to suggest that there is more to Mill's defence of lyric than has been lately been assumed.

One way to introduce the peculiar nature of Swinburne's odes is to draw attention to the different readings of Hegel occasioned by Isobel Armstrong's discussion of the 'double poem' in her study *Victorian Poetry,* and that which follows in my reading of Swinburne's odes. Where Armstrong uses the master-bondsman dialectic to think about the struggle between subjectivity and objectivity as it occurs *within* the 'double poem' (p. 15), I find Hegel's argument regarding self-consciousness fruitful for thinking about the dialectical encounter between the reader and Swinburne's odes.

This is, I would argue, closer to Hegel's view in his *Aesthetics*, in which the struggle between objectivity and subjectivity within the work belongs to a different 'stage of consciousness' and is achieved in drama. For Hegel, lyric poetry is defined, not by changing poles between subjectivity and objectivity within the poem, but through encountering a 'subjective enthusiasm engrossed by the topic'.[26, 27] Hegel is able to maintain this distinction between 'hybrid forms' and 'unadulterated' lyric because he, like Swinburne and Mill, did not find the 'subjective enthusiasm' of lyric, as Armstrong puts it, 'deranged'.[28] In fact, Hegel provides a fairly simple defence of lyric against the accusation of solipsism: the lyric poet need not let go of national interests, politics, or the world outside the poem. Instead, these questions must be subjectively felt and recognized (*Aesthetics*, 1123–24, 1151).[29] Adorno might present the most extreme form of this view by taking lyric poetry's inward turn away from the world as the exemplar for his aesthetic proposition that 'form converges with critique'.[30] However, this connection has not been the point of departure for many recent definitions of lyric poetry.

To continue to assume that Mill protests too much is to risk missing what was of importance for Mill, and by extension, for Swinburne. To put it another way: neither the essayist nor the poet were quite ready to give up on lyric. Swinburne's later odes may be considered valuable precisely so far as they resist both the temptations of eloquence and the technical compromises of the dramatic monologue. They do so in two ways: firstly, in Swinburne's development of a style of ode which does not invite us to imagine a dialectical struggle of 'two voices' within the poem, nor attempt to compel us to action; and secondly in his commitment to lyric as the central emotional focus of his verse-drama.[31] 'Lyric proper' survives in Swinburne's verse-drama because it exists in relation to, yet separate from, the dialogue. The choral odes are very far from being 'poems that contain representations of the linguistic act of a fictional speaker', to quote Culler's recent definition of dramatic monologue.[32] Instead they are encountered as lyrics. These two genres — Swinburne's odes and the chorus of his second Greek play — are not distinct, but form part of the same trajectory in Swinburne's developing odic style. However, before we consider exactly what this involves, it is necessary to reacquaint ourselves with the thesis concerning lyric which found its antithesis in the dramatic monologue, and to do so we must go back to Mill.

Poetry and Eloquence

'Poetry and eloquence are both alike the expression or utterance of feeling: but, if we may be excused the antithesis, we should say that eloquence is *heard*; poetry is *over*heard' — Herbert Tucker puns on 'overhearing' here, taken as 'overmuch' and 'overdone', to suggest the *reductio ad absurdum* of Mill's definition of poetry as it must have appeared to Browning and Tennyson.[33] If instead we take Mill at his word, reanimating this maxim by placing it in the context of his political philosophy, we are better able to grasp what was at stake for Swinburne.

Here is Mill on eloquence and poetry in full:

> Eloquence supposes an audience. The peculiarity of poetry appears to us to lie in the poet's utter unconsciousness of a listener. Poetry is feeling confessing itself to itself in moments of solitude, and embodying itself in symbols which are the nearest possible representations of the feeling in the exact shape in which it exists in the poet's mind. Eloquence is feeling pouring itself out to other minds, courting their sympathy, or endeavoring to influence their belief, or move them to passion or to action.[34]

Mill emphasises the indirectness of poetry in contrast with didacticism. Since poetry has no ambitions to teach, it works with 'symbols' and embodied ideas. This claim would have found retrospective confirmation in Shelley's posthumously published *A Defence of Poetry* (1840), which extends the claims of poetry to include 'All the authors of revolutions in opinion' who 'reveal the permanent analogy of things by images which participate in the life of truth; but as their periods are harmonious and rhythmical, and contain in themselves the elements of verse; being the echo of the eternal music'.[35] For Shelley, 'Poetry strengthens the faculty which is the organ of the moral nature of man, in the same manner as exercise strengthens a limb'. However, it does not do so through instruction, but operates indirectly, through revelation: 'A poet therefore would do ill to embody his own conceptions of right and wrong [...] in his poetical creations, which participate in neither. By this assumption of the inferior office of interpreting himself but imperfectly, he would resign a glory in a participation in the cause' (p. 517).

Mill might have found common cause with another disciple of Shelley in Swinburne, who claimed Mill's *On Liberty* as 'the text-book of my creed as to public morals and political faith'.[36] The influence of Shelley's 'abhorrence' for didacticism, and the sense that poetry must inspire the reader through indirect means, is already evident in Swinburne's thinking in his undergraduate essay 'Of Analogy' discussed in Chapter 2, but which I quote again here:

> Of true analogy we may take two kinds as heads of the division: Poetic and Scientific analogy. To the first we may suppose that Metaphor & such like forms are separable; the perception of likeness and aptitude, of relation & community which give to poetry the powers of comprehension & exposition through which he becomes interpreter & prophet of things unapparent to ordinary men & this we may perhaps define as the special aim of poetry, to which the subordinate analogies of metaphor & rhythm serve as attendants: & rhyme itself thus assumes meaning & reason, if we accept it as a musical balance & relation of sound or responding to the analogy of sense expressed 'thro it; in short, as a metrical & outward analogy of words comprehensible by all as the type and countersign of an inward analogy of perception; which is in fact the use & explanation of verse.[37]

Notably, eloquence, along with the idea that poetry should 'teach and delight', forms no part of his thinking.³⁸ For Shelley and Swinburne, as for Adorno, 'The notion of a "message" in art, even when politically radical, already contains an accommodation to the world: the stance of the lecturer conceals a clandestine entente with the listeners, who could only be rescued from deception by refusing it'.³⁹ For Mill too, poetry's rescue can only be accomplished by a refusal of eloquence. A similar impulse is discernible in his subsequent separation of 'living beliefs' from 'habit'. A thorough overview of the relationship between Mill's earlier aesthetic essays and his later political philosophy is not possible here. However, it is impossible to understand what was at stake for Mill in attempting to rescue lyric, without also considering the claim he makes in *On Liberty*, that 'Over himself, over his own body and mind, the individual is *sovereign*'.⁴⁰

Mill envisages society as a debating chamber in which a community of free subjects debate their habitual beliefs, which, through a process of being tested, are either discarded or again enlivened. The need for such a society was not lost on the undergraduate Swinburne, who reinterpreted Mill's terms in his term essay 'On Political and Speculative Liberty':

> It is a common saying, if not a common belief, that all men in whom habit and teaching have not supplanted nature, desire the possession and the active exercise of reasonable freedom. No common assertion contains a graver error than this. Men, as a rule, do not love liberty: they love their own opinions, their own customs, the systems of their time, the morals and manners of their country. Such residue of regard as they keep for liberty lies mainly in words and vague impotent tradition.⁴¹

Swinburne's essay takes Mill's argument about the dangers of a society governed by habitual belief as his theme, commenting that 'this has been so thoroughly proved and reasoned out by the great writer above quoted, that one cannot hope to do more than touch on the heads of his argument'. Yet how is this wished-for 'political' liberty to be won? And more particularly: how might poetry work to bring about political liberty without, as Shelley put it, 'resigning a glory'? Swinburne does not get so far in his undergraduate essay. Ultimately, this was a problem that he would come to solve elsewhere and in another genre. For the moment, we can find a provisional answer in Mill, who rejects the idea that a desire for freedom can be instilled in another in his discussion of 'genius':

> I am not countenancing the sort of 'hero-worship' which applauds the strong man of genius for forcibly seizing on the government of the world and making it do his bidding in spite of itself. All he can claim is freedom to point out the way. The power of compelling others into it, is not only inconsistent with the freedom and development of all the rest, but corrupting to the strong man himself.⁴²

Once we connect this restriction on the man of genius with the restriction placed on poetry — which Mill, twenty-six years earlier, imagined as a poet singing alone in his cell, overheard in the next room — we might question the connections between the kind of lyricism which Mill encountered reading Shelley, and a political philosophy that was to become, in Stefan Collini's terms, the 'essential moral basis' of modern liberalism.⁴³ For as Mill suggests in a later article of 1833, 'The Two Kinds of Poetry', poetry and eloquence are not simply two different conceptions of poetry. They also correspond to two distinct poetic modes.⁴⁴

Having first reminded his reader of the distinction between eloquence and poetry, Mill goes on to 'illustrate it by a parallel between the two English authors of our own day', Shelley and Wordsworth. The discussion that unfolds suggests a preference for the technical repertoire he encounters in Shelley over that which he encounters in Wordsworth. At points, he is polemical:

> Wordsworth's poetry is never bounding, never ebullient; has little even of the appearance of spontaneousness: the well is never so full that it overflows. There is an air of calm deliberateness about all he writes, which is not characteristic of the poetic temperament [...] He never seems *possessed* by any feeling: no emotion seems ever so strong as to have entire sway, for the time being, over the current of his thoughts. He never, even for the space of a few stanzas, appears entirely *given up* to exultation, or grief, or pity, or love, or admiration, or devotion, or even animal spirits [...] the genius of Wordsworth is essentially unlyrical. (p. 719)

Spontaneous, possessed, emotional, and exulting — could we add 'enthusiastic' and 'intoxicating'? These are the qualities of poetry which Mill discerns as lacking in Wordsworth.⁴⁵ However, they are also precisely those qualities which prompted Tillyard's suspicion of Swinburne's 'Hertha'. I want to suggest that we find in Mill an alternative series of coordinates for thinking about what was at stake in the relationship between eloquence, poetry and liberty in nineteenth-century poetry, one which makes an alternative reading of Swinburne's lyricism possible. Tucker and others have demonstrated that the high demands which Mill and, I would add, Swinburne, placed on lyric found one answer in the dramatic monologue. Yet might this struggle between poetry and eloquence have also played out in the losing genre: the ode or higher lyric? So long as our argument stays at the level of commentary, we remain within the zone of pure conjecture. I want to turn now to consider, as one test case for this hunch, the style of the losing genre in the work of the losing poet.

The Development of Swinburne's Odes

Walter Pater writes that 'the chief question which a critic has to answer' is the 'peculiar quality of pleasure' an artist's work has for us, 'that which we cannot get elsewhere'.⁴⁶ One way of pursuing the 'peculiar quality' of Swinburne's odes that has already proved provocative in this study is comparative analysis. As Swinburne argues, it is impossible to grasp the precise peculiarity of any ode without understanding its place in relation to 'the work of the leading poets of our own country and century' ('Dedicatory Epistle', p. xiv). Once divided 'after the old Roman fashion into sections and classes', Swinburne's odes show a development away from an ode style in which the reader appears compelled to listen, towards a more fluid, vigorous ode style in which, as Adorno puts it, the speaker sounds forth.

Swinburne is perhaps ungenerous in not mentioning that just such an attempt to place his odes in relation to the tradition had been made by his friend Edmund

Gosse in his anthology *English Odes* (1880). Perhaps he disagreed with the final selection. The anthology clearly provoked debate, as seen in Swinburne's letter of acknowledgement:

> I must lose no time in thanking you for the exquisite little book which arrived last night [...] I am proud to be found worthy of the last place in it — and amused to see who is my neighbor, and what are his ideas of lyric style and the structure of an ode. I think you have been rather cruel to the Laureate: it was hard on him to reprint two such pieces as you have given: but perhaps the man who could be capable of writing either may be said to deserve that neither should be charitably forgotten.
>
> I think your favourite Cowley might have been better represented. Is not his Ode to Brutus a finer sample of his better style than these? To my mind also there is too much of Gray: but I should say that despite my respect for Matthew Arnold's opinion I am a heretic — and always have been — as to 'The Progress of Poesy' — about which I am rather disposed to agree with Dr. Samuel Johnson [...]
>
> I have completed about a quarter or so of an ode addressed to the Greeks which I hope and expect will be worthier of the subject than that on the rising in Crete.[47]

This letter, written four years after the publication of *Erechtheus*, shows Swinburne thinking retrospectively and comparatively about the specific styles of different odes. Some of his critical remarks are unsurprising. Opposed to the irregular ode, Swinburne's 'amusement' to find his own 'To Victor Hugo in Exile' following Coventry Patmore's highly irregular odes and in the company of Tennyson's more explicitly Cowleyan — not to mention royalist — compositions is easy to account for. However, his apparently unorthodox dislike of Gray's later, more ambitious odes, his preference for Cowley's 'Ode to Brutus', and his joke about Tennyson's 'Ode to Memory' are more subtle. His remarks also channel something else about the ode which he felt keenly: its competitiveness. Elsewhere in his correspondence Swinburne writes of continually striving to outdo his earlier compositions, a fact that registers in the development of his ode style. In giving an overview of the main stylistic developments, I will concentrate on three odes: the 'Ode to Mazzini' (written while Swinburne was still an undergraduate), the 'Ode on the Insurrection' (which prompted Mazzini's rousing letter) and the third choral ode of *Erechtheus*. These first two odes are not Swinburne or Gosse's favourites, nor the most successful.[48] Yet, read successively, they present three stages in Swinburne's development: from a kind of ode in which the stanza does not quite cohere and the verse plods, to a style in which the reader is entirely swept up in its movement. Since these poems are difficult to come by, and since it may help to give a sense of Swinburne's development if they are read successively, I shall quote from all three of them at some length:

> I
>
> A voice comes from the far unsleeping years,
>   An echo from the rayless verge of time,
>   Harsh, with the gathered weight of kingly crime,
> Whose soul is stained with blood and bloodlike tears,

And hearts made hard and blind with endless pain,
    And eyes too dim to bear
    The light of the free air,
And hands no longer restless in the wonted chain,
    And valiant lives worn out
    By silence and the doubt
That comes with hope found weaponless and vain;
    All these cry out to thee,
    As thou to Liberty,
All, looking up to thee, take heart and life again.

II

Too long the world has waited. Year on year
    Has died in voiceless fear
Since tyranny began the silent ill,
And Slaughter satiates yet her ravenous will.
    Surely the time is near---
    The dawn grows wide and clear;
And fiercer beams than pave the steps of day
    Pierce all the brightening air
    And in some nightly lair
The keen white lightning hungers for his prey,
    Against his chain the growing thunder yearns
    With hot swift pulses all the silence burns,
And the earth hears, and maddens with delay.

III

Dost thou not hear, thro' the hushed heart of night,
The voices wailing for thy help, thy sight,
    The souls, that call their lord?
    'We want the voice, the sword,
We want the hand to strike, the love to share
    The weight we cannot bear;
The soul to point our way, the heart to do and dare.
    We want the unblinded eye,
    The spirit pure and high,
And consecrated by enduring care:
    For now we dare not meet
    The memories of the past;
They wound us with their glories bright and fleet,
    The fame that would not last,
    The hopes that were too sweet;
    A voice of lamentation
Shakes the high places of the thronèd nation,
The crownless nation sitting wan and bare
    Upon the royal seat.' ...[49]

Swinburne's first extant praise-poem for Mazzini is heavy, unwieldy and long. We can account for this by considering the structure of stanzas, the lack of enjambment combined with end-pointing, and his 'mixed' metaphors. The 'Ode to Mazzini' combines three-beat, five-beat and six-beat lines in irregular stanzas, so that no single metrical set ever becomes fully established. The result of this is that there is no norm to break with. Therefore transitions between one line length and another hardly register as variants, producing tension, but they are encountered as another kind of line entirely. Hence this composition is edging towards collapse before it has even got off the ground. Take the first stanza: the opening five lines, which show a tendency for the last syllable to be stressed, achieve a kind of rhythmic parallelism which falls heavy on the ear. Despite the variation in the first foot of the third line, each line appears to confirm the intimation of a heavy, plodding rhythm. These lugubrious five-beat lines are broken by shorter skipping intervals — we might call them hemistichic couplets — of three beats, interspersed with the option (or so it appears) of a six-beat line. However, although the stanza ostensibly moves to and from a five-beat base, the verse feels as if it is cobbled together, composed of lines which bear no relation to each other.

That this need not be the necessary result of combining lines of varying length is suggested by comparison with two other odes of a similar construction, one of which it is certain that Swinburne knew well.[50] Although he also combines five-beat lines with hemistichic lines and hemistichic couplets — let us call the former a 'stop' and the latter a 'skip' for short — we do not doubt, reading Coleridge's 'Dejection: An Ode', that the incorporation of different line lengths deviates from the base rhythm:

> A stifled, drowsy, unimpassioned grief,
> Which finds no natural outlet, no relief,
> In word, or sigh, or tear —
> O Lady! in this wan and heartless mood,[51]

Here the 'stop' in the third line quoted halts, breaking off before the apostrophe in the next line. In comparison, the 'stop' in the second verse of Swinburne's ode throws the reader:

> Too long the world has waited. Year on year
> Has died in voiceless fear
> Since tyranny began the silent ill.

The effects continue into the next line, when the effort to right the rhythm tempts me to overegg the duple rhythm. There is a sense of juncture here, which is not present in Coleridge's stops or skips (see for example, lines 37–44). Coleridge's stops and returns to the five-beat base feel like dips: the verse stops and eddies, and the couplet rhyme has the effect of lifting the line as if in an upsurge of song. That Coleridge is able to hint at the 'joy' which is the subject and longed-for object of this poem without commenting upon it suggests a poet who has lost himself within and is thinking fluently within his form. Swinburne, in this early poem, is more heavy-handed. The skip in the first verse aims to create a parallelism between the *misérables* who cry to Mazzini, and Mazzini as an intervening saint calling on the goddess Liberty. Yet the effect of the skip after such ponderous lines means the rhetorical parallelism is roughly passed over. It is as if the figure has been shoe-horned into the shorter lines.

In a similar way, Swinburne's use of the six-beat line here feels forced in a way which is only once true of his later experiments with the English alexandrine in *Tristram of Lyonesse*. (The line I have in mind is: 'Toward light they turn to music love the blue strong skies'; *Poems,* IV, p. 16.) Dryden has the capacity to incorporate a six-beat line mid-stanza without it feeling like a deviation from the norm, or a closure:

> Even love (for love sometimes her muse exprest)
> Was but a lambent flame which play'd about her breast,
> Light as the vapours of a morning dream ...[52]

The second line quoted stretches out a little further than expected — a little frisson — but we have no trouble returning to the pentameter base. In Swinburne's ode one is less sure of the steps, and the mid-stanza six-beat line is simply another change to cope with.

Further reasons for the tendency for Swinburne's lines to throw us are found in the end-pointing. One reason why the enjambment in the second line of the second stanza of the 'Ode to Mazzini' throws us so far is because it breaks with the general trend to encounter one sense-unit per line. Generally speaking, the argument edges forwards one line at a time, and explains why some lines appear thin on content. Take, for example, 'By silence and the doubt' (l.10) which sounds a little like a filler. Couple this with the fact that Swinburne here is working with a relatively small set of rhymes (the virtuosic polysyllabic rhymer who could match 'Colonus' with 'enthrone us' in the 'Ode to Athens' is still a long way off), which always return right on cue, corresponding to lines of like length at a distance of no more than two lines, and it is easy to see why the lines feel so tight and bounded.

This gradual emergence of the argument has the effect of building the conceit before our ears. Yet Swinburne's attempt to give voice to that roar which lies on the other side of silence is not quite successful. The metaphors are, to adopt an adjective often used of Milton's metaphors, 'mixed', but not successful. To question why the beams of the new dawn which Mazzini's republicanism presents should 'pave' the steps of day, as well as pierce the air, or why the tears, coupled with blood, must be bloodlike too, is not to split hairs — as Eliot did when writing of the lines 'Time with a gift of tears / Grief with a glass that ran' in *Atalanta* — but appears a legitimate question (*Selected Essays*, p. 326). Reversals of syntax add to the sense of multiple contortions taking place. It is hard to know who is who in the last three lines of the first stanza without backtracking. Swinburne would mix his metaphors and play with syntax successfully in his later odes, but plodding and heavy as the pace is, his metaphors and imagery fall flat.

The 'Ode to Mazzini' was not published in Swinburne's lifetime. Edmund Gosse speculates that the political events it responds to were over too soon to make its publication relevant.[53] However, he also reflects that a further reason for this oversight has to do with its form:

> It is an irregular ode, of the Pindaresque sort, on the model which was invented by Cowley, and constantly employed during the close of the seventeenth century, but exposed, in a brilliant and learned essay, by Congreve, as founded on a total misconception of the law of Pindar's prosody. Later Swinburne

perceived the falsity of the Pindaresque ode, and his mature poems are types of disciplined evolution. There were therefore reasons of various kinds, external and internal, why the Ode to Mazzini, if not printed soon after it was written, could not be printed by Swinburne.[54]

Gosse's argument rather overstates Congreve's scholarship, but is in line with his argument in the introduction to *English Odes*, which anticipates Swinburne in preferring the regular ode. As Swinburne would insist in his epistle:

> The title of ode may more properly and fairly be so extended as to cover all lyrical poems in stanzas or couplets than so strained as to include a lawless lyric of such irregular and uneven build as Coleridge only and hardly could make acceptable or admissible among more natural and lawful forms of poetry. Law, not lawlessness, is the natural condition of poetic life; but the law must itself be poetic and not pedantic, natural and not conventional (I, pp. xv–xvi).

This statement is made retrospectively and presumably has in mind the odes of *Erechtheus* more than these early odes.[55] Nevertheless, Gosse's conclusions require some qualification: the 'Ode to Mazzini' is not as Cowleyan as he would have it in two basic respects. First, it does not see-saw quite as much as Cowley does in its combination of lines of different length in the same stanza.[56] Secondly, Swinburne's early mode of stanza construction also prompts a further realisation of how Swinburne's early ode style sets him apart from Cowley and other ode writers in this tradition. Reading Swinburne's early odes, we become aware that when transitions within a stanza form appear arbitrary, we seek reasons why this shift or that change might be happening. This tendency must be connected to the fact that the irregular ode is so often reflexive. We might think here of Dryden's 'Alexander's Feast', which Gosse did not include in his anthology, or William Collins's 'The Passions', a poem that Swinburne valued far less highly than he did his 'Ode to Evening':

> And ever and anon he beat
> The doubling drum with furious heat;
> And though sometimes each dreary pause between,
> Dejected Pity at his side
> Her soul-subduing voice applied,
> Yet still he kept his wild unaltered mien,
> While each strained ball of sight seemed bursting from his head.[57]

Four-beat for the drum, a respite in the five-beat line, alliteration and assonance to smooth the lines describing pity, before the line *strains* out, ending with six beats to describe the pressure of revenge. Yet this wilful courting of a mimetic reading is hardly ever seen in Swinburne, even in this early irregular ode. There is some hint as to Swinburne's own thoughts on this tendency in his much later comments on Wordsworth's 'Immortality Ode', 'which by the way is no more an ode than it is an epic'. For five stanzas it is very 'great' indeed, but after the seventh it 'falls suddenly far down':

> The details which follow on the close of this opening cadence do but impair its charm with a sense of incongruous realism and triviality, to which the suddenly halting and disjointed metre bears only too direct and significant a correspondence.[58]

The lines which Swinburne mentions in the seventh verse move between five-beat, four-beat and three-beat lines in quick succession to demonstrate the way the now no longer newborn child 'cons' his way through different roles: 'As if his whole vocation / Were endless imitation'. I use the word 'demonstrate' because these lines, like Pope and Collins before them, mimic their meaning. Yet they may also have appeared unacceptable to Swinburne in their argument, namely the endorsement of 'trivialities', the habits the child learns, what he calls, in his undergraduate essay on liberty: 'opinions', 'customs', 'systems'.[59] Might this technique of having the verse act them out via verbal mimesis have counted in Swinburne's mind as a kind of eloquence? From the very beginning, then, Swinburne's odes appear to be averse to the kinds of reflexivity or verbal mimesis which we find in Pope, Collins, Gray, and here, too, in Cowley's teetering ode 'In Praise of Pindar':

> *Pindar's unnavigable Song*
> Like a swoln *Flood* from some steep *Mountain* pours along,
> The *Ocean* meets with such a *Voice*
> From his enlarged *Mouth*, as drowns the *Oceans* noise.[60]

Where Swinburne's odes do aim to inspire his reader with a sense of boundless freedom and energy, they achieve this by very different means.

Some of these are already present in his next audacious attempt at a 'regular' ode, the 'Ode on the Insurrection in Candia' (II, pp. 200–07). This contains five strophes, all of different length and construction, followed by five corresponding antistrophes, but never reusing the same rhyme words exactly. *Rime riche*, or polysyllabic rhyme, is clearly preferable, and the usual suspects in Swinburne's rhyme repertoire (such as 'breath/death'; 'sea/me'), are kept in reserve far longer. Strophes combine four-beat, five-beat and six-beat lines, with the four-beat line sometimes being realised as a three-beat line with a single unrealized offbeat, which leads to a pause. This is the same set of materials as Swinburne employed in the 'Ode to Mazzini', yet the result is very different. These differences include: a tightening up of the different line lengths into units, corresponding adjustments in the rhyme scheme, experiments with enjambment, and the discovery of a speed and ease achieved by combining lines of proportional metrical sets together. Yet despite regularisation, the relationship of line to syntax, and the way the argument is constructed line by line, it is still plodding. Swinburne's sense that this ode might incur charges of 'formality' (I, p. xiv) reveals him as his own acutest critic. I quote the poem at full length, in order to give the reader a sense of its complexity and ambition:

> Str. 1
>
> I laid my laurel-leaf
> At the white feet of grief,
> Seeing how with covered face and plumeless wings,
> With unreverted head
> Veiled, as who mourns his dead,
> Lay Freedom couched between the thrones of kings,
> A wearied lion without lair,
> And bleeding from base wounds, and vexed with alien air.

Str. 2

Who was it, who, put poison to thy mouth,
 Who lulled with craft or chant thy vigilant eyes,
O light of all men, lamp to north and south,
 Eastward and westward, under all men's skies?
For if thou sleep, we perish, and thy name
 Dies with the dying of our ephemeral breath;
And if the dust of death o'ergrows thy flame,
 Heaven also is darkened with the dust of death.
If thou be mortal, if thou change or cease,
If thine hand fail, or thine eyes turn from Greece,
Thy firstborn, and the firstfruits of thy fame,
God is no God, and man is moulded out of shame.

Str. 3

Is there change in the secret skies,
 In the sacred places that see
  The divine beginning of things,
   The weft of the web of the world?
Is Freedom a worm that dies,
 And God no God of the free?
  Is heaven like as earth with her kings
   And time as a serpent curled
    Round life as a tree?

From the steel-bound snows of the north,
 From the mystic mother, the east,
  From the sands of the fiery south,
   From the low-lit clouds of the west,
A sound of a cry is gone forth;
 Arise, stand up from the feast,
  Let wine be far from the mouth,
   Let no man sleep or take rest,
    Till the plague hath ceased.

Let none rejoice or make mirth
 Till the evil thing be stayed,
  Nor grief be lulled in the lute,
   Nor hope be loud on the lyre;
Let none be glad upon earth.
 O music of young man and maid,
  O songs of the bride, be mute.
   For the light of her eyes, her desire,
    Is the soul dismayed.

It is not a land new-born
 That is scourged of a stranger's hand,
  That is rent and consumed with flame.
   We have known it of old, this face,

With the cheeks and the tresses torn,
    With shame on the brow as a brand.
        We have named it of old by name,
            The land of the royallest race,
                The most holy land.

Str. 4

        Had I words of fire,
            Whose words are weak as snow;
        Were my heart a lyre
            Whence all its love might flow
In the mighty modulations of desire,
In the notes wherewith man's passion worships woe;

        Could my song release
            The thought weak words confine,
        And my grief, O Greece,
            Prove how it worships thine;
It would move with pulse of war the limbs of peace
Till she flushed and trembled and became divine.

        (Once she held for true
            This truth of sacred strain;
Though blood drip like dew
            And life run down like rain,
It is better that war spare but one or two
Than that many live, and liberty be slain.)

        Then with fierce increase
            And bitter mother's mirth,
        From the womb of peace,
            A womb that yearns for birth,
As a man-child should deliverance come to Greece,
As a saviour should the child be born on earth.

Str. 5

        O that these my days had been
        Ere white peace and shame were wed
        Without torch or dancers' din
        Round the unsacred marriage-bed!
        For of old the sweet-tongued law,
        Freedom, clothed with all men's love,
        Girt about with all men's awe,
        With the wild war-eagle mated
        The white breast of peace the dove,
        And his ravenous heart abated
        And his windy wings were furled
        In an eyrie consecrated
        Where the snakes of strife uncurled,
        And her soul was soothed and sated
        With the welfare of the world.

Ant. 1

But now, close-clad with peace,
   While war lays hand on Greece,
The kingdoms and their kings stand by to see;
   "Aha, we are strong," they say,
   "We are sure, we are well," even they;
   "And if we serve, what ails ye to be free?
   We are warm, clothed round with peace and shame;
But ye lie dead and naked, dying for a name."

Ant. 2

O kings and queens and nations miserable,
   O fools and blind, and full of sins and fears,
With these it is, with you it is not well;
   Ye have one hour, but these the immortal years.
These for a pang, a breath, a pulse of pain,
   Have honour, while that honour on earth shall be;
Ye for a little sleep and sloth shall gain
   Scorn, while one man of all men born is free.
Even as the depth more deep than night or day,
The sovereign heaven that keeps its eldest way,
So without chance or change, so without stain,
The heaven of their high memories shall nor wax nor wane.

Ant. 3

As the soul on the lips of the dead
   Stands poising her wings for flight,
     A bird scarce quit of her prison,
       But fair without form or flesh,
So stands over each man's head
   A splendour of imminent light,
     A glory of fame rearisen,
       Of day rearisen afresh
         From the hells of night.

In the hundred cities of Crete
   Such glory was not of old,
     Though her name was great upon earth
       And her face was fair on the sea.
The words of her lips were sweet,
   Her days were woven with gold,
     Her fruits came timely to birth;
      So fair she was, being free,
       Who is bought and sold.

So fair, who is fairer now
   With her children dead at her side,
     Unsceptred, unconsecrated,
       Unapparelled, unhelped, unpitied,
With blood for gold on her brow,
   Where the towery tresses divide;

> The goodly, the golden-gated,
>> Many-crowned, many-named, many-citied,
> Made like as a bride.

And these are the bridegroom's gifts;
> Anguish that straitens the breath,
>> Shame, and the weeping of mothers,
>>> And the suckling dead at the breast,
White breast that a long sob lifts;
> And the dumb dead mouth, which saith,
>> "How long, and how long, my brothers?"
>>> And wrath which endures not rest,
>>> And the pains of death.

Ant. 4

> Ah, but would that men,
>> With eyelids purged by tears,
> Saw, and heard again
>> With consecrated ears,
All the clamour, all the splendour, all the slain,
All the lights and sounds of war, the fates and fears;

> Saw far off aspire,
>> With crash of mine and gate,
> From a single pyre
>> The myriad flames of fate,
Soul by soul transfigured in funereal fire,
Hate made weak by love, and love made strong by hate.

> Children without speech,
>> And many a nursing breast;
> Old men in the breach,
>> Where death sat down a guest;
With triumphant lamentation made for each,
Let the world salute their ruin and their rest.

> In one iron hour
>> The crescent flared and waned,
> As from tower to tower,
>> Fire-scathed and sanguine-stained,
Death, with flame in hand, an open bloodred flower,
Passed, and where it bloomed no bloom of life remained.

Ant. 5

> Hear, thou earth, the heavy-hearted
> Weary nurse of waning races;
> From the dust of years departed,
> From obscure funereal places,
> Raise again thy sacred head,
> Lift the light up of thine eyes;
> Where are they of all thy dead
> That did more than these men dying

In their godlike Grecian wise?
Not with garments rent and sighing,
Neither gifts of myrrh and gold,
Shall their sons lament them lying,
Lest the fame of them wax cold;
But with lives to lives replying,
And a worship from of old.

Epode

O sombre heart of earth and swoln with grief,
    That in thy time wast as a bird for mirth,
Dim womb of life and many a seed and sheaf,
    And full of changes, ancient heart of earth,
From grain and flower, from grass and every leaf,
    Thy mysteries and thy multitudes of birth,
From hollow and hill, from vales and all thy springs,
    From all shapes born and breath of all lips made,
From thunders, and the sound of winds and wings,
    From light, and from the solemn sleep of shade,
From the full fountains of all living things,
    Speak, that this plague be stayed.
Bear witness all the ways of death and life
    If thou be with us in the world's old strife,
        If thou be mother indeed,
        And from these wounds that bleed
Gather in thy great breast the dews that fall,
        And on thy sacred knees
        Lull with mute melodies,
Mother, thy sleeping sons in death's dim hall.
        For these thy sons, behold,
        Sons of thy sons of old,
Bear witness if these be not as they were;
        If that high name of Greece
        Depart, dissolve, decease
From mouths of men and memories like as air.
        By the last milk that drips
        Dead on the child's dead lips,
By old men's white unviolated hair,
        By sweet unburied faces
        That fill those red high places
Where death and freedom found one lion's lair,
        By all the bloodred tears
        That fill the chaliced years,
The vessels of the sacrament of time,
        Wherewith, O thou most holy,
        O Freedom, sure and slowly
Thy ministrant white hands cleanse earth of crime;
        Though we stand off afar
        Where slaves and slaveries are,
Among the chains and crowns of poisonous peace;

> Though not the beams that shone
> From rent Arcadion
> Can melt her mists and bid her snows decrease;
> Do thou with sudden wings
> Darken the face of kings,
> But turn again the beauty of thy brows on Greece;
> Thy white and woundless brows,
> Whereto her great heart bows;
> Give her the glories of thine eyes to see;
> Turn thee, O holiest head,
> Toward all thy quick and dead,
> For love's sake of the souls that cry for thee;
> O love, O light, O flame,
> By thine own Grecian name,
> We call thee and we charge thee that all these be free.

One can only wonder what a day (and night) that must have been for the typesetters at *The Fortnightly Review*. This first strophe bears some resemblance to the skips interspersed with pentameter lines which we saw in the earlier ode. However, instead of employing different line lengths without any regularity, Swinburne builds different lengths of lines into units. This is underpinned by the rhyme scheme, which has also been regulated to form connections between correspondent line lengths: $3a3a5b3c3c5b4d6d$. The effect is therefore one of two slow opening eddies, a running line, two corresponding eddies, and a run answering the *b* rhyme, before a new rhyme line which hits the previously unsounded fourth beat, finishing in a line which audibly stretches out. Perhaps Swinburne, in this new scheme, had one ear on Samuel Johnson's criticism of Gray: 'His stanzas are too long, especially his epodes; the ode is finished before the ear has learned its measures, and consequently before it can receive pleasure from their consonance and recurrence'.[61] Regularising his measures allows Swinburne to produce pleasure from the satisfaction of established norms, and furthermore (what Johnson does not mention) tension when deviating from them.

What Swinburne did have in mind is the hymnic part of Milton's ode 'On the Morning of Christ's Nativity'. That Swinburne thought highly of Milton's poem is suggested by his postscript in a letter to William Michael Rossetti discussing 'The Eve of Revolution', which refers to the last hexameter of verse quoted below as 'my favourite of any alexandrine in the language'.[62] The first strophe and antistrophe of the Candiote Ode is identical in construction.[63] However, if Swinburne is avoiding 'triviality', and making room in the structure of his ode for the pleasure of recurrence and consonance, then why this undeniable 'formality'? Something in Milton's verse, differently handled in Swinburne's ode, gives us the clue:

> Nor is Osiris seen
> In Memphian Grove, or Green,
>   Trampling the unshow'rd Grasse with lowings loud:
> Nor can he be at rest
> Within his sacred chest,
>   Naught but profoundest Hell can be his shroud:
> In vain with Timbrel'd Anthems dark
> The sable stoled Sorcerers bear his worship't Ark.[64]

There is nothing stilted here, in metre, enjambment or syntax. The reversal of the adjective and noun in the third line hardly registers, so smooth is the instrumentation.

By contrast, Swinburne's deployment of syntax within the line is so focused on the line as an individual unit that the stanza can end up feeling cobbled together out of individual lines. This is handled very differently in Milton's poem. In the stanza quoted the preceding four-beat line arranges adverbial clause and noun in such a way that the reader must rush over the line to complete the sense.[65] The speed and fluency of the movement is aided by the instrumentation — alliteration, assonance, consonance.[66] In Swinburne's poem, the impression that the poet is still trying to make many lines of different lengths cohere into an unwieldy whole registers in the way in which enjambment always feels odd, and the six-beat line arrives like an appendage. The syntax of the lines 'O fools and blind, and full of sins and fears, / With these it is, with you it is not well;' feels stilted and artificial, far from the spontaneity that Mill recommends.[67] The spatial conceit in the last line, which compares the honour of fallen heroes to the heavens: 'Even as the depth more deep than night or day,' only just holds together. Swinburne's take on the nativity ode stanza is not bounding, not ebullient. Instead we are put more in mind of the 'air of calm deliberateness [...] [which] never seems *possessed* by any feeling: no emotion seems ever so strong as to have entire sway, for the time being, over the current of his thoughts', which Mill associated with Wordsworth. This opening strophe feels more like being moved along, rather than being carried, through the different changes and textures.

Perhaps it will take off in the second stanza, when the uniform presence of a five-beat line culminating with a six-beat line in the last line, means that the reader will not be troubled by the rapidly shifting combination of different line lengths. The second strophe of twelve lines sets the precedence for four-line sets of alternating rhyme, then moves into couplets in the last four lines, introducing a new rhyme, but repeating the third rhyme in the final line: $5a5b5a5b5c5d5c5d5e5e5f6f$. However, the enjambment does not work. In the antistrophe 'scorn' clunks into place like an afterthought, from which the rhythm of the line takes a moment to recover. Yet we were hardly waiting for it. In fact, this second stanza as a whole is full of redundancies which speak of what Simon Jarvis aptly refers to as 'chewing your pen': 'even they;' seems calculated to fill the line and match a rhyme.[68] This ode is like one of Falstaff's soliloquies, those early games in Eastcheap, in which he acts out acting and appears absurd. Is this thought prompted by the use of personification in Swinburne's opening strophe, in which freedom is described in similar imagery, as a lairless, maimed lion, whimpering between the thrones of shameless kings? The diction, like Milton's, is of a high register here, but missing Milton's naturalness in the handling of syntax and line. Perhaps Swinburne knew all this, for after this point he begins to compose monostrophic strophes, or to combine lines with a proportional relationship together.

Here, within this ode which Swinburne repudiated, there are occasional flashes of flexibility which, in their balance of syntax against line, rival even Shelley:

> In one iron hour
> > The crescent flared and waned,
> > As from tower to tower,
> > Fire-scathed and sanguine-stained,
> Death, with flame in hand, an open bloodred flower,
> Passed, and where it bloomed no bloom of life remained. (II, p. 206)

Death's dominion, which Swinburne figures as a levelling force that should provoke all lovers of liberty to rise up, is beautifully handled here. The consonance of three four-beat lines with a final unrealised offbeat (which registers as a pause) allows for recurrence and consonance, before the fourth beat is sounded to our satisfaction, in the fourth line, and the poem shifts into two six-beat lines. Yet the transition here is easy, fluid and energetic when compared to similar jumps in the 'Ode to Mazzini'.

Pushed to account for this, we can observe how the different line lengths are related. The three-beat line with a pause adds together to make a six-beat line, a fact that registers in the strong tendency the reader feels to pause midway through Swinburne's last two lines. The tendency for Swinburne's longer measures to reveal themselves as made up of smaller units is more marked than most, as George Saintsbury notes. This is:

> a peculiarity which does not appertain to the bounties of Bacchus in their larger receptacles. They have a wicked habit of 'splitting themselves up' and saying, 'You may write me how you like, but you cannot read me at full length.' They do this so obstinately — they are so thoroughly English in all their qualities — that even the poet's malicious afterthought, in trying to make the split impossible by making it occur in the middle of a word, does not prevent them.[69]

The movement from one metrical set to a proportional metrical set feels natural, though a tension, produced by the perception of similarity in difference, is still discernible. Here, Swinburne has discovered the method of strophe construction which he would develop in his later 'Ode on the Proclamation', where he again plays with a combination of three-beat and six-beat lines in the third strophe. For now, it is enough to note that this ease, arising from the technique of combining proportionally similar lines within a stanza, makes it possible to see where the choral odes of *Erechtheus* come from.[70] However, they are no less astonishing when they arrive.

The Choral Odes of Erechtheus

Writing to the engraver, poet and fellow disciple of Mazzini, W. J. Linton, in 1883, Swinburne expresses his wish to be represented in a volume of 'English Verse' by the 'Ode to Athens' or *Erechtheus*, specifically the 'Rape of Oreithya [...] or the sea battle [...] rather than any of his earlier work' (*Letters*, V, p. 40). The same preference is also recorded by Gosse, who notes that '[Swinburne's] best choral writing [...] is to be found in his unequalled drama of *Erechtheus*'. A summary of this play is very easy, since it contains very little in the way of plot. The question at hand is freedom, the natural condition of the Athenians, which is threatened by the invasion of Eumolpus, high priest of Eleusis. As in the dramaturgy of Aeschylus, the second of Swinburne's two acknowledged models, the play does not derive its tension from events. It has been revealed to Erechtheus, ruler of Athens, that he must sacrifice his daughter Chthonia for the redemption of her country. However, Chthonia is overjoyed to lay down her life for the city. The tension therefore lies in the inner turmoil of those lovers of freedom, who wait to see whether the gods will grant their city — and by implication the whole community of free people — the grace to continue. As *The Edinburgh Review* put it: 'Through the whole course of the drama we are made to thrill to the chances that are trembling in the scales, as we throw our vision forward through a long vista of historical glories'.[71] The chorus of Athenian elders gives voice to this unfolding emotional situation.

It is a peculiarity of Swinburne's choral odes that, despite their appearance in a verse-drama, they do not read like dramatic monologues. At no point does the dialogue 'present' these lyrics, asking us to attend to their lyrical character, or to discern two voices at work within the ode. Instead, Swinburne appears to keep faith with his models by constructing his play along a division between the dialogue and chorus, a difference which Hegel thought 'especially elaborated' in ancient Greek drama (*Aesthetics,* p. 1172). One of the obvious ways in which Swinburne does this is through metre, using the five-beat line for dialogue, and a variation of the four-beat line for choral song. However, there are other aspects of his play which make any argument for these choral lyrics as dramatic monologues hard to maintain. As one critic of Thomas Noon Talfourd's *Ion* (1836), a play which also turns on the sacrifice of an individual for the city-state, observed:

> If we compare that beautiful play with Mr. Swinburne's 'Erechtheus,' we shall be struck by many points of difference [...] Talfourd's characters are the more lifelike, but [...] of a too modern tone; while Swinburne's are faultlessly correct in attitude [...] but unreal and ghost-like [...] Talfourd very sensibly deserts the Greek for the English stage-tradition, and enacts his catastrophe in the presence of his spectators; while both the first and second catastrophe of the 'Erechtheus' are narrated [...] by the time-honoured lips of our old friend the Messenger. There are no lyric passages in Talfourd's 'Ion' and no chorus; whereas these are by far the strongest points in Mr. Swinburne's play, the ringing resonance of whose chorus charms the ear, even when it fails to convey very distinct notions to the mind.[72]

Far from participating in the technique of the dramatic monologue, which, as Tucker argues, serve to bracket lyric, the choral lyrics of Swinburne's *Erechtheus* are again, like *Atalanta,* 'enchased' within the verse-drama. Swinburne maintains a difference between chorus and dialogue which extends to narration and characterisation. It is in this strict separation of chorus from dialogue, the subjective from the objective, which ensures the survival of what Hegel calls 'unadulterated lyric'. In *Erechtheus* we see a development away from the mode of constructing verse drama first attempted in *Atalanta in Calydon,* where the dialogue and the chorus are brought into rhythmic tension. However, more importantly, I also discover the direct opposite of the synthesis between lyric and drama which dramatic monologue presents: instead the subjective and objective realms (which Hegel associated with lyric and epic respectively) are encountered as a dialectical struggle.

Erechtheus was widely and favourably reviewed and the exceptional lyricism of the third chorus is witnessed in many accounts. For *The London Quarterly Review* it is 'the grandest of its odes'.[73] *The Athenæum* calls it 'A magnificent outburst'.[74] J. A. Symonds distinguishes it from the rest as 'a real triumph of lyrical genius'.[75] Gosse himself notes its 'marvellous power and significance', protesting that 'We cannot resist the temptation of quoting [...]' and citing the second strophe — 'an unrivalled *tour de force*' — at some length.[76] *The Spectator* concludes: 'we think we must select [...] the very beautiful chorus in which the contrast is drawn between the old, far-off sorrow of the rape of the North Wind's bride, and the impending sacrifice of the fair young daughter of Praxithea to redeem the city of Athena'.[77] Occasionally, readers struggled to account for the effect of this ode. *The Saturday Review* is cautious: 'the writer has given the rein too much to his fancy, but [...] the poetry is undeniable'.[78] *Blackwood's Edinburgh Magazine* even suggests an exit clause for the more timorous reader: 'Readers, undesirious [sic] of such fierce music, have a ready pretext for skipping in the *"Excusez-moi monsieur, je n'entends pas le grec"*, of Moliere's [sic] "Henriette" '.[79] Yet this reviewer cannot forego quoting the third ode in its entirety. Readers in 1876 found the third choral odes of *Erechtheus* irresistible. They therefore present a good test case for this investigation into the ways and means of Swinburne's later odes.

> Str. 1.
> Out of the north wind grief came forth,
>   And the shining of a sword out of the sea.
> Yea, of old the first-blown blast blew the prelude of this last,
>   The blast of his trumpet upon Rhodope.
> Out of the north skies full of his cloud,
> With the clamour of his storms as of a crowd
> At the wheels of a great king crying aloud,
> At the axle of a strong king's car
> That has girded on the girdle of war---
> With hands that lightened the skies in sunder
> And feet whose fall was followed of thunder,
>   A God, a great God strange of name,
>   With horse-yoke fleeter-hoofed than flame,
> To the mountain bed of a maiden came,
> Oreithyia, the bride mismated,
> Wofully wed in a snow-strewn bed
> With a bridegroom that kisses the bride's mouth dead;
> Without garland, without glory, without song,
> As a fawn by night on the hills belated,
> Given over for a spoil unto the strong.

Ant. 1.

From lips how pale so keen a wail
   At the grasp of a God's hand on her she gave,
When his breath that darkens air made a havoc of her hair,
   It rang from the mountain even to the wave;
Rang with a cry, Woe's me, woe is me!
From the darkness upon Hæmus to the sea:
And with hands that clung to her new lord's knee,
As a virgin overborne with shame,
She besought him by her spouseless fame,
By the blameless breasts of a maid unmarried,
And locks unmaidenly rent and harried,
   And all her flower of body, born
   To match the maidenhood of morn,
With the might of the wind's wrath wrenched and torn.
Vain, all vain as a dead man's vision
Falling by night in his old friends' sight,
To be scattered with slumber and slain ere light;
Such a breath of such a bridegroom in that hour
Of her prayers made mock, of her fears derision,
And a ravage of her youth as of a flower.

Str. 2.

With a leap of his limbs as a lion's, a cry from his lips as of thunder,
   In a storm of amorous godhead filled with fire,
From the height of the heaven that was rent with the roar of his
                           coming in sunder,
Sprang the strong God on the spoil of his desire.
And the pines of the hills were as green reeds shattered,
And their branches as buds of the soft spring scattered,
And the west wind and east, and the sound of the south,
Fell dumb at the blast of the north wind's mouth,
   At the cry of his coming out of heaven.
And the wild beasts quailed in the rifts and hollows
Where hound nor clarion of huntsman follows,
And the depths of the sea were aghast, and whitened,
And the crowns of their waves were as flame that lightened,
   And the heart of the floods thereof was riven.

Ant. 2.

But she knew not him coming for terror, she felt not her wrong that
                           he wrought her,
   When her locks as leaves were shed before his breath,
And she heard not for terror his prayer, though the cry was a God's
                           that besought her,
   Blown from lips that strew the world-wide seas with death.
   For the heart was molten within her to hear,
   And her knees beneath her were loosened for fear,
   And her blood fast bound as a frost-bound water,
   And the soft new bloom of the green earth's daughter

>   Wind-wasted as blossom of a tree;
>   As the wild God rapt her from earth's breast lifted,
>   On the strength of the stream of his dark breath drifted,
>   From the bosom of earth as a bride from the mother,
>   With storm for bridesman and wreck for brother,
>   As a cloud that he sheds upon the sea.
>
> *Epode.*
>
>   Of this hoary-headed woe
>   Song made memory long ago;
>   Now a younger grief to mourn
>   Needs a new song younger born.
>   Who shall teach our tongues to reach
>   What strange height of saddest speech,
> For the new bride's sake that is given to be
> A stay to fetter the foot of the sea,
> Lest it quite spurn down and trample the town,
> Ere the violets be dead that were plucked for its crown,
>   Or its olive-leaf whiten and wither?
>   Who shall say of the wind's way
>   That he journeyed yesterday,
> Or the track of the storm that shall sound to-morrow,
> If the new be more than the grey-grown sorrow?
> For the wind of the green first season was keen,
> And the blast shall be sharper than blew between
>   That the breath of the sea blows hither.

This ode (IV, pp. 361–64) pushes off, returns, sweeps, rushes and pauses, allowing an isolated image to blossom and crystallise for a moment, then changes tack again, building tension and releasing it as it the lines stretch out long or pull back tight. We go through it all over again twice, and in each case the movements are similar but different. The pace slows in the epode, trembling with echoes of former speed, which threaten to break out, yet it keeps its own track. It is hard to keep up. It is impossible not to keep up. It is no wonder that contemporary accounts had recourse to onomatopoeic or mimetic readings which conflate style and content, the irresistible verse style with the advance of an irresistible god. However, we should not be so hasty. While the reader is instantly swept up in a dance which shows no signs of faltering, making it very hard, as Gosse notes, to extract, this is not the relentless speed that we encounter in some of the monostrophic choruses of *Atalanta*. Instead it is full of stops, eddies, pauses — in short, it has poise.

The clue to the gestural aspect of this ode lies in its combination of short and long lines proportionally like each other. A two-beat line is half a four-beat line, something that Swinburne's internal rhyme seems to demonstrate from the off. Likewise, a three-beat line with a pause, often offering some of the most beautiful images in the poem, is in fact a four-beat line with a final unsounded beat that registers as a pause. Therefore, though the lines appear to be different lengths, they are all related. Perhaps the closest analogy in dance would be a Scottish reel, which can be notated as 2/2 or 4/4 time, depending on the whim of the recording authority. The result is an ode that carries the reader through various transitions without throwing them, combined with a rhythmic propulsion that Swinburne's earlier odes never fully realise, though the early beginnings of it are clear as early as 1867. Yet the resulting ode remains far from automatic. Housman's comparison of Swinburne's lyric to a sausage-machine, mechanically cranking out the lines, might be true of other odes formed on a strong rhythmical base.[80] However, here Swinburne allows the rhythm to build up by joining lines of like rhythmical (and sometimes also syntactical) structure together, producing mesmeric effects which often register in performance as a tendency to make pitch uniform, there remains a remarkable degree of variation.

The late M. L. West noted that in

> the marching anapaests of drama, cretic-paeonic, and certain others used in choral song [...] the equivalence between a long and a short appears to be more absolute, and the substitution of one for the other does not seem to put the rhythm under any strain as it does in the hexameter. Here, presumably, the discipline of music and/or movement has imposed a stricter mathematical relationship upon the long and short positions of the metrical scheme, and the pronunciation of the syllables is adjusted accordingly.[81]

West's description of the special case which choral song presents suggests an ancient analogue for the equivalence which Swinburne appears to have found, between one, two, and even three unstressed syllables, between beats. In this we discover an analogous principle of the subtle alterations, swift changes, eddies and swirls of Swinburne's song of the apotheosis of Oreithya.

To characterise this ode as a four-beat line with immense flexibility in the number of unstressed syllables between beats would be correct, but would miss the brilliance of Swinburne's variation. Compare the different rhythmical textures of the following lines from the first strophe: 'A God, a great God strange of name' ('iambic', with trochaic inversion); 'With a bridegroom that kisses the bride's mouth dead;' ('anapestic', with a final iambic foot); or the punchline: 'woefully wed in a snow-strewn bed' (hyper-catalectic 'anapestic', with a falling tendency). In the second antistrophe two six-beat lines occur and recur, yet because these lines have a clear proportional relationship to the metrical base, they do not throw us. This said, though we have the measure of the line, we are put through our paces.

The result of this principle of construction is perhaps best demonstrated when encountering several lines about which one has to make a decision as to whether to sound all the possible stresses without any kind of hierarchy, or to give in to the rhythm. I could read 'Yea, of old the first-blown blast blew the prelude of this last,' as two four-beat lines run together. Internal rhyme even suggests that this is a couplet strung together into an eight-beat line. Yet this line has cemented itself in my memory as dipodic, that is, as having two possible levels of stress, meaning that the speed of the line increases to double time, and we stress 'old', 'blast', 'pre-' and 'last'. Coventry Patmore writes about dipodic rhythms in his 'Essay on English Metrical Law', but there is nothing like this instinctual metrical pull in Patmore's odes.[82] There is a canny rhythmic-syntactical cooperation present here, as the arrangement of the line read thus links the 'old' 'blast' as a type of 'last' sacrifice, allowing us to connect the subject of this ode with the sacrifice of Chthonia for the salvation of Athens. We also encounter lines which could be read as having three or four stressed syllables. Do we read the line 'The blast of his trumpet upon Rhodope' (l.558) as having four beats, stressing the second syllable of 'upon' (which feels slightly ponderous)? Or do we read three swift beats (on 'blast-', 'trump-', '-pe'), realising the last, fourth beat as a pause, in line with Swinburne's punctuation? The same dilemma is also present in the last line of the first strophe. In each case there is a strong pull towards the quicker reading, which is also supported by manuscript evidence.

Very unusually for Swinburne, the working draft of this ode in the manuscript of *Erechtheus* contains several 'scansions' in the margins to lines 556, 558, and 561.[83] These do not themselves suggest that Swinburne was working with a fixed metrical scheme since, even if one could be derived from three lines, no schema readily suggests itself. More likely he was noting the rhythmic texture of his more complex lines and dividing them according to word-end, as an aide-memoire for responsion in the antistrophe. The scansion for line 558 suggests that Swinburne preferred the quicker reading (here taking a breve to indicate an unstressed syllable, and the long to indicate a stressed one): '⌣–|⌣⌣–⌣|⌣⌣⌣–. (For the record, the scansion appended for the other two lines is as follows: l. 556: ⌣⌣–⌣|⌣⌣–|⌣⌣⌣–; l. 561: ⌣⌣–|⌣⌣⌣–|⌣⌣–.) However, to factor out these decisions, producing scansions after our encounter with the poem, is merely to make explicit what we do by instinct. These lines, which ask us to accommodate runs of up to three unstressed syllables, speeding English triple rhythm towards the third paeonic, and to do so mid-dance, require that we give ourselves over to an overwhelming lyrical impulse.

Two contemporary reviewers, including the classicist J. A. Symonds, compared Swinburne's odes to Aeschylus's *The Suppliant Maidens* and *Seven Against Thebes*.[84] I have argued in chapter one that Swinburne discovers, through translating Aristophanes, that English is a language 'to which all variations and combinations of anapestic, iambic or trochaic metre are as natural and as pliable as all dactylic and spondaic forms of verse are unnatural and abhorrent' (V, p. 42). Following Swinburne's lead, any attempt to find a classical precedent for the rhythms of the choruses of *Erechtheus* must remain cautious. However, there does appear to be a form of prosodic hospitality at work here between Swinburne's verse and Aeschylus's choruses which proves insightful.[85]

Following the reviewers' hints reveals that two odes in Aeschylus's *Seven Against Thebes* which come close to *Erechtheus* in theme and imagery are in what A. M. Dale notes as 'very regular' dochmiac rhythm.[86] The chorus's song of agitation which prompts Eteocles' anger resembles Swinburne's battle-chorus in its imagery (the sound of the horses' hooves; the simile of the invading armies as waves) and is 'lucidity itself (metrically speaking)'.[87] Likewise, the dochmiacs of the chorus's later attempt to encourage Eteocles 'are so regular that the rhythm is unmistakable'. On first glance, the most commonly found extant form of the dochmiac colarion does not look particularly friendly to English prosody, as it contains two stressed syllables side by side: ⌣–––⌣.⁸⁸ However, as Dale observes, this arrangement has a particularly 'Protean diversity of form [...] accounted for by the extent to which it avails itself of two principles of equation, quantity and syllable counting'.[89] This is the same equivalence that West has in mind when accounting for the easy interchangeability of two short syllables for a long syllable in tragic metres. Therefore, running two dochmiacs together into a dimeter (as Dale notes often occurs) and resolving them so as to avoid the two stressed syllables in a row (which Swinburne found 'unnatural and abhorrent') might be accommodated within strict stress metre in English.

In a number of ways, the four-beat line in the choral odes of *Erechtheus* suggests that Swinburne may have found an English home for the tragic iambo-dochmiac: a principle of equivalence allows for one, two, or even three unstressed syllables to realise an offbeat, and this flexibility can, like the Greek dochmiac, allow for iambicity, which can have a *rallentando* or blunting effect, something we often see in the second half of Swinburne's lines in the third choral ode.[90] The dochmiac, as a colarion, can be built into larger or smaller lines much like the way in which the *Rape of Oreithya* can contain two-beat lines, but also six-beat lines, without throwing the reader. Yet there is also a further, connotative meaning attached to this form which answers to its particular emotional force. As Dale observes: 'All three tragedians use it freely to express strong feeling, grief, fear, despair, horror, excitement, occasionally triumph or joy [...] Its characteristic use is for the panic of the Theban women under siege, the half-articulate prophecies of Cassandra, Theseus's lament for Phaedra, the ravings of Agave, the howls of the blind Polymester, the extravagant joy of the female in a scene of ἀναγνώρισις'.[91] Once one considers that the dochmiac was the particular province of Aeschylus, and used in a modified form by Pindar — Swinburne's two acknowledged models for *Erechtheus* — it becomes clear why the contemporary reviewers made this connection.

Yet this is not all that Swinburne took from Aeschylus and Pindar. The third choral ode also abounds in response and πνίγη, or 'pnîgos' ('breathlessness'), which West defines as 'a very long period in uniform rhythm' (West, *Greek Metre*, p. 49 and glossary). Swinburne took pains to reproduce the rhythm of individual lines exactly in the answering antistrophe. This allows Swinburne to forge momentary comparisons or contrasts across the ode. Response at lines 570 and 590 allows the reader to connect the wedding of Oreithya and the vision 'vain, all vain' of a dead man, perhaps linking the dreaded death of Erechtheus back to an original myth. Response between lines 574 and 594 forges a contrast between the 'spoil' perceived by the god, and the flower-like fall encountered by Oreithya, thereby balancing their perspectives. In a similar way, the isolated images which emerge in the two-beat and three-beat lines (ll. 603, 608, 617, 622, 633) are understood to have a relation to each other because of their rhythmical similarity. This allows Swinburne to create an ode in which part answers part, much like the organicism which Carne-Ross claims as one of the glories of Pindar's odes.[92]

Rhyme, in addition to its capacity to determine how the end of a line falls out rhythmically, and to bind isochronic lines into units, also creates interest through straying from couplets (and in some cases triplets) and returning to them. The end-rhyme moves from and back to couplets, building to triplets, which speeds the lines further (e.g. ll.566–68). This leads to sections where rhymes are allowed a greater range, enabling a different kind of aural texture to emerge. Shorter lines or 'stops' which occur mid-sentence, or three-beat lines with a pause (which often coincide with the end of a sentence) often use a rhyme which has occurred a few lines previously (e.g. ll.603, 608 and antistrophe; 633, 640) to pause or complete a movement. Rhyme can carry us quickly over short bursts, or gracefully, over long distances: it eddies, whirls, and pauses, but we never cease, never miss a beat.

The result is a style of ode in which the reader is neither thrown, tripped, moved along, or compelled to notice, but is instead carried. As one contemporary reviewer puts it, this play abounds in 'magnificent passages which we feel should be transcribed bodily if we are to do justice to their sense and spirit'.[93] The reviewer has caught the 'peculiar' quality of Swinburne's later odes: a grace, vigour and pliant dexterity that do not appear to 'compel' us, but instead avail themselves of their 'freedom to point the way'.

I have argued that Swinburne's peculiar ode style shows a clear development, discernible once we read Swinburne's odes together, yet two questions remain: how far do these poems present a stylistic solution to Mazzini's request? And how might Mill's understanding of lyric poetry offer an alternative reading of Swinburne's lyricism to that of Tillyard and others, who connect Swinburne's intoxicating lyricism with fascist politics? The remainder of this chapter will endeavour to answer these questions, and to do so I shall stay with this most magnificent of all Swinburne's later odes.

'The Rape of Oreithya'

Writing of *Atalanta*, T. S. Eliot caught the all-encompassing effect of Swinburne's lyrics in a single sentence: 'This is not merely "music"; it is effective because it appears to be a tremendous statement, like statements made in our dreams'. However, Eliot continues, 'when we wake up' we find that Swinburne's verse does not make sense. The reader of the third choral ode of *Erechtheus* faces a greater challenge than the reader of *Atalanta*. When we wake up we find that our dream was of rape. Francis O'Gorman's judgement that 'for much of Swinburne's political poetry, the recognition of violence was hardly real, and scenes of slaughter hardly registered' becomes harder to maintain here.[94] The reaction of a reader who has been swayed by its music may be doubly violent: how can a poem which possesses us, and then leaves us with the dawning consciousness that we have been reading about a violent abduction, have anything to do with freedom? Tillyard's connection between an all-absorbing lyricism and the loss of individuality which totalitarianism invites might well come back to haunt the critic: 'The intoxication of these ideas is well known [...] And the intoxicating quality of Swinburne's verse represents such a process only too well.'

And yet at no point in my encounter with 'The Rape of Oreithya' have I been encouraged to think about what Swinburne's verse 'represents'. In fact, my own encounter has been the exact opposite of verbal mimesis, or pointing: what I encounter in the most magnificent of all of Swinburne's odes is a sense of ebullient, boundless freedom, an 'infinitude of consciousness', in Hegel's phrase.[95] The relationship between form and content, between lyric and narrative possession is not so simple. In order to account for the rape of Oreithya, we must deal with this poem on its own terms. And to do so requires us to recognise that Tillyard's suspicion rests on several assumptions which would not have held for Swinburne.

Specifically, we must engage with the paradox that a sense of freedom may be discovered in a state of bondage; that such a discovery may also cause one to view one's individuality in the light of larger universals; and that such an understanding depends upon the poem as *metaxu*, a middle space, which not only works on us, but invites us to work upon it. If these three ideas appear Hegelian, this is not to imply a line of intellectual inheritance between Swinburne and German idealism. Swinburne, as I have noted, had no German; the Hegel he encountered through the lectures of Benjamin Jowett at Balliol largely consisted (incredibly) in a suspension of the dialectic.[96] If Swinburne had a definition of dialectic, it was Platonic in character. If, in the following account of Swinburne's lyricism, the reader should be reminded of those moments in Hegel's *Phenomenology of Spirit* 'through which the divided self-consciousness passes in its wretchedness', this is because Hegel's philosophy makes explicit several truths which lyrical verse has always known.

Tying Words Up and Twisting Them Back

John D. Rosenberg jokes that 'The sincerity of Swinburne's attachment to the goddess of Liberty is unassailable, although he composed many of his odes to her while walking to a brothel where he paid to be flogged'.[97] Rosenberg appears baffled and amused. However, the irony of his comment escalates once we consider that this apparently paradoxical fact about Swinburne's writing routine also contains a truth about the experience of reading Swinburne's verse. Freedom and bondage are inextricably, not paradoxically, involved in each other (*Phenomenology*, p. 117). However, before we are reduced to gossip, we should recall that this understanding of freedom in bondage was also one of Swinburne's preferred analogies for the workings of verse. I have already quoted Swinburne's remarks in *Lesbia Brandon* at some length ('Things in verse hurt one, don't they? hit and sting like a cut.'[98]). Leaving Swinburne's trips to Verbena Lodge aside, might he have discovered a kind of freedom in his encounters with verse written in an overpowering style?

There is a curious moment in a footnote to his early *William Blake: A Critical Essay*, in which he seems to suggest just that. Critics are fond of quoting from this footnote, since it contains Swinburne's statement of *l'art pour l'art*: 'The pure artist never asserts; he suggests, and therefore his meaning is totally lost upon moralists and sciolists, is indeed irreparably wasted upon the run of men who cannot work out suggestions'. However, what he goes on to say about Balzac's style has proved somewhat less extractable:

> So profound and extensive a capacity of moral apprehension no other prose writer, no man of mere analytic faculty, ever had or can have. [...] Once consent to forget or overlook the mere entourage and social habiliment of Balzac's

> intense and illimitable intellect, you cannot fail of seeing that he of all men was fittest to grapple with all strange things and words, and compel them by divine violence of spiritual rape to bring forth flowers and fruits good for food and available for use.[99]

How can Balzac's style be likened to spiritual rape? Surely Swinburne's characteristic hyperbole has gone too far here. However, if we read this in the context of Swinburne's critical writing, and consider it in relation to the third choral ode of *Erechtheus*, it becomes clear that Rosenberg has dislodged a truth greater than his intention. There was, for Swinburne, an ineluctable connection between the constraints of verse, the constraints of bondage, and the effervescent state which Hegel describes in his exploration of the master-bondsman dialectic. Might this, rather than any elaborate mimetic equation between verse and the lash — what Yopie Prins calls 'metrical discipline' — be the more serious side to Swinburne's scurrilous equation of the two in his flagellatory poems?[100] If so, the test of this will lie, not in what Swinburne says about the relationship between bondage and verse, but in our encounter with the poem.

And yet, if so, we shall also require a very different understanding of the kind of participation lyric poetry involves. For Tillyard, lyric intoxication is something done to us. Yet as Swinburne's own analogy suggests, self-consciousness is also reactive. Verse 'wouldn't hurt us if we had no blood and no nerves [...] You have the nerve of poetry — the soft place it hits on, and stings'. What Tillyard, and perhaps Plato, too, miss is the way in which we also respond to the poem as an independent influence. This is surely the only way in which we can understand Walter Pater's answer to the question he poses in his essay on Winckelmann: 'Can art represent men and women in these bewildering toils so as to give the spirit at least an equivalent for the sense of freedom?' That is the task of the poet and artist: 'so to rearrange the details of modern life, so to reflect it, that it may satisfy the spirit'.[101] For Pater, whose aesthetic encounters often take the form of ravishment, as for his teacher Hegel, and, I suggest, for Swinburne also, to encounter art, to have it work upon you, as you work upon it, is to be 'in the presence of self-consciousness in a new shape' (p. 120).

And yet, for Tillyard, as for the historian Emilio Gentile, lyric intoxication, like a politics of religion, involves the extinguishment of individuality in the name of the community:

> The resulting religion of politics is a religion in the sense that it is a system of beliefs, myths, rituals and symbols that interpret and define the meaning and end of human existence by subordinating the identity of individuals and the collectivity to a supreme entity.[102]

However, for Hegel, community is not the end which reduces everyone to the condition of slaves, but the gift which awaits the free self-consciousness. For the former, sacrifice is fascistic; for the latter, it is dialectical: 'the experience of what Spirit is — this absolute substance which is the unity of the different independent self-consciousnesses which, in their opposition, enjoy perfect freedom and independence: "I" that is "We" and "We" that is "I"' (pp. 110–11). This last idea

— that one might, through working upon something, come to understand one's free individuality in relation to the universal — may seem to stray very far from Swinburne's third choral ode. In fact, what Hegel suggests about coming to view one's individuality in terms of the universal is something which poetry, and praise poetry in particular, has always known.

Marcel Detienne has drawn attention to the way in which ancient understandings of memory differ from our own. Memory is not simply a psychological function; instead, the poet collaborates with 'setting the world in order'. Detienne shows how truth in ancient poetry was connected with being remembered. A person was therefore only worth so much as his name, or *logos*, and people might be said to be 'granted memory' more than they are remembered.[103] In ancient society, praise poetry thus has two roles. It may win the victor recognition in the present moment. However, it also involves the revelation of their participation in what Hegel would call 'the Unchangeable': 'I' that is 'We' and 'We' that is 'I'. It is precisely this movement between the individual and the universal, between seeing myself as an individual, and seeing myself as a participant in a community of individuals, which makes Pindar's *epinikia* so hard to understand for readers today. D. S. Carne-Ross, who draws on Detienne in his study of Pindar, observes:

> Even so good a critic as Burton can speak of 'the fantasy of the dead kings listening [...] To the hymns in praise of their posterity' [...] Fantasy for us, yes, but perhaps not for Pindar, whose world was possessed of a sense of the unity of all being, a great vital continuum embracing divine, human and natural, in which the dead, the living, and the unborn are bound more closely than we can imagine.[104]

We should be suspicious of Carne-Ross's modesty, for it is precisely his capacity to accept this unity which makes him such an astute reader of Pindar. Though his popularity among classical scholars is less than it once was, Carne-Ross's grasp of how readers might come to participate in a community which reaches beyond the present is particularly Swinburnean:

> This event — a sacred marriage between a god and an ancestral heroine of the victor's city it may be, or some great deed of bravery performed by an ancestor — is the origin of today's triumph, the seed from which it grew [...] What grants the enormous joy breathing through the odes, before which we stand abashed and awed, is that for a brief stretch of profane time a place here on earth is bathed in the sacred light of the origins.[105]

We have already seen that something like this understanding underpins Swinburne's sense of a community of verse-makers which stretches all the way back: 'I wonder who first thought of tying words up and twisting them back to make verses, and hurt and delight all the verses in the world forever.'[106] In thinking about the relation between poetry and freedom by way of Hegel, and Pindar's praise poetry, we have in fact come full circle.

I have suggested that Swinburne found in Pindar and the choral odes of Aeschylus a model of ode construction. However, it is only once we begin to get to grips with the assumptions on which Swinburne's poetry rests that we come to appreciate fully what going back to Pindar really meant to Swinburne. This might be better explained by retelling the joke that Swinburne makes about the two odes by Tennyson which appeared in Gosse's anthology *English Odes*. Gosse has been 'cruel' to the laureate in republishing these odes, but 'perhaps the man who could be capable of writing either may be said to deserve that neither should be charitably forgotten'. The odes in question were the 'Ode on the Death of the Duke of Wellington' and the very early 'Ode to Memory'. Swinburne's mockery of the laureate's regrettably unforgettable act of commemorating the duke is clear enough. However, in order to understand the subtleties of Swinburne's wit, we need to return to the opening lines of Tennyson's 'Ode to Memory'. Tennyson's apostrophe is unmistakably directed towards Pindar. The coincidence of the two symbols — 'divine fire', with which Longinus crowned his style, and Horace's famous characterisation of Pindar's song as a mighty flood — would not have been lost on Swinburne:

> Thou who stealest fire,
> From the fountains of the past,
> To glorify the present; oh, haste,
>   Visit my low desire!
> Strengthen me, enlighten me!
> I faint in this obscurity,
> Thou dewy dawn of memory.[107]

This apostrophe presents a self-enclosed, self-defeating movement: the laureate asks Pindar, the poet of efficacious speech, who is capable (of 'putting the world in order'), to make his speech efficacious, because he is not capable. Yet this is also an intensely self-reflexive moment. The gaudy internal rhyme plus couplet, which becomes the poem's refrain, has an energy which sits awkwardly with the energy it argues it is incapable of conjuring: the rhyme rotates but does not leave the ground. Of course, Tennyson's ode is not the only poem to draw attention to its own incapacity. Frank O'Hara's 'Ode' jokes that 'Evening! your breeze is an obstacle'.[108] More recently, Keston Sutherland's *Odes to TL61P* reduce the individual poet's participation in the whole to a kind of cannibalism:

> [...] and with
> growling stomach and powdered flower
> roots to snort in dust steps on
> the podium of odium to trill this elegy:
> *I have a dream of every man I ate in*
> *all my life ...*[109]

For Sutherland and O'Hara, as for Tennyson, 'the podium of odium' can only end in death; the poet who attempts to write an ode can only sing an elegy to what is no longer possible for lyric poetry. 'Forget it!' Swinburne winks at Gosse, 'these poets just don't seem to understand how Pindar's praise poetry works!'

We might grasp something of the way it does work in the distinction which the poet Charles Péguy makes between history and memory:

> L'histoire consiste essentiellement à passer au long de l'événement. La mémoire consiste essentiellement, étant dedans l'événement, avant tout à n'en pas sortir,

> à y rester, et à le remonter en dedans. [History consists essentially in running through the event. Memory consists essentially in being in the event, above all not to go outside of it, to stay there, and to get back into it from the inside.][110]

'Étant dedans l'événement [...] et à le remonter en dedans'. In this phrase we discover the ambition of Swinburne's odes: to reconnect his reader with the fate of Athens, so that the fear, the sense of resulting independence, and the realisation of one's place in the larger order of free individuals is something which we, too, might also undergo 'from the inside'. This and nothing less is the ambition of the third choral ode of *Erechtheus*. Once we grasp this, and the assumptions on which it rests, we can begin to understand and appreciate the peculiar lyricism which we encounter in the Oreithya ode.

'I' that is 'We' and 'We' that is 'I'

Swinburne admired Pindar's ability to tell an anecdote in lyric stanzas.[111] However, it is often hard to understand the relation between the myth which Pindar uses and the event which is being celebrated. Carne-Ross suggests that 'the best course is to look for some general consonance without trying to set up any mechanical point-for-point correspondence, leaving the mind free to ponder the deeper relations which bind the myth to its ode'.[112] However, in *Erechtheus*, the reader must do so twice: first, to understand the relation between Oreithya's fate and the sacrifice of Chthonia, and secondly to understand the relation between Chthonia's offering and the reader's own situation. The glory of Oreithya and Chthonia's sacrifice, and the glory of Athens, must inspire the reader with a dream of a world in which things would be different. However, the way that Swinburne manages this is not through narrative, or argument, but through the prolongation of the lyric present.[113]

The lack of enjambment in this ode means that each line has an independence of its own: the god's approach takes place in immense detail, though swiftly. We then undergo the same present moment again from the point of view of Oreithya in the answering antistrophe. The reader therefore encounters Oreithya's ravishment from multiple perspectives. Another way in which Swinburne achieves this is through his handling of syntax. Lines 575–78, which describe Oreithya's scream, resist narrative sequence. Instead, by shifting focus from her pale lips, to her scream, to the god's hand, before the verb 'gave' is allowed to take responsibility for the foregoing elements, Swinburne invites the reader to undergo something of the shock and terror which Oreithya feels. Likewise the enforced delay of the verb 'sprang' to describe the action of the god at the opening of the second strophe seems more true to immediate, momentary experience. Swinburne is here inviting his reader to experience the moment from the inside, rather than narrating the event.

This lyricism also explains the way in which it seems hardly possible to think of Oreithya as a 'sort of person [...] in [...] circumstances [...] with an attitude', to use Culler's definition of dramatic monologue. Plutarch's Spartan accused the nightingale of being 'vox et praetera nihil' [a voice and nothing else]. The same might be said of Oreithya's outburst *'Woe's me, woe is me!'* Oreithya's only utterance appears in italics, without quotation marks, and is hardly heard, subsumed within the text and rhythm of the poem, a fact which answers to Swinburne's lyrical expertise. Yet there is more to this, too. It is at this moment that one might grasp the challenge that Swinburne's poetry presents, since it is here that we encounter the reverse of the dramatic monologue. Instead of a lyrical moment, encased in a dramatic frame, sorrow flashes past, another drop in the lyrical outrush. Like the description of Mariam's performance of Leopardi's 'Canzone all' Italia' in George Eliot's *Daniel Deronda*, all personal pronouns seem to cease their usual function here.[114] There is nothing dramatic, nothing bounded, nothing safe about this lyrical abandonment. This is what Mill means when he writes that 'purely pathetic music commonly partakes of soliloquy'. We are made to undergo emotions, rather than witness a personality, just as Péguy suggests that memory, as opposed to history, stays in the moment.

Much has been written about the curious way in which the lyric 'I' operates as a space into which the reader seamlessly enters.[115] However, Swinburne's ode proves something of a special case when we reflect that what the chorus appears to be inviting the reader to undergo is an imaginative encounter with ravishment and death. 'For the heart was molten within her to hear,' — in this line, Swinburne invites his reader to consider what Hegel calls 'the absolute melting-away of everything stable'. No wonder Tillyard sensed something intensely dangerous in Swinburne's lyricism. *Excusez-moi monsieur*, we might might say, *je n'entends pas le grec*. Yet this encounter is not simply an end, but the beginning, since this melting away of everything solid presents: 'the simple, essential nature of self-consciousness, absolute negativity, *pure being-for-self*, which consequently is *implicit* in this consciousness' (*Phenomenology*, p. 117). That Swinburne might have thought similarly is suggested by the way in which Oreithya does not vanish entirely, but is transmogrified: ravaged, wind-wasted, she becomes 'a flower', 'blossom of a tree', 'a cloud that he sheds upon the sea'. These are similes of a raw vulnerability, but also of springtime and new life.

Oreithya's almost-apotheosis is in continuity with the way in which the chorus places this current event in the light of all nature. One of the principle ways in which Swinburne achieves this is through polysyndeton: Oreithya's 'wail' rings out three times — in the first line of the antistrophe, the fourth line and the sixth — reaching across ever vaster distances. Hence all of nature appears to participate in this one event. Anaphora has a ripple effect which takes place in time, but implies simultaneity, a single, shared, present moment in which all nature stands confused and silent. This has two effects. First it allows the reader to connect Oreithya's independence — and, by invitation, their own — with all nature, and so to see it in relation to everything which might be conceived as an independent consciousness. Secondly, it also prepares the way for the chorus's argument in the epode, that Oreithya, as an individual, is also a particular individual with a relation to the universal: 'We that is I [...] I that is we'.

For Swinburne, as for Hegel, this participation does not simply involve all of nature in the present tense, but connects, in Carne-Ross's phrase, the reader, the chorus and Oreithya in a 'great vital continuum': 'Of this hoary-headed woe / Song made memory long ago; / Now a younger grief to mourn / Needs a new song younger born'. How, the chorus asks, can one song unite both the old song and the new; the mythic sacrifice of Oreithya, and the current fate of Chthonia; the fate of Athens, and the nineteenth-century experiments in democratic republicanism which Swinburne welcomed with such enthusiasm in his odes? The rhetorical question can only serve as an invitation to the reader to recognise explicitly what she has already undergone implicitly in the act of reading. The rhythm drops down here into duple, falling rhythm, meaning that the questions emerge slowly and with a clarity and a tenderness not present in the previous onrush. Once we realise that the chorus, too, seems to be confronting their own death, the epode gains in poignancy: if Athens should perish, who shall be charged with the task of remembering, of putting the world in order?

It is only then that one realises that the fate of Athens is also tied up with the fate of poetry. When we factor these lines out, we find that the chorus is only claiming that past sadness was difficult, and future sadness will be worse than what happens in between. However, this does not do justice to the elegance of Swinburne's handling. Parallelism in the penultimate couplet draws a connection between the past and the future, and brings them both to bear on the present in the next line, a move which invites the reader to perceive our place in a grand continuum of free people. Adorno grasps something like this movement when he writes of the temporality of utopias: 'Ever since Plato's doctrine of anamnesis the not-yet-existing has been dreamed of in remembrance, which alone concretizes utopia without betraying it to existence'.[116] In the case of this ode, this is achieved, not through preaching, but through the act of praising.

It is on this understanding that *Erechtheus*, rather than his earlier odes or the collection *Songs before Sunrise*, should be considered as Swinburne's real response to Mazzini's request for a series of 'lyrics for the crusade'. In this poem Swinburne has achieved, not the eloquence that would 'compel' his reader, but poetry — that which avails itself of its 'freedom to point the way'. The manuscript of *Erechtheus* reveals that Swinburne was thinking about Mazzini's request when composing the opening lines of the epode.[117] In his first attempt he writes: 'Now a new song younger born [...] needs a nobler sword of song', the same phrase that Swinburne used in his 1871 dedication poem to Mazzini. Yet he abandons this characterisation of song as a 'sword', preferring instead to characterise poetry as a 'new song younger born'. Younger, perhaps, but still inextricably bound up with Pindar, Aeschylus and the dream of Athens.

Swinburne's choral odes are exceptional, both in their mode of construction, and in their fidelity to a lyricism which subsequent critics have been inclined to assume was ideal. They prompt us to reconsider that Mill's characterisation of lyric can only appear absurd if one conceives of poetry's task being one of compulsion, or of poetry as a 'sword of song'. This is an argument of which Swinburne remained suspicious all his writing life. Perhaps we might instead grasp, in Mill's more recent reception, the perplexity of the modern reader: unable to trust to efficacious speech, yet suspicious of the idea that poetry should compel the reader to do anything, the poet is caught in the crossfire between the barricades and the prisoner's cell. Swinburne thought differently about poetry, preferring that 'spontaneous loyalty to those laws of no man's making, which forgetfulness may never but for a season put to sleep — laws wherein the God of song shows himself mighty, and waxes not old'.[118] Such a quality could even be found, it transpires, in the poetry of Wordsworth. It is only right that Swinburne should be read and appreciated on his own terms.

Notes to Chapter 4

1. *Fortnightly Review*, March 1867, pp. 284–89.
2. Reprinted in Georges Lafourcade's *La Jeunesse de Swinburne*, 2 vols (Paris: Les Belles Lettres, 1928), I, pp. 253–54.
3. Quoted in Rikky Rooksby, *A. C. Swinburne: A Poet's Life* (Aldershot: Scolar, 1997), p. 145.
4. Ibid., p. 176.
5. *The Swinburne Letters*, ed. by Cecil Y. Lang, 6 vols (New Haven: Yale University Press, 1959–1962) I, p. 242.
6. Susan Stewart, 'What Praise Poems Are For', *Publications of the Modern Language Association*, 120, 1 (1995), p. 237.
7. George Shuster notes three tendencies in the development of the ode throughout the Victorian period: for academic or popular celebration, classical imitation or as a continuation of the Romantic lyric (see *The English Ode from Milton to Keats* (New York: Columbia University Press, 1940), p. 246). For a recent overview of the critical literature which argues, to the contrary, that 'ode practice began to wane after 1820' (p. 16) see T. E. Durno, 'Poetics of the English Ode, 1786–1820' (unpublished doctoral thesis, University of Cambridge, 2013), pp. 16–17.
8. Penelope Wilson, 'The Knowledge and Appreciation of Pindar in the Seventeenth and Eighteenth Centuries' (unpublished doctoral thesis, University of Oxford, 1974), p. 350.
9. This distinction is far from watertight and English poetry contains many examples of odes which contain elements of both. However, to venture a general definition: Cowleyan ('irregular') odes establish a metrical set only to break from it, involve leaps in length between lines, have no requirement to answer a proceeding strophe by reproducing a similar pattern later on, and combine near rhyme with rhymes answering each other across distances which challenge the reader's rhyme recall. Congrevian ('regular') odes, usually proceed by means of strophe, antistrophe and epode, with responsion required between answering strophes and antistrophes, and rhyme working over shorter distances.
10. Apart from the work of Congreve (more useful to Swinburne for his reassessment of Pindar than his ode style) examples of regular odes in English are rarer. However, we might include here Collins's 'Ode to Evening' and aspects of Abraham Cowley's ode 'Brutus'.
11. Jerome McGann and Charles H. Sligh's edition of Swinburne's *Major Poems and Selected Prose* (New Haven: Yale University Press, 2004) includes no odes and overlooks *Erechtheus*. Alex Wong's *Selected Verse* (Manchester: Fyfield Books, 2015) gives us the monostrophic choral odes of *Atalanta*, but none of the regular odes and nothing of *Erechtheus*. Francis O'Gorman's new edition, *Algernon Charles Swinburne* (Oxford: Oxford University Press, 2016), includes Swinburne's early Cowleyan experiment, the 'Ode to Mazzini', and the monostrophic odes on March and Russia. However, the regular odes and *Erechtheus* are not included..
12. A. C. Swinburne, *William Blake: A Critical Essay* (London: James Camden Hotten, 1868), p. 103.
13. Rikky Rooksby argues that Swinburne transgresses the principle of *l'art pour l'art* in *Songs before Sunrise* and *Songs of Two Nations*. See *A. C. Swinburne: A Poet's Life*, p. 161.
14. Julia Saville, 'Cosmopolitan Republican Swinburne, the Immersive Poet as Public Moralist', *Victorian Poetry*, 47 (2009), 691–713.
15. Stephanie Kuduk-Weiner, *Republican Politics and English Poetry* (New York: Palgrave Macmillan, 2005), p. 159.
16. Marion Thain, 'Desire Lines: Swinburne and Lyric Crisis' in *Algernon Charles Swinburne: Unofficial Laureate*, ed. by Stefano Evangelista and Catherine Maxwell (Manchester: Manchester University Press, 2013), pp. 138–54.

17. Linda K. Hughes, *The Cambridge Introduction to Victorian Poetry* (Cambridge: Cambridge University Press, 2010), pp. 52–53.
18. 'Swinburne', in *The Oxford History of Classical Reception in English Literature*, ed. by Norman Vance and Jennifer Wallace (Oxford: Oxford University Press, 2015) IV, p. 636.
19. Once Swinburne's Mazzinian belief in the fated glory of certain nations is understood, O'Gorman argues, this opponent of monarchy and organized Christianity and Home Rule in Ireland appears 'remarkably consistent' (p. 454). See 'Swinburne and Ireland', *Review of English Studies*, 64, 265 (2013), 454–74.
20. E. M. W. Tillyard, *Five Poems 1470–1870: An Elementary Essay on the Background of English Literature* (London: Chatto & Windus, 1948), p. 101.
21. Herbert Tucker, *Epic: Britain's Heroic Muse 1790–1910* (Oxford: Oxford University Press, 2008), p. 530n.
22. 'Ion' in *The Dialogues of Plato*, trans. By B. Jowett Oxford: Oxford University Press, 1892), p. 494.
23. Matthew Reynolds, *The Realms of Verse English Poetry in a Time of Nation-Building* (Oxford: Oxford University Press, 2001), p. 41.
24. Isobel Armstrong argues that whereas 'Schopenhauer wrote of the lyric poet as uttering between two poles of feeling, between the pure undivided condition of unified selfhood, and the needy, fracturing self-awareness of the interrogating consciousness. The Victorian poet does not swing between these two forms of utterance but dramatizes and objectifies their simultaneous existence. There is a kind of duplicity involved here, for the poet often invites the simple reading by presenting the poem as lyric expression as the perceiving subject speaks (p. 12)' (See *Victorian Poetry: Poetry, Poetics, Politics* (London and New York: Routledge, 1993), pp. 12–15, and Chapter 5 *passim*.) In Herbert Tucker's essay 'Dramatic Monologue and the Overhearing of Lyric' (see *Lyric Poetry: Beyond New Criticism*, ed. by C. Hosek and P. Parker (Ithaca: Cornell University Press, 1985), pp. 226–43) the rise of the dramatic monologue in the nineteenth century is understood to be intimately bound up with the history of lyric poetry. His examples are drawn from the early experiments of Browning and Tennyson, which, he notes, often place lyrical moments within a context that calls attention to them *as* lyrical moments. In so doing, he writes, 'Browning was confessing to the open secret of spontaneous lyricism, but in ways that disowned it' (p. 227). The account of lyric offered by J. S. Mill in his 1833 essay (J. S. Mill, 'What Is Poetry?', *Monthly Repository* , 7, 73 (January 1833), 60–70) which Tucker takes as his starting point, is understood as the readerly equivalent of this desire. Tucker's recourse to the technique of poems, and his provocation that the dramatic monologue involves readers in a compensatory version of lyric which renders Mill's longed-for lyrical freedom as a 'late ceremony' has been foundational for my argument.
25. Mill's sense of a radical distinction between poetry and eloquence informs Culler's invitation to 'Consider what the model of lyric as dramatic monologue misses', in which he tacitly acknowledges the critical *status quo* while seeking to overcome it ('Why Lyric?', *Publications of the Modern Language Association*, 123, 1 (2008), p. 201); for Culler's earlier engagement with Mill see *The Pursuit of Signs* (London: Routledge and Kegan Paul, 1981, p. 137). Mill's article also provides the point of departure for Tucker's investigation into how Mill's definition of poetry must have appeared to pioneers of the dramatic monologue. Jackson and Prins, in the introduction to *The Lyric Reader: A Critical Anthology* (Baltimore: Johns Hopkins University Press, 2014) recognize the importance of Mill's ideas about lyric, but conclude, prematurely, I think, that Mill must have known 'that his requirement that the lyric poet be unconscious of the audience already posed a problem' (p. 4).
26. *Aesthetics: Lectures on Fine Art*, trans. by T. M. Knox, (Oxford: Clarendon Press, 1998), II, p. 1141. All subsequent references will be to the page numbers of this edition and will be given in the text.
27. Presumably Hegel would not count dramatic monologue as a species of 'lyric proper' since the 'leaning of lyric towards the vivacity of drama is essentially restricted to the fact that though without proceeding to describe an action that moves forward into conflicts, the lyric poem is a conversation and can therefore adopt the external form of a dialogue. However, these transitional stages and hybrid kinds we will leave on one side and only consider briefly those forms in which the proper principle of lyric is asserted unadulterated' (*Aesthetics*, p. 1138).

28. I borrow Armstrong's adjective to describe Browning's reaction to Mill in poems such as 'Porphyria's Lover' and 'Johannes Agricola' (Armstrong, *Victorian Poetry*, pp. 140–41). For a recent defence of 'lyric proper' as separate from 'dramatic monologue' see Jonathan Culler, *The Theory of Lyric* (Cambridge and London: Harvard University Press, 2015), pp. 116–17.
29. Jennifer Benjamin, *The Bonds of Love* (London: Virago, 1988), pp. 42–43.
30. See 'Lyric Poetry and Society' in *Notes to Literature* (New York: Columbia University Press, 1991), I, p. 40; *Aesthetic Theory* (London: Continuum, 1997), p. 189.
31. The structure of Swinburne's *Atalanta*, explored in Chapter 1, suggests that he is in the same tradition as Hegel, who holds that the difference between chorus and dialogue, subjective and objective elements, is 'especially elaborated' in Greek drama: 'whereas in modern drama this difference disappears because the material given to the chorus in Greek drama is now put into the mouths of the characters themselves' (Hegel, *Aesthetics*, p. 1172).
32. Culler, *The Theory of Lyric*, p. 108.
33. Tucker, 'Dramatic Monologue and the Overhearing of Lyric', pp. 228–29.
34. J. S. Mill, 'What Is Poetry?', pp. 64–65.
35. P. B. Shelley, 'A Defence of Poetry', *Shelley's Poetry and Prose*, ed. by Donald H. Reiman and Neil Fraistat, 2nd edn (New York and London: Norton, 2002), p. 515.
36. *The Swinburne Letters*, II, p. 293.
37. A. C. Swinburne, 'Of Analogy', College Essays [1856–1858], London, British Library, Ashley MS.4349.
38. The seeds of his pronouncement in his *William Blake* that the poet must prioritise 'Art for art's sake first of all, and afterwards we may suppose all the rest shall be added to her' is already apparent here in the description of the poet as 'prophet and interpreter' rather than teacher (A. C. Swinburne, *William Blake*, p. 91).
39. Adorno, 'Commitment', trans. by Francis McDonagh in *Aesthetics and Politics* (London: Verso, 2007), p. 193.
40. J. S. Mill, *On Liberty and Other Writings*, ed. by Stefan Collini (Cambridge: Cambridge University Press, 1989), p. 13. For a recent attempt to consider Mill's aesthetic writing in relation to his political philosophy see David Russell, 'Aesthetic Liberalism: John Stuart Mill as Essayist', *Victorian Studies*, 56,1 (2013), pp. 7–30.
41. 'On Political and Speculative Liberty', transcribed by Rikky Rooksby in *The Victorians Institute Journal*, 18 (1990) and subsequently made available via the NINES website <http://www.nines.org/exhibits/swinburne_manuscripts?page=> [accessed 26 April 2018] Swinburne's undergraduate notebooks at the University of Leeds, Balliol and Worcester Colleges, Oxford, and the British Library feature very rarely in criticism of Swinburne to date.
42. Mill, *On Liberty and Other Writings*, pp. 66–67.
43. Collini, 'Introduction', *On Liberty and Other Writings*, p.vii.
44. J. S. Mill, 'The Two Kinds of Poetry', *Monthly Repository*, 7, 80 (August 1833), p. 717.
45. It is impossible to prove that Swinburne had Mill's essay in mind when he wrote his long intervention 'Wordsworth and Byron'. However, Swinburne's own aesthetic preferences show a strong affiliation with Mill, evident in his claim that: 'to neither [Wordsworth or Keats] was it given, as it was given to Shelley, to rise beyond these regions of contemplation and sensation [...] to breathe, in Shakespeare's audaciously subtle and successful phrase the very "spirit of sense" itself, to transcend at once the sensuous and the meditative elements of poetry, and to fuse their highest, their keenest, their most inward and intimate effects, in such verse as utters what none before could utter, and renders into likeness of form and sound such truths of inspired perfection, such raptures of divine surprise, as no poet of nature may think to render again'. ('Wordsworth and Byron', *Miscellanies* (London: Chatto &Windus, 1895), pp. 63–156 (p. 155).) Swinburne also prefers Collins's lyricism to Gray's eloquence: 'Here, in the twilight which followed on the splendid sunset of Pope, was at last a poet who was content to sing out what he had in him — to sing and not to say, without a glimpse of wit or a flash of eloquence'. See 'Introduction' to William Collins, in *The English Poets*, ed. Thomas Humphry Ward, 2nd edn (London: Macmillan and co., 1884), III, p. 294.
46. Walter Pater, *The Renaissance*, ed. Adam Phillips (Oxford: Oxford University Press, 1998), p. 33.
47. *The Swinburne Letters*, IV, pp. 208–09.

48. Swinburne's own entry 'To Victor Hugo in Exile' was a reprint of an ode first published in *Poems and Ballads*. Whether this was a late move on Swinburne's part to emphasize the continuity between the earlier and later poetry is hard to say. It was not Gosse's first or second choice. Gosse suggested the 'Ode on the Insurrection', yet Swinburne refused, arguing that he would prefer not 'to be represented by so merely occasional a piece as the Candiote Ode': 'altogether a palpably hasty and comparatively inferior piece of work. Watts thinks — and I with him — most decidedly that my representative Ode is *The Eve of Revolution*' (*Letters*, IV, p. 173). Why the Hugo ode, and not the 'Eve of Revolution', made the final cut must remain the subject of conjecture.
49. *Ode to Mazzini; The Saviour of Society; Liberty and Loyalty: Unpublished Mss. Discovered Among The Author's Effects After His Death*, with a preface by Edmund Gosse (Boston: The Bibliophile Society, 1913)
50. Swinburne writes that the 'superb and enchanting' music of Coleridge's 'Dejection: An Ode' is a true achievement, but, because it lacks 'an accurately corresponsive or antiphonal scheme of music', it cannot compare to 'such a poem as his ode on France' See the 'Dedicatory Epistle' in *The Poems of Algernon Charles Swinburne* (London: Chatto & Windus, 1905; first printed 1904) 'p.xv.
51. Samuel Taylor Coleridge, 'Dejection: An Ode', *The Major Works*, ed. H. J. Jackson (Oxford: Oxford World Classics, 1985), p. 114.
52. 'To The Pious Memory of Mrs. Anne Killigrew', *English Odes*, ed. by Edmund Gosse, (London: Kegan Paul, 1881), p. 56.
53. Edmund Gosse, 'Preface' to Swinburne, *Unpublished Mss. Discovered among the Author's Effects after his Death*, p. 11.
54. Ibid., pp. 10–11.
55. 'The Ode to Mazzini' is not the only 'Cowleyan' ode Swinburne wrote. In addition to his early 'Ode to Music' and 'To the Nightingale', an early notebook also contains a fragmented chorus. From the different lengths of indentation, and the uncertain metrical set, it is clear that this is an early attempt to combine lines of different length into a single stanza. The poem was probably abandoned. If Swinburne later rejected the irregular ode, it was not out of ignorance. See *Poetical Notebook* used by A. C. Swinburne [1857]. London, British Library, Ashley MS.4453.
56. See Cowley's ode 'In Praise of Pindar' quoted below.
57. *English Odes*, p. 118.
58. Swinburne, 'Wordsworth and Byron', *Miscellanies*, p. 135.
59. *English Odes*, p. 151. Might this also lie at the heart of Swinburne's alleged dislike for Gray, and in particular for 'The Progress of Poesy'? The lines in which Gray imagines the muse giving Shakespeare a pencil (*English Odes*, pp. 106–07) to paint the seasons with must have seemed dubious to a poet convinced that the study of Shakespeare was 'traceable by ear and *not* by finger' (see Swinburne's 'Preface' in *A Study of Shakespeare* (London: Chatto &Windus, 1880), unpaginated).
60. 'The Praise of Pindar', *English Odes*, p. 41.
61. Samuel Johnson, *Lives of the English Poets*, ed. George Birkbeck Hill, (Oxford: Clarendon Press, 1905), III, pp. 438–39.
62. *The Swinburne Letters*, II, p. 109.
63. The 'Eve of Revolution' which Swinburne also offered to Gosse for inclusion in *English Odes*, also plays in its closing lines with a movement between a five-beat, four-beat and a six-beat line. Swinburne also uses an almost identical form in his slightly earlier 'Ode to Victor Hugo' (1866), the poem included in Gosse's anthology. Running *3a3a5b3a3a5b4c6c*, the Hugo Ode also experiments with this lengthening of lines, but with a tighter rhyme scheme which links the first and second skips by rhyme. This means the development from the first three lines into the second unit of three lines is not so marked as it is in Milton's ode and 'Ode on the Insurrection'.
64. *English Odes*, p. 35.
65. We might consider, as a further point of comparison, Shelley's even speedier approaches to the six-beat line, in which syntax has completely overleapt the line breaks: 'As foam from a ship's swiftness, when there came / A voice out of the deep: I will record the same' ('Ode to Liberty',

English Odes, p. 194). This is not to claim that Shelley does not also take the opportunity the unit of the line affords to arrange his syntax to great effect: 'They seize me — I must speak them — be they fate.'; 'If hope and truth and justice can avail ...' ('Ode to Naples', *English Odes*, p. 209). However, for Shelley both options — enjambment and rhetorical balance within the line — were possible.

66. For this use of the term 'instrumentation' see V. M. Zhirmunsky, *Rifma: eyo istoriya i teoriya* ed. Dmitrij Tschižewski et al., with a new preface by the author, Slavische Propyläen: Texte in Neu- und Nachdrucken, 71, (St Petersburg, 1923,repr. Munich: Fink, 1970, Chapter 1. My thanks to Simon Jarvis for his help with the translation of this term.
67. This kind of syntactical omission is also present in the ode 'To Victor Hugo', e.g., 'freedom a man may have, he shall not peace'. See *English Odes*, p. 253.
68. Simon Jarvis, 'Lyric Thinking: The English Ode from Cowley to Tennyson': Congreve, Pope and the Fate of Grand Lyric', lecture, Faculty of English, Cambridge, 2014.
69. Sainstbury, *A History of English Prosody* (London, 1910), III, p. 350.
70. In construction, this strophe recalls Shelley's 'Ode to Liberty', which Swinburne admired. However it is in the sixth strophe, which is a four-beat line, that the verse attains a fluency unseen in Swinburne's previous ode work. In the answering antistrophe, this scheme has finesse:

> And from their eyes in thine there gazes
> A spirit other far than sorrow —
> A soul triumphal, white and whole
> And single, that salutes thy soul. (II, p. 287)

71. 'Mr. Swinburne's Erechtheus', *Edinburgh Review*, 144, 295 (July 1876), p. 153.
72. 'Ion', *Blackwood's Edinburgh Magazine*, 126, 768, October 1876, p. 419.
73. Unsigned Review, 'Swinburne's Erechtheus', *London Quarterly Review*, 46, 91 (April 1876), pp. 249–54 (p. 251).
74. Unsigned Review, 'Mr. Swinburne's *Erechtheus*', *Athenæum*, 2514, 1 January 1876, 13–14, p. 14.
75. Unsigned Review, *Academy*, 8 January 1876, pp. 23–24 (p. 24).
76. Edmund Gosse, '*Erechtheus*', *Examiner*, 3545, 8 January 1876, p. 42.
77. Unsigned Review, 'Mr. Swinburne's Erechtheus', *Spectator*, 1 January 1876, p. 23.
78. Unsigned Review, 'Swinburne's Erechtheus', *Saturday Review*, 41, 1054 (8 January 1876), pp. 50–51 (p. 50).
79. 'Ion', *Blackwood's Edinburgh Magazine*, 126, 768, October 1876, pp. 419–34 (p. 422).
80. We might consider the later monostrophic ode 'To Athens' (1881) where a long strophe in seven-beat lines, an antistrophe in six-beat lines and an epode in eight-beat lines repeats three times. In this ode monostrophism, coupled with the coincidence of sense-unit and line, come to seem relentless (V, pp. 194–213).
81. M. L. West, *Greek Metre* (Oxford: Oxford University Press, 1982), pp. 20–21.
82. Coventry Patmore, *Essay on English Metrical Law*, ed. Sister Mary Augustine Roth (Washington, D. C.: Catholic University of America Press, 1961), p. 26.
83. A. C. Swinburne, 'Erechtheus', autograph draft [1875], London, British Library, Ashley MS.5263.
84. 'Swinburne's Erechtheus', *London Quarterly Review*, 46, 91 (April 1876), pp. 249–54; *The Academy*, 8 January 1876, pp. 23–24.
85. I am adapting Paul Ricœur's understanding of translation as 'linguistic hospitality'; see *On Translation*, trans. by Eileen Brennan (Abingdon: Routledge, 2006).
86. A. M. Dale, *The Lyric Metres of Greek Drama* (Cambridge: Cambridge University Press, 1968), p. 111.
87. Aeschylus, *Aeschylus*, ed. and trans. by Alan H. Sommerstein, Loeb Classical Library Series: 145, (Cambridge, MA: Harvard University Press, 2008) I, pp. 160 ff., pp. 226 ff.; Dale, *The Lyric Metres of Greek Drama*, p. 111.
88. Dale, *The Lyric Metres of Greek Drama*, p. 105.
89. Ibid., p. 104.
90. Ibid., p. 107.
91. Ibid., p. 110.

92. D. S. Carne-Ross, *Pindar* (New Haven: Yale University Press, 1985), p. 144.
93. Unsigned Review, 'Mr. Swinburne's Erechtheus', *Edinburgh Review*, 144, 295 (July 1876), p. 163.
94. Francis O'Gorman, 'Swinburne and Ireland', p. 469.
95. G. W. F. Hegel, *The Phenomenology of Spirit*, trans. A. V. Miller (Oxford: Oxford University Press, 1977), p. 120.
96. Jowett prefers Hegel 'out of its dialectical form'; see E. Abbott and L. Campbell, *Life and Letters of Benjamin Jowett*, 2 vols (London: John Murray, 1897), I, p. 130; A. C. Swinburne, 'On the Dialectic of Plato', Undergraduate Essays on Philosophy [between 1856 and 1860], Worcester College Library, Oxford, MS.243.
97. John D. Rosenberg, 'Swinburne', *Victorian Studies*, 11.2 (December 1967), p. 142.
98. A. C. Swinburne, *Lesbia Brandon*, ed. Randolph Hughes (London: Falcon Press, 1952), p. 148.
99. A. C. Swinburne, *William Blake: A Critical Essay*, p. 103n.
100. Yopie Prins, 'Metrical Discipline: Algernon Swinburne on The Flogging Block' in *Algernon Charles Swinburne: Unofficial Laureate*, ed. Stefano-Maria Evangelista and Catherine Maxwell (Manchester: Manchester University Press, 2013), pp. 95–124.
101. Pater, *The Renaissance*, pp. 148–49.
102. Emilio Gentile, *Politics as Religion* (Princeton: Princeton University Press, 2006), p. xiv, italics original.
103. Marcel Detienne, *Masters of Truth in Archaic Greece* (New York: Zone Books, 1996), pp. 48–49.
104. Carne-Ross, *Pindar*, pp. 120–21. For a recent theoretical account of the social contributions of lyric see Culler, *The Theory of Lyric*, p. 305.
105. Ibid., p. 19.
106. A. C. Swinburne, *Lesbia Brandon*, p. 148.
107. 'Ode to Memory', in *The Poems of Tennyson*, ed. Christopher Ricks, 2nd edn (London: Longman, 1987), I, p. 231.
108. *The Collected Poems of Frank O'Hara*, ed. Donald Allen (New York: Alfred A. Knopf, 1972), p. 196.
109. Keston Sutherland, *The Odes to TL61P of Keston Sutherland* (London: Enitharmon, 2013), p. 18.
110. *Clio, dialogue de l'histoire et de l'âme païenne*, VIII, 285–86, quoted in Emmanuel Mournier, *La Pensée de Charles Péguy* (Paris: Plon, 1931), p. 82. Charles Taylor's translation of 'remonter' as 'to relive' (*A Secular Age* (Cambridge, MA: Harvard University Press, 1997), p. 746) strikes me as not quite right, because to 'relive' something might still conceive of it as happening in the past. Péguy's phrase draws on the figurative sense of *'remonter la pente'* — 'to get back on one's feet', to resume an activity from where one left off.
111. *The Swinburne Letters*, IV, p. 306.
112. Carne-Ross, *Pindar*, p. 18.
113. Jonathan Culler argues in his article 'Why Lyric?' that 'narrative', in its domination of discussions of lyric poetry, has come to be thought of as 'the very condition of experience' (p. 201). However, to conceive this lyric as 'as a fictional imitation of the act of a speaker, [...] to work out what sort of person is speaking, in what circumstances and with what attitude or, ideally, drama of attitudes' is difficult. Swinburne's ode resists narrative. The 'condition of experience' achieved in this ode is a lyric present, which invites us to stay within the moment of Oreithya's abduction, with little room for exit.
114. George Eliot, *Daniel Deronda*, ed. Terence Cave (London: Penguin, 1995), pp. 483–84.
115. See, for example, Anne Williams, *Prophetic Strain: The Greater Lyric in the Eighteenth Century* (Chicago: University of Chicago Press, 1984), p. 15.
116. Adorno, *Aesthetic Theory*, p. 174.
117. A. C. Swinburne, 'Erechtheus', autograph draft [1875], London, British Library, Ashley MS 5263.
118. A. C. Swinburne, *Miscellanies*, p. 151.

CONCLUSION

'[S]urely you have noticed', Paul Valéry writes:

> the curious fact that some word which is perfectly clear when you hear it or use it in current language, and causes no trouble when it is caught in the quick pace of an ordinary phrase, becomes magically embarrassing, introduces a strange resistance, and foils all effort of definition as soon as you take it out of circulation to examine it apart, and seek a meaning in it after having removed it from its momentary function?[1]

There is something curious and potentially embarrassing about the use of the word 'style' in this study. Often it is used in passing as a synonym for Swinburne's verse. I have written of 'two styles in *Atalanta*', of 'the repetitive style', 'a triplet more in the style of Dryden or Pope', and of Swinburne's later 'ode style'. Here a number of other words such as 'technique', 'structure' and 'verse' might have done. In such cases, it is simply, as Valéry puts it, like 'one of those light boards thrown across a ditch or over a mountain crevasse to support the passage of a man in quick motion' (p. 211). Yet I have also argued about 'taking Swinburne's style seriously', noted 'peculiar fact[s] about Swinburne's style' and, in doing so, tried to come to terms with the 'peculiar character of Swinburne's style'. At some point in the course of thinking about Swinburne's poetry, this word became so indispensable as to appear in my title. Isolated in this way, the word 'takes revenge' (p. 211).

Valéry suggests a strategy for dealing with such words. Where they do not answer to a problem which he feels, they are dismissed as 'other people's problems' (p. 212). Yet the persistence of 'style' suggests that it does present a problem, which may tell us something about Swinburne's poetry. If so, then 'style' would appear to be neither an embarrassment, nor a bridge, but crucial to our encounter with Swinburne's poetry. We must do exactly what Valéry warns us not do, and 'loiter to dance on the thin board to try its resistance' (p. 211). In doing so, we might try it against two other terms which could reasonably have been used instead: 'form' and 'verse-thinking'.

Critics working under the banner of cultural neo-formalism, or historical poetics, might find their *raison d'être* in the remoteness of Swinburne's verse. To talk of Swinburne's form would allow his poetry to become the object of a culturally and historically informed reading, by way of a reconstruction of the explicit thinking surrounding his form.[2] Yet Swinburne's poetry remains remarkable for its resistance to such approaches. His recent omission from a *Victorian Poetry* special issue on prosody is a case in point. The lacuna is striking, first, since he is a major poet, but especially so considering that no Victorian poet better deserves the title given to him by Saintsbury, of 'prosodist magician'.[3] Pushed to explain this, the editors suggest the reason lies in his 'refusal to engage with poetic debates' (p. 152). That Swinburne did enter into poetic debates — often, as I have shown, with great fury — need not be the first response to this claim.

Instead, this method is checked by Swinburne's poetry. His verse challenges a conception of reading which limits itself to the interpretative frames that paralinguistic contexts — such as prosodic theory — may be said to provide.[4] Not even Eliot proposes that we can no longer hear Swinburne. However, since the advent of free verse we have grown unaccustomed to his manner. Recent approaches to Swinburne's poetry that assume the necessity of mediation are only one possible response to this remoteness. As such, they risk not approaching his poetry at all. This study has sought to encounter Swinburne's poetry by another way.

In my introduction I argued that it is the 'shape' of words which Swinburne's poetry asks us to attend to, the 'contaminations' that, as Prynne notes, are 'especially marked in strongly formed and complex traditions of literary expression'.[5] In this connection, Pierre Bourdieu's definition of *habitus*, or practical knowledge, has much in common with the argument about literary language advanced by Prynne, and is worth dwelling on at some length for what it demonstrates about the inadequacy of the understanding of form outlined above for a poet such as Swinburne.

Once we move from the structure of a language to its function, Bourdieu argues, one realises very quickly that the reduction of language to the status of a code gives a very imperfect sense of what is taking place. Context and situation are just as important:

> the very content of the communication, the nature of the language and all the forms of expression used (posture, gesture, mimicry etc.) and above all, perhaps, their style, are affected by the structure of the social relation between the agents involved.[6]

Bourdieu quotes here from the linguistic anthropologist Charles Bally, whose search for a fuller anthropology of language led him to coin the term *indices* to refer to those linguistic aspects of meaning which were demoted by his teacher Saussure.[7] For Bourdieu, the analogy between the style of the speaking subject and the style of artworks is unavoidable. Poets are born and made within the realm of the *habitus*, that complex collision of inherited practices, acceptable techniques and topics in which art has meaning:

> Each agent, wittingly or unwittingly, willy nilly, is a producer and reproducer of objective meaning. Because his actions and works are the product of a *modus operandi* of which he is not the producer and has no conscious mastery, they contain an 'objective intention', as the Scholastics put it, which always outruns his conscious intentions.[8]

This definition entails a modified understanding of freedom — 'conditional and conditioned' — which defines style as the poet's exercise of freedom in her own particular direction. According to Bourdieu, to seek after the 'sign-manual' of Swinburne is to ask in what manner Swinburne's style differs from that of other poets, and to consider what place he holds within the tradition of English verse.

This comes closer to Swinburne's own understanding of 'style', in so far as he had a definition of it. *A Study of Shakespeare* sought

> to examine by internal evidence alone the growth and the expression of spirit and of speech, the ebb and flow of thought and style, discernible in the successive periods of Shakespeare's work; to study the phases of mind, the changes of tone, the passage or progress from an old manner to a new, the reversion or relapse from a later to an earlier habit, which may assuredly be traced in the modulations of his varying verse, but can only be traced *by ear and not by finger*.[9]

This phrase suggests why there could be no method to this study, no hypothesis or way of proceeding, except the cue the poem gives. 'Dialectics does not give any instructions for the treatment of art, but inheres in it'.[10] I have attempted to understand the gesture in the *habitus*, the word in the genre. But why not talk, then, of 'Swinburne's verse thinking'? Why insist on talking about Swinburne's style?

The collocation of 'verse' and 'thinking' appears often in the work of Simon Jarvis, whose criticism develops many of the fundamental insights of Adorno's *Aesthetic Theory* as it might pertain to poetry.[11] In particular, his work demands that we rethink the mental work involved in reading poetry, taking its impetus, like Adorno, from music:

> were prosody to take its cue from the philosophy of music as cognition, one essential requirement would be a different conception of the relationship between substance and method in prosodic enquiry. Perhaps an approach which placed the individual poetic authorship at its centre, not as natural, but as traditional, and therefore not simply liquidable, unit, might have its methodologism continually chastised by the complexity of the subject matter.[12]

This suggestion is especially pertinent to Swinburne's verse, in which there often appears to be more sound than sense. In fact, it was this proposal, made in an article which explores 'Prosody as Cognition' that first suggested

> a reading of Swinburne in which the evacuation of semantic content in his work could be understood not as a self-indulgent pursuit of ersatz musicality, but as a cognitively astute practice of degeneration apprised of the historical decay of certain aspects of late romantic verse technique.[13]

So why not verse thinking? Why persist in talking about Swinburne's style? The answer lies in this apt description of Swinburne's poetry: 'cognitively astute'. It is here that one begins to doubt the strength of the term 'verse thinking' to accommodate Swinburne's verse, to wonder whether it might require a different word, one which answers to the problem that Swinburne's verse poses for the conception of tradition.

William Empson was one of the first to understand the risk of Swinburne's verse, recognising that it 'depended on a tradition that its [own] example was destroying.'[14] This observation is perhaps better explained if we consider Swinburne's status as a virtuoso, but not quite in the way that Pierre Bourdieu imagines. For Bourdieu the virtuoso is an artist for whom:

> the schemes of thought and expression he has acquired are the basis for the

intentionless intervention of regulated improvisation. Endlessly overtaken by his own words, with which he maintains a relation of 'carry and be carried' [...] the virtuoso finds in the *opus operatum* new triggers and new supports for the *modus operandi* from which they arise, so that his discourse continually feeds off itself like a train bringing along its own rails.[15]

By contrast, in the work of Swinburne, the 'scheme of thought and expression' he has acquired becomes the basis for an informed intervention, as if he has taken the 'objective intention' of the *habitus* and made it intentional. Whether that involves taking certain inherent characteristics in the language to their logical extreme, as he did by experimenting with triple rhythm within the five-beat line, or developing existing tendencies, as he did with the regular ode, his verse is knowingly classic, 'cognitively astute'. Bourdieu's assumption that agents operating within the *habitus* undergo a kind of *genesis amnesia* is troubled here.[16] In a sense, Swinburne's poetry knows what it is doing, and also knows it.

Recognising the curious virtuosity that we encounter in Swinburne's verse allows us to explain why Swinburne's personal style proves so difficult to talk about. Tennyson's description of Swinburne as 'a reed through which all music blows' is still apt.[17] Instead of fluently working within the tradition until he could forge his own manner, Swinburne took it upon himself to channel all of the most recognisable aspects of the tradition. This perhaps explains why our view of what is 'Swinburnean' remains so selective. Rather than his ballads written in pitmatic dialect, or the choral odes of *Erechtheus*, Swinburne's popular readership tends to remember the rhythmico-metrical feats of *Poems and Ballads: First Series*. It is a testament to the endurance of lyric that it is the lyrical aspects of his verse that we most respond to.

Swinburne has no personal style, because he had many styles. Eliot understood this when he recognise that 'It is impersonal, and no one else could have made it' (*Selected Essays*, p. 327). Eliot's essay, 'Tradition and the Individual Talent', presents his fullest critical response to the problem that Swinburne's verse poses. This essay, which argues that no poet, or artist, is an island, is the critical equivalent of the owl of Minerva. It theorises, at the same time as it seeks to resist, the triumph of style — which is individualised, objective and historically situated — over tradition. After this moment, a poet cannot be said to move between the poles of archaism and innovation in quite the same way.[18]

Consider as an example the different treatments of Pindar by Swinburne, Pound and Veronica Forrest-Thomson. Swinburne, as I have suggested, sought to return to Athens by seeking to do something in the style of Pindar in English, and doing it superbly. Here, by contrast, is Pound:

> The roots go down to the river's edge
> and the hidden city moves upward
> white ivory under the bark ...[19]

Eliot writes that 'The good poet welds his theft into a whole of feeling which is unique, utterly different from that from which it was torn; the bad poet throws it into something which has no cohesion'.[20] Pound's theft is expert. Yet we have a sense that Swinburne would have never thought of his own relation to Pindar as a kind of thievery. In 'Cordelia', Forrest-Thomson apes the rhythms of Pound, Eliot, and Swinburne (and others) in broad daylight, and even jokes about it:

> And as for this line I stole it from T. S. Eliot
> And Ezra Pound and A. C. Swinburne. All very good
> Poets to steal from since they are all three dead.[21]

Very good, if you are concerned about copyright. But also dead in the further sense that their 'posture, gesture, mimicry' prove recyclable, recognisable, stylised.

Was the tradition dead for Swinburne? This study, which has had to cope with numerous innovations, suggests not. Yet we can see in the astuteness of his verse the germ of that reflexivity which led Eliot to conceive of poetic tendencies as something individualized that could be stolen (or, worse, borrowed) and which I understand by the word 'style'.

We might take as one example of that reflexivity Swinburne's request, in an undated scrap of a letter, that his unknown correspondent 'Accept these lines':

> [...] I spent a quarter of an hour (timed per watch) upon it this morning:
>> 'Yea then, Although love be sweet, what memories
>> Are left of lovers from the royal time
>> Now all the measure of remembrance is
>> Closed in the compass of some various rhyme?[22]

Other poets have used rhyme as a synecdoche or synonym for verse. However, here the form of attention in which the different-but-similar and the similar-but-different appear and take effect is extended from verse-thinking towards a perception of difference which we might call historical. Yet what if, following the figure, the poet were to conceive of himself as a 'ruined rhyme', as the speaker does in 'The Triumph of Time'? Eliot knew what he was talking about when he argued that the poet cannot 'take the past as a lump, an indiscriminate bolus' (*Selected Essays*, p. 16). Swinburne's refusal to take the past 'as a lump', his quest to stay within the *genesis amnesia*, motivates his at times exhausting quest to renew the connection between contemporary verse and its past. As Nietzsche identifies in *The Birth of Tragedy*:

> This is indeed the characteristic sign of that 'break' of which everyone customarily speaks as constituting the original suffering of modern culture, that the theoretical man, horrified and dissatisfied by the consequences of his predicament, no longer dares to entrust himself to the fearful icy current of existence, but instead runs anxiously up and down the river bank.[23]

The *Untimely Meditations* would go on to explore the suprahistorical viewpoint. However, here Nietzsche is more concerned with how 'our art reveals this universal distress':

> it is in vain that one relies on all the great productive periods and natures for models to imitate, it is in vain that one assembles the whole of 'world literature' around modern man in order to console him and surrounds him with the artistic styles and artists of all times, so that he might, like Adam with the animals, give them a name: he still remains eternally hungry, the weak and joyless 'critic', the Alexandrian man, who is basically a wretched librarian and proof-reader blinded by book dust and printers' errors (p. 100).

What Nietzsche's description allows us to grasp is the peculiar nature of Swinburne's style. Swinburne is one of the first English poets to view his material as traditional, and the last who was capable of the *genesis amnesia* required to overcome this.

This ambivalence is captured in an equally ambivalent obituary that appeared in *The Spectator*. Swinburne's poetry is understood as a graft onto, rather than an organic offshoot of, English poetry.[24] The reviewer reflects on Swinburne's cultivation of Edmund Waller's song 'Hylae, oh Hylae, why sit we mute': 'Like a scientific gardener, he took the flower, transplanted it, crossed it, and developed it till he gave the world such a measure as that of "Hesperia" [*sic*]: — "Out of the golden, remote wild West, where the sea without shore is"'. What the reviewer offers with one hand, he takes away with another:

> Mr. Swinburne [...] was a great master of metre rather than of melody, if by melody we mean [...] the natural and inevitable sense of music in words. Mr. Swinburne understood how to use every metrical device [...] in English verse, but he was not born with that melodious instinct which belonged supremely to Shakespeare, and in a less degree to Wordsworth, to Coleridge, and to Tennyson. We do not, of course, mean by this that Mr. Swinburne had not an extraordinarily acute ear. [...] But his metrical effects were produced by a conscious, or even a mechanical, process rather than by an inborn and unconscious feeling for rhythm and harmony. That is why his verse, which at first astonishes us by its perfection of sound, in the end is apt to weary and prove unsatisfying. There is too much artifice and too little inspiration.[25]

The distinction made here between 'metre' and 'melody', 'artifice' and 'inspiration', recalls Bourdieu's distinction between the *modus operandi* and the *opus operandi*. Swinburne's poetry, it appears, veers too close to the latter. Of course we must reject this statement, drawing attention to the number of times this study has shown Swinburne's innovation. Yet, for all this, there is in Swinburne's verse a certain, fatal, Orphic note: backwards-looking, reflective, Pre-Raphaelite. Though Henry James was commenting on Swinburne's prose style, I must admit that I recognise something in his description of how

> His style [...] is always listening to itself — always turning its head over its shoulders to see its train flowing behind it. The train shimmers and tumbles in a very gorgeous fashion, but the rustle of its embroidery is fatally importunate.[26]

Can verse-thinking accommodate poetry like this? Swinburne's poetry challenges some of the basic assumptions which attend this term. First of all, if prosody is cognitive, then verse-thinking, like Bourdieu's *habitus*, must be liable to change: '[a]rt can be understood only by its laws of movement, not according to any sort of invariants' (*Aesthetic Theory*, p. 3). Secondly, it is because it is traditional that innovations in verse thinking are able to take place — some kind of *genesis amnesia* is therefore necessary. As Adorno notes, 'pre-established forms permit improvisation more securely than do later fully organized and individualized works' (*Aesthetic Theory*, p. 181). Thirdly, since art has a historical truth content, 'No art is ever about itself'. Yet what are we to do with verse which remains so resolutely classic, even while it continues to innovate? Which is so astute that it draws attention to the conditions of its making? How are we to understand verse which — as in Swinburne's use of rhyme as a figure for continuity — seems to be about itself? Does such verse still count as verse-thinking? I think it must, but it is verse thinking of a peculiar style.

An argument running through Adorno's unfinished *Aesthetic Theory* maintains that aesthetics, if it is to have any kind of future, must radically rethink the concept of 'form'. This is how artworks are understood to have a historical truth content. They are utopian, 'windowless monads', a dream of a world in which things would be different (*Aesthetic Theory*, p. 6). Form here is 'the law of the transfiguration of the existing, counter to which it represents freedom' (p. 197). Art achieves this difference by effacing its foundations in empirical reality throughout the entirety of tradition. Yet, as Adorno later acknowledges, '[f]orms too can become material' (p. 202). In this contradiction, we are able to glimpse what is so peculiar about Swinburne's style. Just how can form mediate experience, if after emancipation, form itself becomes the material — that which is mediated — of art? Adorno never resolves this contradiction. Instead, it remains 'uncertain whether art is still possible; whether with its complete emancipation, it did not sever its own preconditions. This question is kindled by art's own past' (p. 2).

It is a question kindled by Swinburne's poetry: this is what it knows. Still able to think within a tradition, but aware that to do so was to risk stylisation, Swinburne's verse drives towards ceaseless innovation. His attempt to conquer almost every style (except the *terza rima*, which he did, of course, later conquer anyway in *Locrine*, despite his previous reservations) are by turns virtuoso and Alexandrian. It is in this sense that we should understand the urgency of Eliot's question: 'where do we go from Swinburne?'[27] Where, indeed, could one go after this?

'The answer appeared to be nowhere': Eliot's answering quip is meant as a joke. But is there a hint of regret here also? There is something intensely painful — is there something blissful, also? — about Swinburne's style: 'Things in verse hurt one, don't they? hit and sting like a cut...' Yet for all that, Eliot did not cease thinking about Swinburne.[28] To ask, in our turn, 'where did we go from Swinburne?' is to ask what it means to write poetry today.[29] We now know that Veronica Forrest-Thomson spent a considerable amount of time before her death in 1976 pursuing this question.[30] As she well knew, you must come to terms with A. C. Swinburne if you are doing poetry.

Notes to the Conclusion

1. Paul Valéry, 'Poetry and Abstract Thought', trans. by Charles Guenther, *Kenyon Review*, 16, 2 (1954), p. 210.
2. In their joint introduction to a special issue of *Victorian Poetry* on Victorian prosody Meredith Martin and Yisrael Levin write of how 'the scholars in this special issue no longer view prosody as an aesthetic category that is distinct from the political or cultural sphere'. See Meredith Martin and Yisrael Levin, 'Victorian Prosody: Measuring the Field', *Victorian Poetry*, 49, 2 (2011), p. 150.
3. George Saintsbury, *History of English Prosody from the Twelfth Century to the Present Day*, 3 vols (London: Macmillan, 1906–10) III, p. 335.
4. In the assumed absence of any personal 'theory' of prosody, critics have been led to provide other

kinds of explicit thinking about Swinburne's poetry. Rhythmical activities such as whipping or swimming may compensate for this perceived lack. See Julia Saville, 'Swinburne's Swimmers: From Insular Peace to the Anglo-Boer War', in *Algernon Charles Swinburne: Unofficial Laureate,* ed. Stefano Evangelista and Catherine Maxwell (Manchester: Manchester University Press, 2012), p. 35; Yopie Prins, 'Metrical Discipline: Algernon Charles Swinburne on the Flogging Block', ibid., p. 95. Yisrael Levin, in an attempt to provide an interpretative structure, traces the influence of Swinburne's poetry on the work of the prosodist T. H. Omond, and reapplies Omond's prosodic theories in order to read Swinburne's poems. See Yisrael Levin (ed.), *A. C. Swinburne and the Singing Word: New Perspectives on the Mature Work* (Farnham: Ashgate, 2010), p. 182.

5. 'Stars, Tigers and the Shape of Words' [the William Matthews lectures 1992 delivered at Birkbeck College, London] (London: Birkbeck College 1993), p. 31.
6. Pierre Bourdieu, *Outline of a Theory of Practice,* trans. Richard Nice (Cambridge: Cambridge University Press, 1977), pp. 25–26.
7. Alessandro Duranti, *Linguistic Anthropology* (Cambridge: Cambridge University Press, 1997), p. 208.
8. Bourdieu, *Outline of a Theory of Practice,* p. 79. As I note in my introduction, it was because of a perceived failure to do this that Adorno dismissed Swinburne's poetry as 'indulgent'.
9. A. C. Swinburne, *A Study of Shakespeare* (London: Chatto & Windus, 1880), p. 16, italics mine.
10. *Aesthetic Theory,* ed. and trans. by Robert Hullot-Kentor (London: Continuum, 1997), p. 192. All subsequent references will be to the page numbers of this edition, and will be given in the text.
11. Jarvis's term 'verse thinking' is not easily defined. Sometimes it is used synonymously with 'style', to indicate the particular characteristic of an individual author (See, for example, *Wordsworth's Philosophic Song* (Cambridge, 2007), p. 31.) However, three further ideas are also at work here. The phrase is, firstly, descriptive, and follows from Jarvis's argument that 'prosody, then, is cognitive; cognition is also prosodic' ('Prosody as Cognition', *Critical Quarterly,* 40, 4 (1998), p. 9) Secondly, it contains an aesthetic claim, drawn and developed from Adorno's aesthetic theory, that poetry has a historical truth content. (Simon Jarvis, 'Why Rhyme Pleases', *Thinking Verse,* 1 (2011), pp. 24–25.) The third usage, which is most relevant to my argument here, is explored in the body of my conclusion above.
12. Jarvis, 'Prosody as Cognition', p. 12.
13. Ibid., p. 12.
14. William Empson, *Seven Types of Ambiguity* (London: Pimlico, 2004), p. 164–65.
15. Bourdieu, *Outline of a Theory of Practice,* p. 79.
16. Bourdieu's definition of *habitus* depends upon a measure of *docta ignorantia.* The artistic equivalent for this is 'genesis amnesia' (p. 79). Working by implication, then, it seems possible that poets might experience a similar *genesis amnesia* in the act of writing, which is one possible excuse for their renowned grumpiness during interviews which seek to unravel the secrets of their practice.
17. Hallam Tennyson, *Alfred Lord Tennyson: A Memoir* (London: Macmillan, 1897), II, p. 285.
18. Simon Jarvis, 'Archaist-Innovators: The Couplet from Churchill to Browning', in *A Companion to Romantic Poetry,* ed. by Charles Mahoney (Oxford: Wiley-Blackwell, 2011), pp. 40–41.
19. Ezra Pound, 'Canto 83', *New Selected Poems and Translations,* ed. by Richard Sieburth (New York: New Directions, 2010), p. 227.
20. T. S. Eliot, *The Sacred Wood* (New York: Methuen, 1921), p. 114.
21. Veronica Forrest-Thomson, *Collected Poems and Translations* (London: Agneau 2, Allardyce, Barnett, 1990),p. 153.
22. A. C. Swinburne, untitled manuscript, Georgetown University, John. S. Mayfield Papers: Swinburne Series, 1:29/ GAMMS470.1.29 MS#199.
23. Friedrich Nietzsche, *The Birth of Tragedy from the Spirit of Music,* trans. by Douglas Smith (Oxford: Oxford University Press, 2000), p. 100.
24. Curiously, Paul Valéry also makes use of the same figure when he parodies the idea that 'by meditating on his art, with a rigor of reasoning like that applied to the culture of roses, a poet

can only be led astray [...] Possibly this opinion contains a grain of truth, although its simplicity makes me suspect it is of academic origin.' See Valéry 'Poetry and Abstract Thought', p. 208.
25. Unsigned Obituary, 'Mr. Swinburne as a Master of Metre', *Spectator*, 17 April 1909, pp. 9–10. Doubtless the writer means the poem 'Hesperides'.
26. Henry James, 'Essays and Studies by Algernon Charles Swinburne', in *Henry James: Literary Criticism*, ed. Leon Edel (New York: Literary Classics of the United States, 1984), p. 1282. James's review of Swinburne's essay collection was first published in *Nation,* July 29, 1875. My thanks to James Lello for drawing my attention to James's comments on Swinburne here.
27. T. S. Eliot, *Inventions of the March Hare* (London: Faber & Faber, 1996), p. 388.
28. See, for example, Eliot's lecture 'The Music of Poetry', the W. P. Ker Memorial Lecture (Glasgow: Jackson, 1942).
29. This study has argued with Adorno that 'The specifically artistic in art must be defined concretely from its other; that alone would fulfill the demands of a materialistic-dialectical aesthetics' (*Aesthetic Theory*, p. 3).
30. *The Chicago Review* 56.2/3 (Autumn 2011), 10–76, features three unpublished essays by Forrest-Thomson on Modernism and Victorian poetry.

BIBLIOGRAPHY

ABBOTT, C. C., ed., *The Letters of Gerard Manley Hopkins to Robert Bridges* (London: Oxford University Press, 1935)
ABBOTT, E., and L. CAMPBELL, *Life and Letters of Benjamin Jowett*, 2 vols (London: John Murray, 1897)
ABRAMS, M. H., *The Mirror and the Lamp: Romantic Theory and the Critical Tradition* (New York: Norton, 1958)
ADORNO, THEODOR W., *Quasi Una Fantasia: Essays on Modern Music* (London: Verso, 2011)
—— *Notes to Literature*, ed. by Ralph Tiedemann, trans. by Shierry Weber Nicholsen, 2 vols (New York: Columbia University Press, 1991)
—— 'Theses Upon Art and Religion Today', *Kenyon Review*, 7.4, (1945), pp. 678–79
—— *Aesthetic Theory*, ed. and trans. by Robert Hullot-Kentor (London: Continuum, 1997)
—— 'Commitment' trans. by Francis McDonagh, in *Aesthetics and Politics* (London and New York: Verso, 2007), pp. 177–95
AESCHYLUS, *Aeschylus*, ed. and trans. by Alan H. Sommerstein, Loeb Classical Library Series, 145, 146, 505, 3 vols (Cambridge, MA: Harvard University Press, 2008)
AGAMBEN, GIORGIO, *The End of the Poem*, trans. by Daniel Heller-Roazen (Stanford: Stanford University Press, 1999)
ALBRIGHT, DANIEL, *Untwisting the Serpent: Modernism in Music, Literature, and Other Arts* (Chicago: University of Chicago Press, 2000)
ALPERS, SVETLANA, and MICHAEL BAXANDALL, *Tiepolo and the Pictorial Intelligence* (New Haven: Yale University Press, 1994)
ARMSTRONG, ISOBEL, *Victorian Poetry: Poetry, Poetics, Politics* (London and New York: Routledge, 1993)
—— ed., *Victorian Scrutinies: Reviews of Poetry, 1830–1870* (London: Athlone Press, 1972)
—— 'The Victorian Poetry Party', *Victorian Poetry*, 42, 1 (2004), 9–27
ARNOLD, MATTHEW, *Complete Prose Works*, ed. by R. H. Super, 11 vols (Ann Arbor: University of Michigan Press, 1960–77)
—— *Poems of Matthew Arnold*, ed. by Kenneth Allott (London: Longman, 1965)
—— *Culture and Anarchy And Other Writings*, ed. by Stefan Collini (Cambridge: Cambridge University Press, 1993)
ASHTON, ROSEMARY, *The German Idea: Four English Writers and the Reception of German Thought 1800–1860* (London: Libris, 1994)
ATTRIDGE, DEREK, *The Rhythms of English Poetry* (London: Longman, 1982)
—— 'The Case for the English Dolnik; or, How Not to Introduce Prosody', *Poetics Today*, 33.1 (Spring 2012), 1–26.
AUGUSTINE OF HIPPO, SAINT, *Confessions*, ed. and trans. by Henry Chadwick (Oxford: Oxford University Press, 2008)
BALDICK, CHRIS, *The Social Mission of English Criticism, 1848–1932* (Oxford: Clarendon Press, 1987)
BARTHES, ROLAND, *The Pleasure of the Text*, trans. Richard Miller (Oxford: Blackwell, 1990)

—— *Camera Lucida: Reflections on Photography* (London: Vintage, 1993)
BARR, ALAN P., 'The Irony of Swinburne's *Atalanta in Calydon*', *Victorian Poetry*, 51.1 (2013), 1–13
BAUDELAIRE, CHARLES, *Baudelaire as a Literary Critic*, intro. and trans. by Lois Boe Hyslop and Francis E. Hyslop Jr. (University Park: Pennsylvania State University Press, 1964
BAXANDALL, MICHAEL, *Painting and Experience in Fifteenth-Century Italy: A Primer in the Social History of Pictorial Style* (Oxford: Oxford University Press, 1988)
BEASLEY, REBECCA, *Theorists of Modernist Poetry: T. S. Eliot, T. E. Hulme, Ezra Pound* (London: Routledge, 2007)
The Bible, Authorized King James Version, with an introduction and notes by Robert Carroll and Stephen Prickett (Oxford: Oxford University Press, 2008)
BENJAMIN, JESSICA, *The Bonds of Love* (London: Virago, 1988)
BENJAMIN, WALTER, *Charles Baudelaire: A Lyric Poet in the Era of High Capitalism*, trans. by Harry Zohn (London: NLB, 1973)
BERNSTEIN, J. M, *Against Voluptuous Bodies: Late Modernism and the Meaning of Painting* (Stanford: Stanford University Press, 2006)
—— *Art and Aesthetics after Adorno* (Berkeley: Townsend Center for the Humanities, 2010)
BEYERS, CHRIS, *A History of Free Verse* (Fayetteville: University of Arkansas Press, 2001)
BIZZOTTO, ELISA, and PAOLA SPINOZZI, *The Germ: Origins and Progenies of Pre-Raphaelite Interart Aesthetics* (Oxford: Peter Lang, 2012)
BLAIR, KIRSTIE, *Form and Faith in Victorian Poetry and Religion* (Oxford: Oxford University Press, 2013)
BLAKE, WILLIAM, *The Complete Poetry and Prose of William Blake*, ed. David V. Erdman (New York: Anchor Books, 1988)
—— *Victorian Poetry and the Culture of the Heart* (Oxford: Clarendon Press, 2006)
BLASING, MUTLU KONUK, *Lyric Poetry: The Pain and Pleasure of Words* (Princeton: Princeton University Press, 2007)
BLOOM, HAROLD, *The Pre-Raphaelite Poets* (New York: Chelsea House Publishers, 1986)
BONNECASE, DENIS, and SÉBASTIEN SCARPA, eds, *Swinburne and France* (Paris: Michel Houdiard, 2012)
—— and SÉBASTIEN SCARPA, eds, *Tombeau Pour Swinburne* (Croissy-Beauborg: Aden, 2010)
BOSWORTH, JOSEPH, and T. NORTHCOTE TOLLER, eds, *An Anglo-Saxon Dictionary* (London: Oxford University Press, 1972)
BOURDIEU, PIERRE, *Outline of a Theory of Practice*, trans. by Richard Nice (Cambridge: Cambridge University Press, 1977)
—— *The Field of Cultural Production: Essays on Art and Literature*, ed. by Randal Johnson (Cambridge: Polity Press, 1993)
BOWRA, C. M., *The Romantic Imagination* (Oxford: Oxford University Press, 1961, repr. 1995)
BRISTOW, JOSEPH, ed., *The Cambridge Companion to Victorian Poetry* (Cambridge: Cambridge University Press, 2000)
BROWNING, ELIZABETH BARRETT, *The Complete Works of Elizabeth Barrett Browning*, ed. by Charlotte Endymion Porter and Helen Clarke (New York: AMS Press, 1973)
BROWNING, ROBERT, *The Poems of Browning*, ed. by John Woolford and Daniel Karlin (Harlow: Longman, 1991)
—— *Strafford; Sordello*, ed. by Ian Jack and Margaret Smith, *The Complete Works of Robert Browning*, II (Oxford: Clarendon Press, 1982)
BURNE-JONES, GEORGIANA, *Memorials of Edward Burne-Jones*, intro. by John Christian, 2 vols (London: Lund Humphries, 1993)
BUDELMANN, FELIX, *The Cambridge Companion to Greek Lyric* (Cambridge: Cambridge University Press, 2009)

BUSH, DOUGLAS, *Mythology and the Romantic Tradition in English Poetry* (Cambridge, MA: Harvard University Press, 1937)
CAMERON, SHARON, *Impersonality: Seven Essays* (Chicago: University of Chicago Press, 2007)
CAMPBELL, MATTHEW, *Rhythm and Will in Victorian Poetry* (Cambridge: Cambridge University Press, 1992)
CARLYLE, THOMAS, *Critical and Miscellaneous Essays,* collected and republished, 2nd edn, 5 vols (London: J. Fraser, 1840)
—— *On Heroes, Hero-Worship and the Heroic in History* (London: Chapman & Hall, 1840)
CARNE-ROSS, D. S., *Pindar* (New Haven: Yale University Press, 1985)
—— *Classics and Translation: Essays,* ed. by Kenneth Haynes (Lewisburg: Bucknell University Press 2010)
CARR, HELEN, *The Verse Revolutionaries: Ezra Pound, H. D. And the Imagists* (London: Jonathan Cape, 2009)
CARROLL, NOËL, *Philosophy of Art: A Contemporary Introduction* (London: Routledge, 1999)
CHEW, SAMUEL C., *Swinburne* (London: John Murray, 1929)
CLARK, T. J., *Farewell to an Idea: Episodes from a History of Modernism* (New Haven and London: Yale University Press, 1999)
—— *The Sight of Death,* (New Haven and London: Yale University Press, 2006
COLERIDGE, SAMUEL TAYLOR, *The Major Works,* ed. by H. J. Jackson (Oxford: Oxford World Classics, 1985)
COLERIDGE, SAMUEL TAYLOR, and WILLIAM WORDSWORTH, *Lyrical Ballads,* ed. by R. L. Brett and A. R. Jones, with a new introduction by Nicholas Roe (London: Routledge, 2005)
COLLIGAN, COLETTE, and MARGARET LINLEY, eds, *Media, Technology, and Literature in the Nineteenth Century: Image, Sound, Touch* (Farnham: Ashgate, 2011)
COLLINI, STEFAN, *Public Moralists: Political Thought and Intellectual Life in Britain 1850–1930* (Oxford: Clarendon Press, 1991)
CREECH, THOMAS, *T. Lucretius Carus, the Epicurean Philosopher, His Six Books De Natura Rerum: Done into English Verse, with Notes* (Oxford: Printed by L. Lichfield for Anthony Stephens, 1682)
CULLER, JONATHAN, *The Pursuit of Signs* (London: Routledge & Kegan Paul, 1981)
—— 'Why Lyric?', *PMLA*, 123, 1 (January 2008), 201–06
—— *The Theory of Lyric* (Cambridge, MA: Harvard University Press, 2015)
CUNNINGHAM, DAVID, and NIGEL MAPP, eds, *Adorno and Literature* (London: Continuum, 2006)
CUSHMAN, STEPHEN, and ROLAND GREENE, eds, *The New Princeton Encyclopedia of Poetry and Poetics,* 4th edn (Princeton: Princeton University Press, 2012)
DALE, A. M., *The Lyric Metres of Greek Drama,* 2nd edn (London: Cambridge University Press, 1968)
DAVIE, DONALD, *Purity of Diction in English Verse and Articulate Energy* (London: Penguin, 1992)
—— *Studies in Ezra Pound* (Manchester: Carcanet, 1991)
DAYAN, PETER, *Music Writing Literature, from Sand Via Debussy to Derrida* (Aldershot: Ashgate, 2006)
DE BOLLA, PETER, *Art Matters* (Cambridge, MA: Harvard University Press, 2001)
DELEUZE, GILLES, *Difference and Repetition,* trans. by Paul Patton (London: Bloomsbury Academic, 2014)
DERRIDA, JACQUES, *The Truth in Painting,* trans. by Geoff Bennington and Ian McLeod, (Chicago: The University of Chicago Press, 1987)

DETIENNE, MARCEL, *Masters of Truth in Archaic Greece,* trans. by Janet Lloyd (New York: Zone Books, 1996)
DIXON, RICHARD WATSON, *The Collected Poems of Canon Richard Watson Dixon, 1833–1900,* ed. by Shirley M. C. Johnson and Todd K. Bender (New York: Peter Lang, 1989)
DOWSON, ERNEST, *The Poetry of Ernest Dowson,* ed. by Desmond Flower (Cranbury: Associated University Presses, 1970)
DURANTI, ALESSANDRO, *Linguistic Anthropology* (Cambridge: Cambridge University Press, 1997)
DURNO, T. E., 'Poetics of the English Ode, 1786–1820' (unpublished doctoral thesis, University of Cambridge, 2013)
DRYDEN, JOHN, *Selected Poems,* ed. by Steven N. Zwicker and David Bywaters (London: Penguin, 2001)
EAGLETON, TERRY, *Criticism and Ideology: A Study in Marxist Literary Theory* (London: Verso, 1978)
—— *Marxism and Literary Criticism* (London: Routledge, 2002)
ELIOT, T. S., *The Sacred Wood* (New York: Methuen, 1921)
—— *Selected Essays* (London: Faber & Faber, 1932)
—— 'The Music of Poetry', the W. P. Ker Memorial Lecture (Glasgow: Jackson, 1942)
—— *Selected Essays,* 3rd edn (London: Faber, 1964)
—— *The Complete Poems and Plays.* 6th ed., (London: Faber, 1982)
—— *Inventions of the March Hare* (London: Faber & Faber, 1996)
EMPSON, WILLIAM, *The Structure of Complex Words* (London: Chatto & Windus, 1951)
—— *Seven Types of Ambiguity* (London: Pimlico, 2004)
ELLMANN, MAUD, *The Poetics of Impersonality: T. S. Eliot and Ezra Pound* (Cambridge MA: Harvard University Press, 1987)
EVANGELISTA, STEFANO-MARIA, and CATHERINE MAXWELL, eds, *Algernon Charles Swinburne: Unofficial Laureate* (Manchester: Manchester University Press, 2013)
FLINT, KATE, *The Victorians and the Visual Imagination* (Cambridge: Cambridge University Press, 2008)
FORREST-THOMSON, VERONICA, *Poetic Artifice: A Theory of Twentieth-Century Poetry* (Manchester: Manchester University Press, 1978)
—— *Collected Poems and Translations* (London: Agneau 2, Allardyce, Barnett, 1990)
—— 'Swinburne as Poet: A Reconsideration', *Journal of Pre-Raphaelite Studies,* 15 (Autumn 2006), 51–71
—— 'His True Penelope Was Flaubert: Ezra Pound and Nineteenth Century Poetry', 'Lilies from the Acorn' and 'Pastoral and Elegy in the Early Poems of Tennyson', *Chicago Review,* 56, 2–3 (Autumn 2011), 10–76
FOWLER, ROGER, 'Three Blank Verse Textures', in *The Languages of Literature: Some Linguistic Contributions to Literature* by Roger Fowler, with an essay written in collaboration with Peter Mercer and two papers by F. W. Bateson (London: Routledge and Kegan Paul, 1971), pp. 184–99.
FRIED, MICHAEL, *Art and Objecthood: Essays and Reviews* (Chicago: University of Chicago Press, 1998)
GALIMBERTI, ALICE, *L'Aedo d'Italia* (Palermo: Sandron, 1925)
GAUTIER, THÉOPHILE, *Mademoiselle de Maupin* (Paris: Librairie Générale Française, 1994)
—— *Mademoiselle de Maupin,* trans. Helen Constantine (London: Penguin, 2005)
GENTILE, EMILIO, *Politics as Religion,* trans. by George Staunton (Princeton: Princeton University Press, 2006)
GILLESPIE, STUART, and PHILIP HARDIE, eds, *The Cambridge Companion to Lucretius* (Cambridge: Cambridge University Press, 2007)

GOSSE, EDMUND, 'Erechtheus', *The Examiner*, 8 January 1876, pp. 41–43
—— *The Life of Algernon Charles Swinburne* (London: Macmillan, 1917)
—— ed., *English Odes* (London: Kegan Paul, 1881)
GRIFFITHS, ERIC, *The Printed Voice of Victorian Poetry* (Oxford: Clarendon Press, 1989)
GROSS, JOHN, *The Rise and Fall of the Man of Letters* (Harmondsworth: Penguin, 1991)
HALL, JASON DAVID, *Meter Matters: Verse Cultures of the Long Nineteenth Century* (Athens GA: Ohio University Press, 2011)
HAMMERMEISTER, KAI, *The German Aesthetic Tradition* (Cambridge: Cambridge University Press, 2002)
HARDING, DENYS, *Words into Rhythm: English Speech Rhythm in Verse and Prose* (Cambridge: Cambridge University Press, 1976)
HARDY, THOMAS, *The Complete Poetical Works of Thomas Hardy*, ed. by S. Hynes, 3 vols (Oxford: Clarendon Press, 1984)
HARGREAVES, H. A., 'Swinburne's Greek Plays and God, "The Supreme Evil"' *Modern Language Notes* 76 (1961), 607–16
HAYNES, KENNETH, *English Literature and Ancient Languages* (New York: Oxford University Press, 2003)
HEGEL, G. W. F., *The Phenomenology of Spirit*, trans. by A. V. Miller (Oxford: Oxford University Press, 1977)
—— *Aesthetics: Lectures on Fine Art*, trans. by T. M. Knox, 2 vols (Oxford: Clarendon Press, 1998)
HEIDEGGER, MARTIN, *Poetry, Language, Thought* (New York and London: Harper and Row, 1975)
—— *Being and Time*, trans. by John Macquarrie and Edward Robinson (Oxford: Blackwell, 1967)
HELSINGER, ELIZABETH K., *Poetry and the Pre-Raphaelite Arts: Dante Gabriel Rossetti and William Morris* (New Haven: Yale University Press, 2008)
HOPKINS, GERARD MANLEY, *The Major Works*, ed. by Catherine Phillips (Oxford: Oxford University Press, 2002)
HOŠEK, CHAVIVA, and PATRICIA PARKER, eds., *Lyric Poetry: Beyond New Criticism* (Ithaca: Cornell University Press, 1985)
HOUGH, GRAHAM, and ERIC WARNER, eds, *Strangeness and Beauty: An Anthology of Aesthetic Criticism, 1840–1910* (Cambridge: Cambridge University Press, 1983)
HOUSMAN, A. E., 'Swinburne', *Cornhill Magazine*, 177 (Autumn 1969, written 1910), pp. 380–400
HUGHES, JOHN, *The End of Work: Theological Critiques of Capitalism* (Oxford: Blackwell, 2007)
HUGHES, LINDA K., *The Cambridge Introduction to Victorian Poetry* (Cambridge: Cambridge University Press, 2010)
HUHN, TOM, ed., *The Cambridge Companion to Adorno* (Cambridge: Cambridge University Press, 2004)
HULME, T. E., *The Collected Writings of T. E. Hulme*, ed. by Karen Csengeri (Oxford: Clarendon Press, 1996)
HURLEY, MICHAEL, 'George Saintsbury's *History of English Prosody*', *Essays in Criticism*, 60, 4 (2010), 336–60
HYDER, C. K., *Swinburne's Literary Career and Fame* (Durham, NC: Duke University Press, 1933)
—— ed., *A. C. Swinburne: The Critical Heritage*, (London: Routledge, 1995: first published 1970 as *Swinburne: The Critical Heritage*)
ISER, WOLFGANG, *Walter Pater: The Aesthetic Moment*, trans. David Henry Wilson (Cambridge: Cambridge University Press, 1987)

JACKSON, VIRGINIA, and YOPIE PRINS, eds, *The Lyric Theory Reader: A Critical Anthology* (Baltimore: Johns Hopkins University Press, 2014)
JAMES, CLIVE, 'Loves in a Life', *TLS*, 5798, 14 May 2014, TLS Online Archive, <http://www.the- tls.co.uk/tls/public/article1410176.ece> [last accessed 1st October 2015]
JAMESON, FREDRIC, *The Prison-House of Language: A Critical Account of Structuralism and Russian Formalism* (Princeton: Princeton University Press, 1972)
JARVIS, SIMON, 'Prosody as Cognition', *Critical Quarterly*, 40, 4 (1998), 3–15
—— *Theodor W. Adorno: Critical Evaluations in Cultural Theory* (London: Routledge, 2004)
—— *Wordsworth's Philosophic Song* (Cambridge: Cambridge University Press, 2007)
—— 'The *Melodics of Long Poems*', *Textual Practice*, 24, 4 (2010), 607–21
—— 'Why Rhyme Pleases', *Thinking Verse*, 1, (2011), 17–43, available at <www.thinkingverse.com>[last accessed 26 April 2018]
—— 'Archaist-Innovators: The Couplet from Churchill to Browning', in *A Companion to Romantic Poetry*, ed. by Charles Mahoney (Oxford: Wiley-Blackwell, 2011), pp. 25–43
—— 'Swinburne: The Insuperable Sea', in *The Oxford Handbook of Victorian Poetry*, ed. by Matthew Bevis (Oxford: Oxford University Press, 2013), pp. 521–35
—— 'What is Historical Poetics?', in *Theory Aside*, ed. Jason Potts and Daniel Stout (Durham, NC: Duke University Press, 2014), pp. 97–116
—— 'Lyric Thinking: the English Ode from Cowley to Tennyson': Congreve, Pope and the Fate of Grand Lyric' Lecture, Faculty of English, University of Cambridge, 2014
JAUFRÉ RUDEL, *The Songs of Jaufré Rudel*, ed. by Rupert T. Pickens, Studies and Texts Series: 41 (Toronto: Pontifical Institute of Mediaeval Studies, 1978)
JAY, MARTIN, *Dialectical Imagination: A History of the Frankfurt School and the Institute of Social Research, 1923–1950*, (Berkeley: University of California Press, 1996)
JOHNSON, SAMUEL, *Lives of the English Poets*, ed. by George Birkbeck Hill, 3 vols (Oxford: Clarendon Press, 1905)
JOUGHIN, JOHN J., and SIMON MALPAS, *The New Aestheticism* (Manchester: Manchester University Press, 2003)
JUMP, JOHN, (ed.) *Lord Alfred Tennyson: The Critical Heritage* (London: Routledge, 1995)
Juvenal and Persius, trans. by G. G. Ramsay, Loeb Classical Library (unnumbered) (London: Heinemann, 1918)
KANT, IMMANUEL, *Critique of Pure Reason*, ed. and trans. by. Paul Guyer and Allen W. Wood (Cambridge: Cambridge University Press, 2006)
—— *Critique of Judgement*, trans. by James Creed Meredith, rev. and ed. by Nicholas Walker (Oxford: Oxford University Press, 2008)
KEACH, WILLIAM, *Shelley's Style* (New York and London: Methuen, 1984)
KEATS, JOHN, *The Complete Poems* (Harmondsworth: Penguin, 1996)
KENNER, HUGH, *The Pound Era* (London: Pimlico, 1991)
KERMODE, FRANK, *The Romantic Image* (London: Routledge & Kegan Paul, 1957)
KIERKEGAARD, SØREN, *Fear and Trembling; Repetition,* ed. and trans. by Howard V. Hong and Edna H. Hong (Princeton: Princeton University Press, 1983)
KUDUK-WEINER, STEPHANIE, *Republican Politics and English Poetry* (New York: Palgrave Macmillan, 2005)
KRAMER, LAURENCE, *Music and Poetry: The Nineteenth Century and After* (Berkeley: University of California Press, 1984)
KUGEL, JAMES, *The Idea of Biblical Poetry: Parallelism and its History* (New Haven: Yale University Press, 1981)
LAFOURCADE, GEORGES, *La Jeunesse de Swinburne (1837–1867)*, 2 vols (Paris: Les Belles Lettres, 1928)
LANDOR, WALTER SAVAGE, *Poems, Dialogues in Verse and Epigrams*, 2 vols (London: Dent, 1892)

LaPorte, Charles, 'Victorian Literature, Religion, and Secularization', *Literature Compass*, 10 (2013), 277–87
Leighton, Angela, *On Form: Poetry, Aestheticism, and the Legacy of a Word* (Oxford: Oxford University Press, 2007)
Lessing, Gotthold Ephraim, *Laocoön; or, the Limits of Poetry and Painting*, trans. by William Ross (London: J. Ridgway and Sons, 1836)
Levin, Yisrael, ed., *A. C. Swinburne and the Singing Word: New Perspectives on the Mature Work* (Farnham: Ashgate, 2010)
—— and Meredith Martin, 'Victorian Prosody: Measuring the Field', *Victorian Poetry*, 49.2 (Summer 2011): 149–60
Levin, Yisrael, 'But the Law Must Be Poetic', in *Meter Matters*, ed. by Jason David Hall (Athens [GA.]: Ohio University Press, 2011), pp. 178–95
—— *Swinburne's Apollo: Myth, Faith and Victorian Spirituality* (Farnham: Ashgate, 2013)
Lichtmann, Maria R., *The Contemplative Poetry of Gerard Manley Hopkins* (Princeton: Princeton University Press, 1989)
Littré, Emile, (ed.) *Dictionnaire de la langue française* (1872–1877), made searchable by the ARTFL Project maintained by the University of Chicago <https://artfl-project.uchicago.edu/content/dictionnaires-dautrefois> [last accessed 25 April 2018]
Louis, M. K., 'Wise Words and Wild Words: The Problem of Language in Swinburne's "Atalanta"', *Victorian Poetry*, 25.1 (Spring 1987), 45–56
—— *Swinburne and His Gods* (Montreal and London: McGill-Queen's University Press, 1990)
Lyons, Sara, *Algernon Swinburne and Walter Pater: Victorian Aestheticism, Doubt and Secularisation* (London: Legenda, 2015)
Magnus, Laury, *The Track of the Repetend* (New York: AMS Press, 1989)
Mallock, W. H., *Memoirs of Life and Literature* (London: Chapman & Hall, 1920)
Mander, W. J., *British Idealism: A History* (Oxford: Oxford University Press, 2011)
Martin, Meredith, *The Rise and Fall of Meter: Poetry and English National Culture, 1860–1930* (Princeton: Princeton University Press, 2012)
Marx, Karl, *Early Writings*, trans. by Rodney Livingstone and Gregor Benton, intro. by Lucio Colletti (London: Penguin in association with the New Left Review, 1992)
—— *Capital: A Critique of Political Economy*, trans. by Ben Fowkes, intro. by Ernest Mandel, 3 vols (London: Penguin, 1976)
—— *Later Political Writings*, ed. and trans. by Terrell Carver (Cambridge: Cambridge University Press, 1996)
Mathews, Richard, 'Heart's Love and Heart's Division: The Quest for Unity in "Atalanta in Calydon"', *Victorian Poetry*, 9.1–2 (1971), 35–48
Maxwell, Catherine, *Swinburne* (Tavistock: Northcote House, 2006)
—— *Second Sight: The Visionary Imagination in Late Victorian Literature* (Manchester: Manchester University Press, 2008)
McGann, Jerome, *Swinburne: An Experiment in Criticism* (Chicago: University of Chicago Press, 1972)
—— *Dante Gabriel Rossetti and the Game That Must Be Lost* (New Haven: Yale University Press, 2000)
—— 'Wagner, Baudelaire, Swinburne: Poetry in the Condition of Music', *Victorian Poetry*, 47, 4 (2009), 619–32
Medvedev, P. N., and M. M. Bakhtin, *The Formal Method in Literary Scholarship: A Critical Introduction to Sociological Poetics* (Cambridge MA: Harvard University Press, 1985)
Merleau-Ponty, Maurice, *Phenomenology of Perception*, trans. Donald A. Landes (Abingdon: Routledge, 2012)
Meyers, Terry, and Rikky Rooksby, 'Introduction', *Victorian Poetry*, 47.4 ['A Hundred Sleeping Years Ago': Special Issue in commemoration of Algernon Charles Swinburne]

(Winter 2009): 611–18
MILBANK, JOHN, *Theology and Social Theory* (Oxford: Blackwell, 1993)
—— *The Word Made Strange: Theology, Language, Culture* (Oxford: Blackwell, 1997)
MILL, J. S., 'What Is Poetry?', *The Monthly Repository*, 7, 73 (January 1833), 60–70
—— 'The Two Kinds Of Poetry', *The Monthly Repository*, 7, 80 (August 1833), 714–24
—— *On Liberty and Other Writings* ed. Stefan Collini (Cambridge: Cambridge University Press, 1989)
MILNES, RICHARD MONCKTON, 1st Baron Houghton, '*Atalanta in Calydon*: a Tragedy', *Edinburgh Review*, 122, 249, (July 1865): 202–16.
MORRIS, WILLIAM, *The Life and Death of Jason*, 2nd rev. edn (London: Bell and Daldy, 1868)
MOUNIER, EMMANUEL, *La Pensée de Charles Péguy* (Paris: Plon, 1931)
—— *Modernisms: A Literary Guide* (Basingstoke: Macmillan, 1995)
NICHOLLS, PETER, 'The Swinburne Nexus', *Parataxis*, 10 (2001), 33–53
NICOLSON, HAROLD, *Swinburne* (London: Macmillan, 1926)
NIETZSCHE, FRIEDRICH, *The Complete Works of Friedrich Nietzsche*, trans. by T. N. Foulis, ed. by O. Levy, 18 vols (Edinburgh: Foulis 1910)
—— *Untimely Meditations*, trans. by R. J. Hollingdale, ed. by Daniel Breazeale (Cambridge: Cambridge University Press, 1997)
—— *The Birth of Tragedy from the Spirit of Music*, trans. by Douglas Smith (Oxford: Oxford University Press, 2000)
O'GORMAN, FRANCIS, 'Swinburne and Ireland', *Review of English Studies*, 64, 265 (June 2013), 454–74
—— 'Swinburne and Cowardice: Running Away From *Poems and Ballads*, *Journal of Pre-Raphaelite Studies* 26 (2017), 61–80
O'HARA, FRANK, *The Collected Poems of Frank O'Hara*, ed. by Donald Allen (New York: Alfred A. Knopf, 1972)
OLIVER, DOUGLAS, *Poetry and Narrative in Performance* (Basingstoke: Macmillan, 1989)
PATER, WALTER, *Appreciations, with an Essay on Style* (London: Macmillan, 1901)
—— *The Renaissance*, ed. by Adam Phillips (Oxford: Oxford University Press, 1998)
PATERSON, KATIE, ' "Much Regrafted pain": Schopenhauerian Love and the Fecundity of Pain in *Atalanta in Calydon*', *Victorian Poetry*, 47.4 (Winter 2009),715–31
PATMORE, COVENTRY, *Essay on English Metrical Law*, ed. by Sister Mary Augustine Roth (Washington, DC.: Catholic University of America Press, 1961)
PHELAN, J. P. *The Music of Verse: Metrical Experiment in Nineteenth-Century Poetry* (Basingstoke: Palgrave Macmillan, 2012)
PICKSTOCK, CATHERINE, *After Writing: On the Liturgical Consummation of Philosophy* (Oxford: Blackwell, 1997)
—— *Repetition and Identity* (Oxford: Oxford University Press, 2013)
Pindar, ed. and trans. by William H. Race, Loeb Classical Library Series: 56, 2 vols (Cambridge, MA: Harvard University Press, 1997)
PLATO, *The Dialogues of Plato*, trans. by B. Jowett, 3rd edn, 5 vols (Oxford: Oxford University Press, 1892)
POE, EDGAR ALLAN, *Literary Criticism of Edgar Allan Poe*, ed. by Robert L. Hough (Lincoln: University of Nebraska Press, 1965)
POLTEN, ORLA, 'Setting Sea-Serpents in Verse: Momentum and Meaning in Swinburne's Decasyllabic Couplets', *Cambridge Literary Review*, 6 (May 2012), 157–73
—— 'Swinburne's Atalanta in Calydon: Prosody as Sublimation in Victorian 'Greek' tragedy', *Classical Receptions Journal*, 9, 3 (July 2017), 331–49
POPE, ALEXANDER, *The Poems of Alexander Pope*, a one-volume edition of the Twickenham text, ed. by John Butt (London: Routledge, 1965)

PORTER, JAMES I., *Nietzsche and the Philology of the Future* (Stanford: Stanford University Press, 2000)
POUND, EZRA, *Collected Early Poems of Ezra Pound*, ed. by Michael John King, intro. by Louis L. Martz (London: Faber, 1977)
—— 'Swinburne versus Biographers', *Poetry*, 11, 6 (March, 1918): 322–29
—— *The Letters of Ezra Pound, 1907–1941*, ed. D. D. Paige (New York: Haskell House Publishers, 1974)
—— *New Selected Poems and Translations*, ed. by Richard Sieburth (New York: New Directions, 2010)
PREMINGER, ALEX, and T. V. F. BROGAN, eds, *The New Princeton Encyclopedia of Poetry and Poetics*, 3rd edn (Princeton: Princeton University Press, 1993)
PRETTEJOHN, ELIZABETH, ed., *The Cambridge Companion to the Pre-Raphaelites* (Cambridge: Cambridge University Press, 2012)
PRINS, YOPIE, *Victorian Sappho* (Princeton: Princeton University Press, 1999)
—— 'Voice Inverse', *Victorian Poetry*, 42, 1 (2004), 43–59
—— 'Metrical Discipline: Algernon Swinburne on 'The Flogging Block' in *Algernon Charles Swinburne: Unofficial Laureate*, ed. by Stefano-Maria Evangelista and Catherine Maxwell (Manchester: Manchester University Press, 2013), pp. 95–124
PRYNNE, J. H., 'The Elegiac World in Victorian Poetry' [transcript of BBC broadcast talk], *Listener*, 14 February 1963, pp. 290–91
—— 'Stars, Tigers and the Shape of Words' [the William Matthews lectures 1992 delivered at Birkbeck College, London] (London: Birkbeck College 1993)
—— *Poems*, 3rd edn (Hexham: Bloodaxe Books, 2015)
—— 'Mental Ears and Poetic Work', *Chicago Review*, 55, 1 (2010): 126–57
RADFORD, ANDREW, and MARK SANDY, *Romantic Echoes in the Victorian Era* (Aldershot: Ashgate, 2008)
REYNOLDS, MATTHEW, *The Realms of Verse 1830–1870: English Poetry in a Time of Nation-Building* (Oxford: Oxford University Press, 2001)
RIBEYROL, CHARLOTTE, *Etrangeté, passion, couleur: l'hellénisme de Swinburne, Pater et Symonds (1865–1880)* (Grenoble: ELLUG, Université Stendhal, 2013)
—— 'Swinburne', in *The Oxford History of Classical Reception in English Literature* ed. by Norman Vance and Jennifer Wallace (Oxford: Oxford University Press, 2015), IV, 619–42
RICKS, CHRISTOPHER, *Milton's Grand Style* (Oxford: Clarendon Press, 1963)
RICŒUR, PAUL, *On Translation*, trans. by Eileen Brennan (Abingdon: Routledge, 2006)
ROOKSBY, RIKKY, *A. C. Swinburne: A Poet's Life* (Aldershot: Scolar, 1997)
—— AND NICHOLAS SHRIMPTON, eds, *The Whole Music of Passion: New Essays on Swinburne* (Aldershot: Scolar, 1993)
ROSE, GILLIAN, *The Broken Middle: Out of Our Ancient Society* (Oxford: Blackwell, 1992)
ROSENBERG, JOHN D., 'Swinburne', *Victorian Studies*, 11, 2 (1967), 131–52
ROSSETTI, DANTE GABRIEL, *Ballads and Sonnets* (London: Ellis and White, 1881)
—— *Collected Poetry and Prose*, ed. by Jerome J. McGann (New Haven: Yale University Press, 2003)
ROSSETTI, WILLIAM MICHAEL, *Some Reminisces* (London: Brown, Langham, 1906)
—— AND ALGERNON CHARLES SWINBURNE, *Notes on the Royal Academy Exhibition, 1868* (London: James Camden Hotten, 1868)
RUMSEY, LACEY, 'Swinburne et la variation rhythmique', *Études Anglaises*, 62.2 (2009), 186–204
RUSKIN, JOHN, *Elements of English Prosody* (Orpington: George Allen, 1880)
—— *The Works of John Ruskin*, ed. by E. T. Cook and Alexander Wedderburn, 39 vols (London: George Allen, 1903–1912)

The Correspondence of John Ruskin and Charles Eliot Norton, ed. by John Lewis Bradley and Ian Ousby (Cambridge: Cambridge University Press, 1987)

RUSSELL, CORINNA, 'A Defence of Tautology: Repetition and Difference in Wordsworth's Note to "The Thorn"', *Paragraph*, 2 (2005): 104–18

RUSSELL, DAVID, 'Aesthetic Liberalism: John Stuart Mill as Essayist', *Victorian Studies*, 56, 1 (2013), 7–30

RUTLAND, WILLIAM, *Swinburne: A Nineteenth-Century Hellene* (Oxford: Blackwell, 1931)

SAINTSBURY, GEORGE, *Corrected Impressions: Essays on Victorian Writers* (London: Heinemann, 1895)

—— *A History of English Prosody from the Twelfth Century to the Present Day*, 3 vols (London: Macmillan, 1906–10)

—— *A History of English Prose Rhythm* (London: Macmillan and Co., 1912)

—— *Historical Manual of English Prosody* (London: Macmillan and Co., 1910)

SAVILLE, JULIA F., 'Cosmopolitan Republican: Swinburne, the Immersive Poet as Public Moralist', *Victorian Poetry*, 47 (2009), 691–713

SCHUCHARD, RONALD, *The Last Minstrels: Yeats and the Revival of the Bardic Arts* (Oxford: Oxford University Press, 2008)

SCOTT, CLIVE, *Reading the Rhythm: The Poetics of French Free Verse, 1910–1930* (Oxford: Clarendon, 1993)

—— *Channel Crossings: French and English Poetry in Dialogue, 1550–2000* (London: Legenda, 2002)

SEDLEY, DAVID, *Lucretius and the Transformation of Greek Wisdom* (Cambridge: Cambridge University Press, 1998)

SHAW, W. DAVID, *Tennyson's Style* (Ithaca: Cornell University Press, 1976)

SHELLEY, PERCY BYSSHE, *Prometheus Unbound: A Variorum Edition*, ed. Lawrence John Zillman (Seattle: University of Washington Press, 1959)

—— ed. by JACK DONOVAN, CIAN DUFFY, KELVIN EVEREST and MICHAEL ROSSINGTON, 3 vols, (Harlow: Longman, 2011)

—— *Shelley's Poetry and Prose*, selected and edited by Donald H. Reiman and Neil Fraistat, 2nd edn (New York: Norton, 2002)

—— *The Poems of Shelley*, ed. by Kelvin Everest and Geoffrey Matthews, 3 vols (Padstow: Longman, 2000)

SHUSTER, GEORGE, *The English Ode from Milton to Keats* (New York: Columbia University Press, 1940)

SIMMONDS, CLIVE, 'Publishing Swinburne; the Poet, his Publishers and Critics' (unpublished doctoral thesis, University of Reading, 2014)

SPENSER, EDMUND, *The Faerie Queene*, ed. by A. C. Hamilton, Hiroshi Yamashita, and Toshiyuki Suzuki (Harlow: Pearson Education, 2001)

STEAD, C. K., *The New Poetic: Yeats to Eliot* (London: Continuum, 2005)

STEELE, TIMOTHY, *Missing Measures: Modern Poetry and the Revolt against Meter* (Fayetteville: University of Arkansas Press, 1990)

STEWART, SUSAN, 'What Praise Poems Are For', *Publications of the Modern Language Association*, 120, 1 (1995), 235–45

—— *Poetry and the Fate of the Senses* (Chicago: University of Chicago Press, 2001)

SUTHERLAND, KESTON, *The Odes to TL61P of Keston Sutherland* (London: Enitharmon, 2013)

SWIFT, L. A., *The Hidden Chorus: Echoes of Genre in Tragic Lyric* (Oxford: Oxford University Press, 2010)

SWINBURNE, ALGERNON CHARLES, 'Of Analogy', College Essays [1856–58] London, British Library, Ashley MS.4349

—— 'On Political and Speculative Liberty', transcribed by Rikky Rooksby in *The Victorians Institute Journal*, 18 (1990) and subsequently made available via the NINES

website <http://www.nines.org/exhibits/swinburne_manuscripts?page=> [accessed 26 April 2018]
—— Poetical Notebook used by A. C. Swinburne; [1857]. London, British Library, Ashley MS. 4453
—— *Undergraduate Papers; an Oxford Journal (1857–1858)*, ed. Thomas Hill Green, John Nichol, Algernon Charles Swinburne and others. Facsimile reproduction with an introduction by Francis Jacques Sypher (Delmar, NY.: Scholars' Facsimiles and Reprints, 1974)
—— 'On the Dialectic of Plato', Undergraduate Essays on Philosophy [between 1856 and 1860], Worcester College Library, Oxford, MS.243
—— Untitled Manuscript, Georgetown University, John. S. Mayfield Papers: Swinburne Series, 1:29/ GAMMS470.1.29 MS#199
—— *Notes on Poems and Reviews* (London: John Camden Hotten, 1866)
—— *William Blake: A Critical Essay* (London: John Camden Hotten, 1868)
—— 'Erechtheus' Autograph draft [1875], London, British Library, Ashley MS.5263
—— *Essays and Studies* (London: Chatto & Windus, 1875)
—— *A Study of Shakespeare* (London: Chatto & Windus, 1880)
—— 'Introduction' to William Collins, in *The English Poets*, ed. Thomas Humphry Ward, 2nd edn (London: Macmillan, 1884), III, pp. 278–82
—— *Studies in Prose and Poetry* (London: Chatto & Windus, 1894)
—— *Miscellanies*, 2nd edn (London: Chatto & Windus, 1895)
—— *The Poems of Algernon Charles Swinburne*, 6 vols (London: Chatto & Windus, 1905; first printed 1904)
—— *The Tragedies of Algernon Charles Swinburne*, 5 vols (London: Chatto & Windus, 1905–06)
—— *Ode to Mazzini; The Saviour of Society; Liberty and Loyalty: Unpublished Mss. Discovered Among The Author's Effects After His Death*, with a preface by Edmund Gosse (Boston: The Bibliophile Society, 1913)
—— *Lesbia Brandon*, ed. by Randolph Hughes (London: Falcon Press, 1952)
—— *The Letters of Algernon Charles Swinburne*, ed. by Edmund Gosse and Thomas James Wise, 2 vols (London: Heinemann, 1918)
—— *The Swinburne Letters*, ed. by Cecil Y. Lang, 6 vols (New Haven: Yale University Press, 1959–62)
—— *A. C. Swinburne: Major Poems and Selected Prose*, ed. Jerome McGann and Charles Sligh (New Haven: Yale University Press, 2004)
—— *The Uncollected Letters of Algernon Charles Swinburne*, ed. Terry L. Meyers, 3 vols (London: Pickering and Chatto, 2005)
—— *Selected Verse* , ed. by Alex Wong (Manchester: Fyfield Books, 2015)
—— *Algernon Charles Swinburne*, ed. by Francis O'Gorman, 21st Century Oxford Authors Series (Oxford: Oxford University Press, 2016)
SYMONS, ARTHUR, *The Collected Works of Arthur Symons* (London: M. Secker, 1924)
—— *The Symbolist Movement in Literature* (London: Constable and Company, 1911)
—— *Figures of Several Centuries* (London: Constable, 1916)
SYMONDS, J. A., 'Erechtheus: A Tragedy', *The Academy*, 8 January 1876, pp. 23–24
TARLINSKAIA, MARINA, *English Verse* (The Hague: Mouton, 1976)
TAYLOR, CHARLES, *A Secular Age* (Cambridge MA: Harvard University Press, 1997)
TAYLOR, DENNIS, *Hardy's Metres and Victorian Prosody* (Oxford: Clarendon, 1988)
TENNYSON, ALFRED LORD, *Tennyson: A Selected Edition*, ed. by Christopher Ricks (Harlow: Longman, 1989)
—— *The Poems of Tennyson*, ed. by Christopher Ricks, 2nd edn, 3 vols (London: Longman, 1987)

TENNYSON, HALLAM, *Alfred Lord Tennyson: A Memoir*, 2 vols (London: Macmillan, 1897)
THAIN, MARION, 'Desire Lines: Swinburne and Lyric Crisis' in *Algernon Charles Swinburne: Unofficial Laureate,* ed. by Stefano Evangelista and Catherine Maxwell (Manchester: Manchester University Press, 2012), pp. 138–54.
THOMAS, EDWARD, *Algernon Charles Swinburne: A Critical Study* (London: M. Secker, 1912)
TUCKER, HERBERT, 'Dramatic Monologue and the Overhearing of Lyric' in *Lyric Poetry: Beyond New Criticism,* ed. by Chaviva Hošek and Patricia Parker (Ithaca: Cornell University Press, 1985), pp. 226–43
—— 'The Fix of Form: An Open Letter', *Victorian Literature and Culture,* 27, 2 (1999), 531–35
—— *Epic: Britain's Heroic Muse 1790–1910* (Oxford: Oxford University Press, 2008)
TYNIANOV, YURI, 'The Ode as an Oratorical Genre', trans. Ann Shukman, *New Literary History,* 34, 3 (2003), 565–96
UNSIGNED REVIEWS:
—— 'Atalanta in Calydon', *The Times,* 6 June 1865, p. 6
—— 'Atalanta in Calydon', *Spectator,* 15 April 1865, 'Books', pp. 14–16
—— 'Ode on the Insurrection in Candia', *Fortnightly Review,* March 1867, 284–89
—— 'Mr. Swinburne's *Erechtheus*', *Athenæum,* 1 Jan 1876, pp. 13–14
—— 'Mr. Swinburne's Erechtheus', *Spectator,* 1 Jan 1876, 'Books', pp. 23–25
—— 'Swinburne's Erechtheus', *Saturday Review,* 8 January 1876, pp. 50–51
—— 'Swinburne's Erechtheus' , *London Quarterly Review,* April 1876, pp. 249–54
—— 'Mr. Swinburne's Erechtheus', *Edinburgh Review,* July 1876, pp. 147–68
—— 'Ion', *Blackwood's Edinburgh Magazine,* October 1876, pp. 419–34
—— '*Tristram of Lyonesse and Other Poems*', *Athenaeum,* 22 July 1882, pp. 103–05
—— 'Tristram of Lyonesse', *Saturday Review,* 29 July 1882, pp. 156–57
—— 'Mr. Swinburne's Tristram', '*Spectator,* 12 August 1882, 'Books', pp. 15–17
—— *Westminster Review*, October 1882, 'Belles Lettres: Contemporary Literature', pp. 586–87
—— 'Mr. Swinburne as a Master of Metre', *Spectator,* 17 April 1909, pp. 9–10
VALÉRY, PAUL, 'Poetry and Abstract Thought', trans. by Charles Guenther, *The Kenyon Review,* 16, 2 (1954), 208–33
VOLOSHINOV, V. N., *Marxism and the Philosophy of Language*, trans. by Ladislav Matejka and I. R. Titunik. (Cambridge, MA: Harvard University Press, 1986)
WARREN, ALBA H., *English Poetic Theory, 1825–1865* (Princeton: Princeton University Press, 1950)
WARREN, J. LEICESTER, 'Atalanta in Calydon', *Fortnightly Review,* May 15, 1865, pp. 75–80
WEIL, SIMONE, *The Need for Roots: Prelude to a Declaration of Duties Towards Mankind* (London: Routledge, 2002)
—— *Gravity and Grace*, trans. by Emma Crawford and Marion von der Ruhr, intro. by Gustave Thibon (London: Routledge, 2002)
WEIR, MARION, *The Influence of Aeschylus and Euripides on the Structure and Content of Swinburne's 'Atalanta in Calydon' and 'Erechtheus'* (Ann Arbor, MI: George Wahr, 1920)
WENNERSTROM, ANN K., *The Music of Everyday Speech: Prosody and Discourse Analysis* (Oxford: Oxford University Press, 2001)
WESLING, DONALD, *The Scissors of Meter: Grammetrics and Reading* (Ann Arbor: University of Michigan Press, 1996)
WEST, M. L., *Greek Metre* (Oxford: Oxford University Press, 1982)
WHITEHEAD, ANDREW, ed. 'John Sommerfield: Archive' (personal website of Andrew Whitehead, Andrew Whitehead, 2013) <http://www.andrewwhitehead.net/john-sommerfield-archive.html> [last accessed 26 April 2018]
WILDE, OSCAR, *The Complete Works of Oscar Wilde*, ed. by Russell Jackson and Ian Small, 2

vols (Oxford: Oxford University Press, 2005)
WILKINSON, JOHN, *The Lyric Touch: Essays on the Poetry of Excess* (Cambridge: Salt, 2007)
WILLIAMS, ANNE, *Prophetic Strain: The Greater Lyric in the Eighteenth Century* (Chicago: University of Chicago Press, 1984)
WILLIAMS, RAYMOND, *Culture and Society, 1780–1950* (New York: Columbia University Press, 1983)
WILSON, PENELOPE, 'The Knowledge and Appreciation of Pindar in the Seventeenth and Eighteenth Centuries' (unpublished doctoral thesis, University of Oxford, 1974)
WILSON, ROSS, *Theodor Adorno* (London and New York: Routledge, 2007)
WIMSATT, JAMES I., *Hopkins' Poetics of Speech Sound* (Toronto: University of Toronto Press, 2006)
WITTGENSTEIN, LUDWIG, *Major Works: Selected Philosophical Writings* (New York: Harper Perennial, 2009)
—— *Philosophical Investigations,* trans. by G. E. M. Anscombe, 3rd edn (Oxford: Blackwell, 1972)
—— *On Certainty,* ed. by G. E. M. Anscombe and G. H. Von Wright, trans. by G. E. M Anscombe and Denis Paul (Oxford: Blackwell, 1979)
WORDSWORTH, WILLIAM, *The Poems,* ed. by John O. Hayden, 2 vols (Harmondsworth: Penguin, 1982).
WYMER, THOMAS L., 'Swinburne's Tragic Vision in "Atalanta in Calydon"', *Victorian Poetry*, 9, 1/2, (1971), 1–16
YEATS, W. B., *Collected Poems,* ed. by Augustine Martin (London: Vintage, 1992)
YOUNG-BRYANT, ALAN ANDREW, 'Perverse Form and Victorian Lyric' (unpublished doctoral thesis, Cornell University, 2011)
—— 'Swinburne: "The Sweetest Name"', *Victorian Poetry*, 49, 3 (2011), 301–16.
ZUIDERVAART, LAMBERT PAUL, *Refractions: Truth in Adorno's Aesthetic Theory* (Toronto: University of Toronto Press, 1981)

INDEX

adjectives 10, 12–13, 85–87, 92, 94, 101–05, 127, 170
adverbs 94–96
Adorno, Theodor W.:
    aesthetics 22–26, 195
    on art's uncertain future 199
    on commitment 156
    on content 23–24
    dismissal of Swinburne 7, 22
    on the emancipation of art 25, 199
    on form 23–24, 26, 199
    on the historical truth-content of art 24–25, 200 n. 11
    on improvisation 198
    on instrumental reason 22, 25
    on *lingua morta* 106
    on lyric 11, 24, 154, 157
    on material 23–24, 199
    on materialistic-dialectical aesthetics 201 n. 29
    on nostalgia 25, 26, 114 n. 4
    on religious art 121–22, 147 n. 15
    on submitting to the artwork 26
    on temporality 78–80, 83
    on utopia 186
Aeschylus 8, 38, 46, 54, 80, 172, 177–78, 182, 186
aesthetic criticism 3, 30 n. 12, 124
aesthetic experience 22, 32 n. 56
Agamben, Giorgio 115 n. 33
alexandrine 131, 141, 145–46, 161, 169
Aligheri, Dante 89
alliteration 1, 10, 14, 64, 90, 95–99, 127, 130, 162, 170
allusion 91, 94, 103–05, 109, 120
ambiguity 76 n. 82, 102, 104, 107, 113
    see also Empson, William
amplification 89, 91
    see also repetition
anagnorisis 65, 67, 69
analogy 97, 99, 155–56
anapaest *see* greek metrics; triple rhythm; double off-beat
anaphora 73, 88–89, 110, 133, 145, 185
anastasis 96
archaism 11, 74, 130
Aristophanes 30 n. 21, 40, 177
Armstrong, Isobel 153–54, 188 n. 24, 189 n. 28
Arnold, Matthew 37, 39, 41–43, 48, 50–52, 70–71, 80, 92, 122–24, 158
ataraxia 120, 132

attention, modes of 23, 26, 55, 59, 61–62, 72, 80–81, 85–86, 88, 90, 93–114
    see also reading
Attridge, Derek 20–21, 31 n. 25, 40, 44–48, 50–52, 55, 60, 61, 62, 64, 94–95, 148 n. 43
Augustine of Hippo, Saint 78, 100
automatism in verse 8, 90

Bally, Charles 194
Balzac, Honoré de 180–81
Barthes, Roland 35
Barr, Alan P. 34–35, 69
Baudelaire, Charles 11, 20, 36, 72–73, 74 n. 15, 105–06, 110–11
Baxandall, Michael 20, 22, 32 n. 56, 124–25, 147 n. 26
The Bible 1, 95, 100, 103, 105, 114
Benjamin, Jessica 189 n. 29
Benjamin, Walter 110–11
Blair, Kirstie 27, 121–22
blank verse 30 n. 23, 36, 41–42, 48–49, 52–55, 58, 60–64, 70, 85, 100, 132, 134
Blind, Mathilde 123
Bourdieu, Pierre:
    against diagrams 20
    genesis amnesia 196–98, 200 n. 16
    habitus 25, 194–98, 200 n. 16
    intention 30 n. 15
    modus operandi 194, 196, 198
    opus operandi 198
    virtuoso 195–96, 199
Bowra, C. M. [Maurice Bowra] 34, 37, 57, 59, 71
Browning, Elizabeth Barrett 122, 151–52
Browning, Robert 7, 33, 50, 54, 57, 62, 122, 155, 188 n. 24, 189 n. 28
Burne-Jones, Edward 57, 123
Bush, Douglas 35
Byron, Lord [George Gordon Byron; 6th Baron Byron] 41, 189 n. 45

cadence 5–6, 15, 35, 43–44, 57–58, 66, 79, 86, 109, 123–24, 162, 176, 186
caesura 58, 61, 63–64, 66, 69, 71, 85–88, 89, 98–99, 109, 112–13, 126, 129–30, 134–35, 137, 139, 145
Campbell, Matthew 71
Carlyle, Thomas 37, 111, 119
Carne-Ross, D. S. 9, 36, 43, 46, 49, 54, 178, 182, 184–85

Chaucer, Geoffery 44, 88, 123–24, 129–30
characterisation 7, 9, 20, 23, 55, 68, 71–72, 138, 172, 189 n. 31
Chew, Samuel C. 35–36
chorus 9, 21, 33–37, 40–74, 86, 98, 152, 154, 158, 171–73, 176–87, 189 n. 31, 190 n. 55, 196
Coleridge, Samuel Taylor 160, 162, 190 n. 50, 198
Collini, Stefan 156
Collins, William 162–63, 187 n. 10, 189 n. 45
collocation 12, 94, 99–101, 102, 103
Congreve, William 161–62, 187 n. 10
content, see Adorno, T. W.
couplet 9, 15, 23, 25, 28, 43, 51, 63–64, 67, 82, 89, 95, 98, 107, 118–49, 152, 160, 162, 170, 176, 178–79, 183, 186
Cowley, Abraham 158, 161–63, 187 n. 9, 187 n. 10, 187 n. 11, 190 n. 55
Creech, Thomas 132
Culler, Jonathan 153–54, 184, 188 n. 25, 189 n. 28, 192 n. 104

Dale, A. M. 177, 178
Dante, see Aligheri, Dante
Davie, Donald 10, 15, 134
De Bolla, Peter 32 n. 56
Derrida, Jacques 32 n. 70
Detienne, Marcel 182
diction 1, 8–9, 11–13, 15, 25, 53, 64, 90, 92, 105–06, 130, 170
dipodic rhythm 176
Dixon, Richard Watson 39
dol'nik 9, 21, 31 n. 25, 45, 86, 94, 107
double off-beat 9–10, 45, 129, 132, 148 n. 43
Dowson, Ernest 12
duple rhythm 30 n. 21, 40–41, 43–46, 48–54, 58, 61–62, 64–67, 70–71, 86, 101, 109, 160, 176–78, 186
dramatic monologue 33, 49, 58, 72, 79, 82, 85, 91, 106, 111, 114 n. 6, 153–54, 157, 172, 184–85, 188 n. 24, 188 n. 25, 188 n. 27, 189 n. 28
Dryden, John 9, 125–28, 130–33, 137, 139, 142–43, 161–62, 193

Eliot, T. S. 1, 2, 6–8, 10–13, 18, 23, 26, 29 n. 8, 29 n. 10, 30 n. 12, 58–60, 73–74, 76 n. 82, 89, 91–93, 95, 98, 106–08, 110, 161, 179, 194, 196–97, 199
Empson, William 58, 76 n. 82, 104, 116 n. 44, 195
Eliot, George 185
enjambment 6, 53, 70, 87, 95, 109, 113, 119, 125–28, 132–33, 136, 142, 145, 159, 161, 163, 170, 184, 190, 191 n. 65
epic 119, 124, 129, 131, 138, 162, 173
epigrammatic 126–27, 130, 131–33, 137–45
epistrophe 88
epithets 4, 9, 12, 85, 91, 94, 102, 114

Euripides 38, 43
expedient line 64, 70, 134

facism 153, 179, 181
falling rhythm, see cadence
feminine ending, see cadence
five-beat line 46–49, 52, 54–55, 61–62, 64–66, 87, 159–60, 162–63, 170, 172, 196
flagellation, see Swinburne, Algernon Charles; sado-masochism
form, see Adorno, T. W.
Forrest-Thomson, Veronica 1, 10, 30 n. 10, 59, 93–99, 101, 108–09, 196–97, 199
four-beat line 44–55, 58, 60–66, 71, 73–74, 82, 86–88, 162–63, 170–72, 175–76, 178, 191 n. 70
Fowler, Roger 148 n. 40
free verse 2, 3, 22, 25, 60, 124–25, 194

Gautier, Théophile 12
genius 1, 19, 111, 156
Gentile, Emilio 181
Gosse, Edmund 131, 133, 135–36, 158, 161–62, 171, 173, 175, 183, 190 n. 48, 190 n. 63
Gray, Thomas 158, 163, 169, 189 n. 45, 190 n. 59
greek metrics 9, 28, 36, 39–43, 46, 177–78
greek play in English 33, 39, 48–54, 189
greek tragedy 34, 36–38, 57, 67, 72–73, 122, 151, 154, 172, 189
Griffiths, Eric 82, 91, 106, 111

half line, see hemistich
Harding, Denys 9, 36, 43, 50
Hardy, Thomas 8–9, 119
Hargreaves, H. A. 35
Haynes, Kenneth 36, 71
Hegel, G. W. F. 23, 153–54, 172–73, 178, 180–82, 185, 188 n. 27, 189 n. 31
hemistich 35, 48, 64, 67, 160 175
heroic couplet, see couplet
hexameter 42, 169, 176
Historical Poetics 20, 22, 26–28, 193–94
Hollander, John 81–82, 111
homoeleuton 95
homonym 18, 194
homophones 105
Hopkins, Gerard Manley 7, 27, 96–99, 101
Horne, R. H. 123
Housman, A. E. 1, 8–9, 11–12, 14–16, 29, 30 n. 18, 176
Hughes, Linda K. 152
Hugo, Victor 105–06, 151, 158, 190 n. 48, 190 n. 63, 191 n. 67
Hulme, T. E. 2, 148 n. 32

iamb, see cadence; duple rhythm; greek metrics
imagery 7–8, 10, 38, 58–59, 81, 91, 98–99, 103, 106, 108–09, 130, 155, 161, 170, 175, 177–78

innovation 22, 46, 49, 54, 74, 89, 125, 131, 136, 143, 146, 147 n. 23, 151, 196–99
internal rhyme *see* rhyme
iteration, *see* repetition

Jackson, Virginia 153, 188 n. 25
James, Clive 13
Jarvis, Simon 22, 121, 134, 143, 147 n. 23, 170, 195–96, 200 n. 11
Johnson, Samuel 158, 169
Jowett, Benjamin 38, 153, 180, 192 n. 96

Kant, Immanuel 22–23, 25
karole 31 n. 25, 43–46, 48, 52, 67, 74
  see also dol'nik
Keach, William 64, 133–35
Keats, John 7, 103, 111, 130–35, 148 n. 49
Kierkegaard, Søren 113, 117 n. 69
Kirkup, Seymour 18
Knight, Joseph 17
kommos 34, 43, 71, 75 n. 49
Kuduk-Weiner, Stephanie 152
Kugel, James 95, 111

Lafourcade, Georges 34, 43–45, 52, 65
Landor, Walter Savage 48–49, 52–53, 114
Lang, Cecil Y. 2
LaPorte, Charles 147 n. 14
Levin, Yisrael 29 n. 8, 38, 199 n. 2, 200 n. 4
Lichtmann, Maria R. 96–99
line break 58, 66, 70, 127, 129, 133–35, 137–38, 144–45
  see also enjambment
Linton, Eliza Lynn 49
Linton, W. J. 171
Louis, M. K. 36, 81, 100, 105
Lucretius 120, 132, 149 n. 58
Lyons, Sara 17, 123
lyric poetry 11, 14, 16, 24, 29, 33, 35–37, 39, 41–42, 46, 48, 50–51, 54–55, 57, 65, 81, 82, 91, 102, 106, 111–12, 115 n. 29, 125–49, 150–92, 196
  see also ode

Magnus, Laury 95, 101
Malkin, B. H. 18–19
Martin, Meredith 20, 27, 32 n. 60, 199 n. 2
Marx, Karl 20, 32 n. 56
masculine ending, *see* cadence
materialism 123, 140
Mathews, Richard 34, 36
Maxwell, Catherine 81
Mazzini, Giuseppe 150–53, 158–63, 171, 179, 186, 188 n. 19
McGann, Jerome J. 33, 35–36, 72–73, 81, 99
metaphor 81, 97, 115, 159, 161
metre 4, 9–11, 17, 20–21, 25, 27–28, 36, 38–42, 47, 50, 58, 60–67, 70, 74, 94, 107, 123–24, 128, 132, 134–36, 139, 162, 170, 172, 177–78, 198
  see also greek metrics
metrical set 9, 33, 36, 46–55, 61, 63, 71, 73, 160, 163, 171, 187 n. 9, 190 n. 55
Meyers, Terry 29 n. 9
mimesis 10, 17, 24, 31 n. 25, 127, 162–63, 175, 179, 181
Myers, Frederic W. H. 139–41, 149 n. 58
Mill, J. S. 153–57, 170, 179, 185–86, 188 n. 24, 188 n. 25, 189 n. 28, 189 n. 40, 189 n. 45
Milnes, Richard Monckton [1st Baron Houghton] 122
Milton, John 1, 10, 15, 29 n. 7, 41–42, 48, 51–52, 161, 169–70, 190 n. 63
monosyllables 6, 10, 52–54, 57, 64, 66, 73, 77 n. 94, 94, 107, 109, 126, 134
monosyllabic line, *see* monosyllables
Morris, William 7, 123–24, 128–31, 136–37, 71–73, 78, 81, 97–98, 107
musicality 2, 7–8, 23, 41–43, 51, 110–11, 114 n. 4, 155, 195

narrative 16, 22, 29, 82–84, 89, 94, 108, 114, 121, 123, 127–31, 133, 136–37, 141, 144–45, 153, 180, 184, 192 n. 113
Neo-formalism, *see* Historical Poetics
New Formalism, *see* Historical Poetics
Nicholls, Peter 106, 111
Nicolson, Harold 33–36, 54, 71
Nichol, John 41–42
Nietzsche, Friedrich 37–39, 67, 73, 83, 141, 197–98
nouns 10, 12, 30 n. 10, 77 n. 94, 101–02, 105, 127, 129–30, 142, 145, 170, 185

ode 10, 16–19, 23–25, 27, 29, 34, 49, 51, 55, 59–69, 73–74, 98, 133, 150–92, 193–94, 196
O'Gorman, Francis 108, 115 n. 8, 146 n. 4, 152–53, 179, 187 n. 11, 188 n. 19
O'Hara, Frank 183
Oliver, Douglas 20–21, 46

parallelism 73, 77 n. 93, 86–89, 94–99, 101, 103–04, 111, 160, 186
Pater, Walter 3, 30 n. 12, 123–24, 147 n. 24, 147 n. 25, 157, 181
Paterson, Katie 34
Patmore, Coventry 151, 158, 176
pentameter, *see* five-beat line
period ear 3, 100, 124–25, 131
Petrarca, Francesco (Petrarch) 82, 110
Pindar 65, 151–52, 161, 163, 178, 182–84, 187, 196–97
pitch 5, 10, 77 n. 94, 176
  see also stress
Plato 153, 180–81, 186, 192 n. 96
Poe, Edgar Allan 102
Polten, Orla 36, 43, 148 n. 33
Pope, Alexander 9, 12, 64, 119–22, 137, 142, 163, 189 n. 45, 193

Pound, Ezra 1–2, 7–9, 11–14, 29, 74, 92–95, 107, 146, 196–97
prefixes 94
Prins, Yopie 20, 27–28, 32 n. 60, 153, 181, 188 n. 25, 200 n. 4
prolepsis 5, 143
prosodic hospitality 28, 177, 191 n. 85
prosody 11, 18, 26, 33, 35, 39–43, 54, 61, 73, 89, 161, 177, 193, 195, 198, 199 n. 2, 199–200 n. 4, 200 n. 11
Prynne, J. H. 18, 29 n. 6, 91–93, 194

reading 6, 19–20, 22–29, 32 n. 71
redundancy 13, 80, 82, 89, 92, 103–04, 111, 131, 170
reflexivity 17, 81–82, 162–63, 183, 197
refrain 4, 6, 14, 81–82, 102, 183
repetition 3, 5–6, 13, 14, 16, 29, 43–45, 49, 66, 78–118, 120, 126, 146
revenants, *see* repetition
Reynolds, Matthew 153
rhyme:
   as figure 107, 112–13, 197, 199
   internal rhyme 69–70, 126, 162, 175–76, 183
   end-rhyme 3–6, 7, 11, 14, 15–18, 23, 25, 38–39, 41–42, 44, 47–49, 51–52, 88–89, 97–100, 104, 111, 118–49, 155, 160–61, 163, 169–70, 178–79, 183, 187 n. 9, 190 n. 63
rhythm 1, 3, 5–11, 14, 20–21, 23–24, 27–29, 30 n. 10, 30 n. 23, 31 n. 29, 32 n. 70, 33–78, 80, 82, 86–87, 89, 94–95, 97–99, 104, 107, 109, 113–14, 121–22, 132–34, 141, 145, 155, 160, 170, 172, 176–78, 186, 196–98, 200 n. 4
   see also dipodic rhythm; duple rhythm; triple rhythm; cadence
rhythmic tension 33–77, 126, 128–29, 131–33, 160, 169, 171–72, 175
Ribeyrol, Charlotte 152
Ricks, Christopher 1, 29 n. 7
Ricœur, Paul 28, 191 n. 85
rising rhythm, *see* cadence
Rooksby, Rikky 17, 29 n. 9, 79, 187 n. 13
Rose, Gillian 117 n. 69
Rosenberg, John D. 29 n. 10, 59, 180–81
Rossetti, Christina 118
Rossetti, Dante Gabriel 14–15, 17, 123–24, 131
Rossetti, William Michael 11, 84–85, 91–93, 169
Roundel 14, 108, 147 n. 8
Rudel, Jaufré 84, 88–89, 108–09, 113
Rumsey, Lacey 30 n. 10
Ruskin, John 19, 31 n. 49, 57, 61–62
Russell, David 189 n. 40
Rutland, William 38

Saintsbury, George 3, 8, 21, 29, 30 n. 23, 31 n. 25, 33, 36–37, 39–40, 42–46, 49–50, 52, 54, 57–58, 65–67, 73–74, 86, 109, 124–26, 128, 131–32, 136, 148 n. 29, 171, 194

Sappho 8, 27–28, 126–27
Saville, Julia F. 152, 200 n. 4
scansion 20–21, 39, 43–46, 66, 177
Scott, Clive 20
Shelley, Percy Bysshe 15–16, 33, 37, 39, 41, 48–51, 64, 101–02, 118, 120–22, 125, 128, 131, 133–35, 139, 146 n. 6, 155–57, 170, 189 n. 45, 190 n. 65, 191 n. 70
simile 97, 100–01, 119, 126, 128, 136, 177, 185
song rhythm *see* four-beat line
The Song of Solomon, *see* The Bible
Sophocles 43, 80
speech rhythm 5, 9–12, 46, 48–49, 52–54, 60, 62–65, 67–68, 70, 73, 89, 148 n. 29, 195
   see also blank verse, duple rhythm
Spenser, Edmund 13
sprung pentameter, *see* expedient line
sprung rhythm 98
Stedman, Edmund Clarence 118, 121–22, 139
Steele, Timothy 11
Stevens, Wallace 91–92, 112
Stewart, Susan 151
stichomythia 52–54
stress 5, 10, 16–17, 20–21, 23, 40, 43, 45–47, 52, 54, 57, 60–61, 63–64, 66–67, 71, 77 n. 94, 86, 89, 94, 97, 134–37, 160, 176–77
style 1–3, 6–8, 10–11, 17–29, 36–38, 42, 47, 60, 69, 71–73, 81–83, 86, 89–90, 92, 94–96, 99–100, 106–07, 111, 124, 125, 128–29, 133, 136, 142–43, 146, 152–54, 157–58, 162, 175, 179–81, 183, 193–201
Sutherland, Keston 183
Swinburne, Algernon Charles:
   life:
      family 17, 37, 88, 118, 150
      early education 9, 27, 39
      education at Oxford 15, 40–41, 97, 155–56, 163, 180, 192 n. 97
      learning in languages 22, 38, 40–41, 87–88, 105, 123, 169, 177, 180
      obituary 198
      politics 8, 16, 29, 92, 118, 146 n. 4, 153, 150–92, 199 n. 2
      religious views 35, 38, 79, 99, 118–49, 152, 181
      sado-masochism 16–17, 27, 38, 55, 58, 62, 79, 107, 123, 179, 180–81, 200 n. 4
   style, *see* individual index entries
   poems:
      Anactoria 28, 72, 80, 123–26, 128–30, 131, 134, 139, 152
      The Altar of Righteousness 152
      Atalanta in Calydon 21, 29, 29 n. 10, 33–77, 90, 120, 150, 172, 175
      A Ballad of Life 84–85
      A Ballad of Death 84–85
      Before Dawn 84
      Before Parting 84
      A Birth-Song 12

A Century of Roundels 14, 108, 147 n. 8
Choriambics 9
Christmas Antiphones 152
A Dark Month 9
The Death of Rudel 84, 88
Dolores 14, 16, 84
England: An Ode 152
Erechtheus 10, 25, 29, 74 n. 4, 150–204
Erotion 87
Faustine 16
For the Feast of Giordano Bruno 120–21
Félise 79, 84, 100
The Garden of Proserpine 9, 81, 84, 99, 126
The Golden House 88
Hendecasyllabics 9
Hertha 153, 157
Hesperia 84, 198, 201 n. 25
Hymn of Man 152
Itylus 3–6
Laus Veneris 85, 104
A Leave-Taking 84
Memorial Verses for Théophile Gautier 12
Music: An Ode 152
At a Month's End 10, 44
Ode to Athens 161, 171
Ode on the Insurrection in Candia 150, 152, 158, 163–71, 190 n. 48, 190 n. 63
Ode to Mazzini 151, 158–63, 187 n. 11, 190 n. 49, 190 n. 55
Ode on the Proclamation of the French Republic 151, 171
In the Orchard 84, 87, 88
Phaedra 85
Poems and Ballads: First Series 11, 24, 30 n. 23, 78–117
Poems and Ballads: Third Series 12, 44
Queen Yseult 15
'The Rape of Oreithya' 171–80
 see also *Erechtheus*
Relics 12
Sapphics 9
Songs Before Sunrise 10–11, 13, 84, 150, 153, 186, 187 n. 13
The Sun-dew 16
Tristram of Lyonesse 12–13, 25, 29, 72, 80, 109, 118–49, 161
The Triumph of Time 9–11, 29, 34, 64, 74, 81–117
Untitled Manuscript, Georgetown University, John. S. Mayfield Papers: Swinburne Series, 1:29/ GAMMS470.1.29 MS#199 197, 200 n. 22
prose:
 A Study Of Shakespeare 11, 19, 190 n. 59, 195
 Lesbia Brandon 16, 18, 180
 'Of Analogy' 97, 155
 'On the Dialectic of Plato' 180, 192 n. 96
 'On Political and Speculative Liberty' 156
 William Blake: A Critical Essay 73, 152, 180–81, 189 n. 38
 Undergraduate Papers 41
symbol 67, 72, 80–81, 97, 99, 100, 108, 143, 155
Symons, Arthur 3, 11–12, 72, 79–81, 86, 124
Symonds, J.A. 173, 177
symploce 88
syntax 3–5, 8–11, 51, 61, 64, 66, 70, 73, 77 n. 93, 86, 88–89, 98, 109, 126–30, 133–37, 141, 144, 148 n. 49, 161, 163, 170, 184, 190 n. 65, 191 n. 65

tautology 81, 83
Tennyson, Alfred Lord 17, 33, 38, 50, 80, 82, 92–93, 101–04, 108–09, 122–24, 138, 151, 152, 155, 158, 183, 188 n. 24, 196, 198
tension, see rhythmic tension
texture, see verse texture
Thain, Marion 152
Thomas, Dylan 8, 30 n. 19
Thomas, Edward 12, 35–36, 57–58
third paeonic 9, 31, 40, 177
Tillyard, E. M. W. 153, 157, 179–81, 185
tradition 1, 3, 9, 18, 25, 27–28, 33, 39, 48–49, 74, 78, 80, 92, 99, 124–25, 146, 157, 162, 194–99
tragedy, see greek tragedy
translation 28, 36–43, 50, 54, 177, 191 n. 85
 see also prosodic hospitality
Trevelyan, Paulina Jermyn [Lady Trevelyan] 37, 39
triplet 25, 131–49, 178–79
triple rhythm 1, 9, 40, 42–45, 67, 86, 132, 148 n. 43
triple pentameter 60–63
trochee 44–46, 66, 86
 see also cadence, duple rhythm
Tucker, Herbert 34, 108, 124, 129, 138, 153–54, 157, 172, 188 n. 24, 188 n. 25

Valéry, Paul 193
verbs 71, 77, 91–95, 109, 113, 130, 134–35, 139, 144–45
verse history 6, 20–29, 33
 see also reading
verse texture 23–24, 31 n. 38, 58, 88, 130–31, 136–37, 139–46, 148 n. 40, 170, 176–77, 179
verse-thinking 121, 132, 139, 146, 193, 197–99

Wagner, Richard 36, 38, 72–74, 137
Weir, Marion 34
Wennerstrom, Ann K. 5
West, M. L. 176, 178
Wilde, Oscar 80
Wilson, Penelope 151
Wordsworth, William 15, 83, 90, 92, 107–08, 110, 113, 157, 162, 170, 187, 189 n. 45, 198
Wymer, Thomas L. 34

Young-Bryant, Alan Andrew 79, 81, 100

www.ingramcontent.com/pod-product-compliance
Lightning Source LLC
LaVergne TN
LVHW061250060426
835507LV00017B/1999